Shojo Beat

BABY & Me

Vol. 7

Story & Art by **Marimo Ragawa**

BABY & ME   Table of Contents

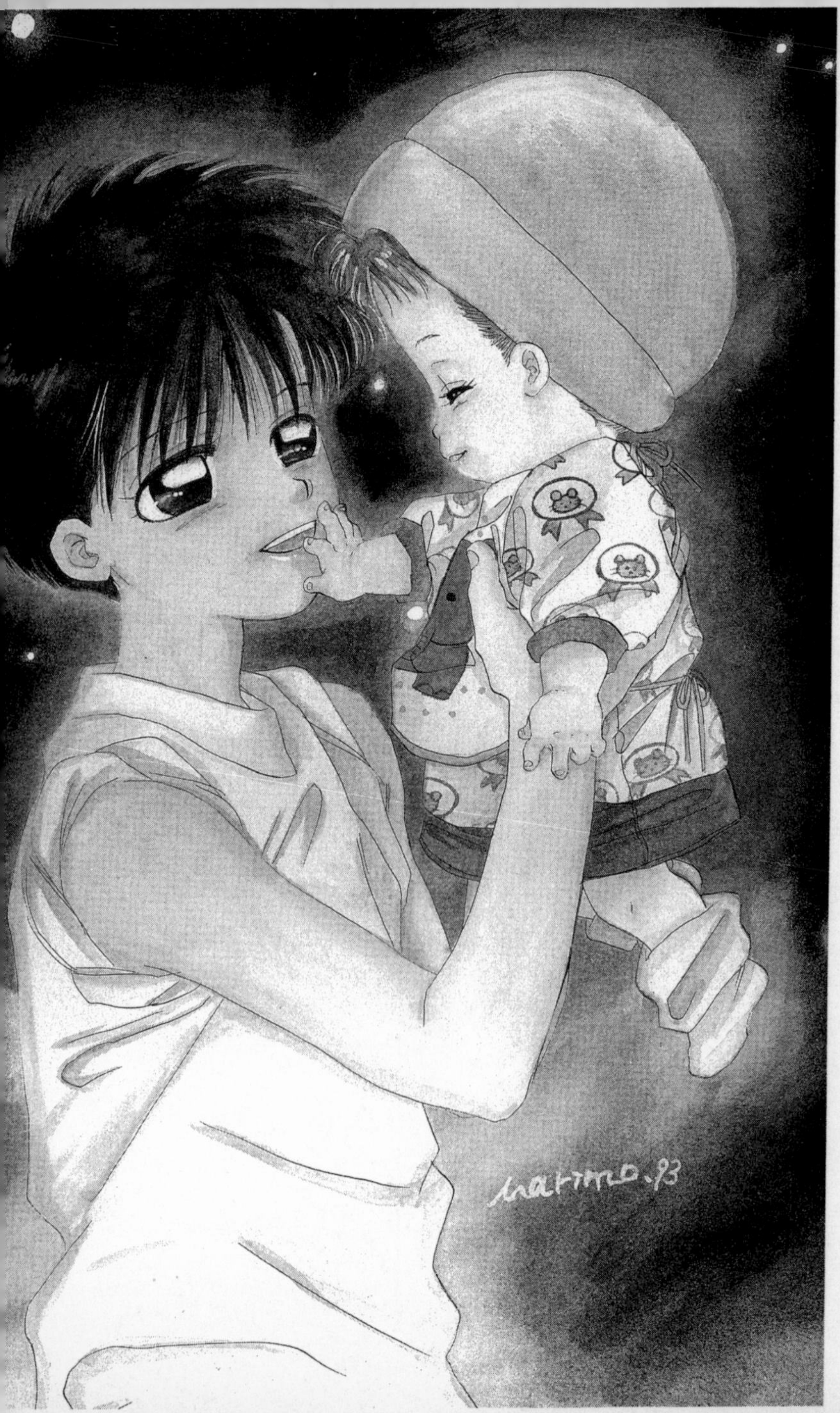

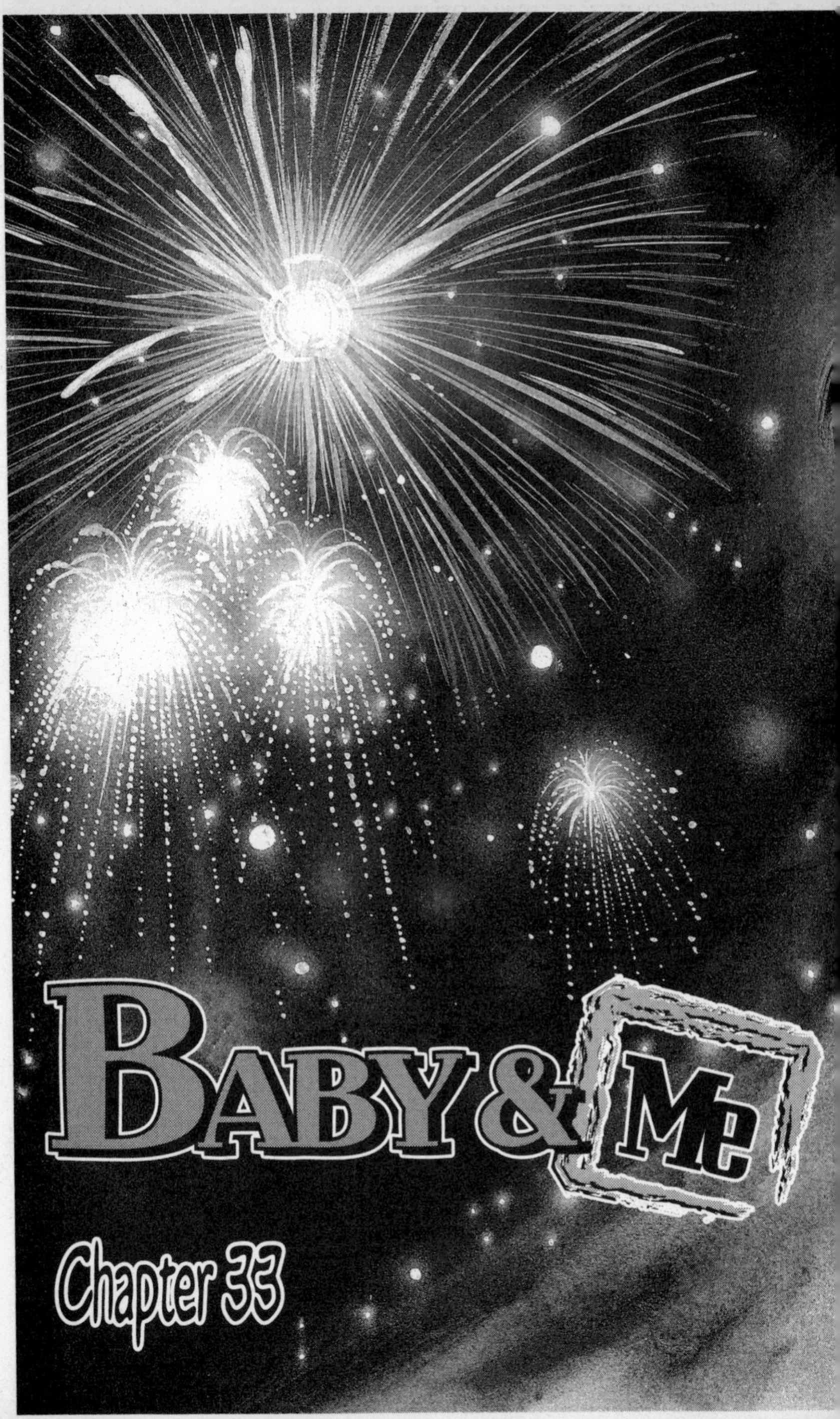
BABY & Me
Chapter 33

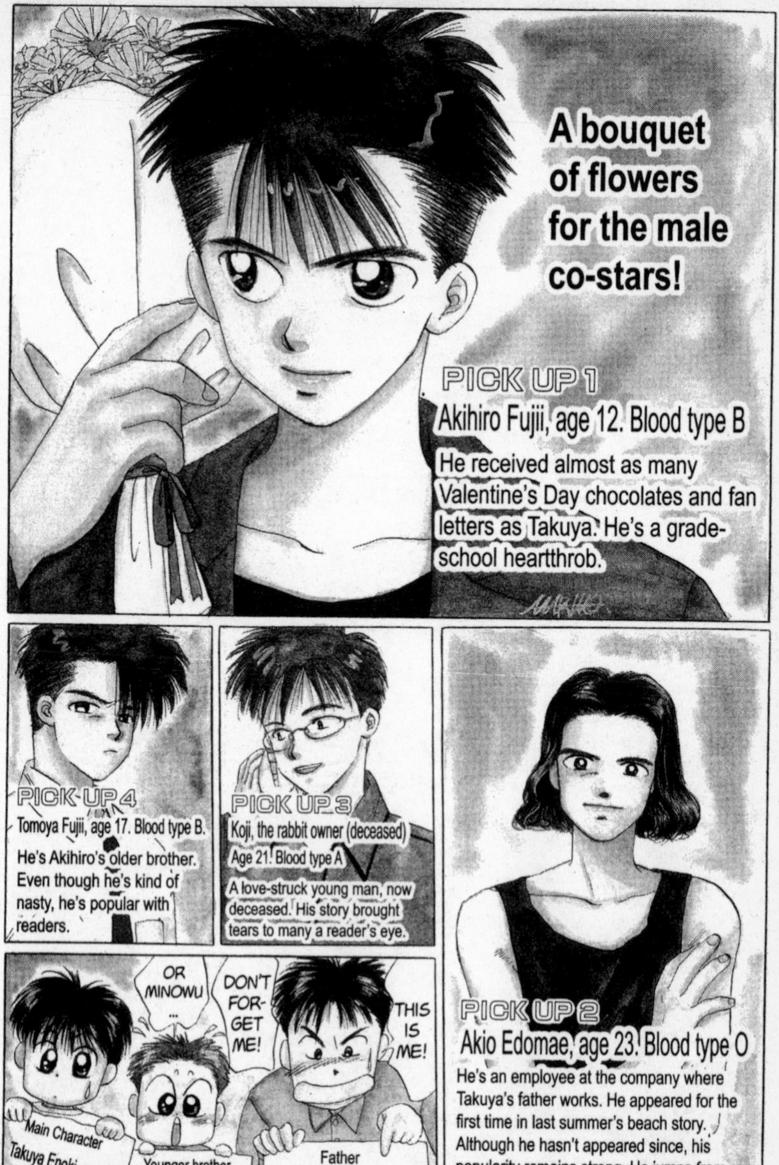
A bouquet of flowers for the male co-stars!
PICK UP 1
Akihiro Fujii, age 12. Blood type B
He received almost as many Valentine's Day chocolates and fan letters as Takuya. He's a grade-school heartthrob.
PICK UP 2
Akio Edomae, age 23. Blood type O
He's an employee at the company where Takuya's father works. He appeared for the first time in last summer's beach story. Although he hasn't appeared since, his popularity remains strong. He jumps from one trend to the next.
PICK UP 3
Koji, the rabbit owner (deceased)
Age 21. Blood type A
A love-struck young man, now deceased. His story brought tears to many a reader's eye.
PICK UP 4
Tomoya Fujii, age 17. Blood type B.
He's Akihiro's older brother. Even though he's kind of nasty, he's popular with readers.
THIS IS ME!
DON'T FOR-GET ME!
OR MINOWU ...
Father
Harumi Enoki, age 34.
Younger brother
Minoru Enoki, age 2.
Main Character
Takuya Enoki, age 12.
Me.

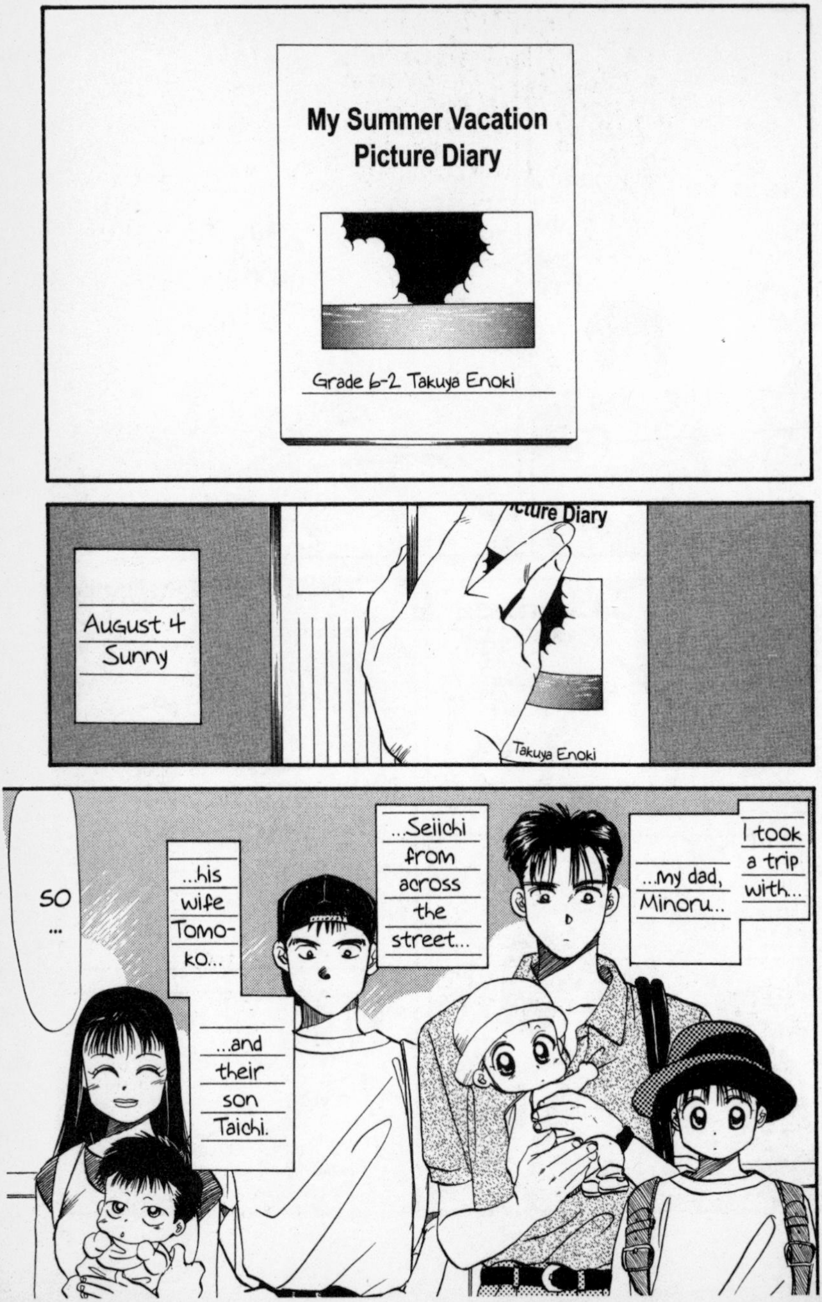
My Summer Vacation Picture Diary
Grade 6-2 Takuya Enoki
icture Diary
Takuya Enoki
August 4 Sunny
I took a trip with...
...my dad, Minoru...
...Seiichi from across the street...
...his wife Tomoko...
...and their son Taichi.
So...

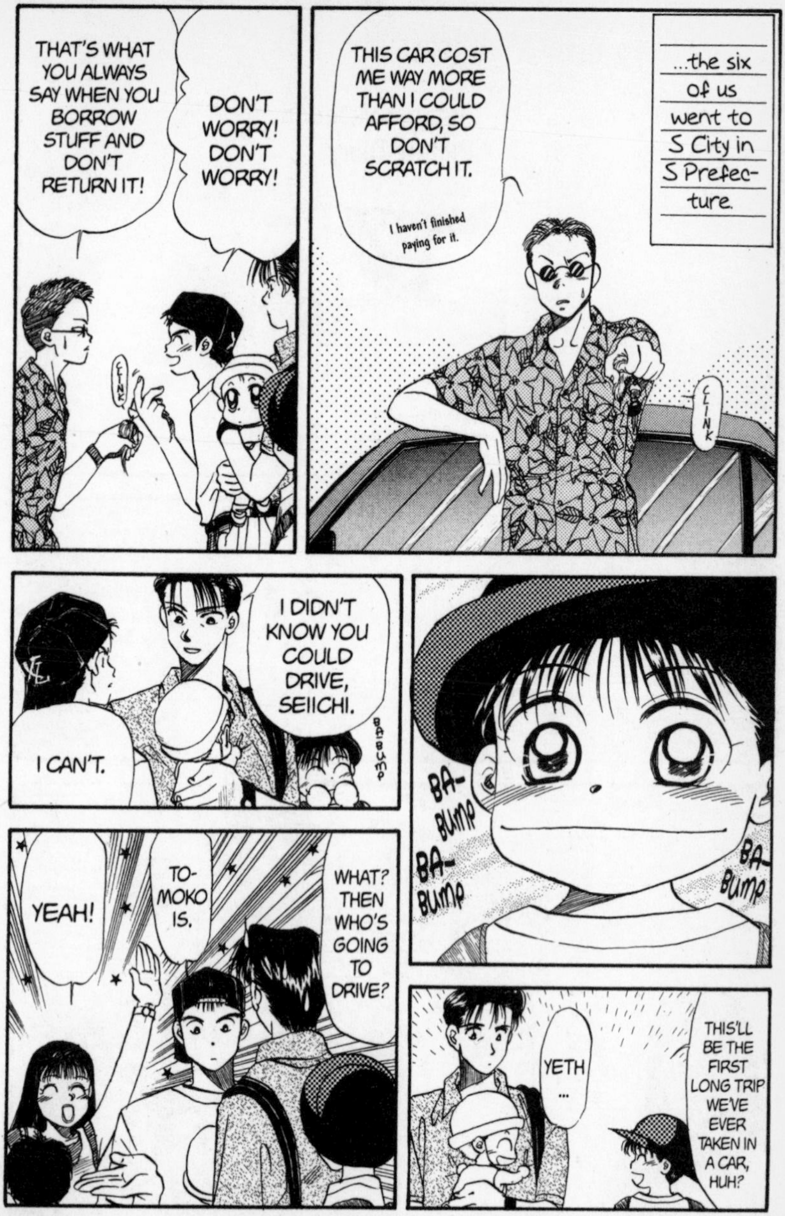
...the six of us went to S City in S Prefecture.
THIS CAR COST ME WAY MORE THAN I COULD AFFORD, SO DON'T SCRATCH IT.
I haven't finished paying for it.
CLINK
DON'T WORRY! DON'T WORRY!
THAT'S WHAT YOU ALWAYS SAY WHEN YOU BORROW STUFF AND DON'T RETURN IT!
CLINK
BA-BUMP
BA-BUMP
BA-BUMP
I DIDN'T KNOW YOU COULD DRIVE, SEIICHI.
BA-BUMP
I CAN'T.
WHAT? THEN WHO'S GOING TO DRIVE?
TO-MOKO IS.
YEAH!
THIS'LL BE THE FIRST LONG TRIP WE'VE EVER TAKEN IN A CAR, HUH?
YETH ...

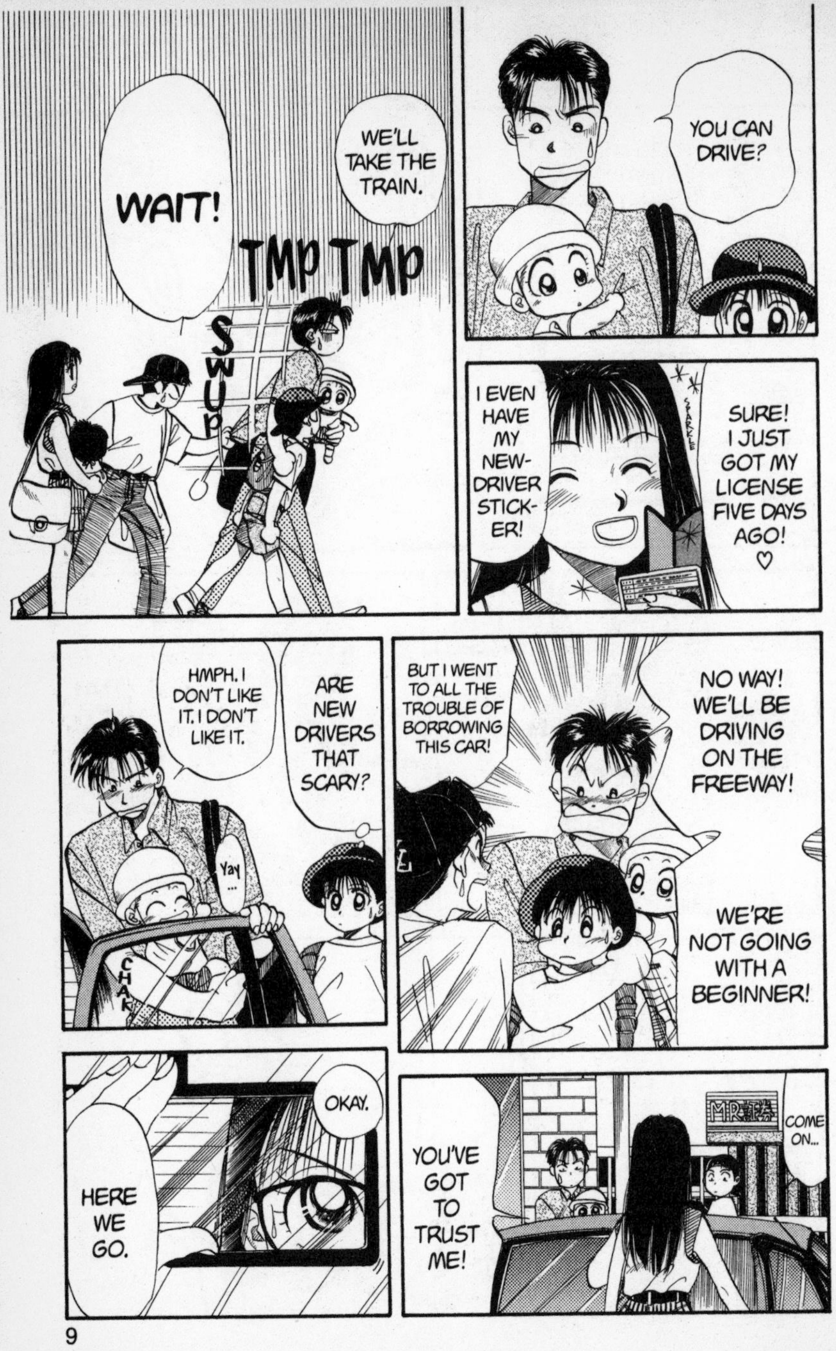
YOU CAN DRIVE?
SURE! I JUST GOT MY LICENSE FIVE DAYS AGO! ♡
SPARKLE
I EVEN HAVE MY NEW-DRIVER STICK-ER!
WE'LL TAKE THE TRAIN.
TMP TMP
WAIT!
SWUP
NO WAY! WE'LL BE DRIVING ON THE FREEWAY!
BUT I WENT TO ALL THE TROUBLE OF BORROWING THIS CAR!
WE'RE NOT GOING WITH A BEGINNER!
ARE NEW DRIVERS THAT SCARY?
HMPH. I DON'T LIKE IT. I DON'T LIKE IT.
Yay ...
CHAK
COME ON...
YOU'VE GOT TO TRUST ME!
OKAY.
HERE WE GO.

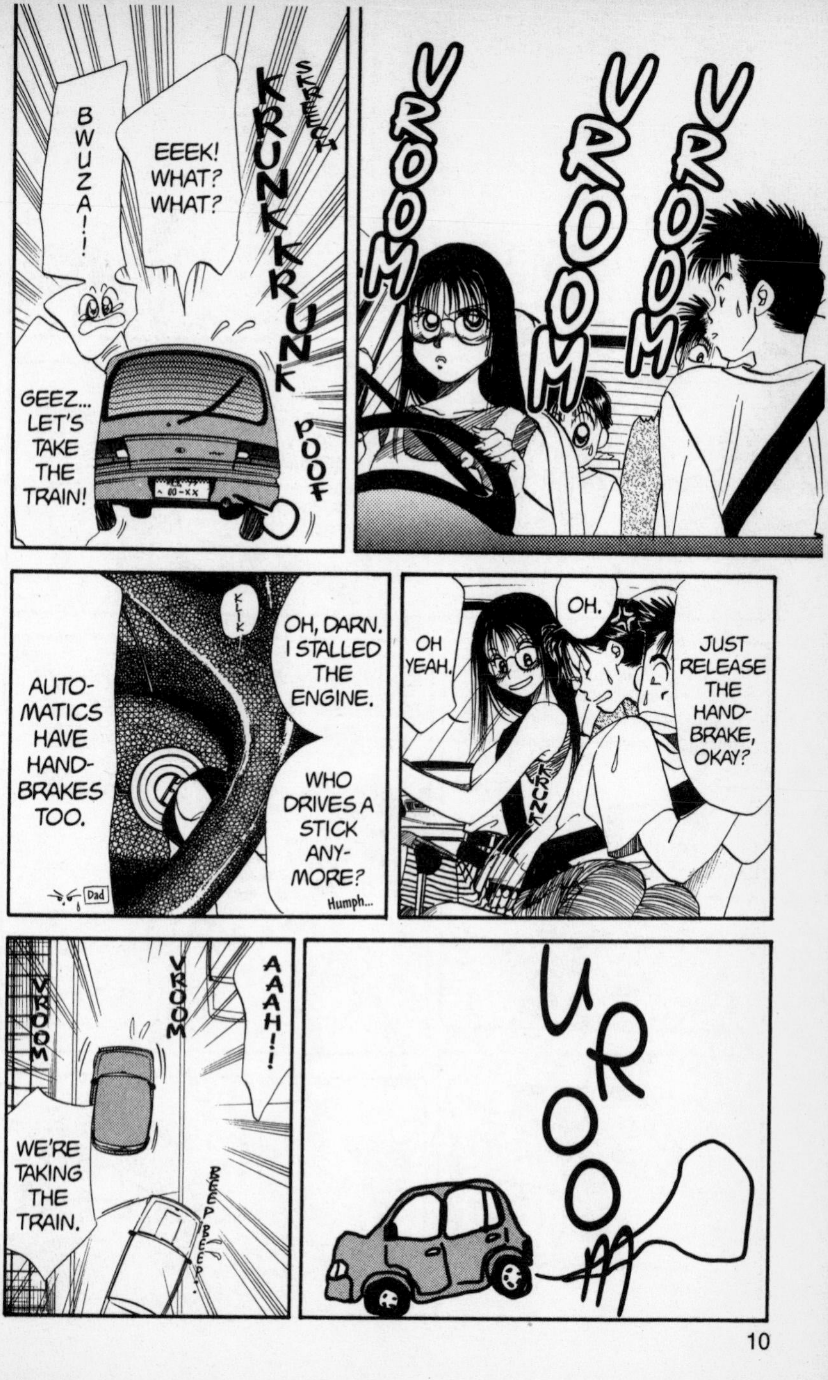
VROOM
VROOM
VROOM
SKRECH
KRUNK KRUNK
EEEK! WHAT? WHAT?
BWUZA!!
POOF
GEEZ... LET'S TAKE THE TRAIN!
JUST RELEASE THE HAND-BRAKE, OKAY?
OH.
OH YEAH.
KRUNK
OH, DARN. I STALLED THE ENGINE.
KLIK
WHO DRIVES A STICK ANY-MORE?
Humph...
AUTO-MATICS HAVE HAND-BRAKES TOO.
Dad
UROOOM
AAAH!!
VROOM
VROOM
BEEP BEEP
WE'RE TAKING THE TRAIN.

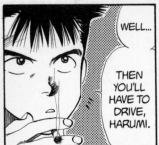

WAAAH
I'VE HAD ENOUGH. I DON'T WANT TO DRIVE ANYMORE...
...
OKAY.
THAT WORKS FOR ME.
Ga-ga...
FWIP
FWIP
Aw...
PAT
PAT
WELL...
THEN YOU'LL HAVE TO DRIVE, HARUMI.
WHAT?!
WHAT'S THE MATTER?
I SAW YOU DRIVE ALL THE TIME WHEN YOU WERE IN COLLEGE. YOU STILL HAVE A LICENSE, DON'T YOU?
WHAT?! YOU HAVE A DRIVER'S LICENSE, DAD?!
YEAH, BUT I HAVEN'T DRIVEN IN YEARS.
Ga-ga...
BUT YOU'RE PROBABLY BETTER THAN I AM!
...
WOW...
SOB
SOB
IMPRESSED
WE'D BEEN PLANNING THIS TRIP FOR THREE MONTHS.
ARE WE GONNA GET BACK ALIVE?

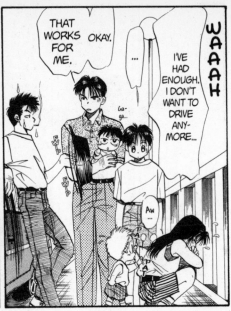

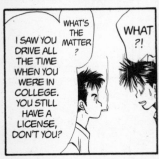

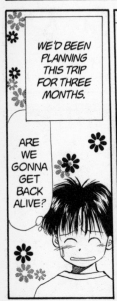

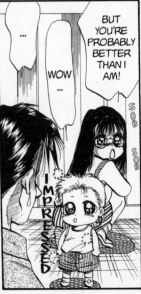

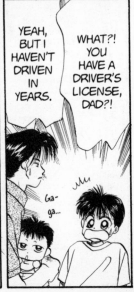

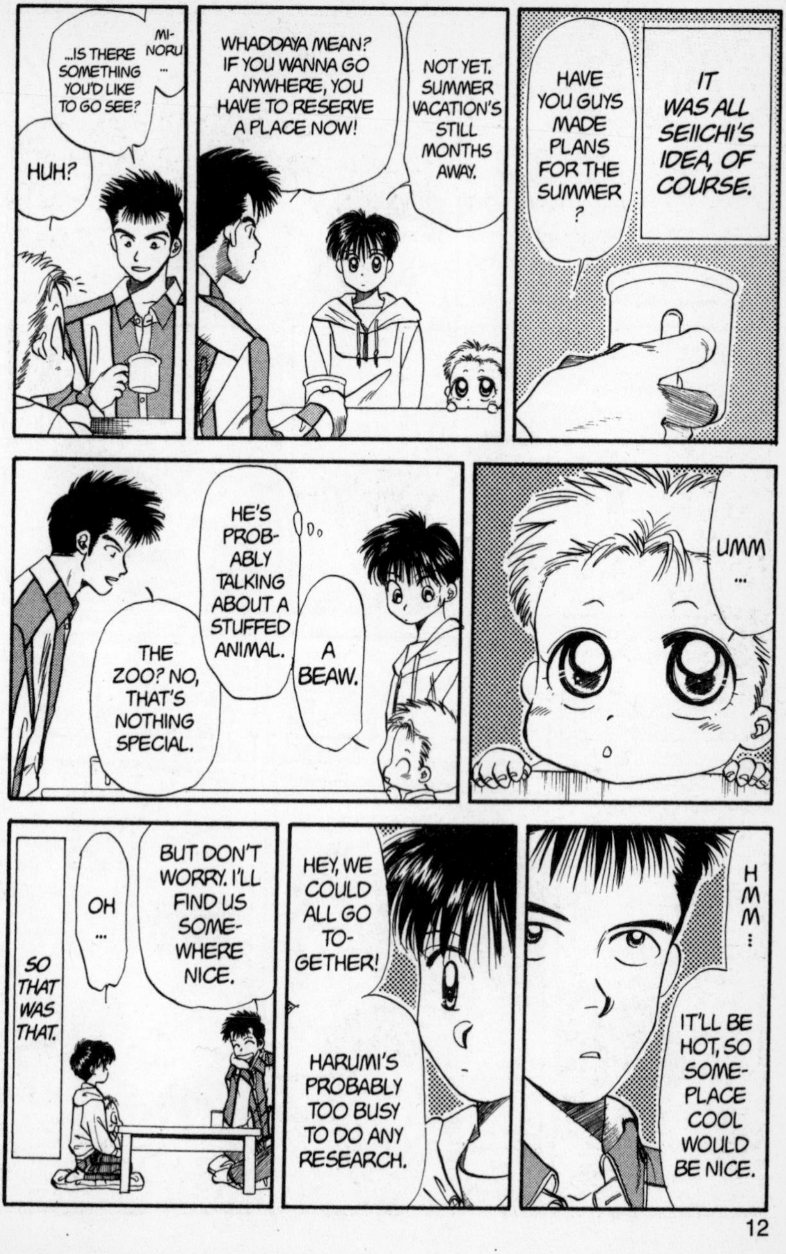
IT WAS ALL SEIICHI'S IDEA, OF COURSE.
HAVE YOU GUYS MADE PLANS FOR THE SUMMER?
NOT YET. SUMMER VACATION'S STILL MONTHS AWAY.
WHADDAYA MEAN? IF YOU WANNA GO ANYWHERE, YOU HAVE TO RESERVE A PLACE NOW!
MI-NORU...
...IS THERE SOMETHING YOU'D LIKE TO GO SEE?
HUH?
UMM...
A BEAW.
HE'S PROBABLY TALKING ABOUT A STUFFED ANIMAL.
THE ZOO? NO, THAT'S NOTHING SPECIAL.
HMM...
IT'LL BE HOT, SO SOMEPLACE COOL WOULD BE NICE.
HEY, WE COULD ALL GO TOGETHER!
HARUMI'S PROBABLY TOO BUSY TO DO ANY RESEARCH.
BUT DON'T WORRY. I'LL FIND US SOMEWHERE NICE.
OH...
SO THAT WAS THAT.

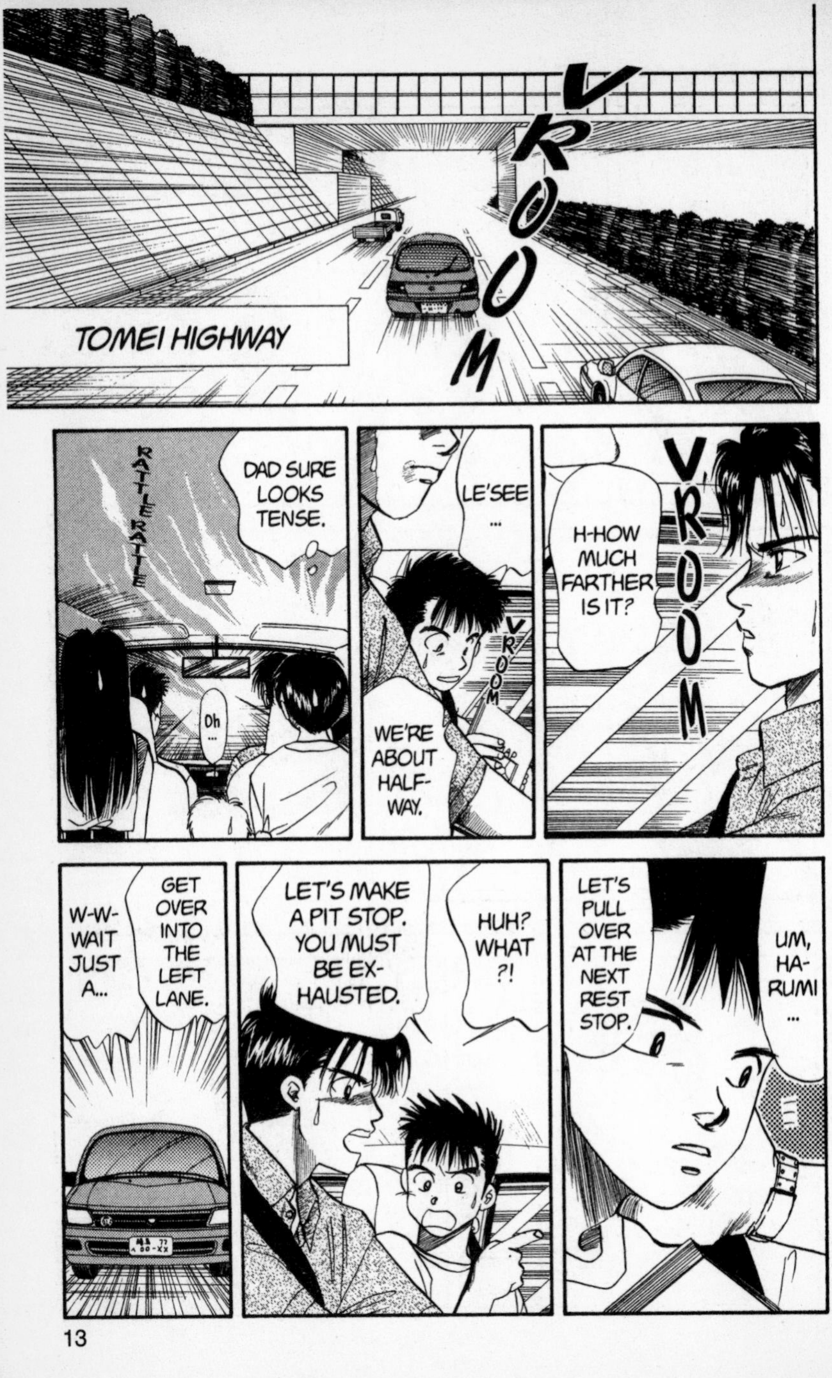
TOMEI HIGHWAY
VROOOM
VROOM
H-HOW MUCH FARTHER IS IT?
LE'SEE ...
VROOM
WE'RE ABOUT HALF-WAY.
DAD SURE LOOKS TENSE.
RATTLE RATTLE
Oh ...
UM, HA-RUMI ...
LET'S PULL OVER AT THE NEXT REST STOP.
HUH? WHAT ?!
LET'S MAKE A PIT STOP. YOU MUST BE EX-HAUSTED.
GET OVER INTO THE LEFT LANE.
W-W-WAIT JUST A...

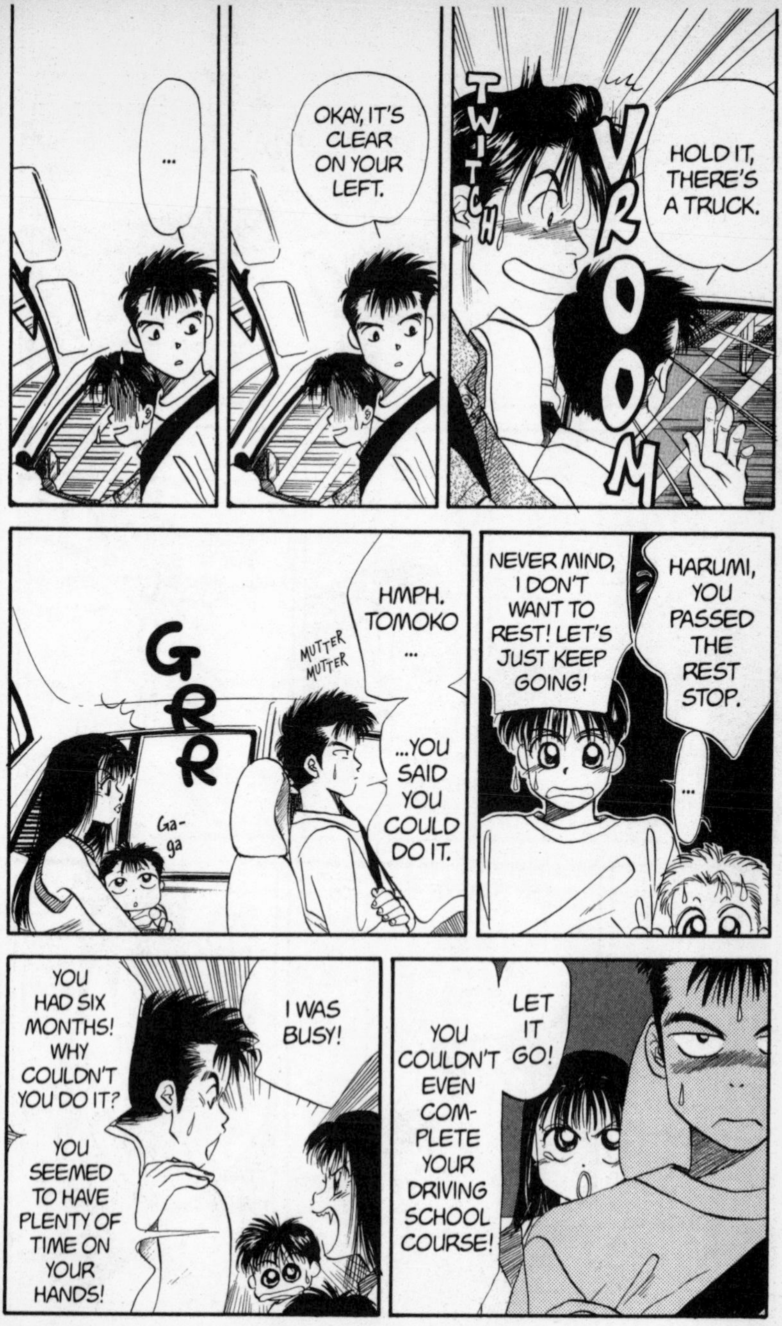
HOLD IT, THERE'S A TRUCK.
VROOM
TWITCH
OKAY, IT'S CLEAR ON YOUR LEFT.
...
HARUMI, YOU PASSED THE REST STOP.
NEVER MIND, I DON'T WANT TO REST! LET'S JUST KEEP GOING!
...
HMPH. TOMOKO ...
MUTTER MUTTER
...YOU SAID YOU COULD DO IT.
GRR
Ga-ga
LET IT GO!
YOU COULDN'T EVEN COM-PLETE YOUR DRIVING SCHOOL COURSE!
I WAS BUSY!
YOU HAD SIX MONTHS! WHY COULDN'T YOU DO IT?
YOU SEEMED TO HAVE PLENTY OF TIME ON YOUR HANDS!

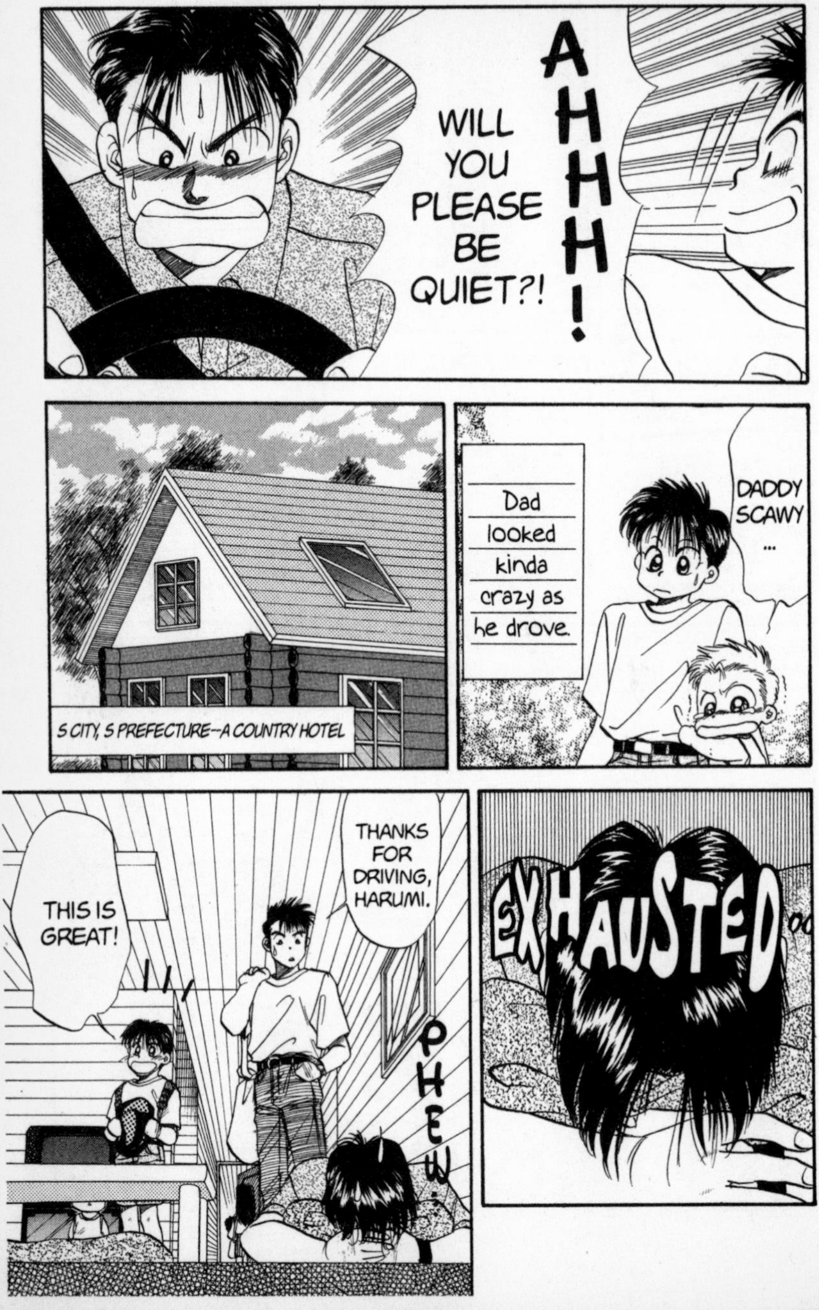
AHHHH!
WILL YOU PLEASE BE QUIET?!
DADDY SCAWY ...
Dad looked kinda crazy as he drove.
S CITY, S PREFECTURE--A COUNTRY HOTEL
EXHAUSTED
THANKS FOR DRIVING, HARUMI.
PHEW...
THIS IS GREAT!

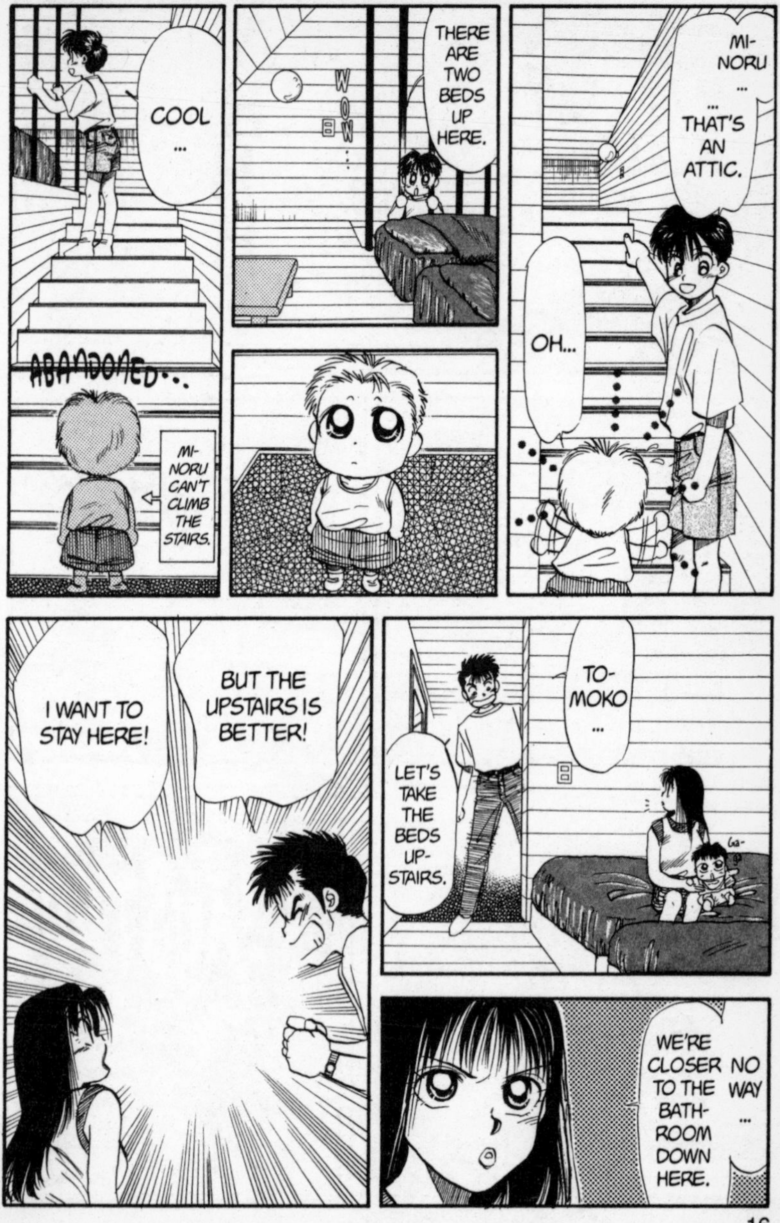
MI-NORU ... ... THAT'S AN ATTIC.
OH...
THERE ARE TWO BEDS UP HERE.
WOW...
COOL ...
ABANDONED...
MI-NORU CAN'T CLIMB THE STAIRS.
TO-MOKO ...
LET'S TAKE THE BEDS UP-STAIRS.
NO WAY ...
WE'RE CLOSER TO THE BATH-ROOM DOWN HERE.
BUT THE UPSTAIRS IS BETTER!
I WANT TO STAY HERE!

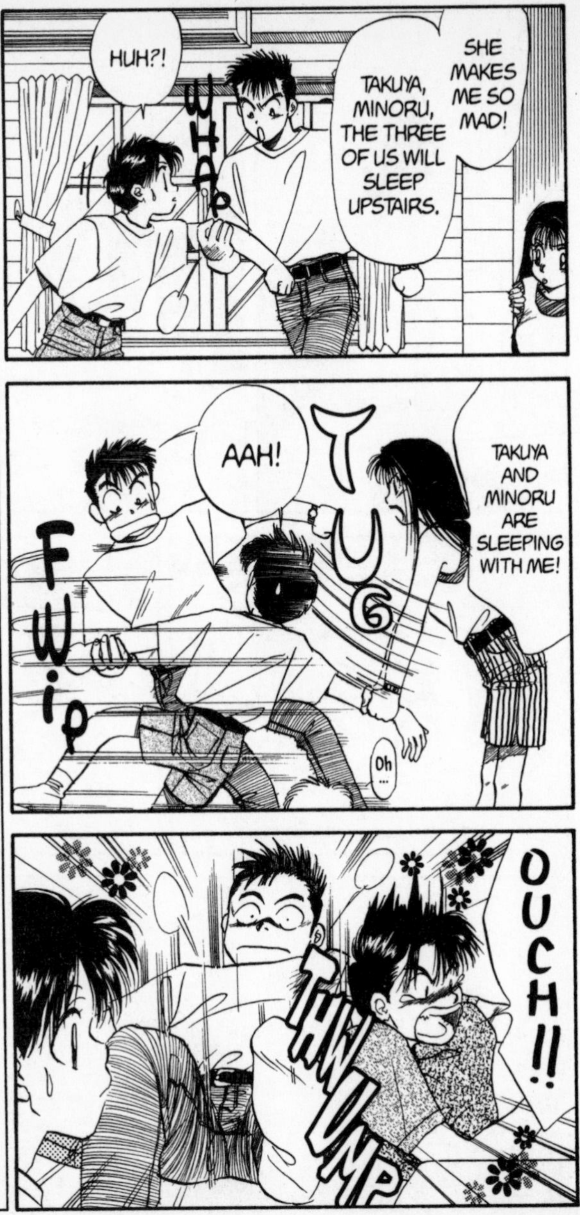
SHE MAKES ME SO MAD!
TAKUYA, MINORU, THE THREE OF US WILL SLEEP UPSTAIRS.
WHAP
HUH?!
TAKUYA AND MINORU ARE SLEEPING WITH ME!
TUG
AAH!
Oh...
FWIP
OUCH!!
THWUMP

Author's Note Part 1

Something That's Been Bothering Me

I'd completely forgotten about it, but a new school year started in Volume 3, so Minoru is now in the Panda Class and Ichika is in the Elephant Class. (see Vol.4, Chap.21) But I still think of Minoru as being in the Chick Class and Ichika in the Turtle Class. This bothers me a little.

Marimo

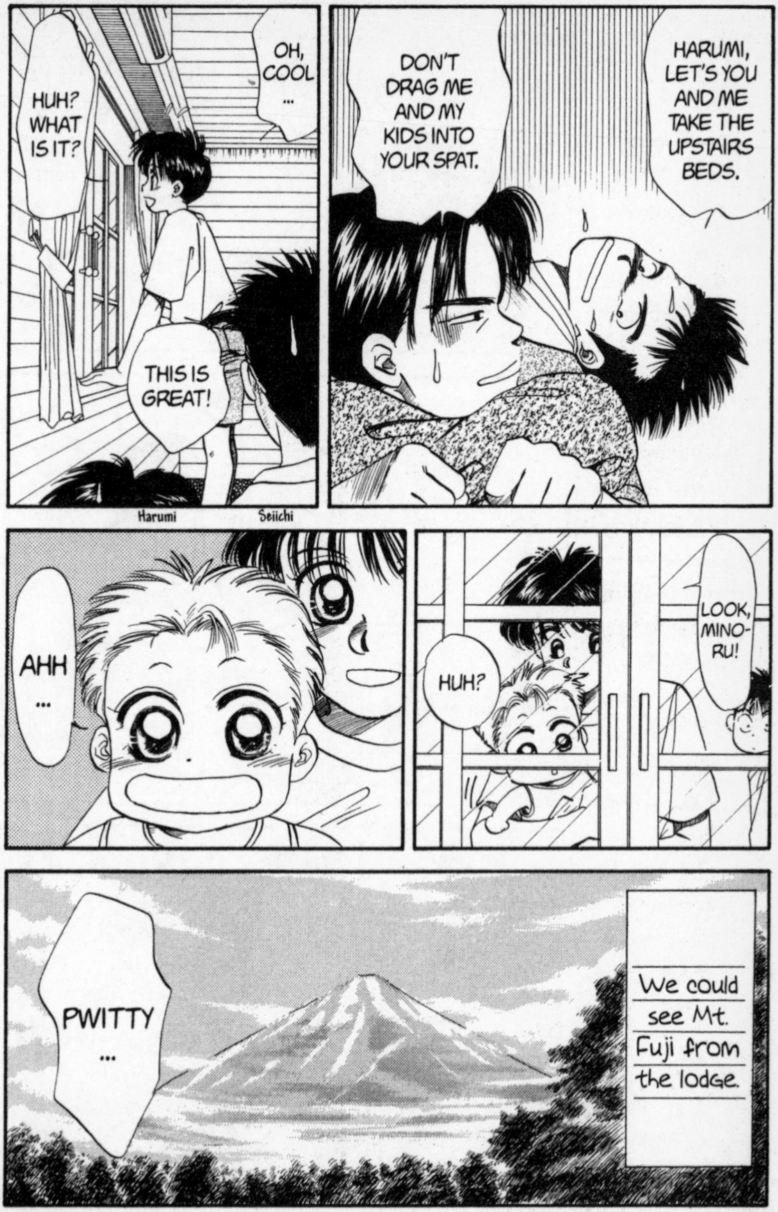
HARUMI, LET'S YOU AND ME TAKE THE UPSTAIRS BEDS.
DON'T DRAG ME AND MY KIDS INTO YOUR SPAT.
OH, COOL ...
HUH? WHAT IS IT?
THIS IS GREAT!
Harumi
Seiichi
LOOK, MINO-RU!
HUH?
AHH ...
We could see Mt. Fuji from the lodge.
PWITTY ...

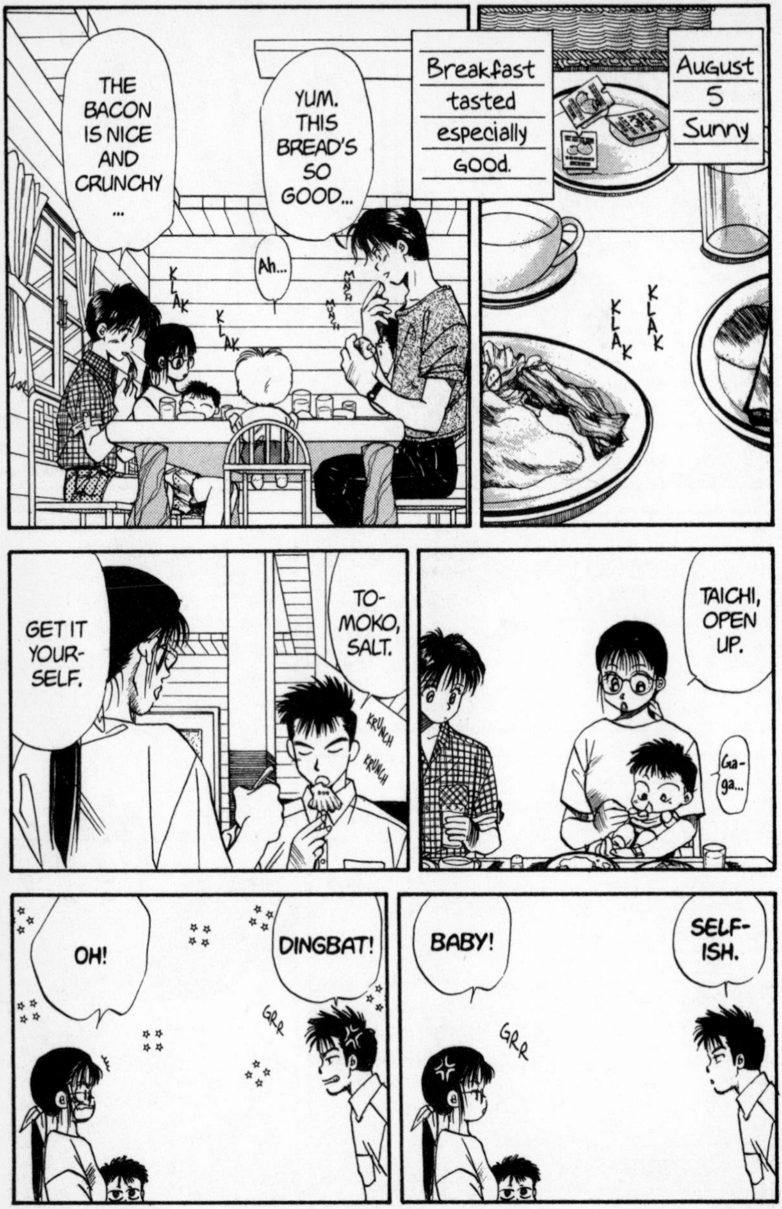
August 5 Sunny
Breakfast tasted especially good.
KLAK
KLAK
YUM. THIS BREAD'S SO GOOD...
THE BACON IS NICE AND CRUNCHY...
Ah...
MUNCH
MUNCH
KLAK
KLAK
TAICHI, OPEN UP.
Ga-ga...
TO-MOKO, SALT.
KRUNCH
KRUNCH
GET IT YOURSELF.
SELF-ISH.
BABY!
GRR
DINGBAT!
GRR
OH!

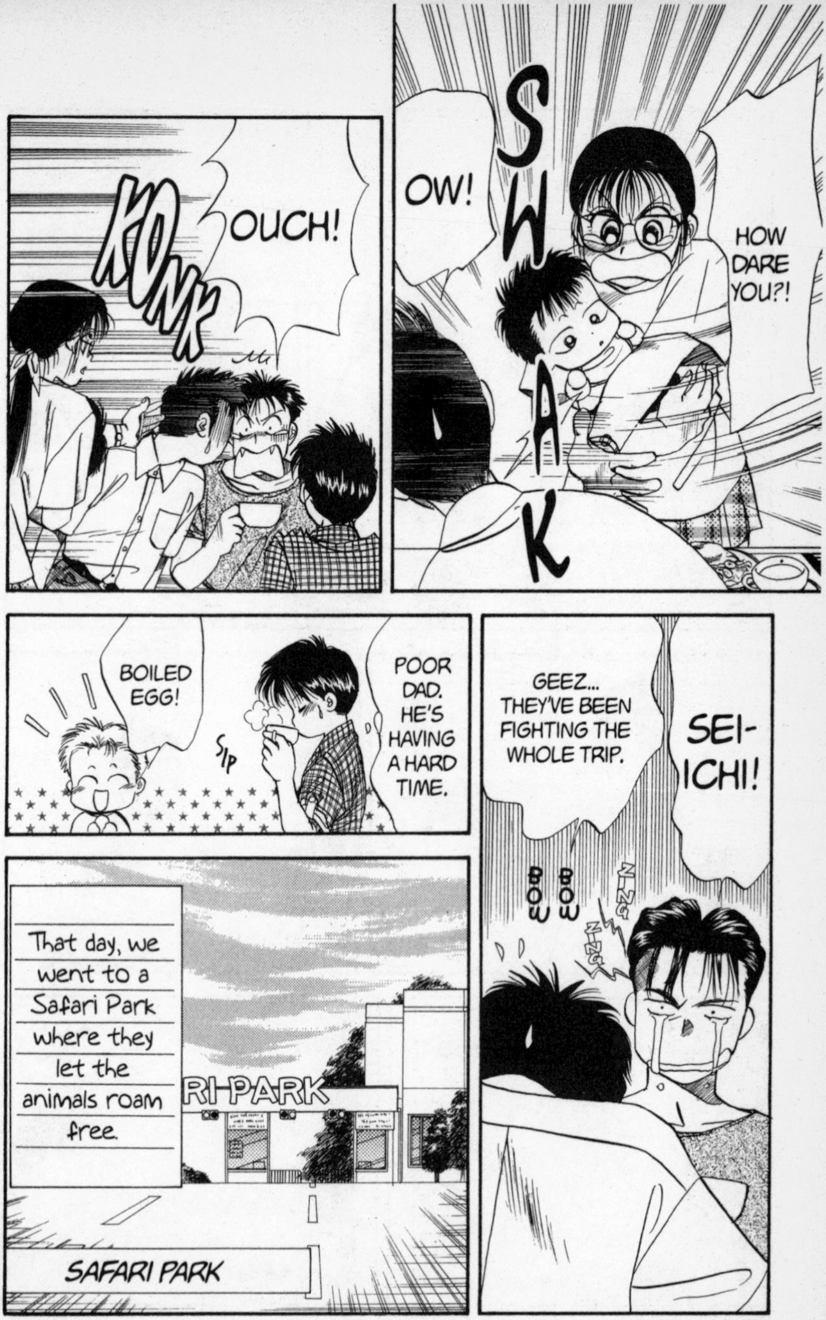
HOW DARE YOU?!
SHAK
OW!
OUCH!
KONK
Mi
SEI-ICHI!
GEEZ... THEY'VE BEEN FIGHTING THE WHOLE TRIP.
ZING ZING
BOW BOW
POOR DAD. HE'S HAVING A HARD TIME.
SIP
BOILED EGG!
That day, we went to a Safari Park where they let the animals roam free.
RI-PARK
SAFARI PARK

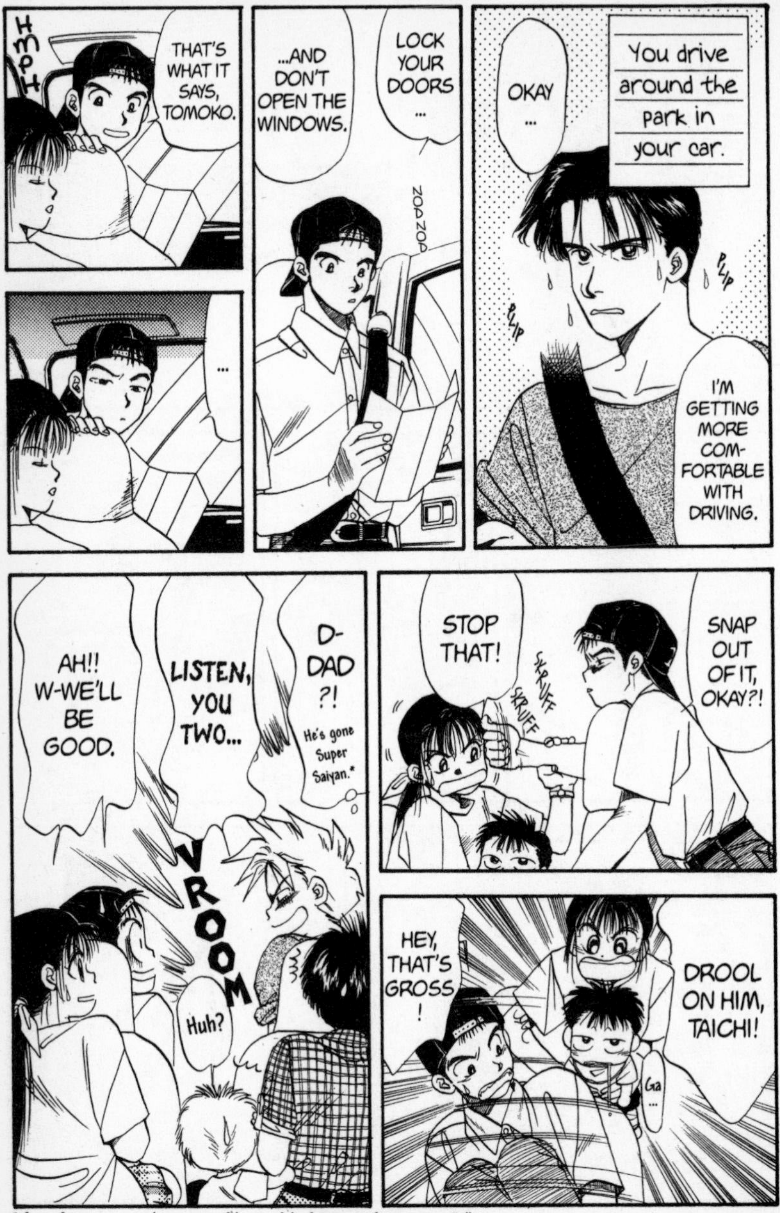
You drive around the park in your car.
OKAY ...
PLIP
PLIP
I'M GETTING MORE COM-FORTABLE WITH DRIVING.
LOCK YOUR DOORS ...
...AND DON'T OPEN THE WINDOWS.
NOD NOD
THAT'S WHAT IT SAYS, TOMOKO.
HMPH
...
SNAP OUT OF IT, OKAY?!
STOP THAT!
SCRUFF SCRUFF
DROOL ON HIM, TAICHI!
HEY, THAT'S GROSS!
Ga ...
D-DAD?!
He's gone Super Saiyan.*
LISTEN, YOU TWO...
AH!! W-WE'LL BE GOOD.
VROOM
Huh?

* Super Saiyan is a special super powerful state of the Saiyan race from *Dragon Ball*.

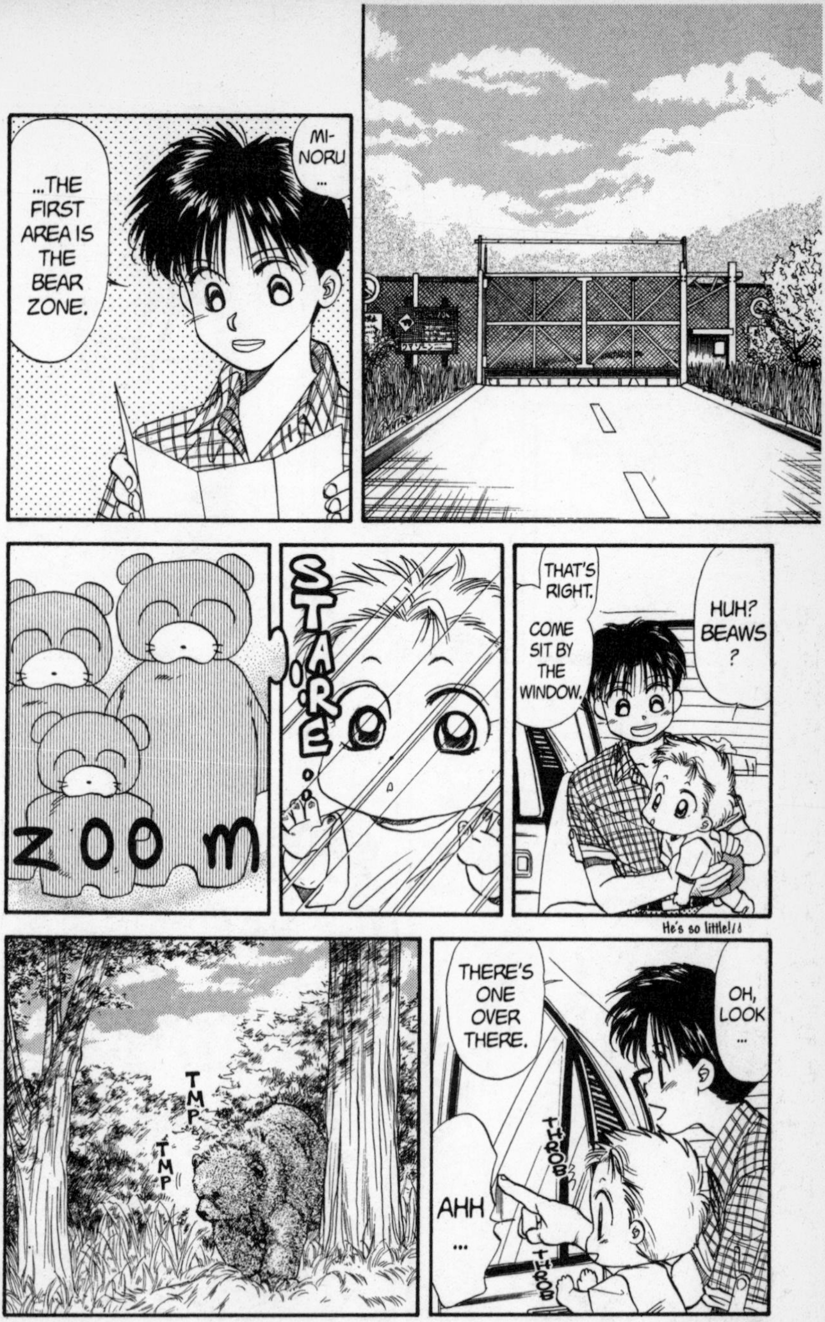
MI-NORU ...
...THE FIRST AREA IS THE BEAR ZONE.
HUH? BEAWS?
THAT'S RIGHT.
COME SIT BY THE WINDOW.
He's so little!!
STARE...
ZOOM
OH, LOOK ...
THERE'S ONE OVER THERE.
THROB
THROB
AHH ...
TMP
TMP

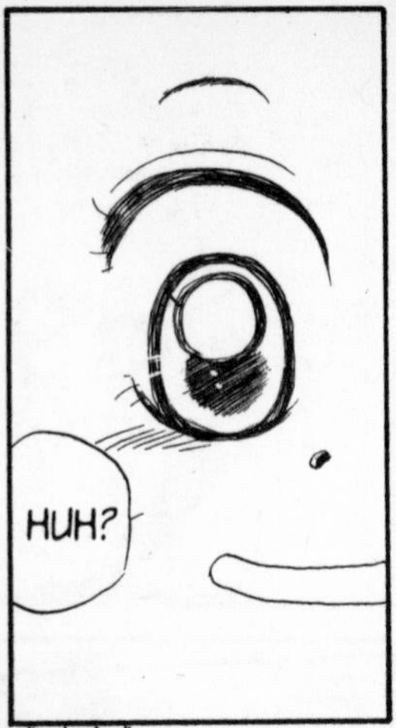
HUH?

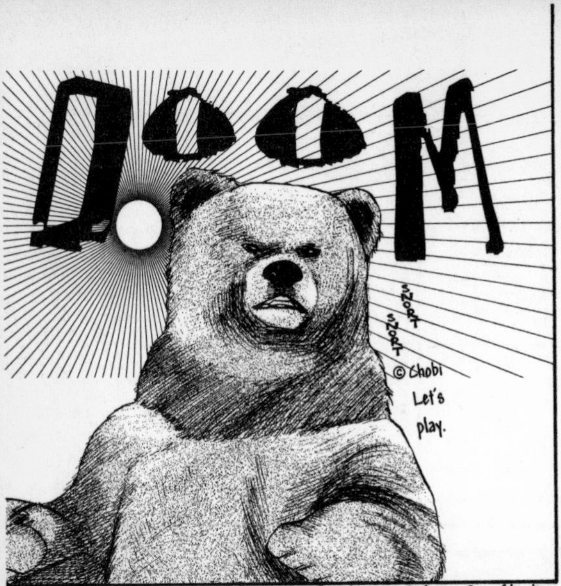
DOOM
SNORT
SNORT
© Chobi
Let's play.

*Chobi is the name of a husky in the manga *Dobutsu no Oishasan.* One of his lines is "Let's play."

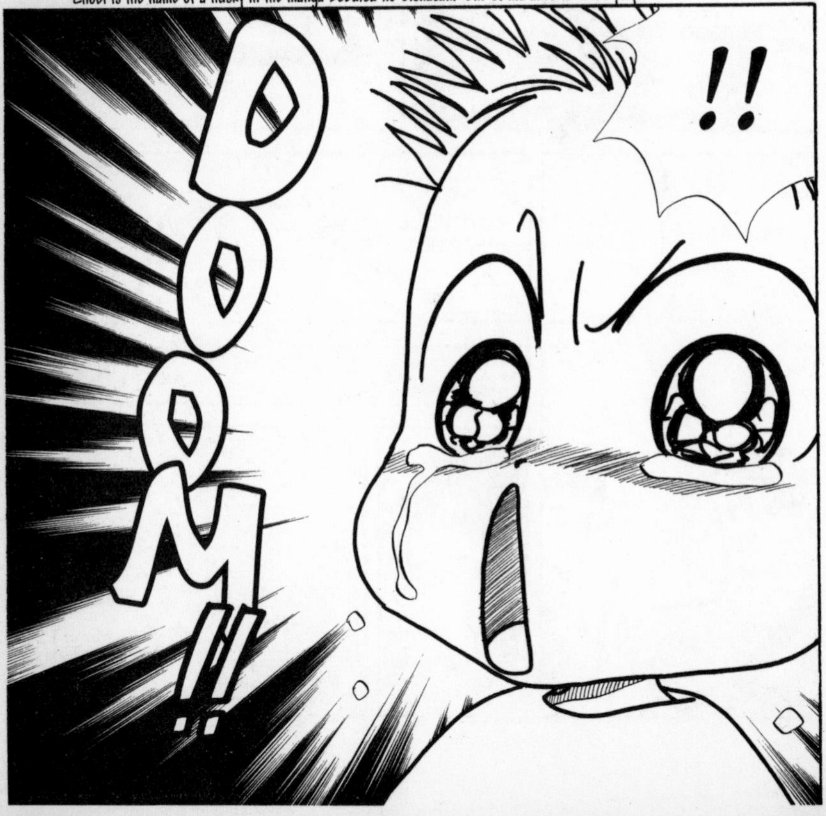
!!
DOOOM!!

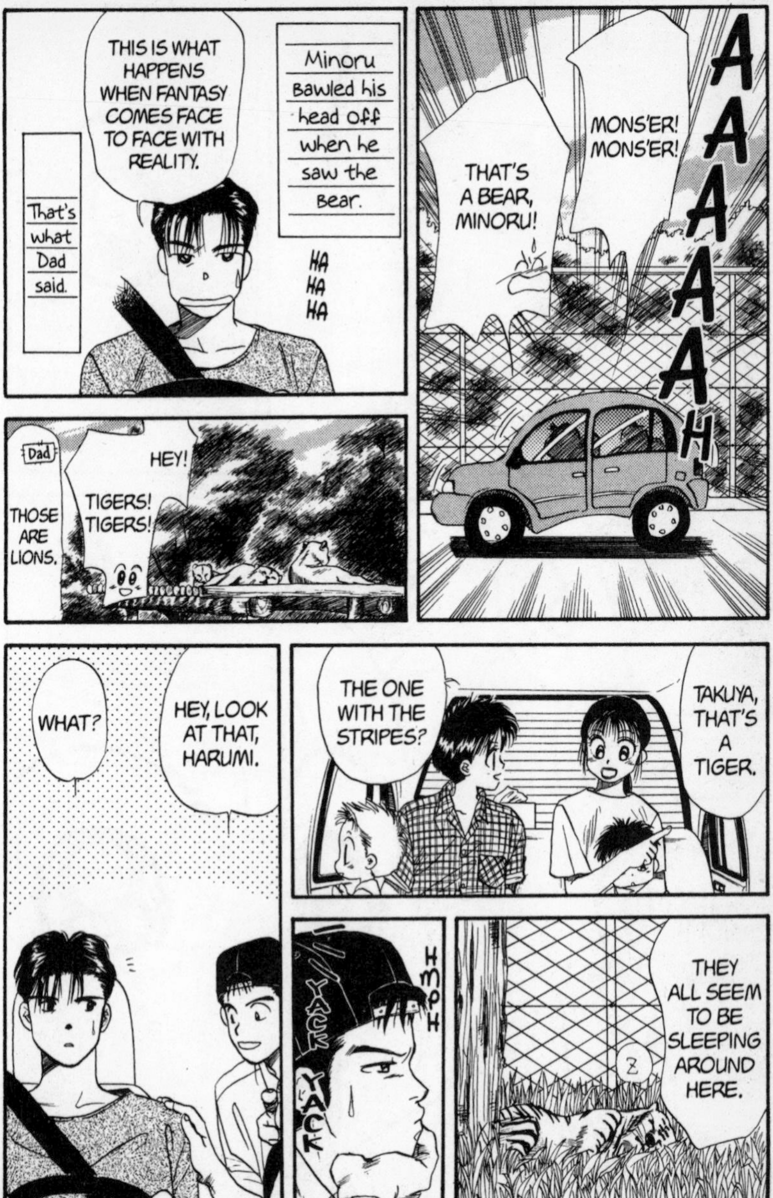
AAAAAAH
MONS'ER! MONS'ER!
THAT'S A BEAR, MINORU!
Minoru bawled his head off when he saw the bear.
THIS IS WHAT HAPPENS WHEN FANTASY COMES FACE TO FACE WITH REALITY.
That's what Dad said.
HA HA HA
HEY!
TIGERS! TIGERS!
Dad
THOSE ARE LIONS.
TAKUYA, THAT'S A TIGER.
THE ONE WITH THE STRIPES?
THEY ALL SEEM TO BE SLEEPING AROUND HERE.
Z
HMPH
YACK YACK
HEY, LOOK AT THAT, HARUMI.
WHAT?

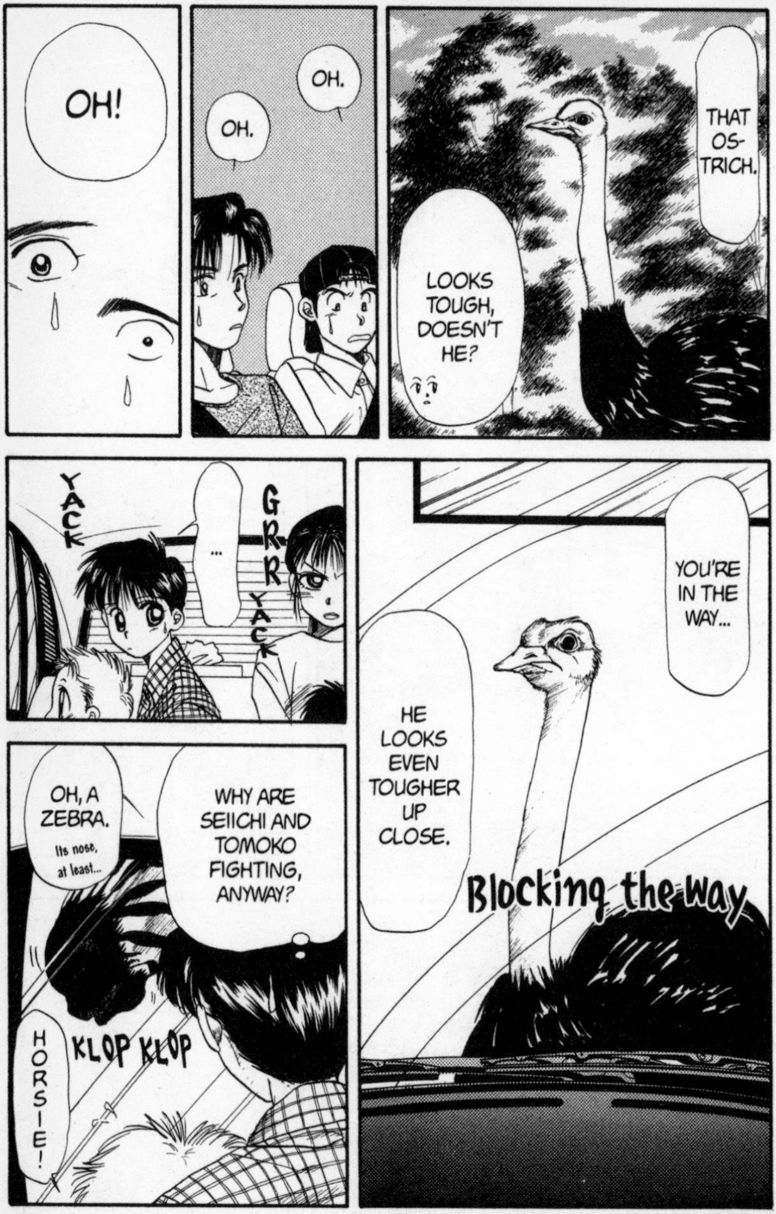
THAT OS-TRICH.
LOOKS TOUGH, DOESN'T HE?
OH.
OH.
OH!
YOU'RE IN THE WAY...
HE LOOKS EVEN TOUGHER UP CLOSE.
Blocking the way
GRR
YACK
...
YACK
WHY ARE SEIICHI AND TOMOKO FIGHTING, ANYWAY?
OH, A ZEBRA.
Its nose, at least...
KLOP KLOP
HORSIE!

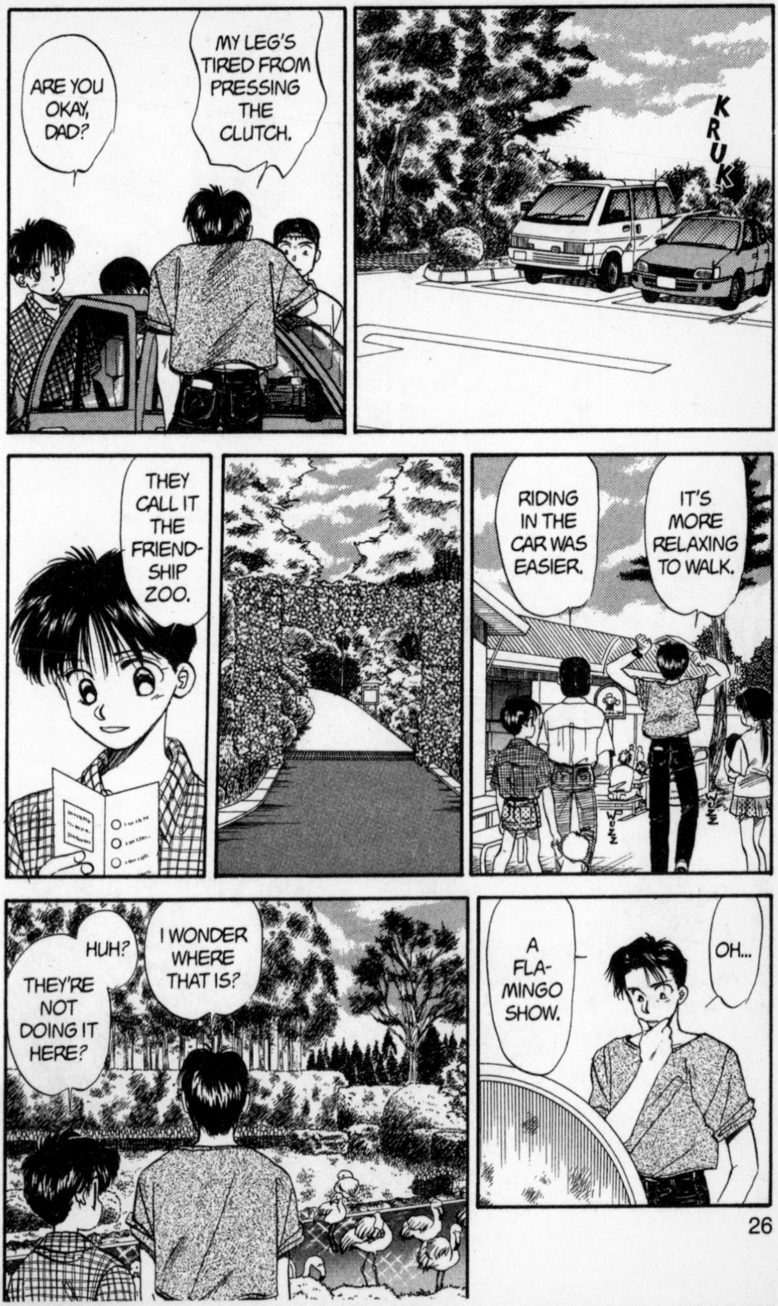
KRUK
MY LEG'S TIRED FROM PRESSING THE CLUTCH.
ARE YOU OKAY, DAD?
IT'S MORE RELAXING TO WALK.
RIDING IN THE CAR WAS EASIER.
WUZZ
WUZZ
THEY CALL IT THE FRIEND-SHIP ZOO.
OH...
A FLA-MINGO SHOW.
I WONDER WHERE THAT IS?
HUH?
THEY'RE NOT DOING IT HERE?

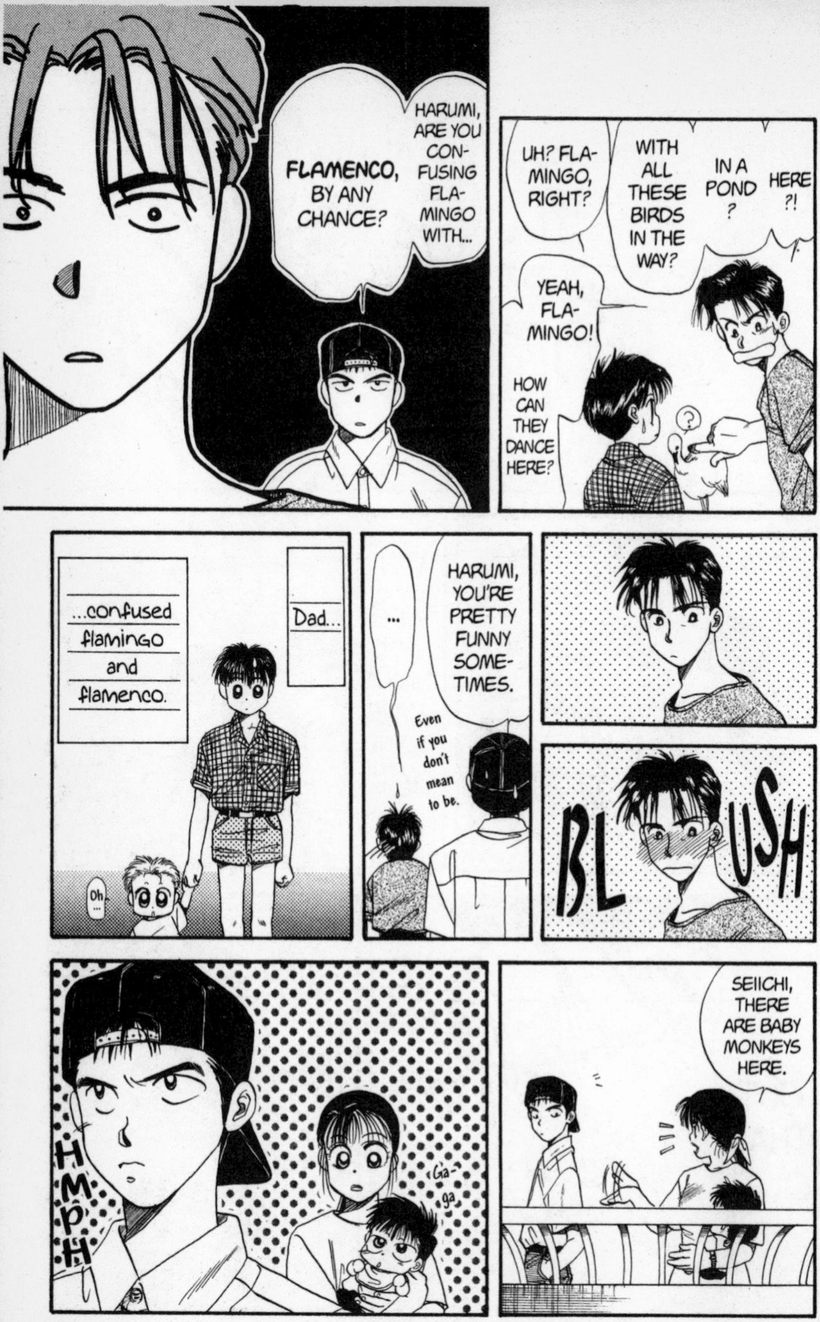
HERE?!
IN A POND?
WITH ALL THESE BIRDS IN THE WAY?
UH? FLAMINGO, RIGHT?
YEAH, FLAMINGO!
HOW CAN THEY DANCE HERE?
HARUMI, ARE YOU CONFUSING FLAMINGO WITH...
FLAMENCO, BY ANY CHANCE?
BLUSH
HARUMI, YOU'RE PRETTY FUNNY SOMETIMES.
...
Even if you don't mean to be.
Dad...
...confused flamingo and flamenco.
Oh...
SEIICHI, THERE ARE BABY MONKEYS HERE.
HMPH
Ga-ga

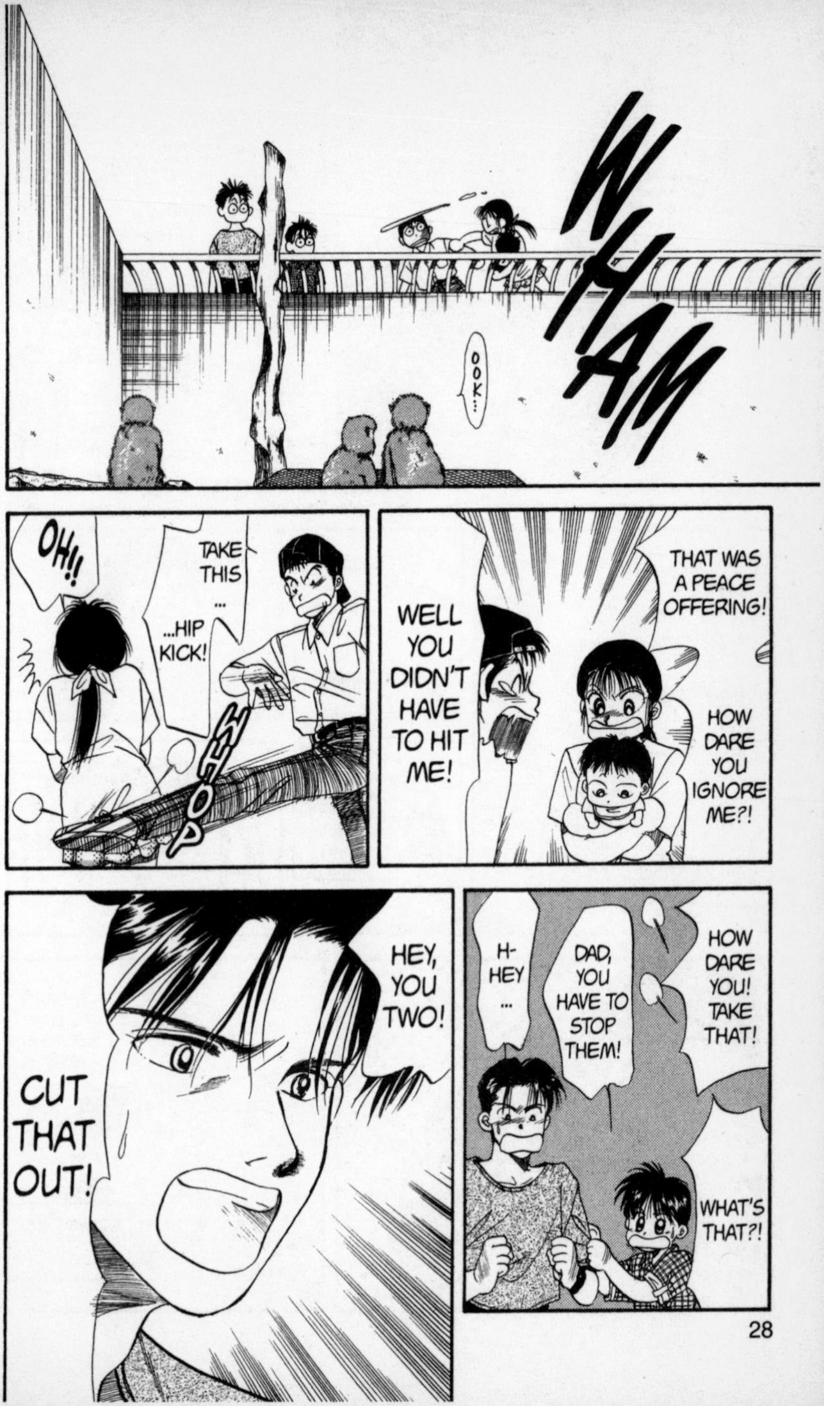
WHAM
OOK...
THAT WAS A PEACE OFFERING!
WELL YOU DIDN'T HAVE TO HIT ME!
HOW DARE YOU IGNORE ME?!
TAKE THIS ...
...HIP KICK!
OH!!
WHOOP
HOW DARE YOU! TAKE THAT!
DAD, YOU HAVE TO STOP THEM!
H- HEY ...
WHAT'S THAT?!
HEY, YOU TWO!
CUT THAT OUT!

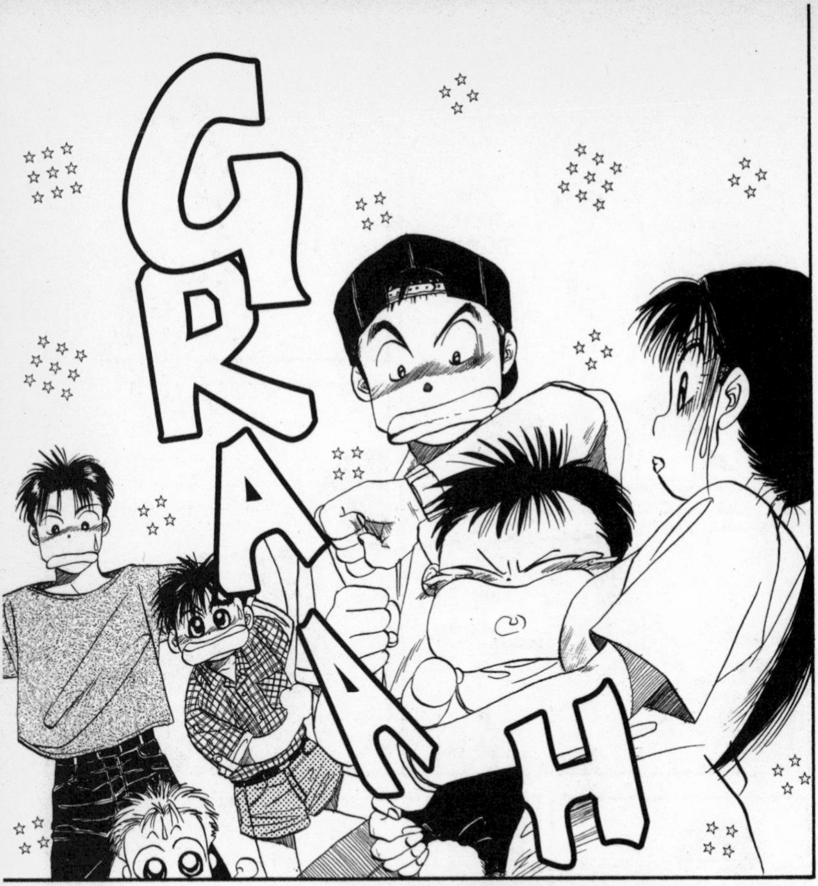
GRAAH

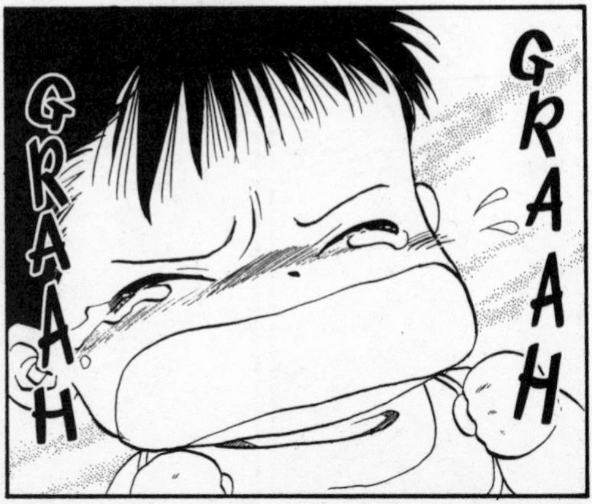
GRAAAH
GRAAH

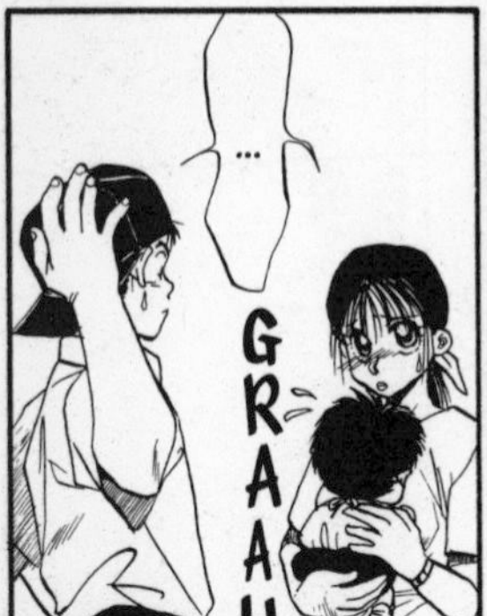
...
GRAAH

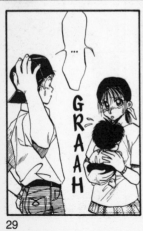

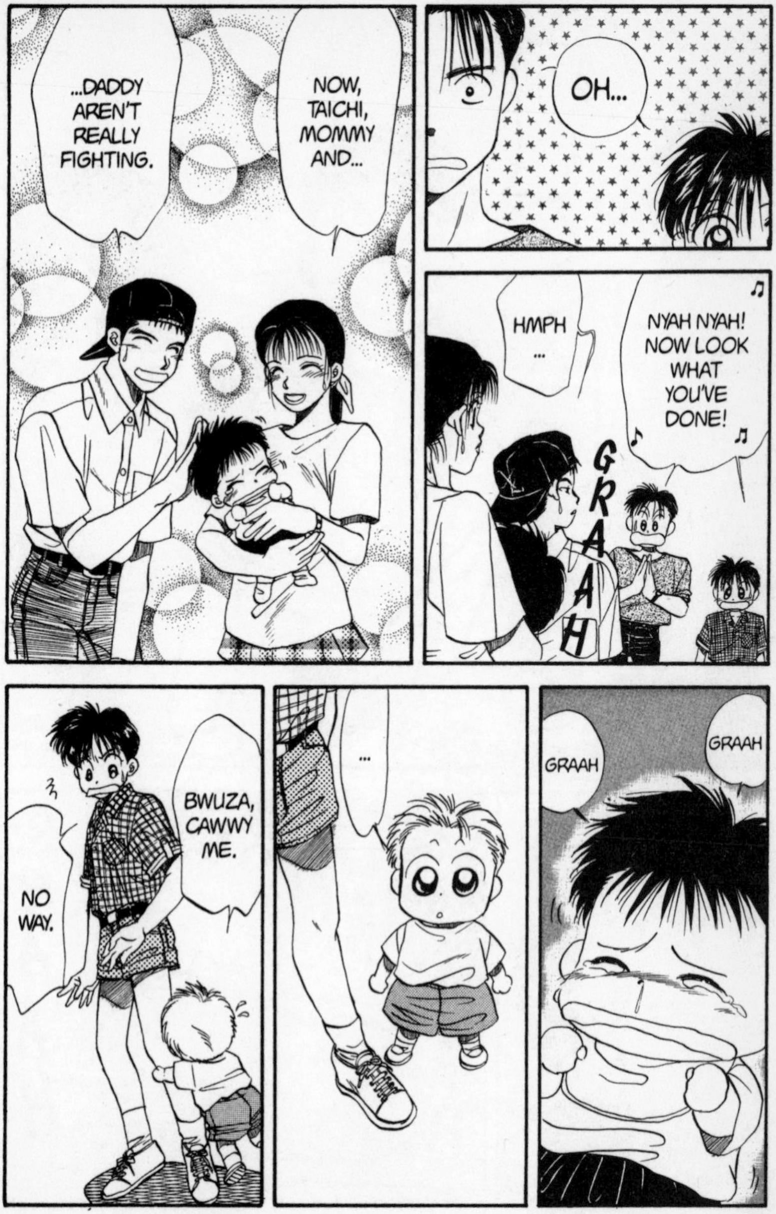
OH...
NYAH NYAH! NOW LOOK WHAT YOU'VE DONE!
HMPH ...
GRAAH
NOW, TAICHI, MOMMY AND...
...DADDY AREN'T REALLY FIGHTING.
GRAAH
GRAAH
...
BWUZA, CAWWY ME.
NO WAY.

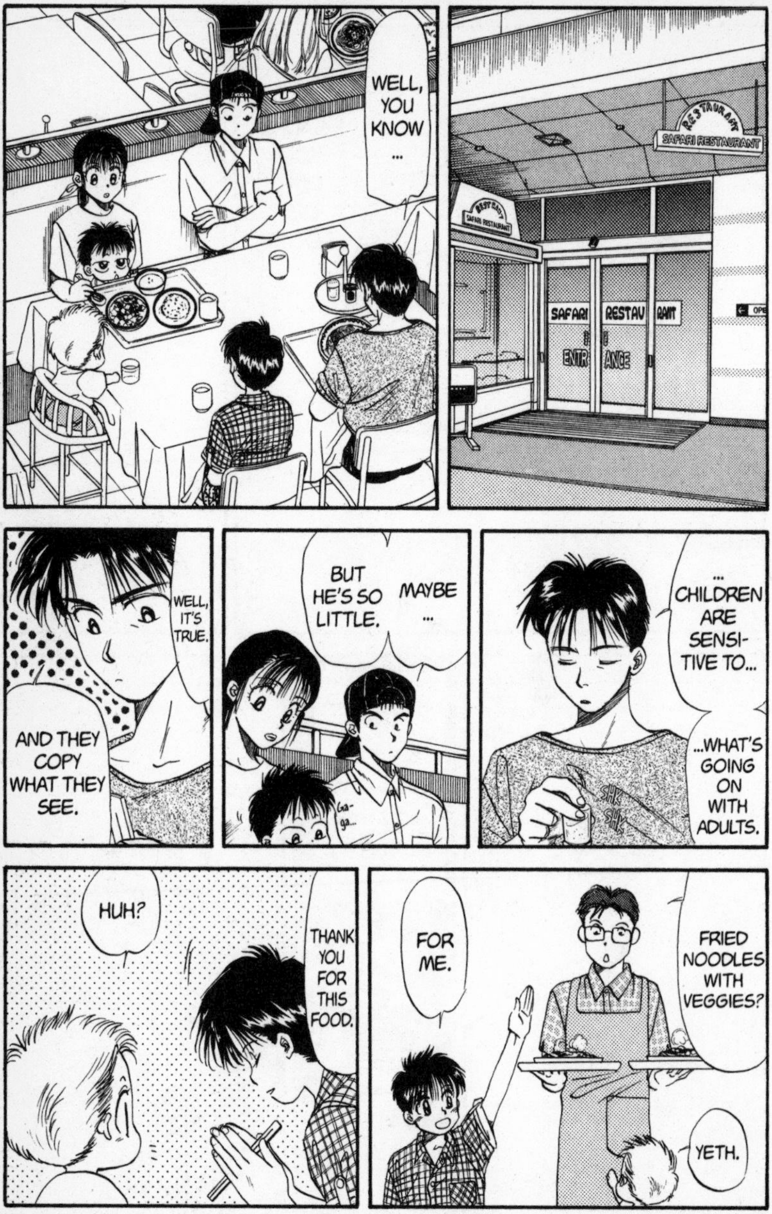
RESTAURANT
SAFARI RESTAURANT
SAFARI RESTAU RANT
ENTR ANCE
WELL, YOU KNOW ...
... CHILDREN ARE SENSI-TIVE TO...
...WHAT'S GOING ON WITH ADULTS.
SHK SHK
MAYBE ...
BUT HE'S SO LITTLE.
Ga-ga...
WELL, IT'S TRUE.
AND THEY COPY WHAT THEY SEE.
FRIED NOODLES WITH VEGGIES?
FOR ME.
YETH.
THANK YOU FOR THIS FOOD.
HUH?

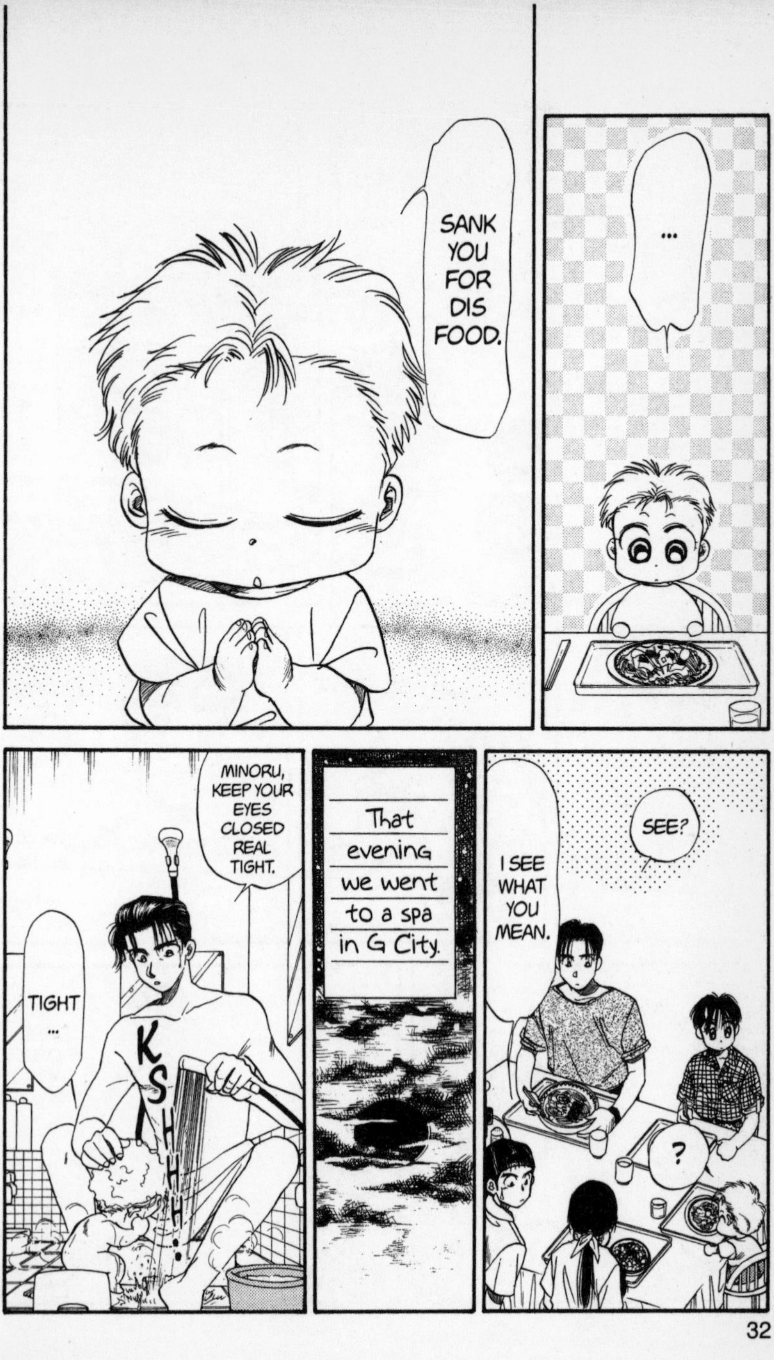
...
SANK YOU FOR DIS FOOD.
SEE?
I SEE WHAT YOU MEAN.
?
That evening we went to a spa in G City.
MINORU, KEEP YOUR EYES CLOSED REAL TIGHT.
KSHHHH
TIGHT ...

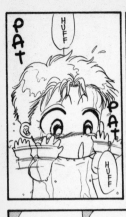

KSHH
JUST A LITTLE LONGER.
OH...
OKAY, MINORU.
*Dad
KSHH
SPUTTER
HUFF
PAT
PAT
HUFF
HERE.
GASP
GASP
HARUMI SURE IS GOOD WITH KIDS.
DAD LIKES TO GIVE MINORU A BATH.
A DOTING FATHER, EH?
YEAH, BUT IT'S NOT JUST THAT...
MINORU MAKES REALLY FUNNY FACES. ♡
HA HA HA HA HA
WEIRD-OES.

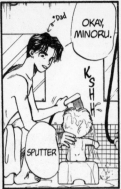

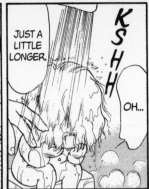

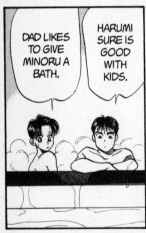

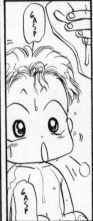

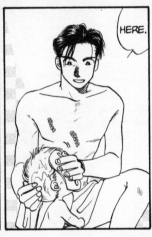

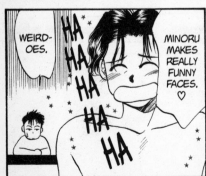

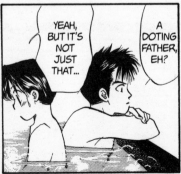

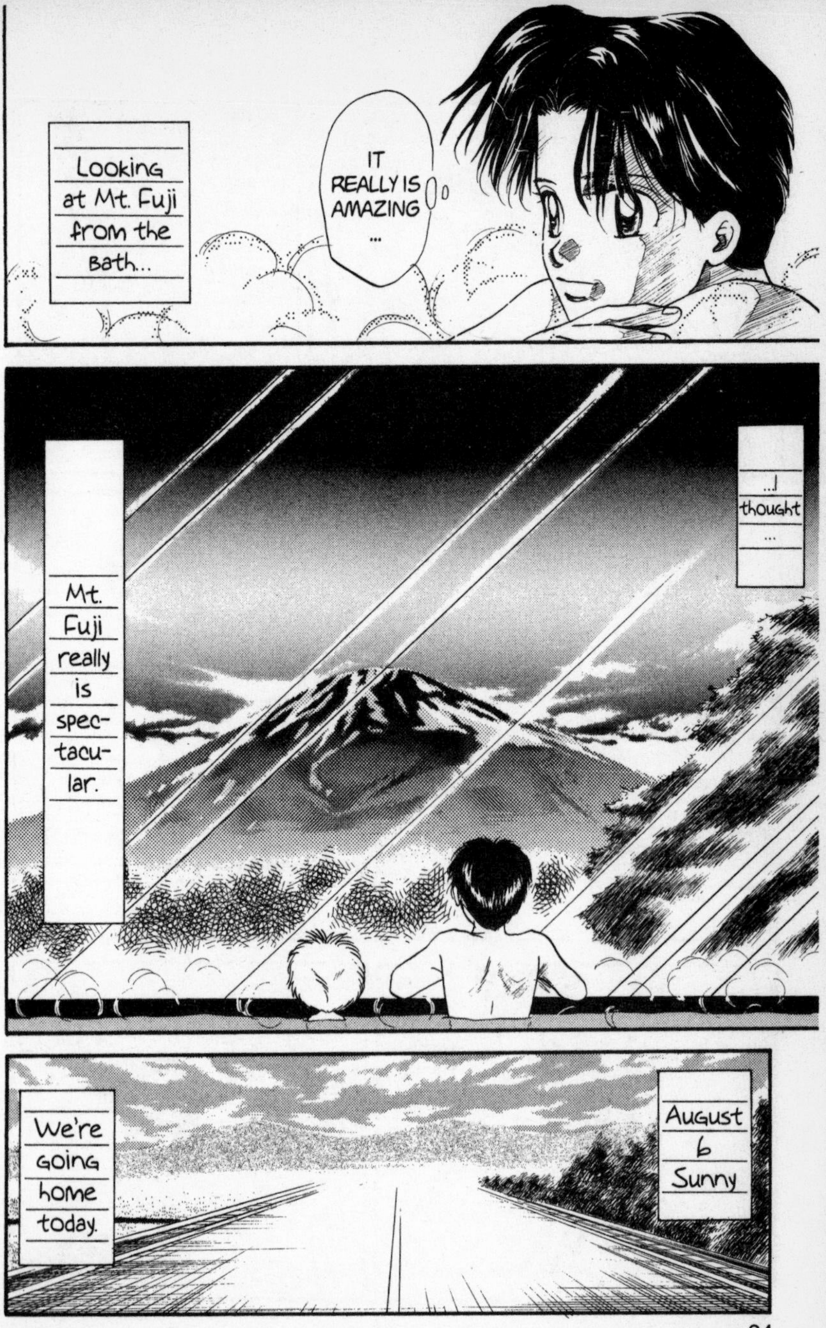
IT REALLY IS AMAZING ...
Looking at Mt. Fuji from the bath...
...I thought ...
Mt. Fuji really is spectacular.
August 6 Sunny
We're going home today.

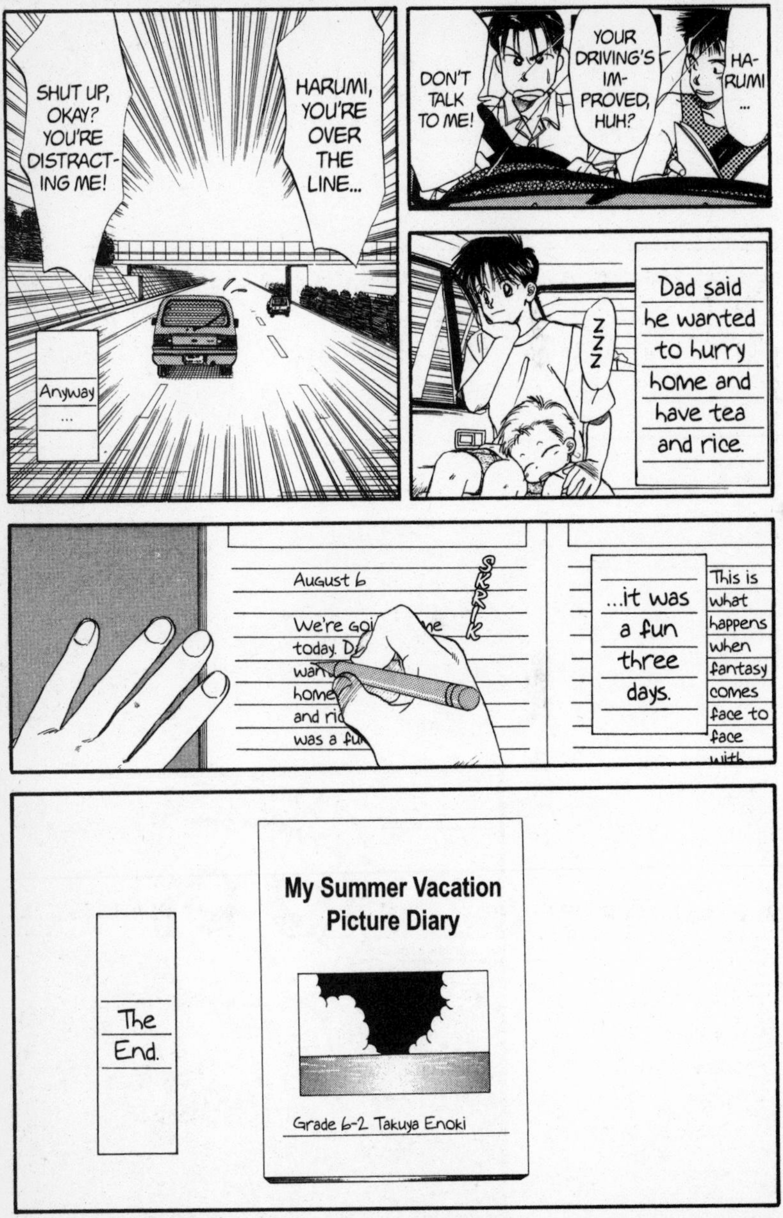
HA-RUMI...
YOUR DRIVING'S IM-PROVED, HUH?
DON'T TALK TO ME!
Dad said he wanted to hurry home and have tea and rice.
ZZZ
HARUMI, YOU'RE OVER THE LINE...
SHUT UP, OKAY? YOU'RE DISTRACT-ING ME!
Anyway ...
This is what happens when fantasy comes face to face with
...it was a fun three days.
SKRIK
August 6
My Summer Vacation Picture Diary
Grade 6-2 Takuya Enoki
The End.

Chapter 33 / The End

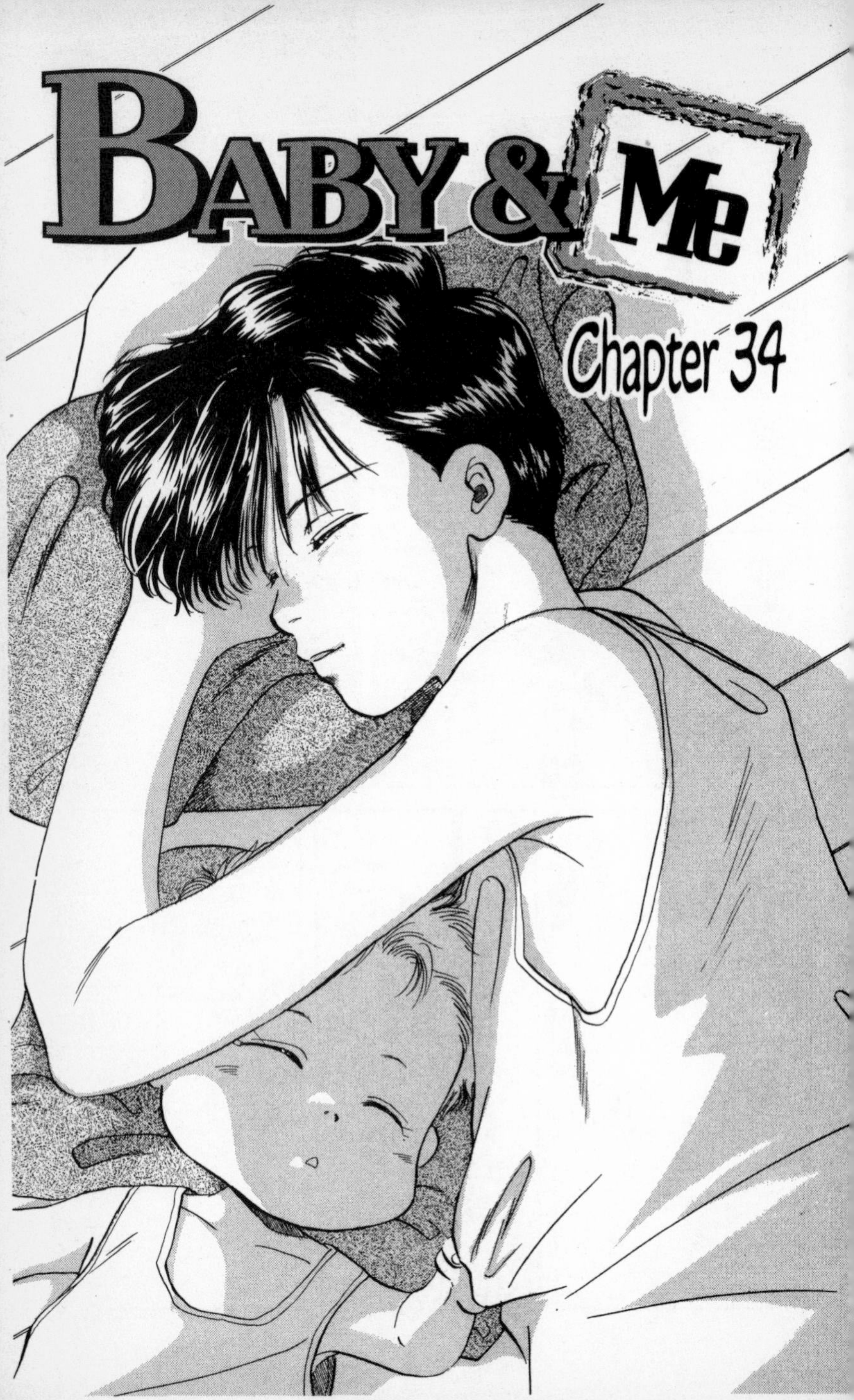
BABY & ME
Chapter 34

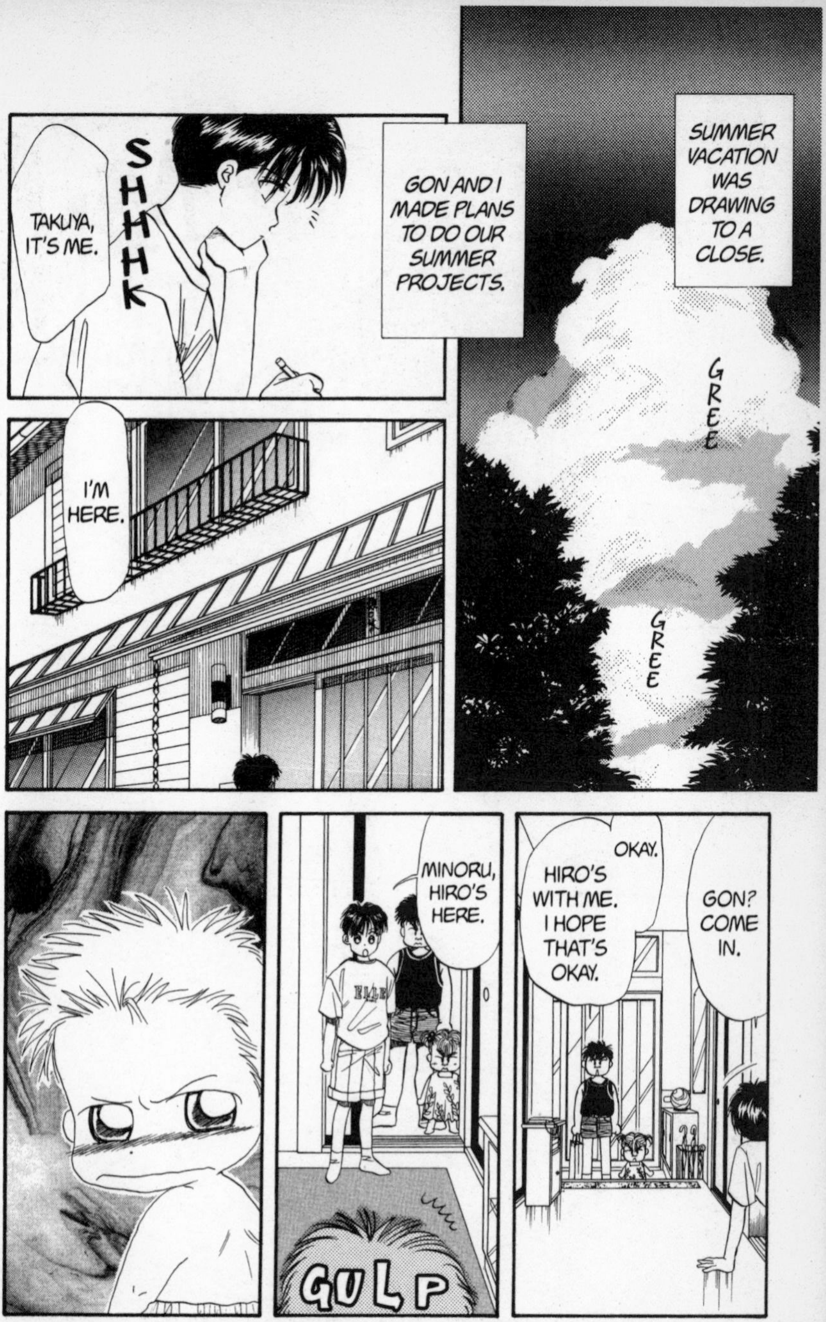
SUMMER VACATION WAS DRAWING TO A CLOSE.
GREE
GREE
GON AND I MADE PLANS TO DO OUR SUMMER PROJECTS.
SHHHK
TAKUYA, IT'S ME.
I'M HERE.
GON? COME IN.
OKAY.
HIRO'S WITH ME. I HOPE THAT'S OKAY.
MINORU, HIRO'S HERE.
GULP

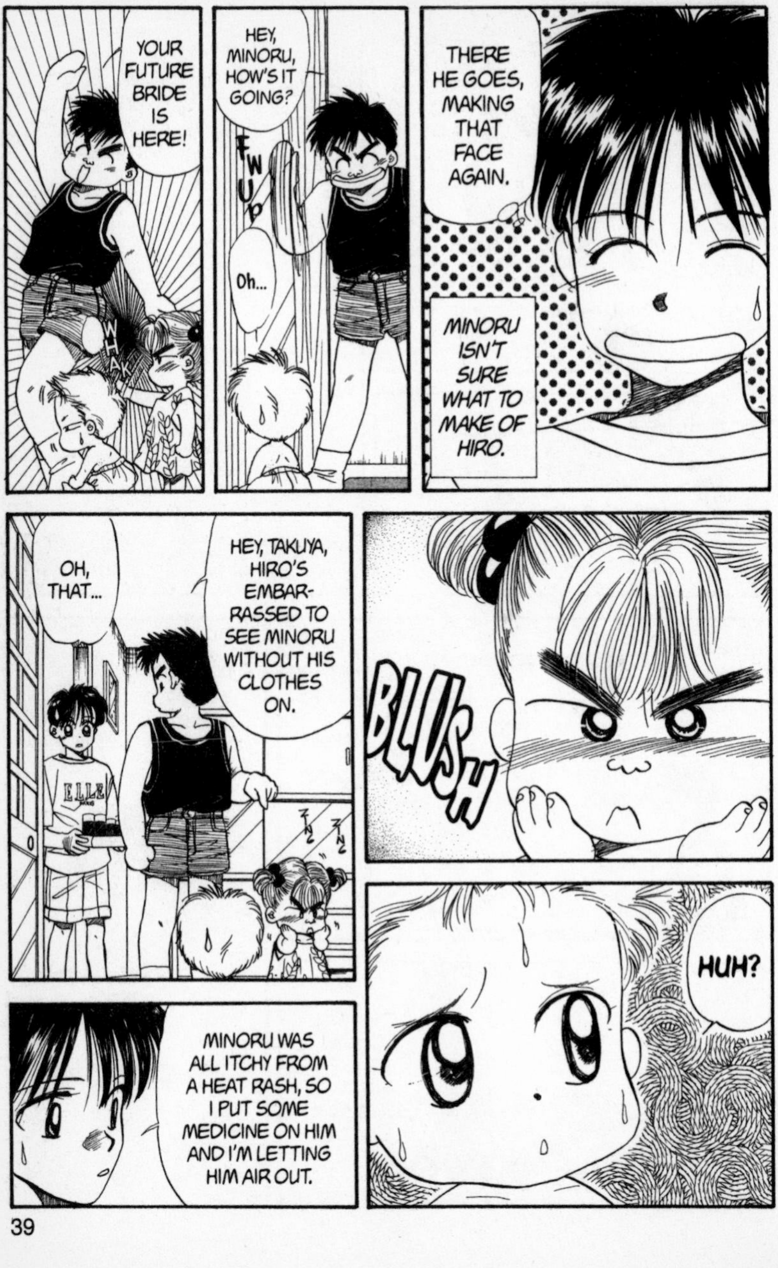
THERE HE GOES, MAKING THAT FACE AGAIN.
MINORU ISN'T SURE WHAT TO MAKE OF HIRO.
HEY, MINORU, HOW'S IT GOING?
FWUP
Oh...
YOUR FUTURE BRIDE IS HERE!
WHAK
BLUSH
HUH?
HEY, TAKUYA, HIRO'S EMBAR-RASSED TO SEE MINORU WITHOUT HIS CLOTHES ON.
OH, THAT...
ELLE
MINORU WAS ALL ITCHY FROM A HEAT RASH, SO I PUT SOME MEDICINE ON HIM AND I'M LETTING HIM AIR OUT.

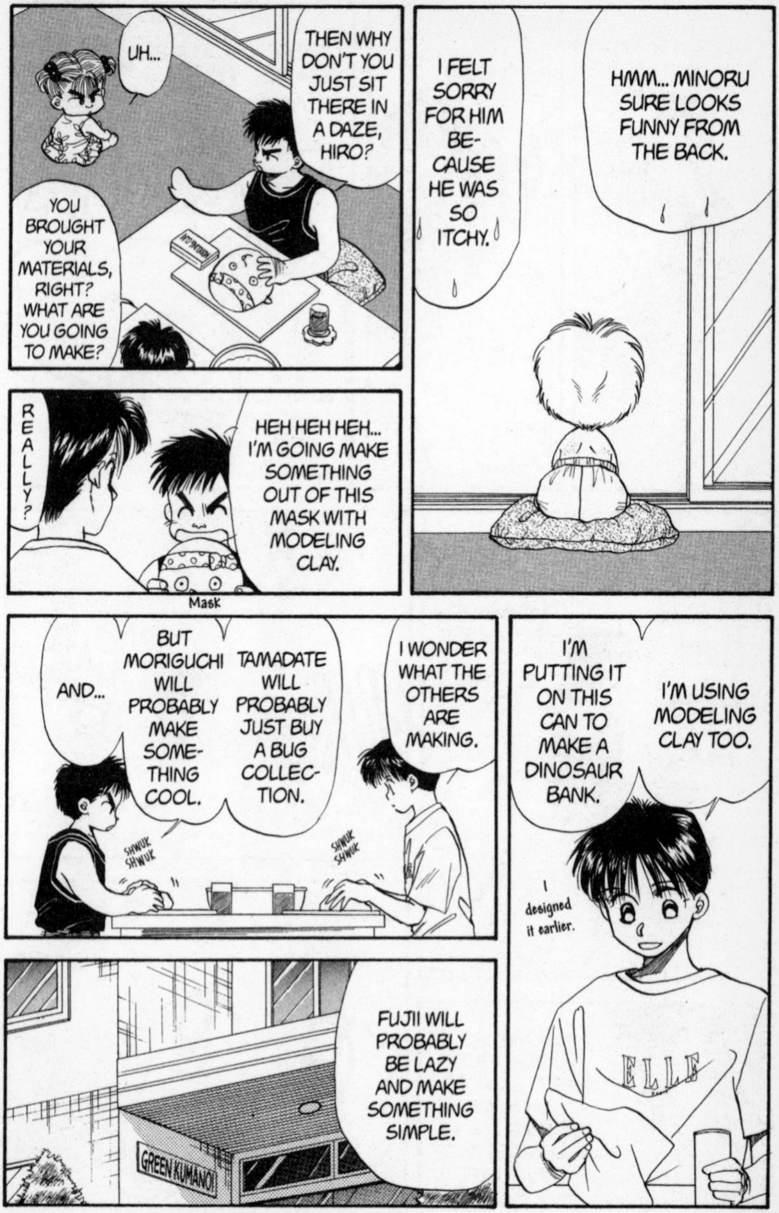
HMM... MINORU SURE LOOKS FUNNY FROM THE BACK.
I FELT SORRY FOR HIM BE-CAUSE HE WAS SO ITCHY.
THEN WHY DON'T YOU JUST SIT THERE IN A DAZE, HIRO?
UH...
YOU BROUGHT YOUR MATERIALS, RIGHT? WHAT ARE YOU GOING TO MAKE?
HEH HEH HEH... I'M GOING MAKE SOMETHING OUT OF THIS MASK WITH MODELING CLAY.
REALLY?
Mask
I'M USING MODELING CLAY TOO.
I'M PUTTING IT ON THIS CAN TO MAKE A DINOSAUR BANK.
I designed it earlier.
I WONDER WHAT THE OTHERS ARE MAKING.
SHWUK SHWUK
TAMADATE WILL PROBABLY JUST BUY A BUG COLLEC-TION.
BUT MORIGUCHI WILL PROBABLY MAKE SOME-THING COOL.
SHWUK SHWUK
AND...
FUJII WILL PROBABLY BE LAZY AND MAKE SOMETHING SIMPLE.
GREEN KUMANOI

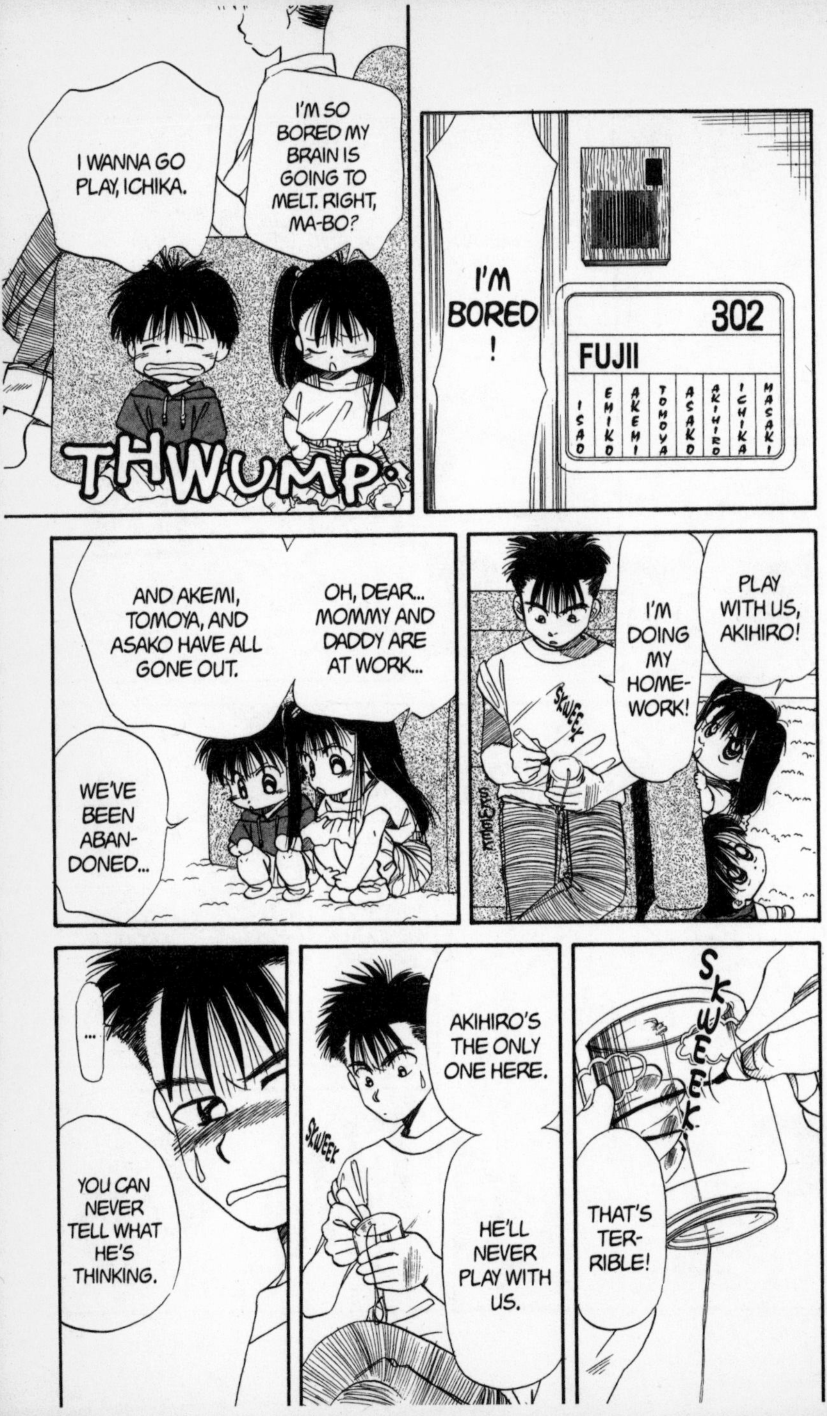
I'M BORED!
302
FUJII
ISAO
EMIKO
AKEMI
TOMOYA
ASAKO
AKIHIRO
ICHIKA
MASAKI
I'M SO BORED MY BRAIN IS GOING TO MELT. RIGHT, MA-BO?
I WANNA GO PLAY, ICHIKA.
THWUMP
PLAY WITH US, AKIHIRO!
I'M DOING MY HOMEWORK!
SKWEEK
SKWEEK
OH, DEAR... MOMMY AND DADDY ARE AT WORK...
AND AKEMI, TOMOYA, AND ASAKO HAVE ALL GONE OUT.
WE'VE BEEN ABANDONED...
SKWEEEK.
THAT'S TERRIBLE!
AKIHIRO'S THE ONLY ONE HERE.
SKWEEK
HE'LL NEVER PLAY WITH US.
...
YOU CAN NEVER TELL WHAT HE'S THINKING.

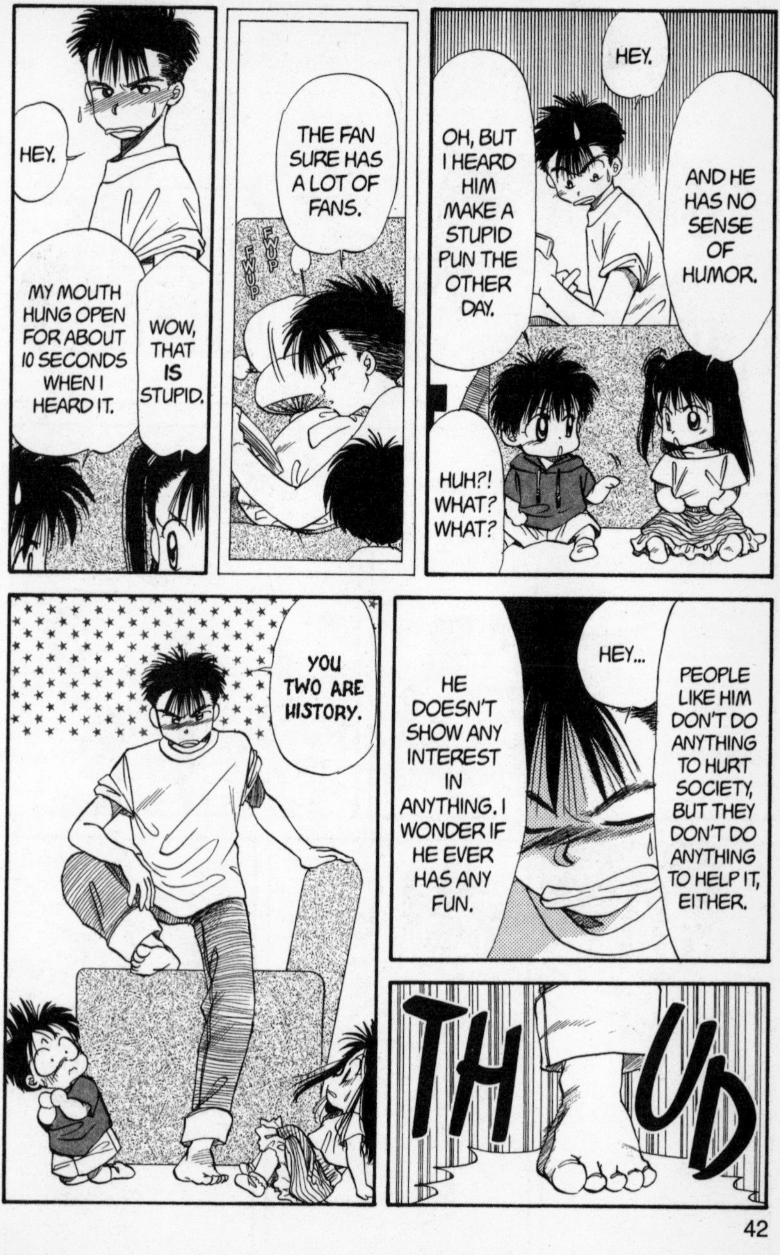
HEY.
AND HE HAS NO SENSE OF HUMOR.
OH, BUT I HEARD HIM MAKE A STUPID PUN THE OTHER DAY.
HUH?! WHAT? WHAT?
THE FAN SURE HAS A LOT OF FANS.
FWUP FWUP
HEY.
MY MOUTH HUNG OPEN FOR ABOUT 10 SECONDS WHEN I HEARD IT.
WOW, THAT IS STUPID.
HEY...
PEOPLE LIKE HIM DON'T DO ANYTHING TO HURT SOCIETY, BUT THEY DON'T DO ANYTHING TO HELP IT, EITHER.
HE DOESN'T SHOW ANY INTEREST IN ANYTHING. I WONDER IF HE EVER HAS ANY FUN.
THUD
YOU TWO ARE HISTORY.

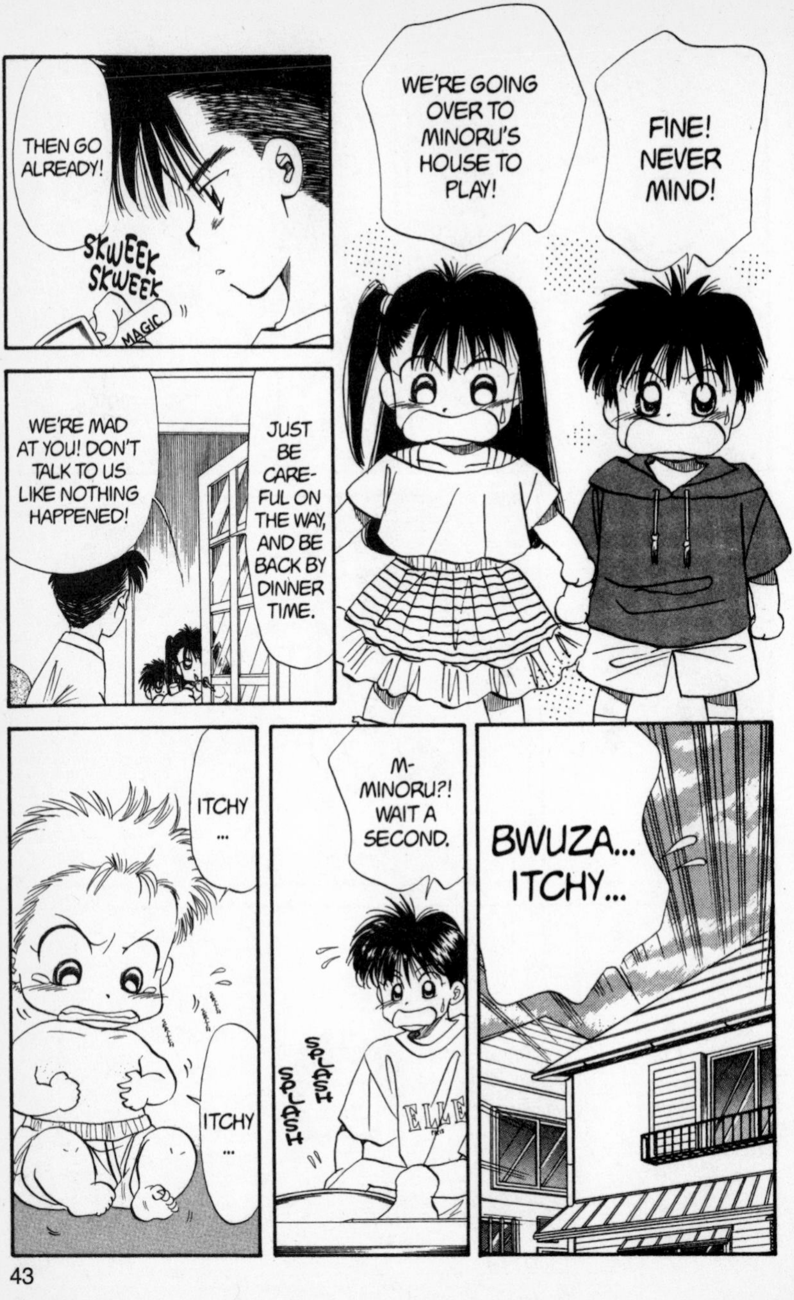
FINE! NEVER MIND!
WE'RE GOING OVER TO MINORU'S HOUSE TO PLAY!
THEN GO ALREADY!
SKWEEK SKWEEK
MAGIC
JUST BE CARE-FUL ON THE WAY, AND BE BACK BY DINNER TIME.
WE'RE MAD AT YOU! DON'T TALK TO US LIKE NOTHING HAPPENED!
BWUZA... ITCHY...
M-MINORU?! WAIT A SECOND.
SPLASH SPLASH
ITCHY ...
ITCHY ...

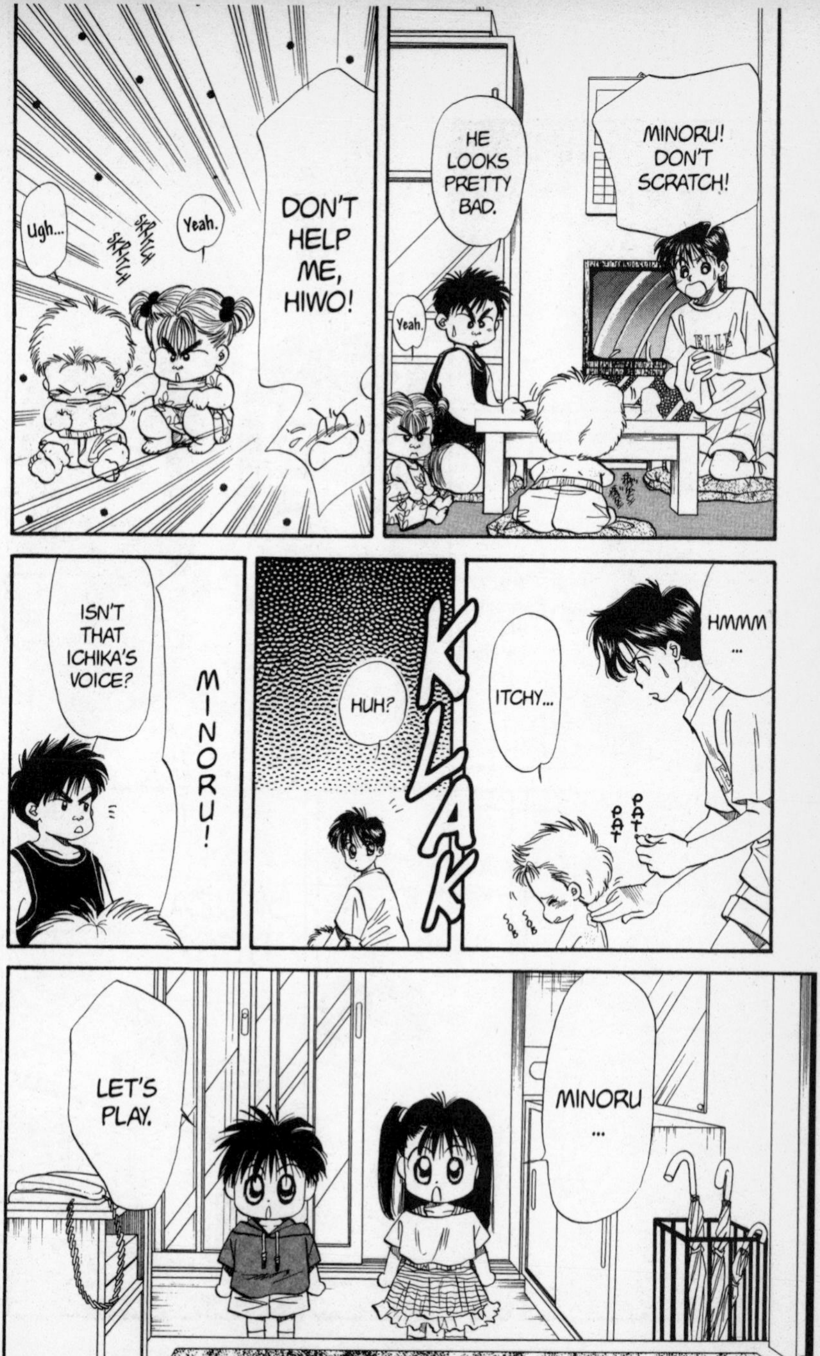
MINORU! DON'T SCRATCH!
HE LOOKS PRETTY BAD.
Yeah.
DON'T HELP ME, HIWO!
Yeah.
SKRITCH SKRITCH
Ugh...
HMMM ...
ITCHY...
PAT PAT
SOB SOB
KLAK
HUH?
ISN'T THAT ICHIKA'S VOICE?
MINORU!
MINORU ...
LET'S PLAY.

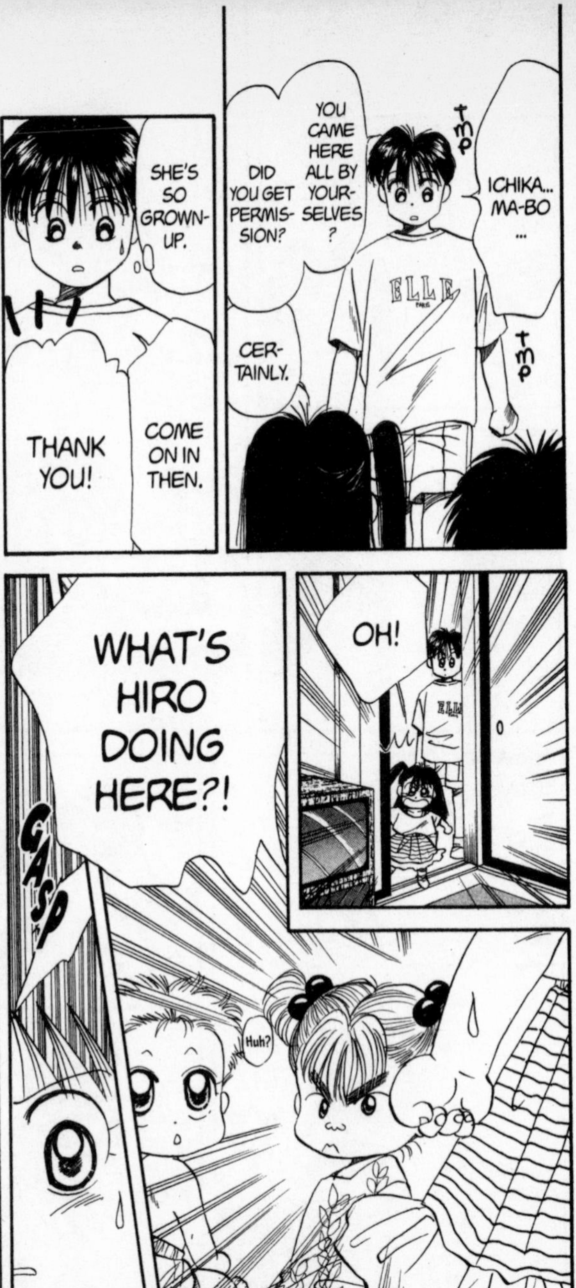
ICHIKA... MA-BO ...
tmp
YOU CAME HERE ALL BY YOURSELVES?
DID YOU GET PERMISSION?
CERTAINLY.
tmp
SHE'S SO GROWN-UP.
COME ON IN THEN.
THANK YOU!
OH!
WHAT'S HIRO DOING HERE?!
GASP
Huh?

Author's Note Part 2

Yoshizo Today--

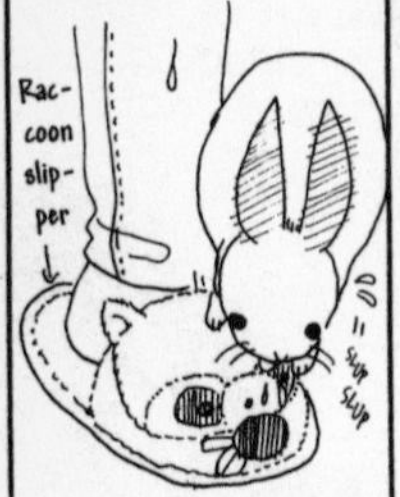
Raccoon slipper
slup slup

When Yoshizo wants attention, she starts grooming my slippers.

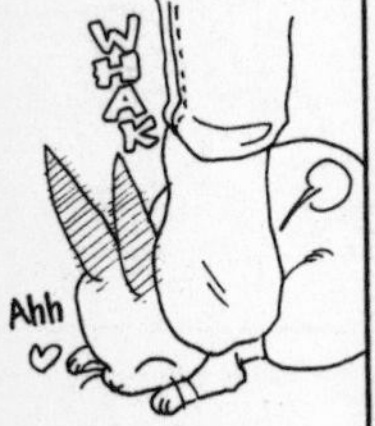
WHAK
Ahh ♡

Even if I give her a kick, Yoshizo seems to think I'm petting her.

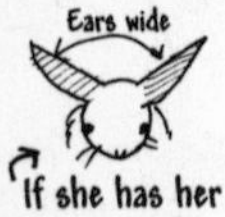
Ears wide

If she has her ears like this...

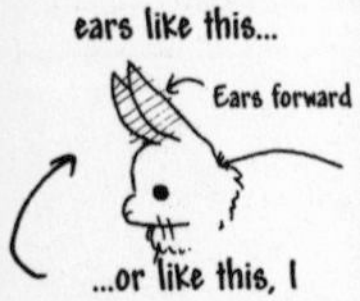
Ears forward

...or like this, I don't mind. But...

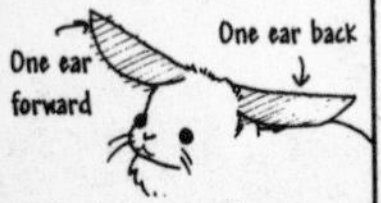
One ear forward
One ear back

I don't like it when her ears are like this.

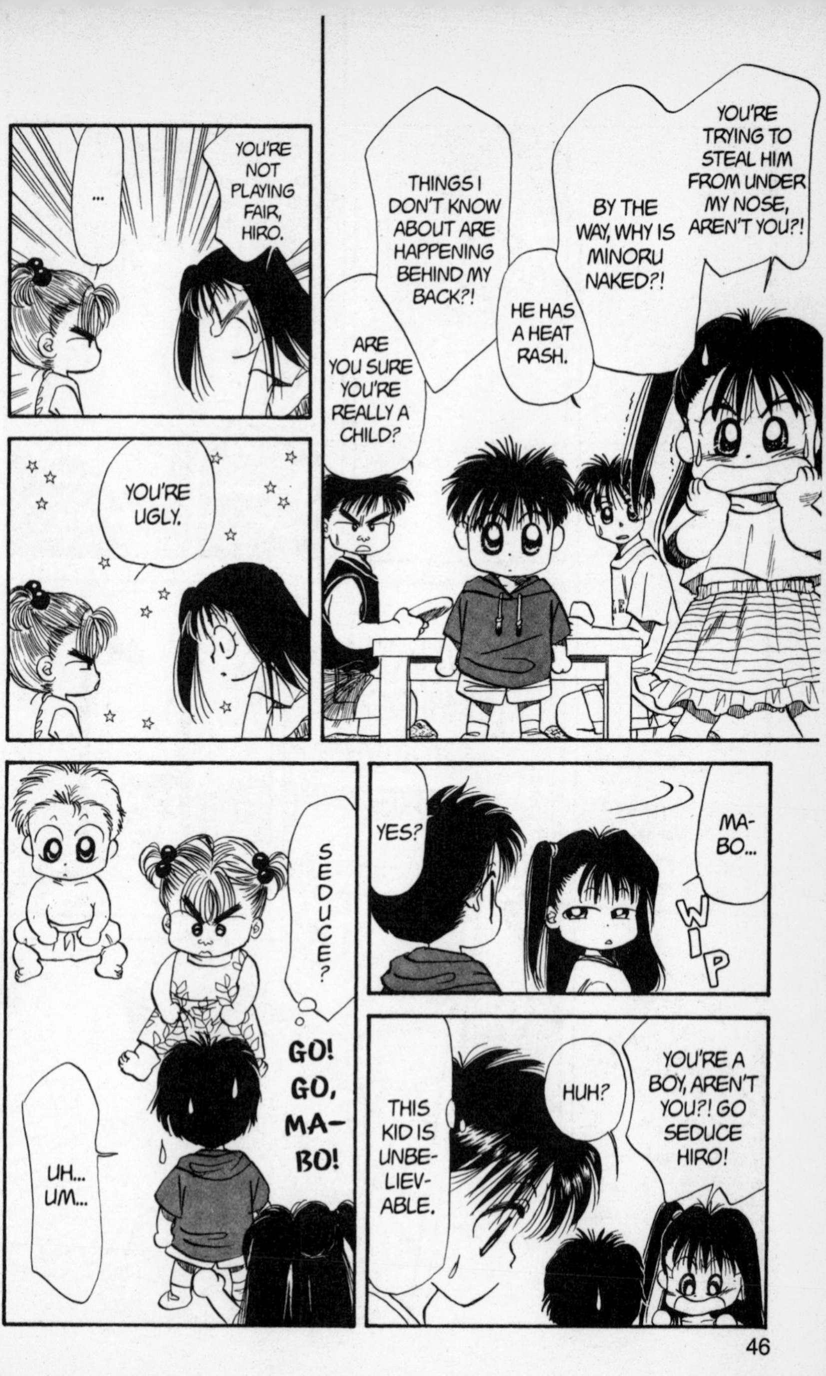
YOU'RE TRYING TO STEAL HIM FROM UNDER MY NOSE, AREN'T YOU?!
BY THE WAY, WHY IS MINORU NAKED?!
HE HAS A HEAT RASH.
THINGS I DON'T KNOW ABOUT ARE HAPPENING BEHIND MY BACK?!
ARE YOU SURE YOU'RE REALLY A CHILD?
YOU'RE NOT PLAYING FAIR, HIRO.
...
YOU'RE UGLY.
MA-BO...
WIP
YES?
YOU'RE A BOY, AREN'T YOU?! GO SEDUCE HIRO!
HUH?
THIS KID IS UNBE-LIEV-ABLE.
SEDUCE?
GO! GO, MA-BO!
UH... UM...

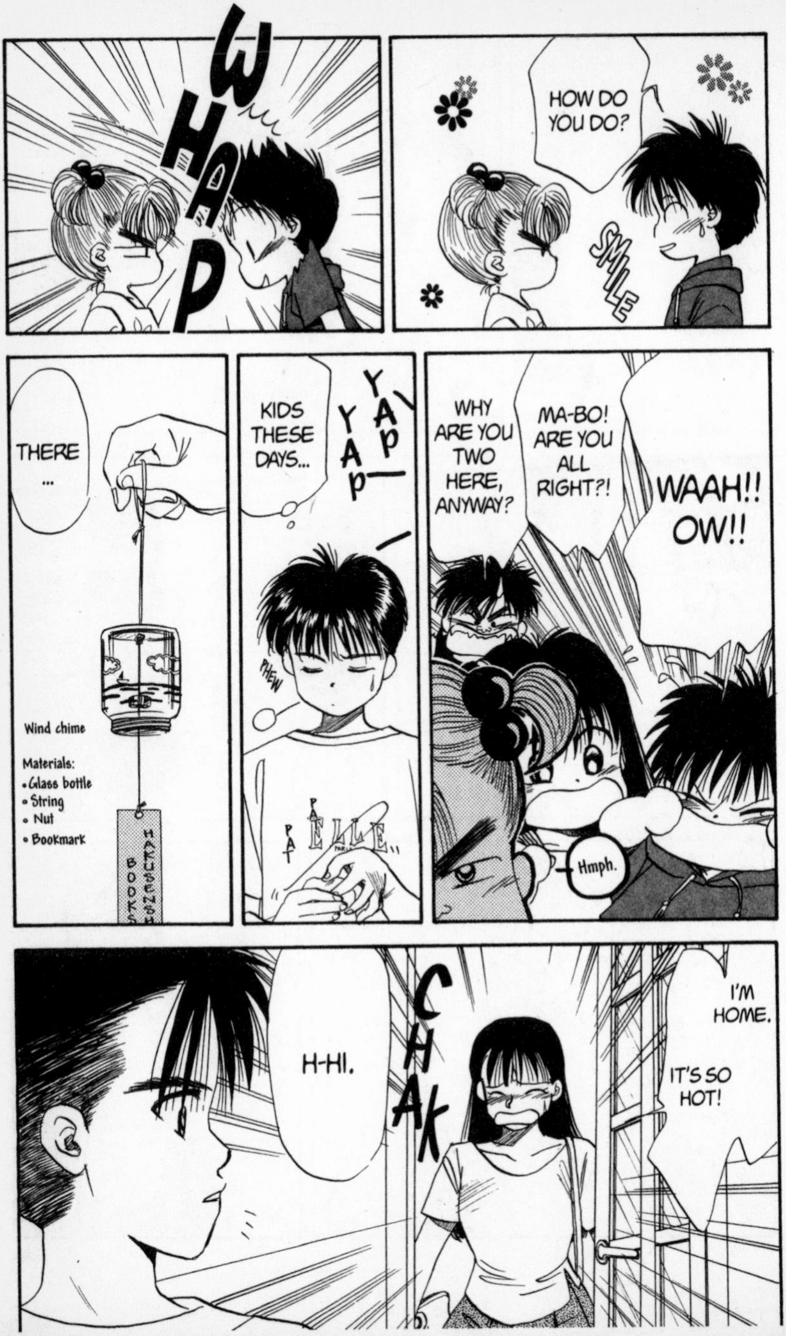
HOW DO YOU DO?
SMILE
WHAP
WAAH!! OW!!
MA-BO! ARE YOU ALL RIGHT?!
WHY ARE YOU TWO HERE, ANYWAY?
Hmph.
YAP YAP—
KIDS THESE DAYS...
PHEW
PAT PAT
THERE ...
Wind chime
Materials:
• Glass bottle
• String
• Nut
• Bookmark
I'M HOME.
IT'S SO HOT!
CHAK
H-HI.

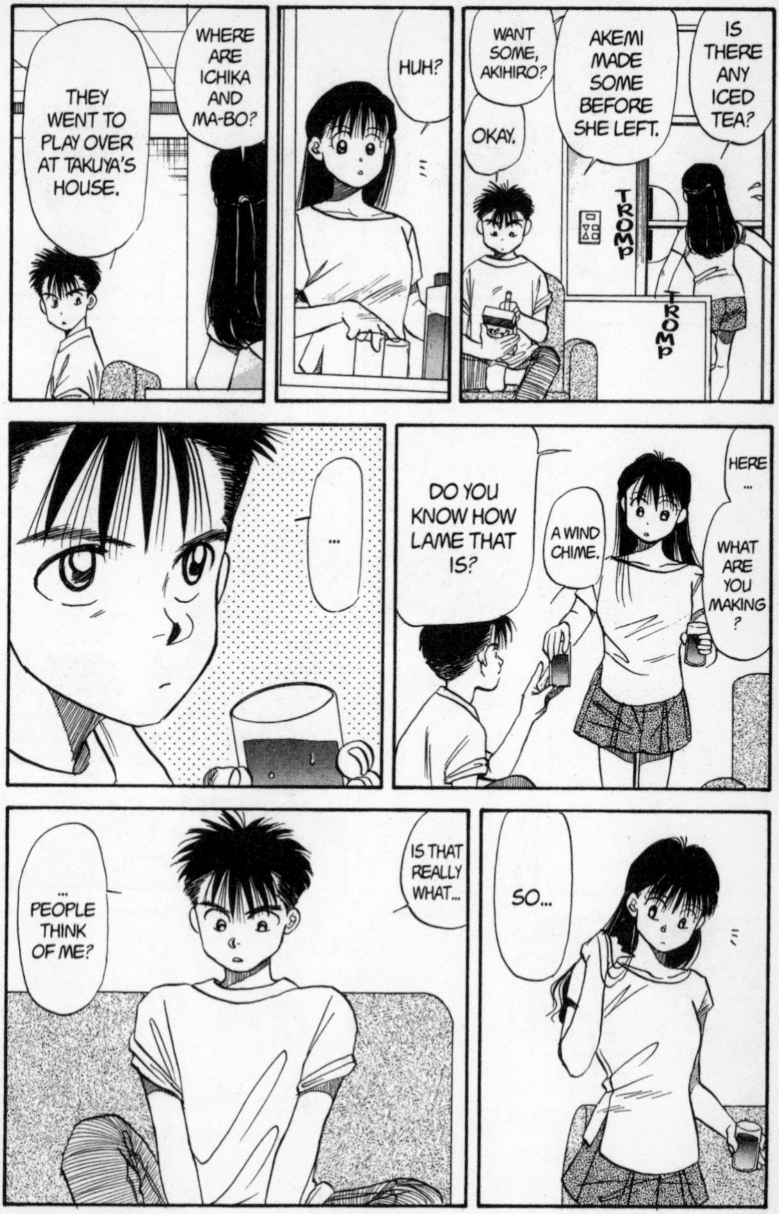
IS THERE ANY ICED TEA?
AKEMI MADE SOME BEFORE SHE LEFT.
WANT SOME, AKIHIRO?
OKAY.
TROMP
TROMP
HUH?
WHERE ARE ICHIKA AND MA-BO?
THEY WENT TO PLAY OVER AT TAKUYA'S HOUSE.
HERE...
WHAT ARE YOU MAKING?
A WIND CHIME.
DO YOU KNOW HOW LAME THAT IS?
...
SO...
IS THAT REALLY WHAT...
... PEOPLE THINK OF ME?

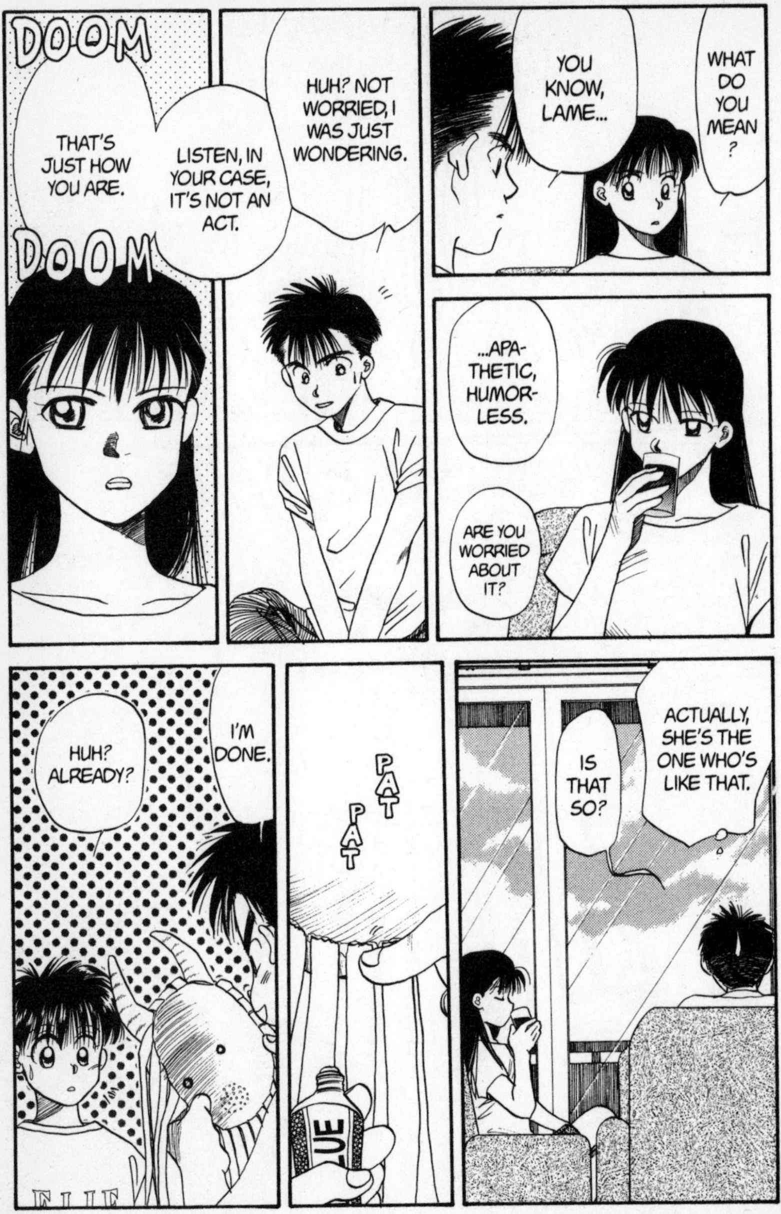
WHAT DO YOU MEAN?
YOU KNOW, LAME...
...APATHETIC, HUMORLESS.
ARE YOU WORRIED ABOUT IT?
HUH? NOT WORRIED, I WAS JUST WONDERING.
LISTEN, IN YOUR CASE, IT'S NOT AN ACT.
THAT'S JUST HOW YOU ARE.
DOOM
DOOM
ACTUALLY, SHE'S THE ONE WHO'S LIKE THAT.
IS THAT SO?
PAT
PAT
I'M DONE.
HUH? ALREADY?

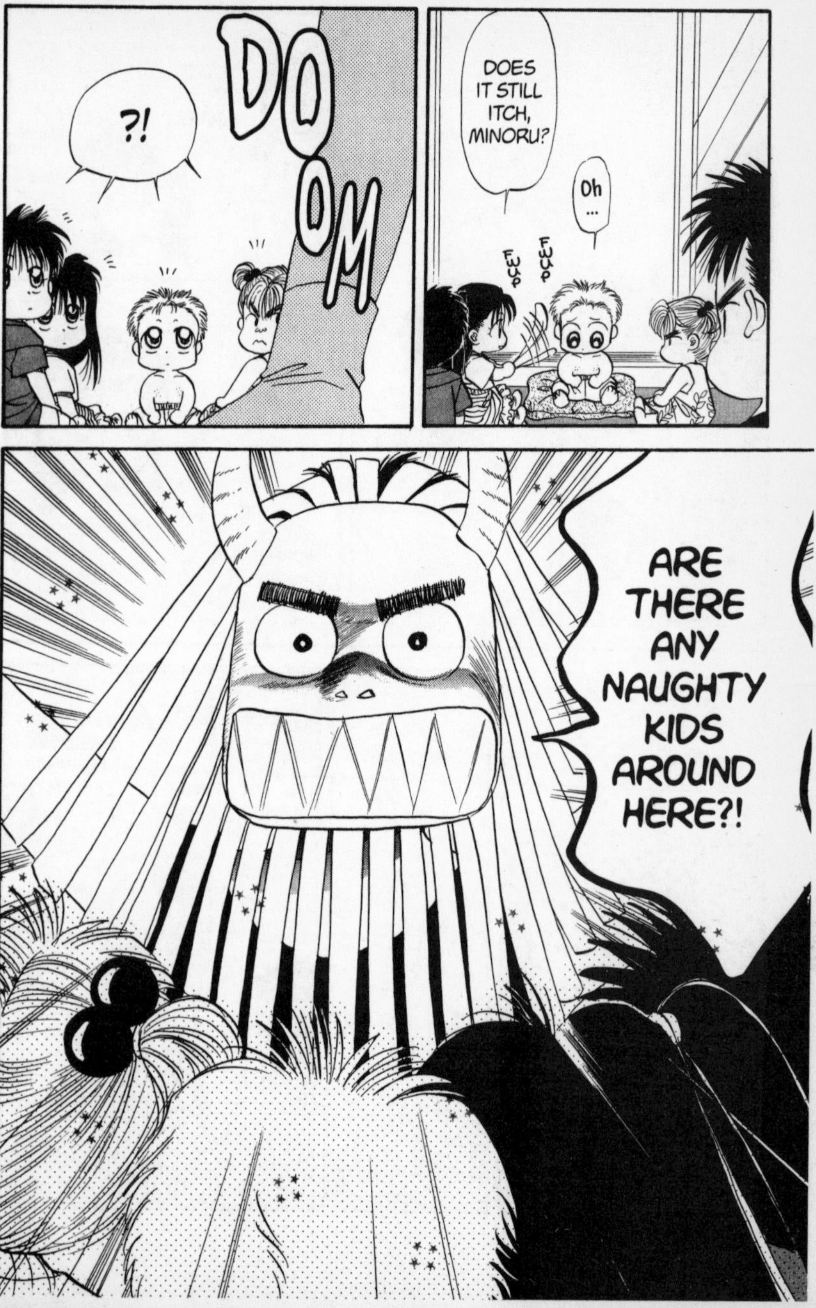
DOES IT STILL ITCH, MINORU?
FWUP FWUP
Oh ...
DOOM
?!
ARE THERE ANY NAUGHTY KIDS AROUND HERE?!

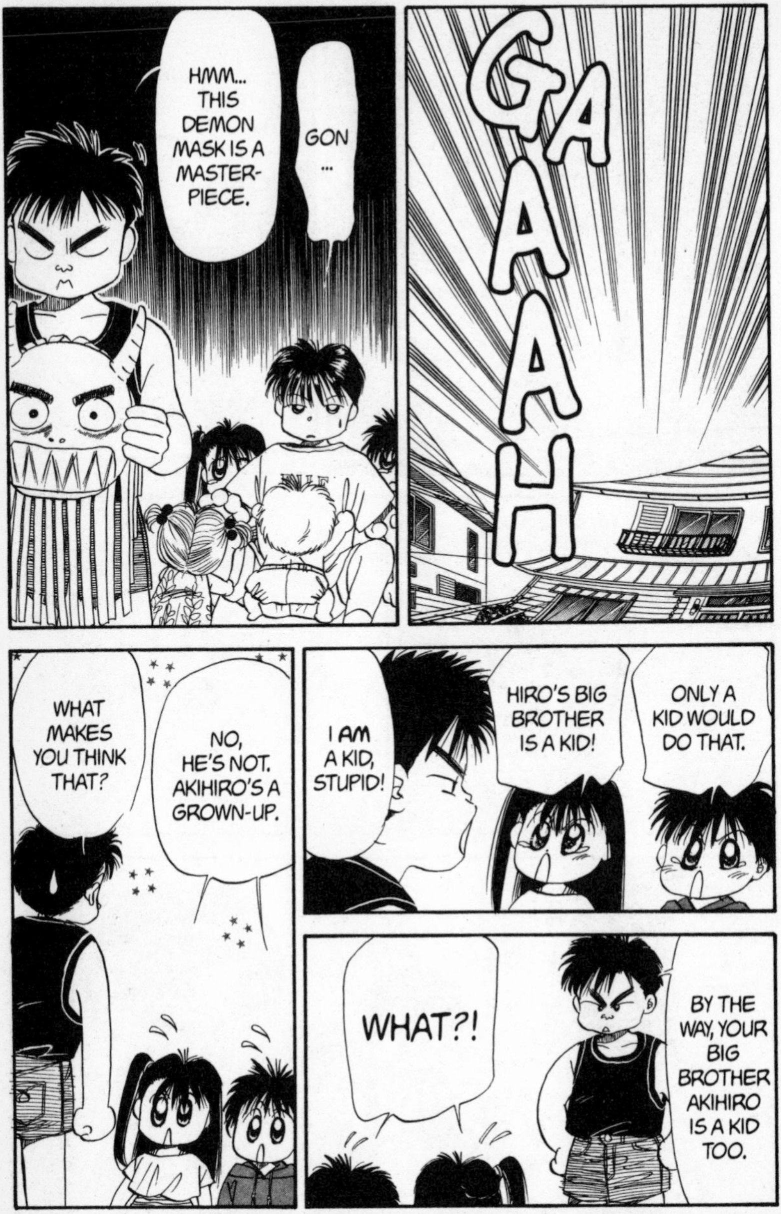
GAAAAH
GON ...
HMM... THIS DEMON MASK IS A MASTERPIECE.
ONLY A KID WOULD DO THAT.
HIRO'S BIG BROTHER IS A KID!
I AM A KID, STUPID!
BY THE WAY, YOUR BIG BROTHER AKIHIRO IS A KID TOO.
WHAT?!
NO, HE'S NOT. AKIHIRO'S A GROWN-UP.
WHAT MAKES YOU THINK THAT?

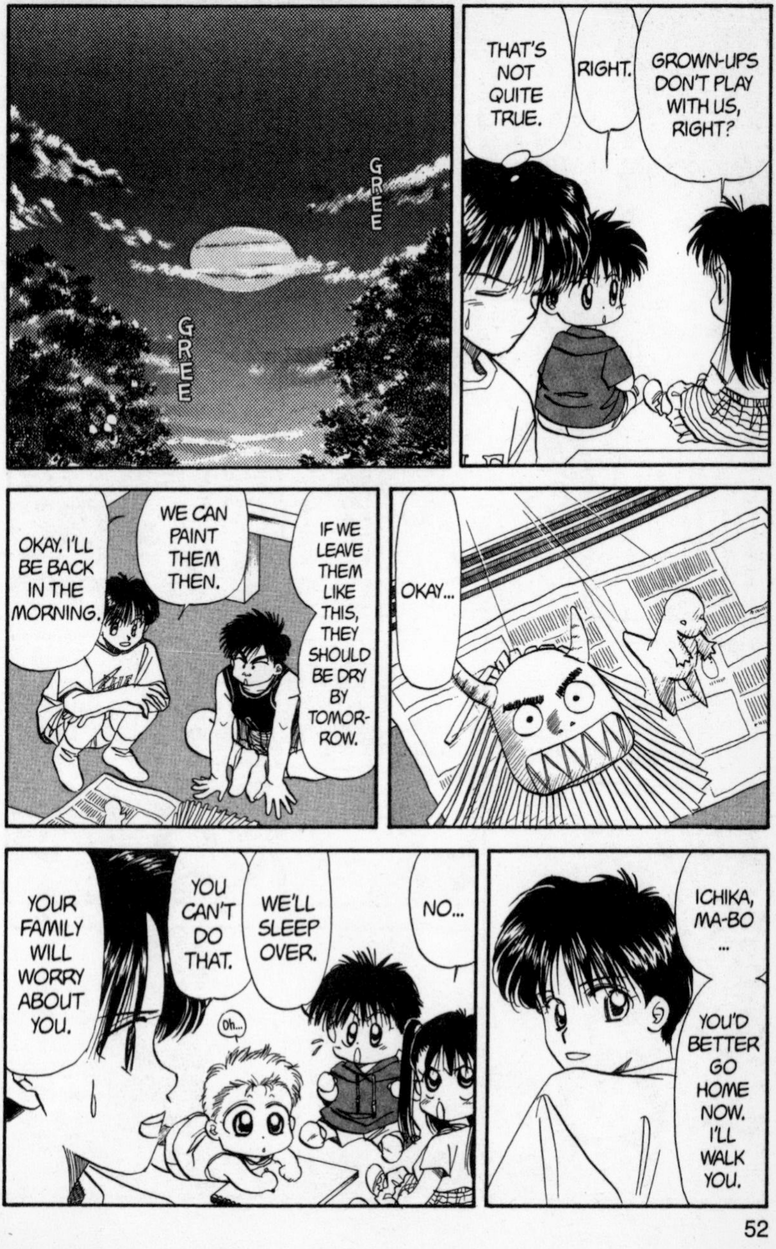
GROWN-UPS DON'T PLAY WITH US, RIGHT?
RIGHT.
THAT'S NOT QUITE TRUE.
GREE
GREE
OKAY...
IF WE LEAVE THEM LIKE THIS, THEY SHOULD BE DRY BY TOMORROW.
WE CAN PAINT THEM THEN.
OKAY. I'LL BE BACK IN THE MORNING.
ICHIKA, MA-BO ...
YOU'D BETTER GO HOME NOW. I'LL WALK YOU.
NO...
WE'LL SLEEP OVER.
YOU CAN'T DO THAT.
Oh...
YOUR FAMILY WILL WORRY ABOUT YOU.

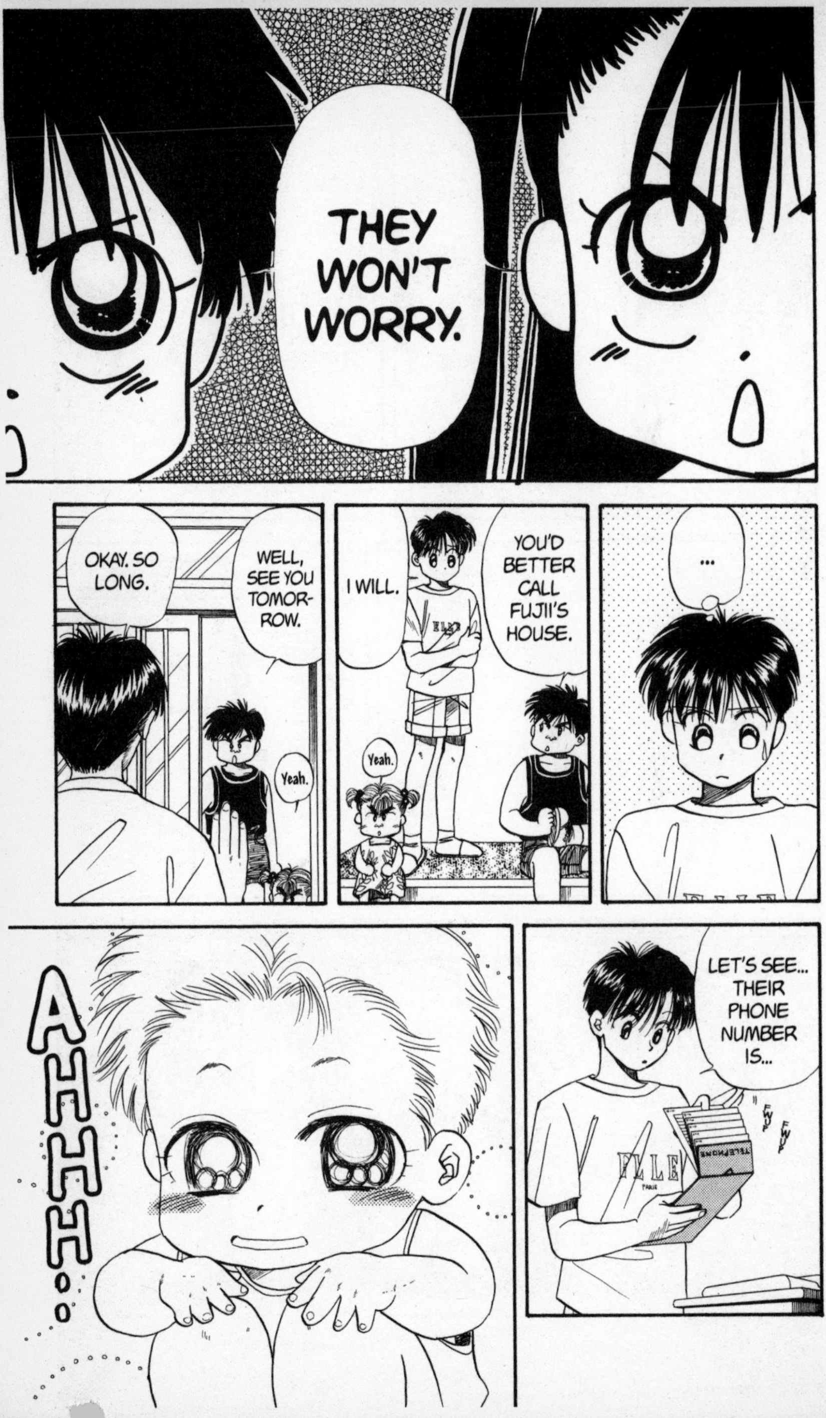
THEY WON'T WORRY.
...
YOU'D BETTER CALL FUJII'S HOUSE.
I WILL.
Yeah.
WELL, SEE YOU TOMOR-ROW.
OKAY. SO LONG.
Yeah.
LET'S SEE... THEIR PHONE NUMBER IS...
FWIP
FWIP
AHHHH...

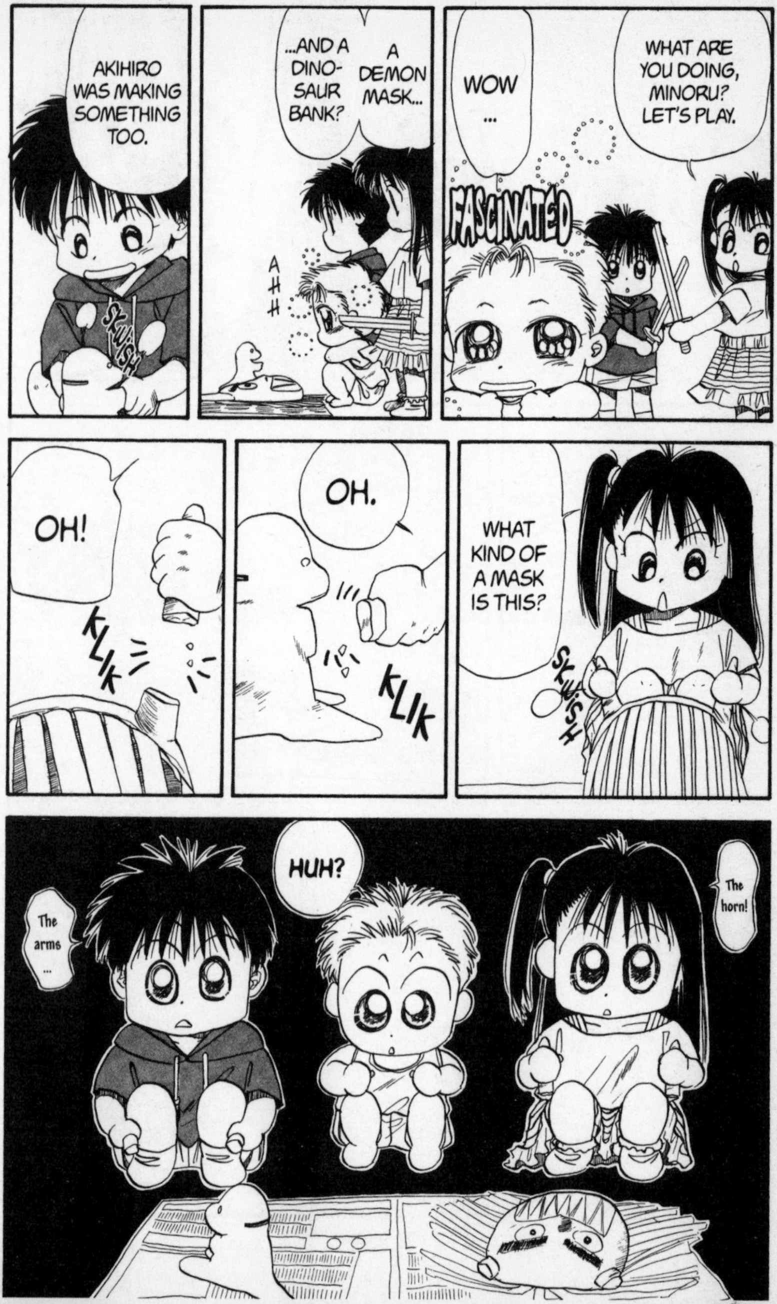
WHAT ARE YOU DOING, MINORU? LET'S PLAY.
WOW ...
FASCINATED
A DEMON MASK...
...AND A DINO-SAUR BANK?
AHH
AKIHIRO WAS MAKING SOMETHING TOO.
SKWISH
WHAT KIND OF A MASK IS THIS?
SKWISH
OH.
KLIK
OH!
KLIK
The horn!
HUH?
The arms ...

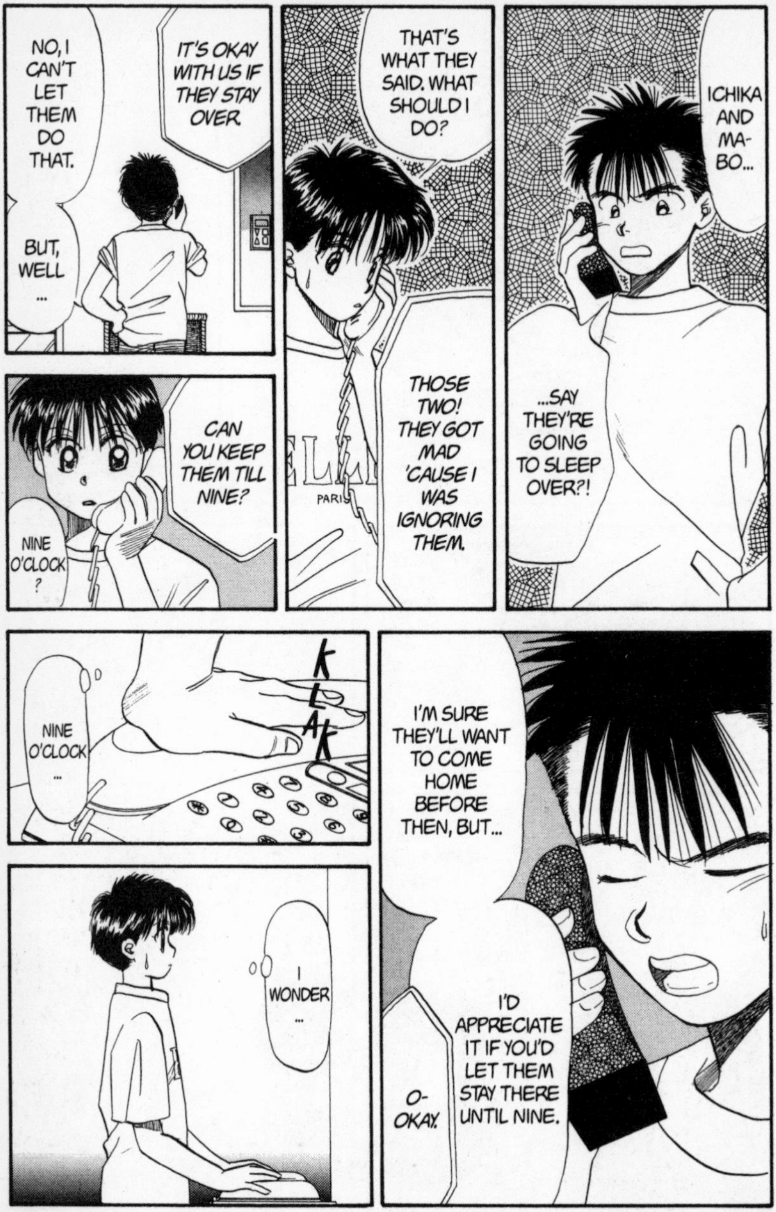
ICHIKA AND MA-BO...
...SAY THEY'RE GOING TO SLEEP OVER?!
THAT'S WHAT THEY SAID. WHAT SHOULD I DO?
THOSE TWO! THEY GOT MAD 'CAUSE I WAS IGNORING THEM.
IT'S OKAY WITH US IF THEY STAY OVER.
NO, I CAN'T LET THEM DO THAT.
BUT, WELL ...
CAN YOU KEEP THEM TILL NINE?
NINE O'CLOCK ?
I'M SURE THEY'LL WANT TO COME HOME BEFORE THEN, BUT...
I'D APPRECIATE IT IF YOU'D LET THEM STAY THERE UNTIL NINE.
O-OKAY.
KLAK
NINE O'CLOCK ...
I WONDER ...

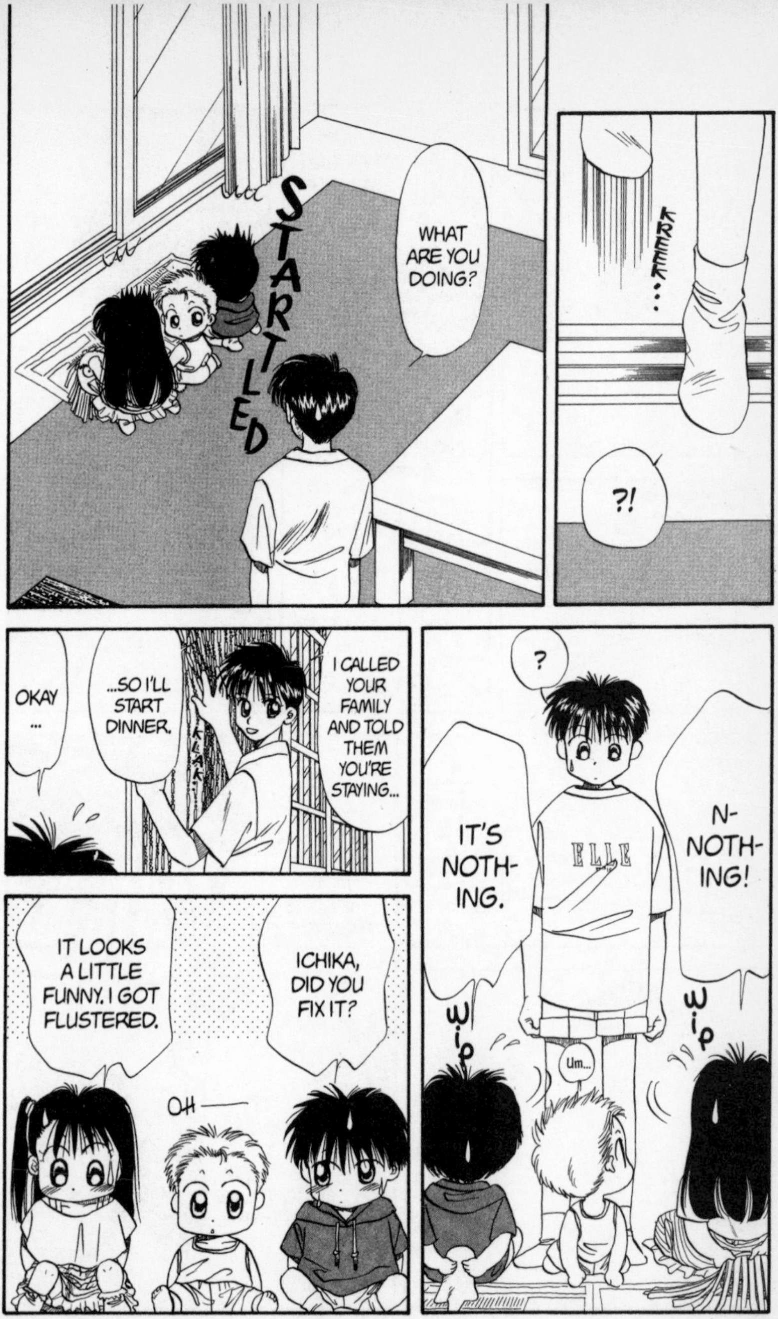

KREEK...
?!
WHAT ARE YOU DOING?
STARTLED
?
N-NOTHING!
IT'S NOTHING.
wip
wip
Um...
I CALLED YOUR FAMILY AND TOLD THEM YOU'RE STAYING...
...SO I'LL START DINNER.
KLAK
OKAY ...
ICHIKA, DID YOU FIX IT?
OH—
IT LOOKS A LITTLE FUNNY. I GOT FLUSTERED.

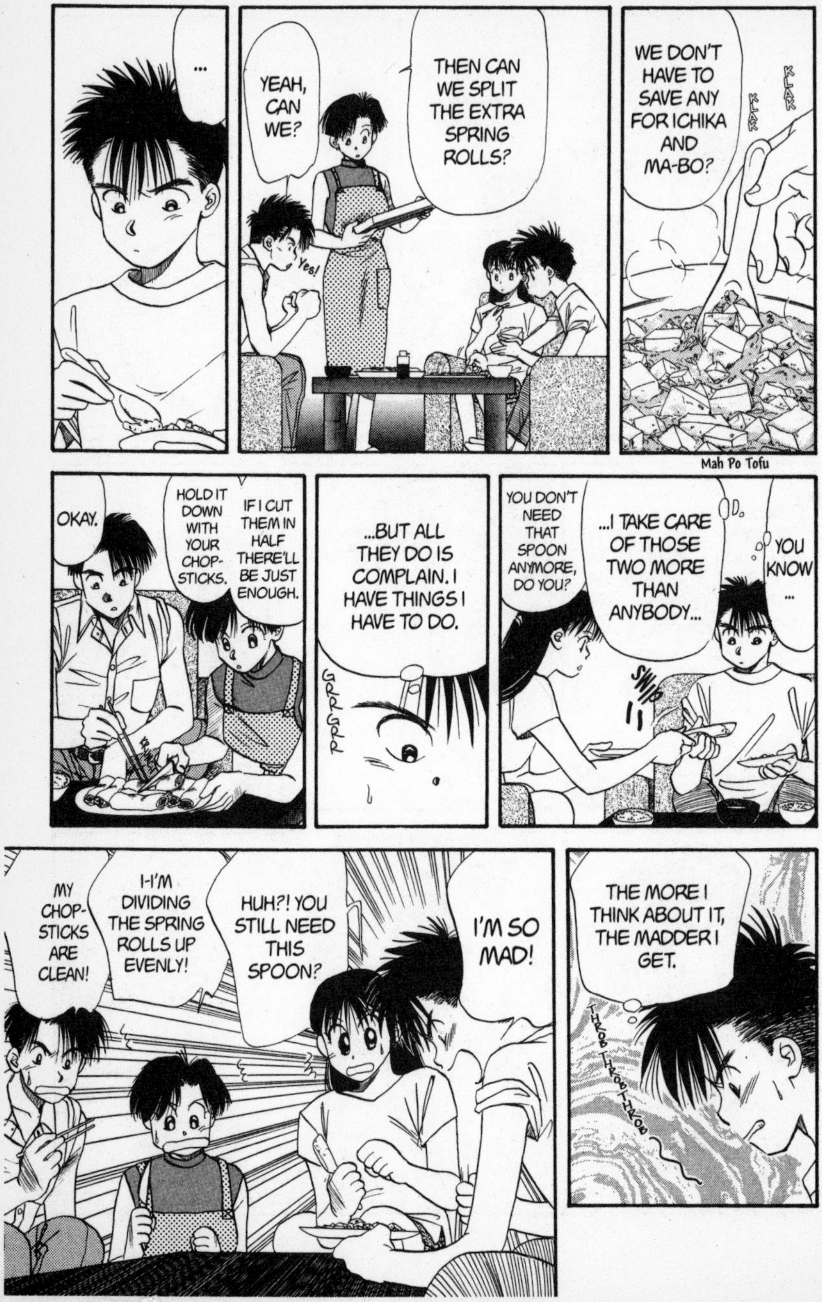
WE DON'T HAVE TO SAVE ANY FOR ICHIKA AND MA-BO?
KLAK KLAK
Mah Po Tofu
THEN CAN WE SPLIT THE EXTRA SPRING ROLLS?
YEAH, CAN WE?
Yes!
...
YOU KNOW ...
...I TAKE CARE OF THOSE TWO MORE THAN ANYBODY...
YOU DON'T NEED THAT SPOON ANYMORE, DO YOU?
SWIP
...BUT ALL THEY DO IS COMPLAIN. I HAVE THINGS I HAVE TO DO.
IF I CUT THEM IN HALF THERE'LL BE JUST ENOUGH.
HOLD IT DOWN WITH YOUR CHOP-STICKS.
OKAY.
THE MORE I THINK ABOUT IT, THE MADDER I GET.
THROB THROB THROB
I'M SO MAD!
HUH?! YOU STILL NEED THIS SPOON?
I-I'M DIVIDING THE SPRING ROLLS UP EVENLY!
MY CHOP-STICKS ARE CLEAN!

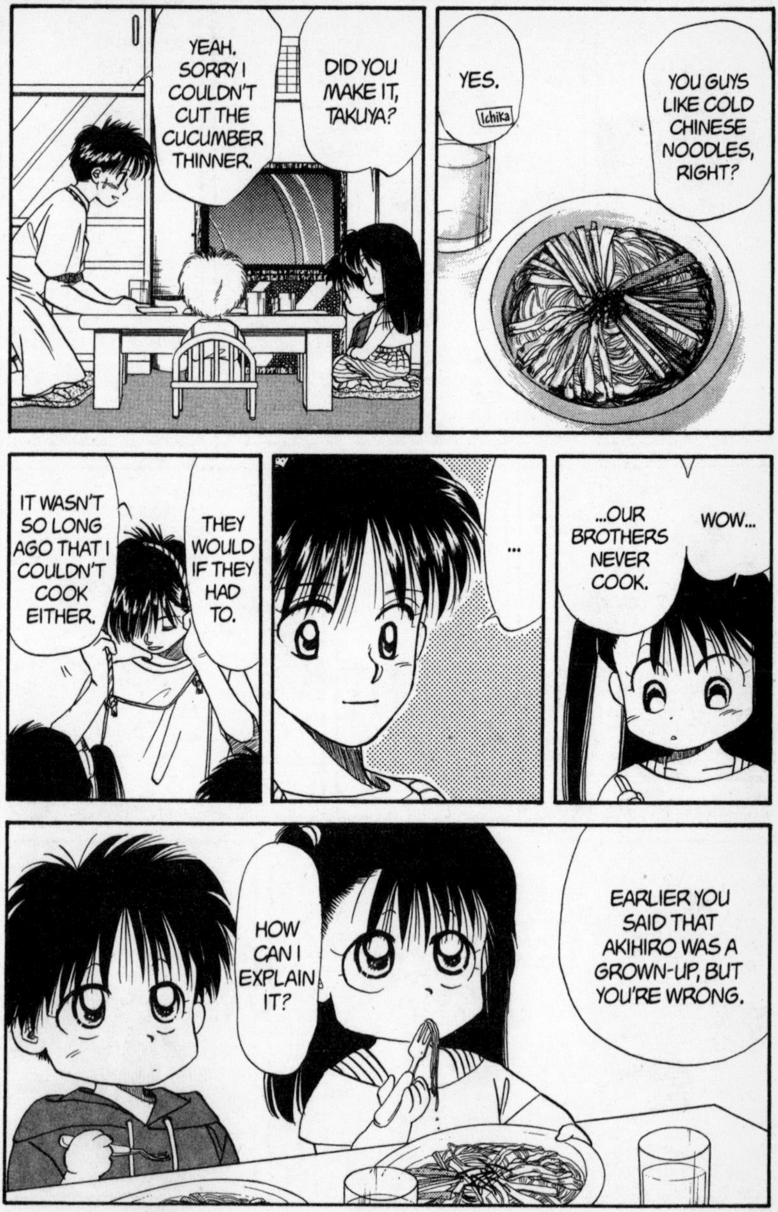
YOU GUYS LIKE COLD CHINESE NOODLES, RIGHT?
YES.
Ichika
DID YOU MAKE IT, TAKUYA?
YEAH. SORRY I COULDN'T CUT THE CUCUMBER THINNER.
WOW...
...OUR BROTHERS NEVER COOK.
...
THEY WOULD IF THEY HAD TO.
IT WASN'T SO LONG AGO THAT I COULDN'T COOK EITHER.
EARLIER YOU SAID THAT AKIHIRO WAS A GROWN-UP, BUT YOU'RE WRONG.
HOW CAN I EXPLAIN IT?

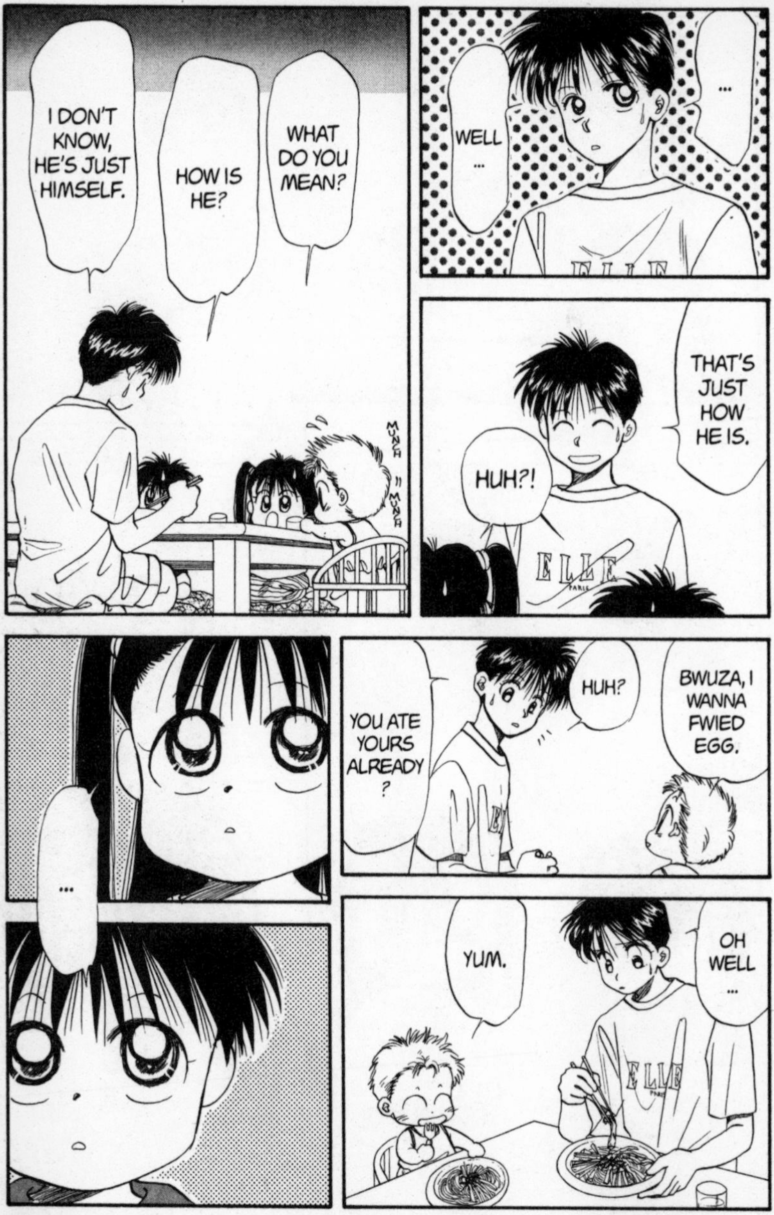
...
WELL ...
THAT'S JUST HOW HE IS.
HUH?!
WHAT DO YOU MEAN?
HOW IS HE?
I DON'T KNOW, HE'S JUST HIMSELF.
MUNCH MUNCH
BWUZA, I WANNA FWIED EGG.
HUH?
YOU ATE YOURS ALREADY?
...
OH WELL ...
YUM.

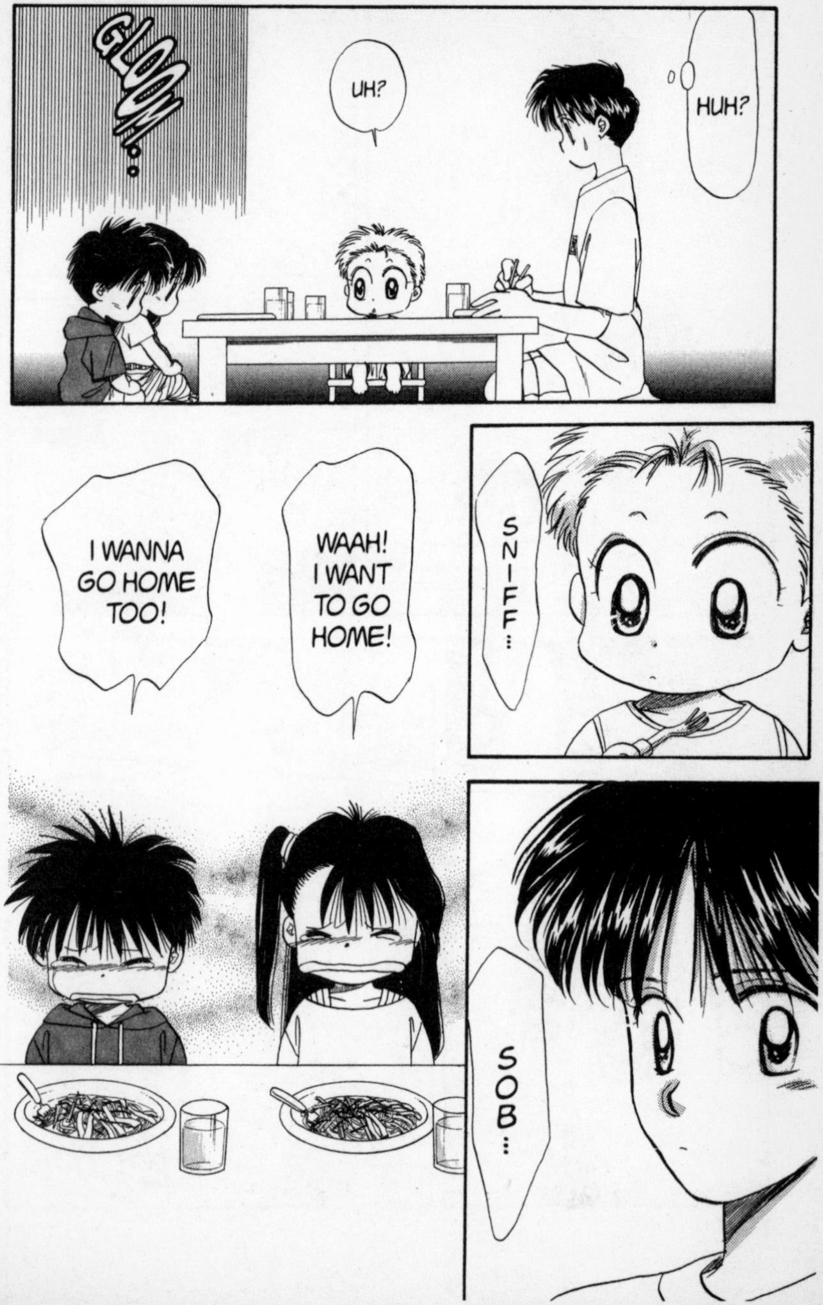
HUH?
UH?
GLOOM..
SNIFF...
WAAH! I WANT TO GO HOME!
I WANNA GO HOME TOO!
SOB...

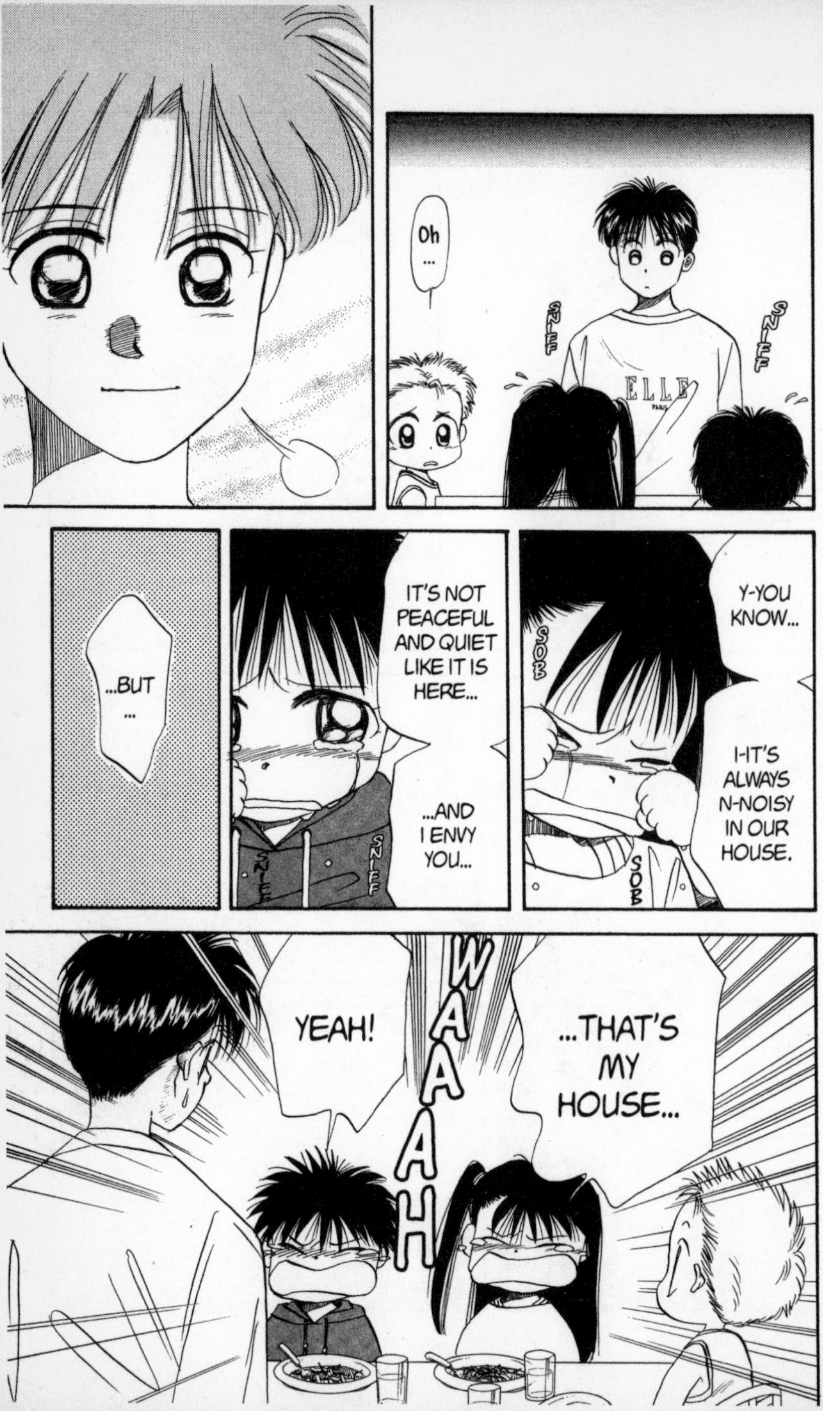
Oh ...
SNIFF
SNIFF
ELLE PARIS
Y-YOU KNOW...
SOB
I-IT'S ALWAYS N-NOISY IN OUR HOUSE.
SOB
IT'S NOT PEACEFUL AND QUIET LIKE IT IS HERE...
...AND I ENVY YOU...
SNIFF
SNIFF
...BUT ...
...THAT'S MY HOUSE...
WAAAAH
YEAH!

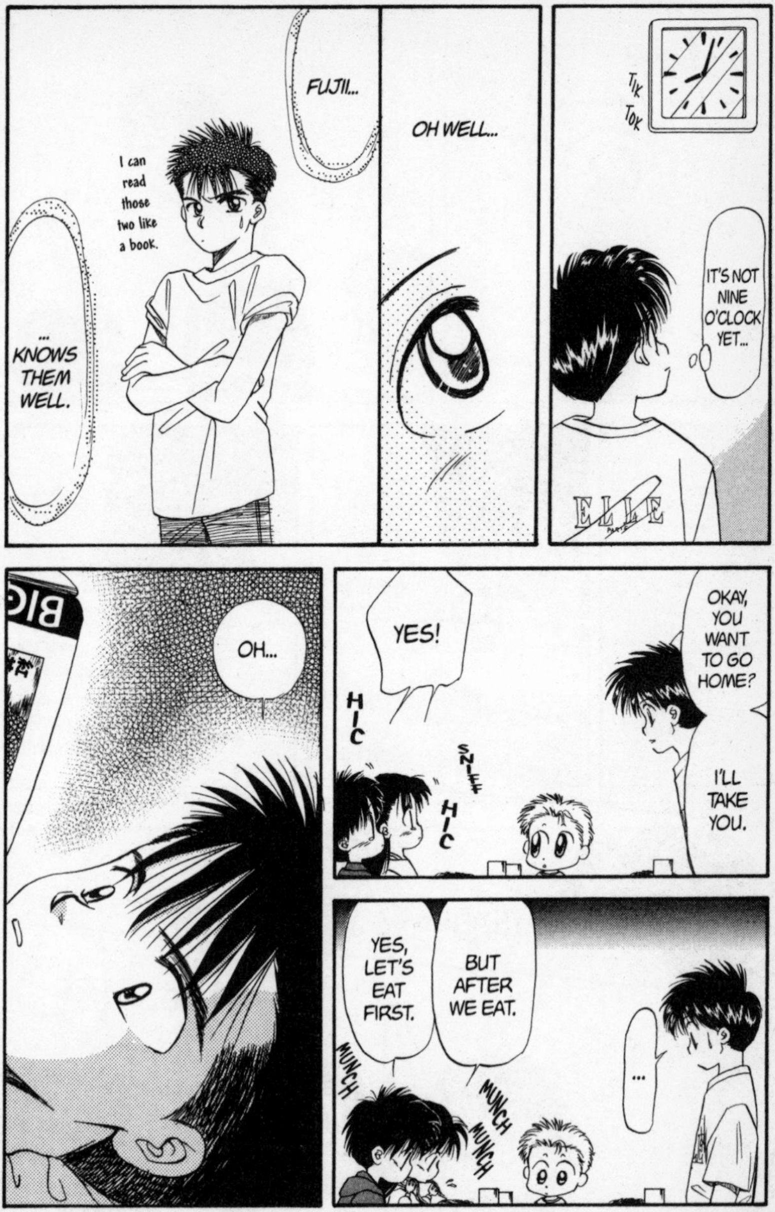
TIK
TOK
IT'S NOT NINE O'CLOCK YET...
OH WELL...
FUJII...
I can read those two like a book.
...KNOWS THEM WELL.
OKAY, YOU WANT TO GO HOME?
I'LL TAKE YOU.
YES!
SNIFF
HIC
HIC
...
BUT AFTER WE EAT.
YES, LET'S EAT FIRST.
MUNCH
MUNCH
MUNCH
MUNCH
OH...

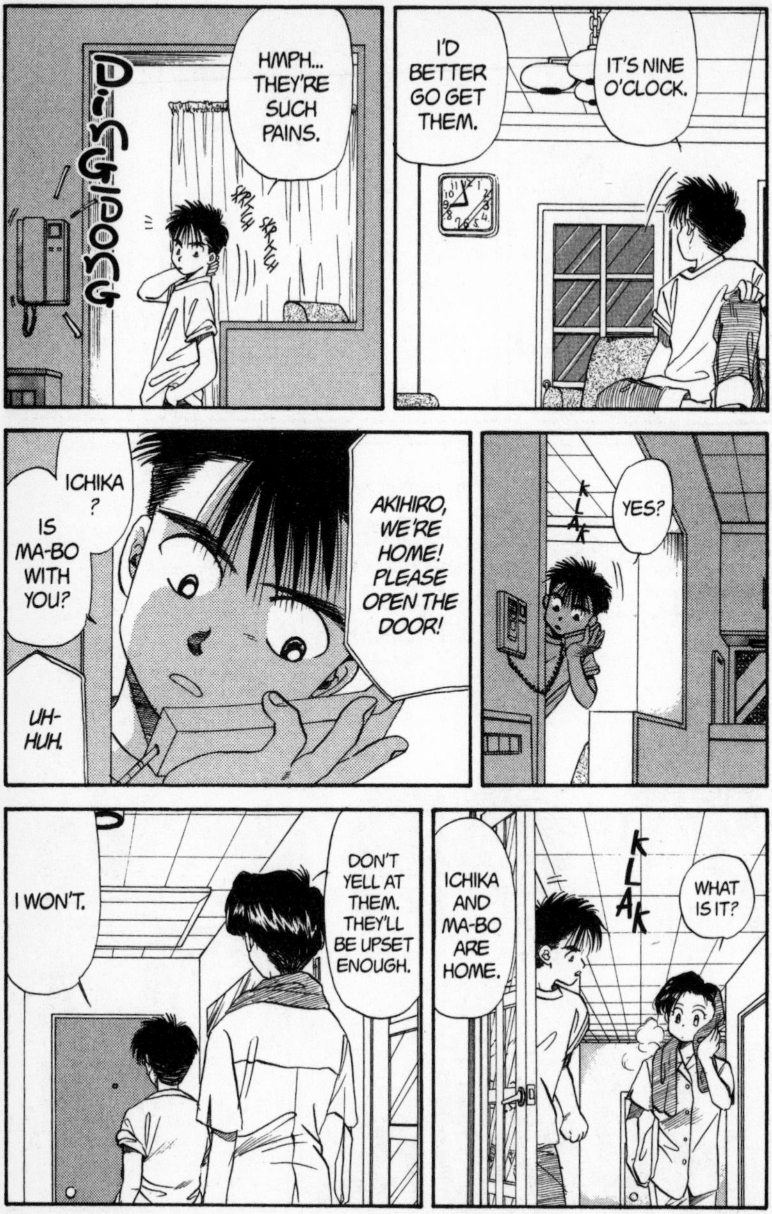
IT'S NINE O'CLOCK.
I'D BETTER GO GET THEM.
HMPH... THEY'RE SUCH PAINS.
SKRTCH
SKRTCH
DING DONG
YES?
KLAK
AKIHIRO, WE'RE HOME! PLEASE OPEN THE DOOR!
ICHIKA?
IS MA-BO WITH YOU?
UH-HUH.
WHAT IS IT?
KLAK
ICHIKA AND MA-BO ARE HOME.
DON'T YELL AT THEM. THEY'LL BE UPSET ENOUGH.
I WON'T.

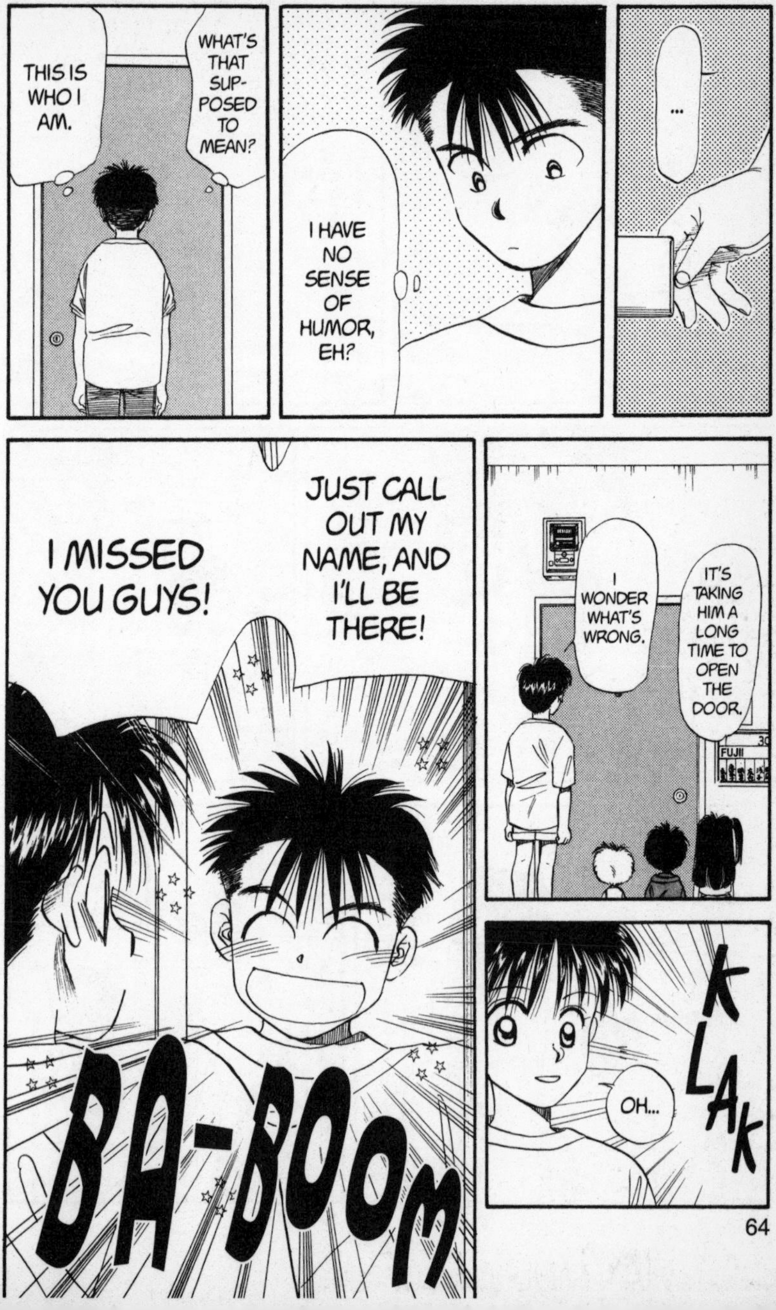
...
I HAVE NO SENSE OF HUMOR, EH?
WHAT'S THAT SUP-POSED TO MEAN?
THIS IS WHO I AM.
IT'S TAKING HIM A LONG TIME TO OPEN THE DOOR.
I WONDER WHAT'S WRONG.
FUJII
KLAK
OH...
JUST CALL OUT MY NAME, AND I'LL BE THERE!
I MISSED YOU GUYS!
BA-BOOM

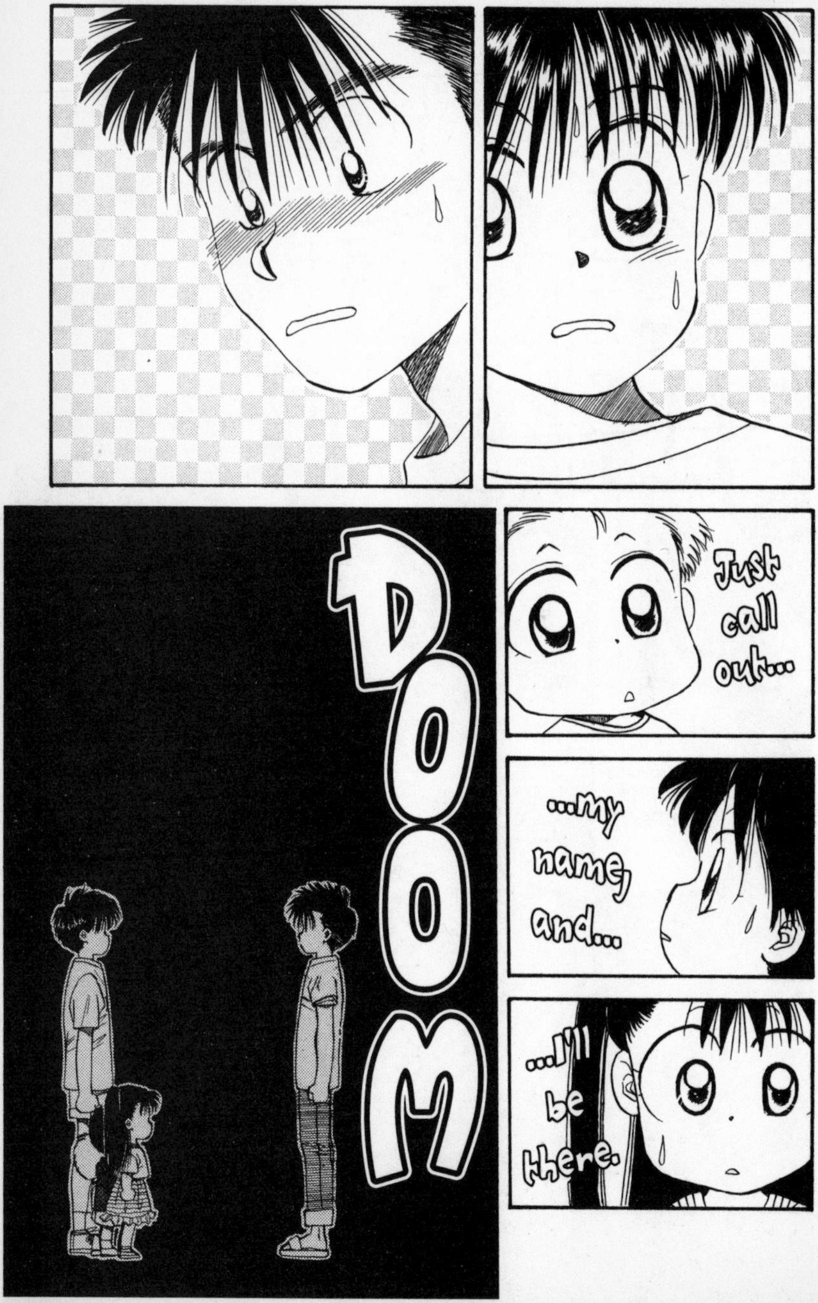
Just call out...
...my name, and...
...I'll be there.
DOOM

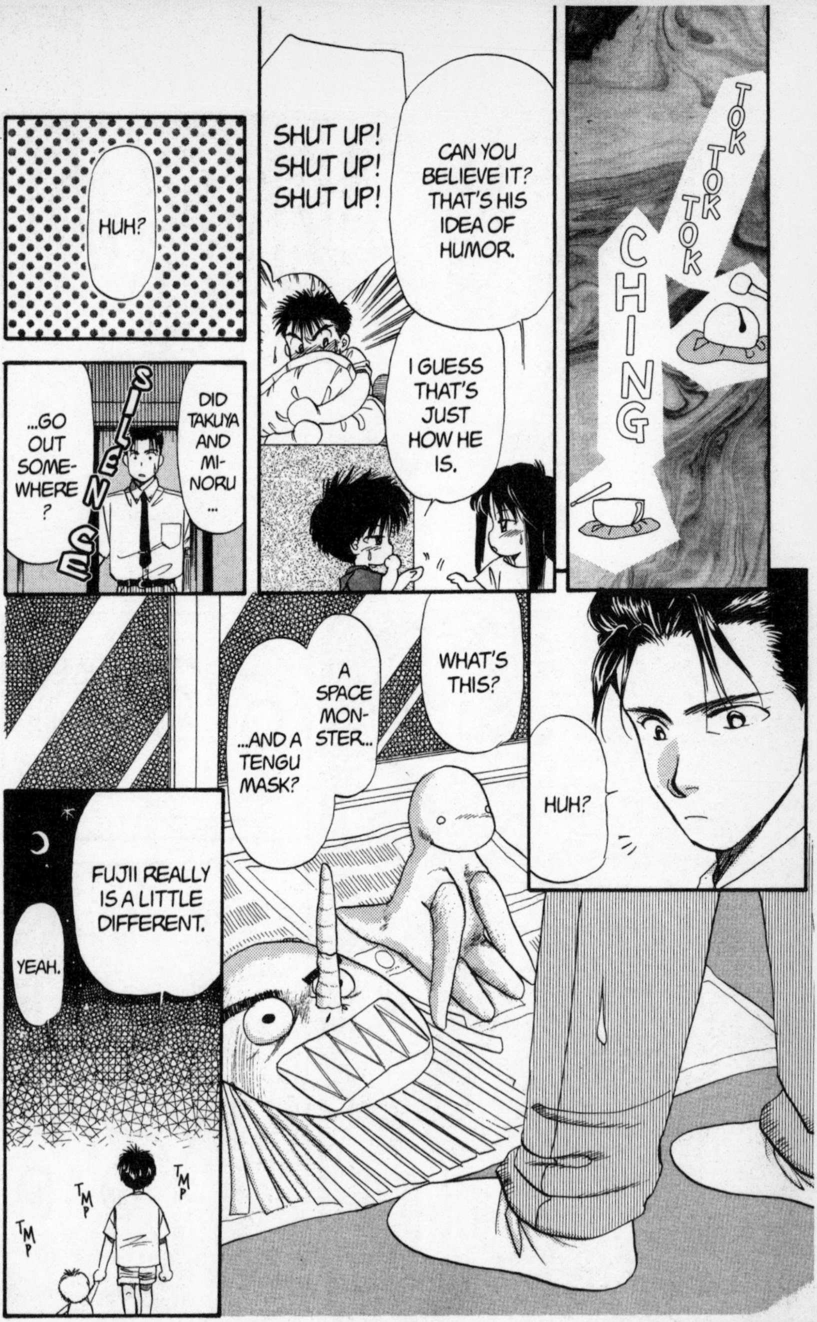
TOK
TOK
TOK
TOK
CHING
CAN YOU BELIEVE IT? THAT'S HIS IDEA OF HUMOR.
SHUT UP! SHUT UP! SHUT UP!
I GUESS THAT'S JUST HOW HE IS.
HUH?
DID TAKUYA AND MI-NORU...
SILENCE
...GO OUT SOME-WHERE?
HUH?
WHAT'S THIS?
A SPACE MON-STER...
...AND A TENGU MASK?
FUJII REALLY IS A LITTLE DIFFERENT.
YEAH.
TMP
TMP
TMP

Chapter 34 / The End

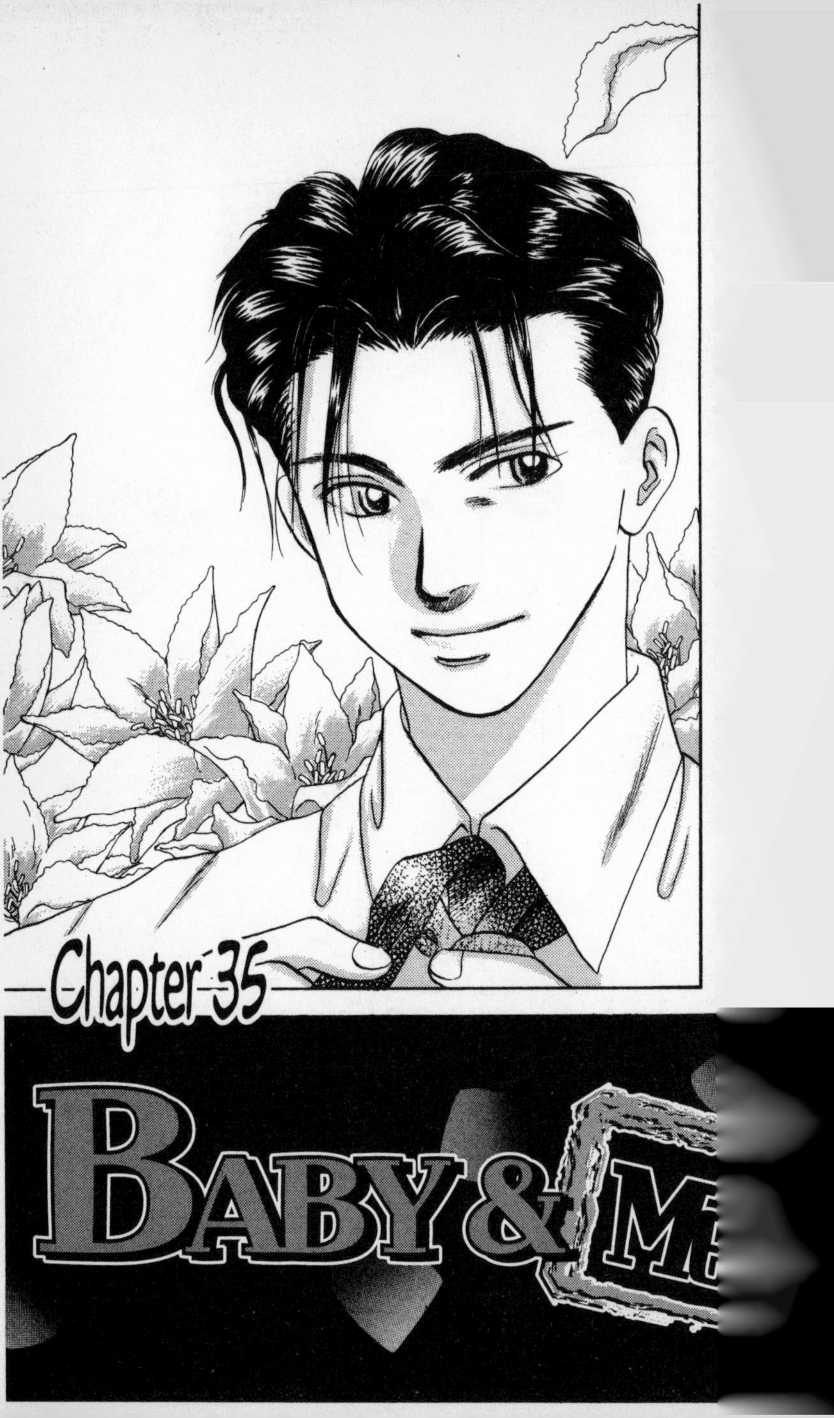
Chapter 35
BABY & ME

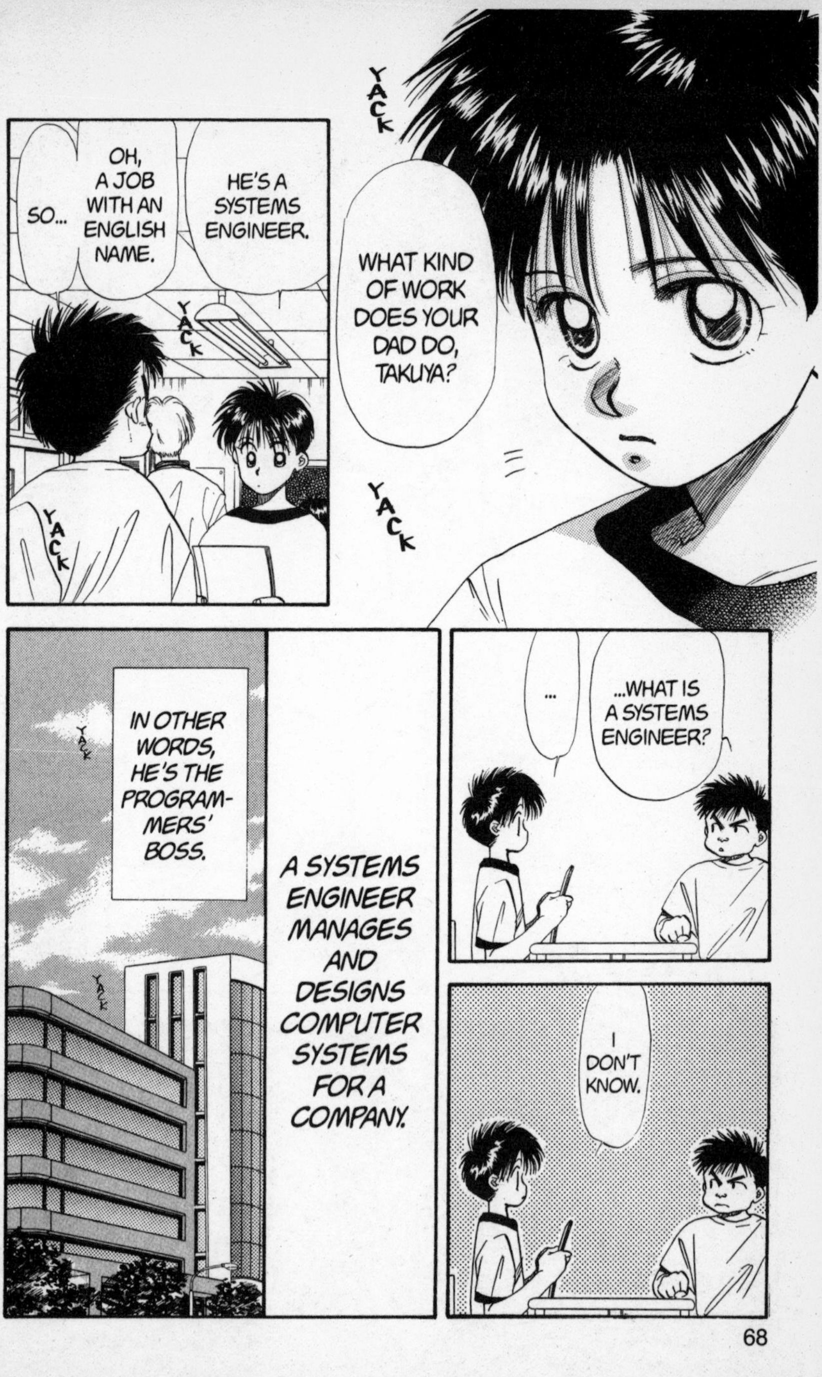
YACK
WHAT KIND OF WORK DOES YOUR DAD DO, TAKUYA?
YACK
HE'S A SYSTEMS ENGINEER.
OH, A JOB WITH AN ENGLISH NAME.
SO...
YACK
YACK
...WHAT IS A SYSTEMS ENGINEER?
...
I DON'T KNOW.
A SYSTEMS ENGINEER MANAGES AND DESIGNS COMPUTER SYSTEMS FOR A COMPANY.
IN OTHER WORDS, HE'S THE PROGRAMMERS' BOSS.
YACK
YACK

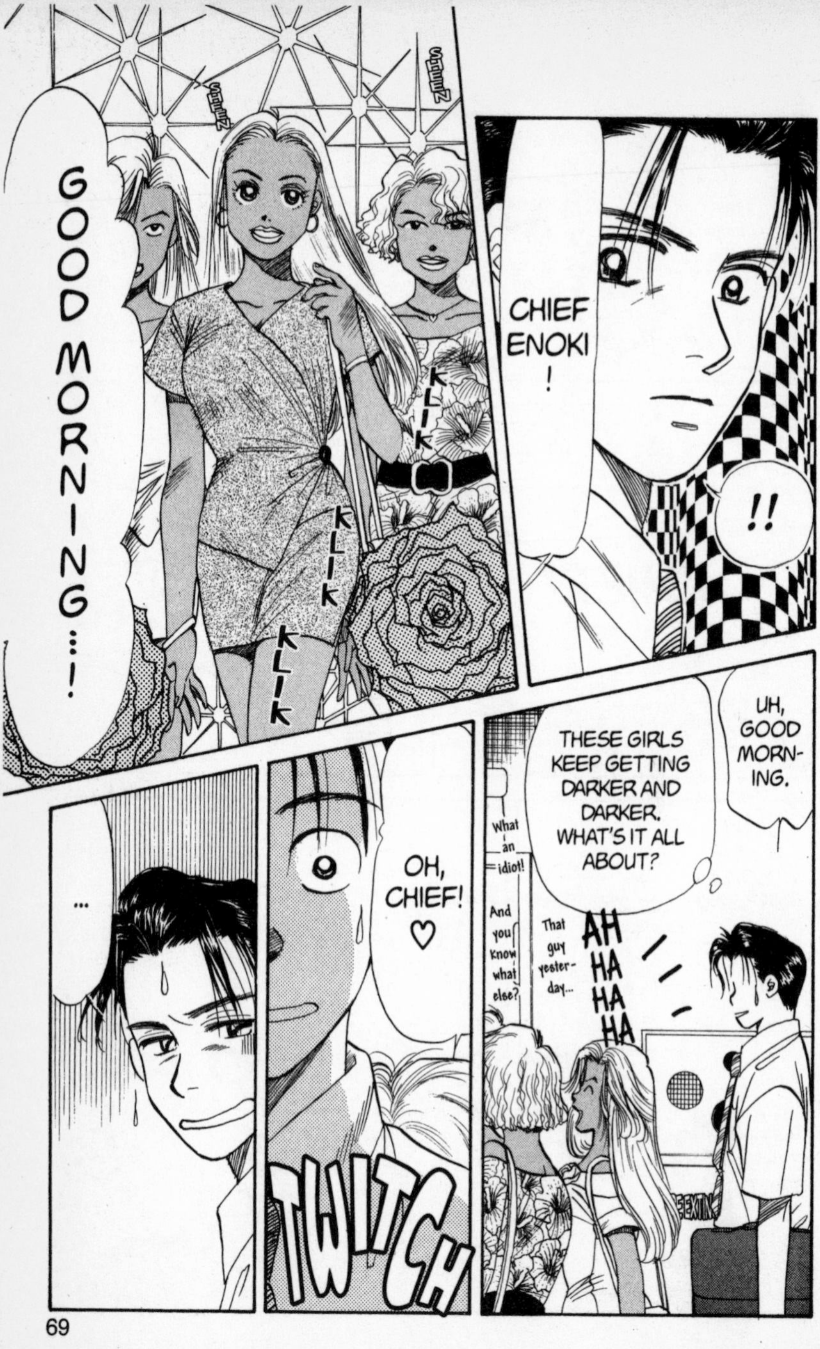
CHIEF ENOKI!
!!
GOOD MORNING...!
SHEEN
SHEEN
KLIK KLIK
KLIK KLIK
UH, GOOD MORNING.
THESE GIRLS KEEP GETTING DARKER AND DARKER. WHAT'S IT ALL ABOUT?
That guy yesterday...
AH HA HA HA
What an idiot!
And you know what else?
OH, CHIEF! ♡
TWITCH
...

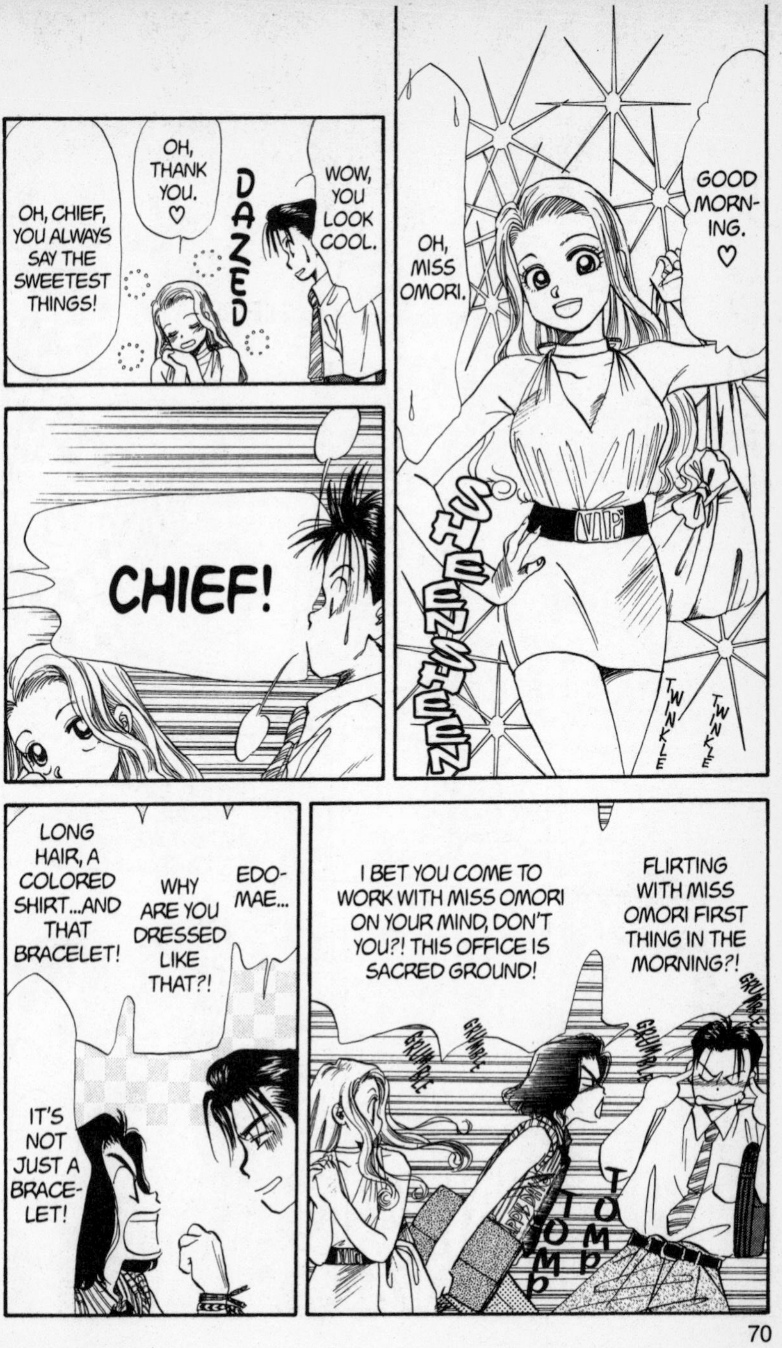

GOOD MORN-ING. ♡
OH, MISS OMORI.
SHEEN SHEEN
TWINKLE
TWINKLE
WOW, YOU LOOK COOL.
DAZED
OH, THANK YOU. ♡
OH, CHIEF, YOU ALWAYS SAY THE SWEETEST THINGS!
CHIEF!
FLIRTING WITH MISS OMORI FIRST THING IN THE MORNING?!
I BET YOU COME TO WORK WITH MISS OMORI ON YOUR MIND, DON'T YOU?! THIS OFFICE IS SACRED GROUND!
GRUMBLE
GRUMBLE
GRUMBLE
GRUMBLE
TOMP
TOMP
EDO-MAE...
WHY ARE YOU DRESSED LIKE THAT?!
LONG HAIR, A COLORED SHIRT...AND THAT BRACELET!
IT'S NOT JUST A BRACE-LET!

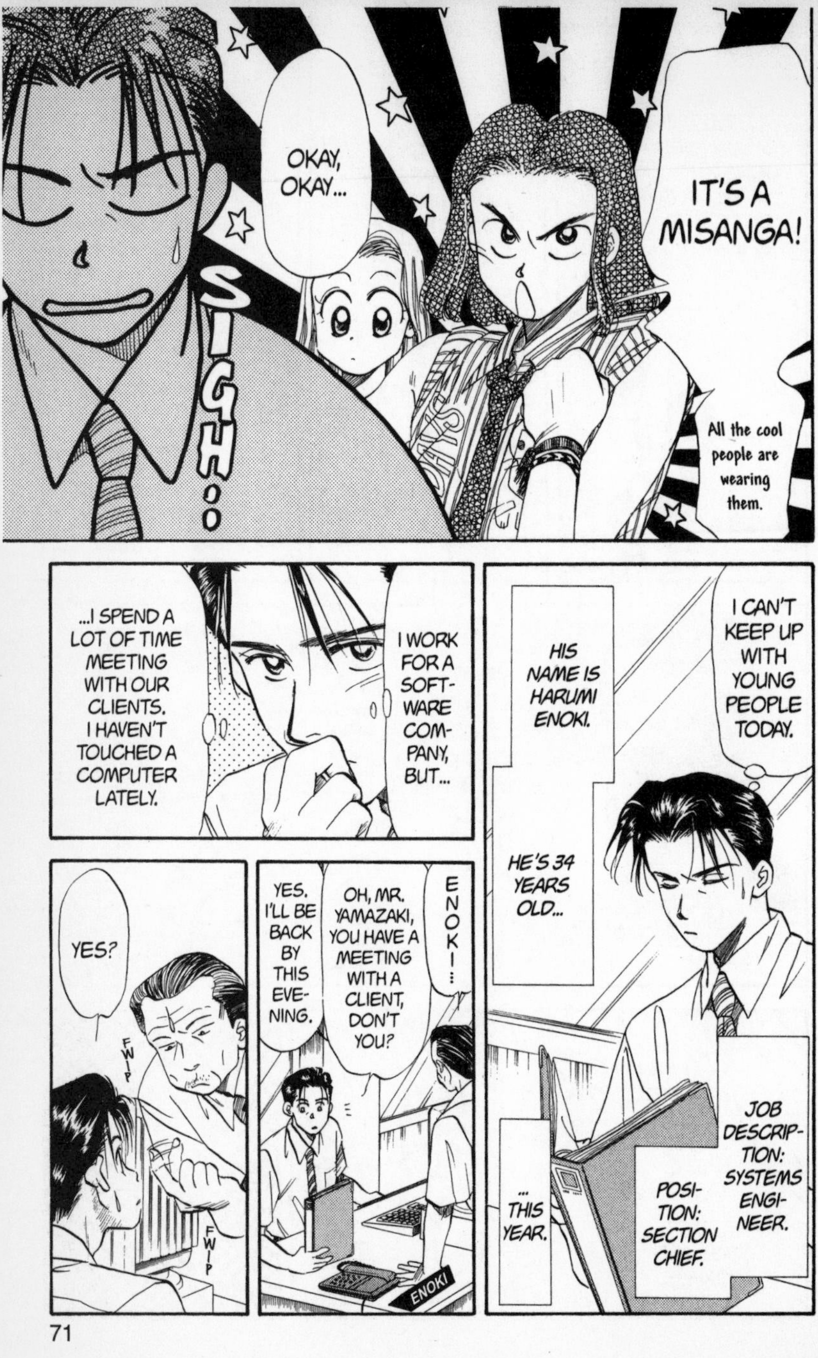
IT'S A MISANGA!
OKAY, OKAY...
All the cool people are wearing them.
SIGH...
I CAN'T KEEP UP WITH YOUNG PEOPLE TODAY.
HIS NAME IS HARUMI ENOKI.
HE'S 34 YEARS OLD...
JOB DESCRIPTION: SYSTEMS ENGINEER.
POSITION: SECTION CHIEF.
...THIS YEAR.
I WORK FOR A SOFTWARE COMPANY, BUT...
...I SPEND A LOT OF TIME MEETING WITH OUR CLIENTS. I HAVEN'T TOUCHED A COMPUTER LATELY.
ENOKI!...
OH, MR. YAMAZAKI, YOU HAVE A MEETING WITH A CLIENT, DON'T YOU?
YES. I'LL BE BACK BY THIS EVENING.
ENOKI
YES?
FWIP
FWIP

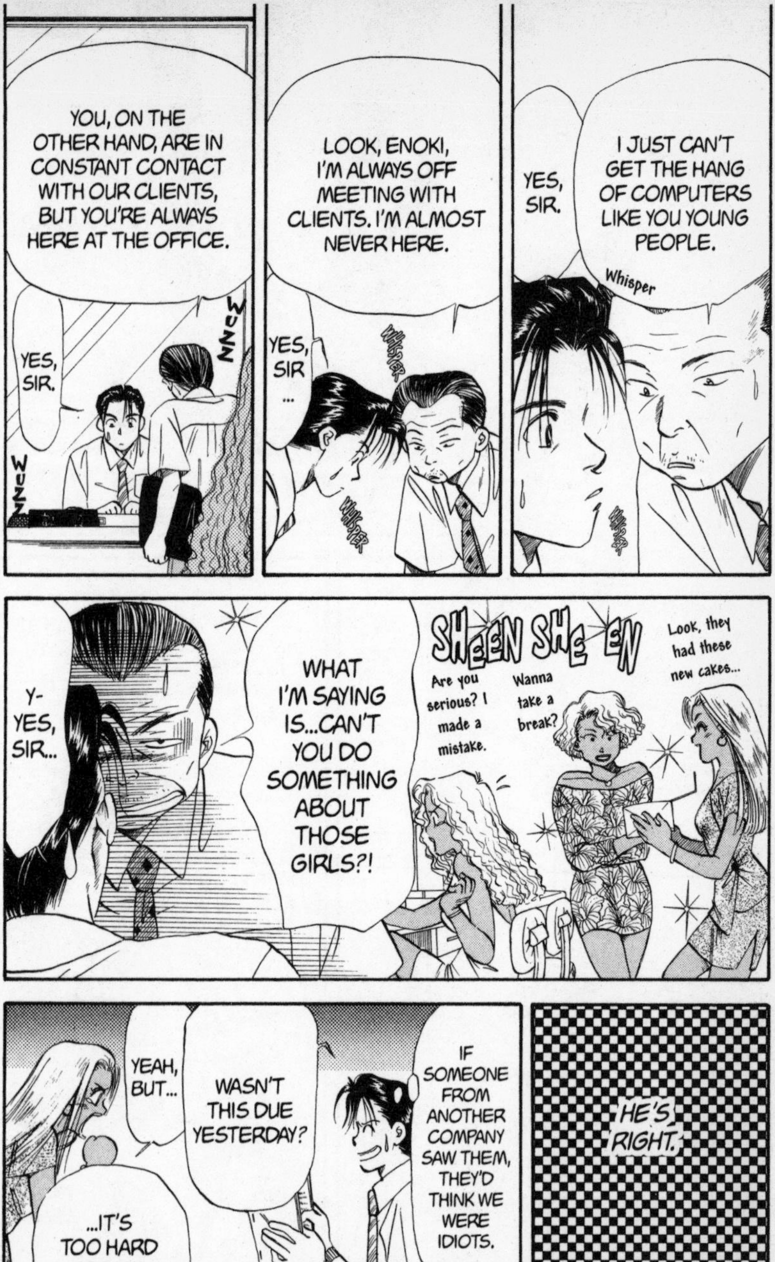
I JUST CAN'T GET THE HANG OF COMPUTERS LIKE YOU YOUNG PEOPLE.
YES, SIR.
Whisper
LOOK, ENOKI, I'M ALWAYS OFF MEETING WITH CLIENTS. I'M ALMOST NEVER HERE.
YES, SIR ...
YOU, ON THE OTHER HAND, ARE IN CONSTANT CONTACT WITH OUR CLIENTS, BUT YOU'RE ALWAYS HERE AT THE OFFICE.
WUZZ
YES, SIR.
WUZZ
Look, they had these new cakes...
Wanna take a break?
Are you serious? I made a mistake.
SHEEN SHEEN
WHAT I'M SAYING IS...CAN'T YOU DO SOMETHING ABOUT THOSE GIRLS?!
Y- YES, SIR...
HE'S RIGHT.
IF SOMEONE FROM ANOTHER COMPANY SAW THEM, THEY'D THINK WE WERE IDIOTS.
WASN'T THIS DUE YESTERDAY?
YEAH, BUT...
...IT'S TOO HARD FOR ME.

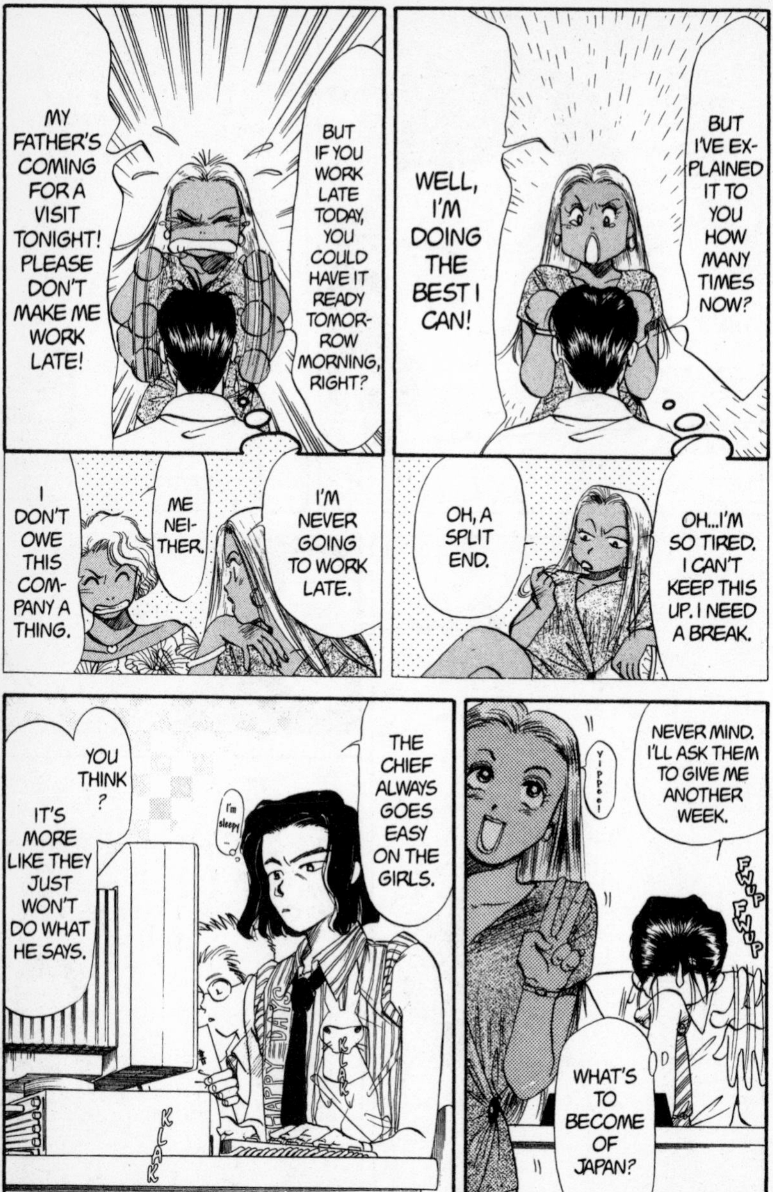
BUT I'VE EX-PLAINED IT TO YOU HOW MANY TIMES NOW?
WELL, I'M DOING THE BEST I CAN!
BUT IF YOU WORK LATE TODAY, YOU COULD HAVE IT READY TOMOR-ROW MORNING, RIGHT?
MY FATHER'S COMING FOR A VISIT TONIGHT! PLEASE DON'T MAKE ME WORK LATE!
OH...I'M SO TIRED. I CAN'T KEEP THIS UP. I NEED A BREAK.
OH, A SPLIT END.
I'M NEVER GOING TO WORK LATE.
ME NEI-THER.
I DON'T OWE THIS COM-PANY A THING.
NEVER MIND. I'LL ASK THEM TO GIVE ME ANOTHER WEEK.
FWUP FWUP
Yippee!
WHAT'S TO BECOME OF JAPAN?
THE CHIEF ALWAYS GOES EASY ON THE GIRLS.
YOU THINK?
IT'S MORE LIKE THEY JUST WON'T DO WHAT HE SAYS.
I'm sleepy...
HAPPY DAYS
KLAK
KLAK

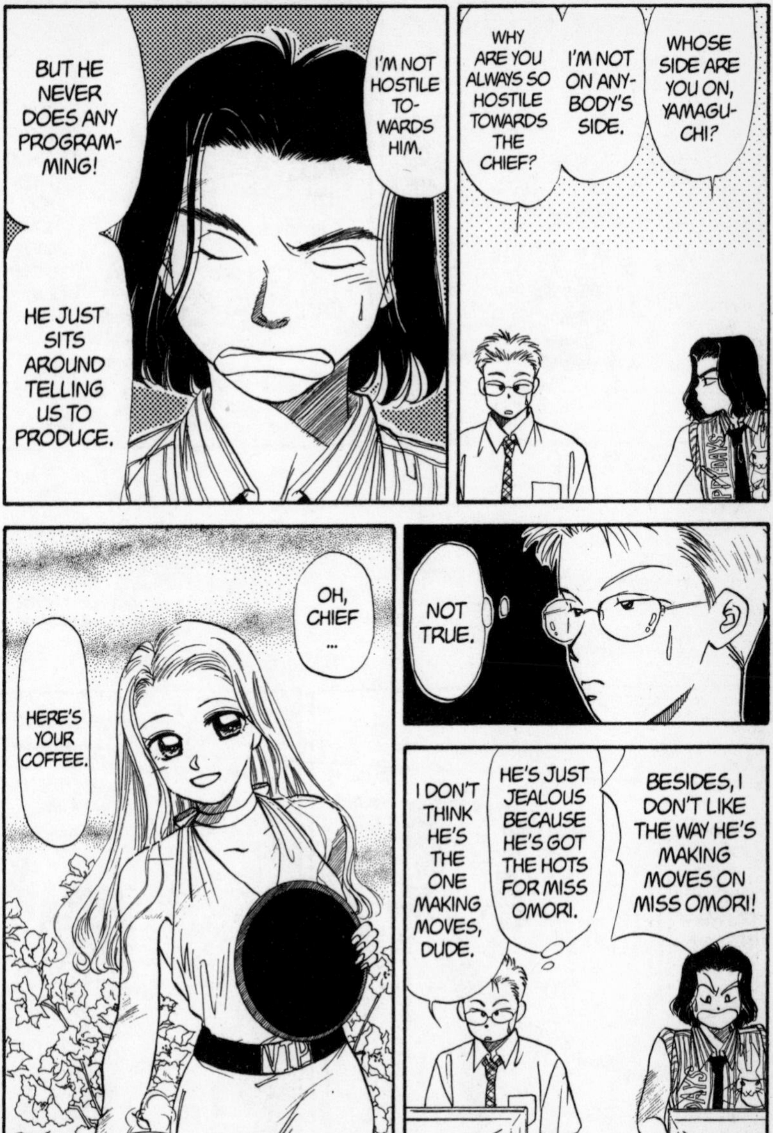
WHOSE SIDE ARE YOU ON, YAMAGUCHI?
I'M NOT ON ANYBODY'S SIDE.
WHY ARE YOU ALWAYS SO HOSTILE TOWARDS THE CHIEF?
I'M NOT HOSTILE TOWARDS HIM.
BUT HE NEVER DOES ANY PROGRAMMING!
HE JUST SITS AROUND TELLING US TO PRODUCE.
NOT TRUE.
BESIDES, I DON'T LIKE THE WAY HE'S MAKING MOVES ON MISS OMORI!
HE'S JUST JEALOUS BECAUSE HE'S GOT THE HOTS FOR MISS OMORI.
I DON'T THINK HE'S THE ONE MAKING MOVES, DUDE.
OH, CHIEF ...
HERE'S YOUR COFFEE.

HUH? OH...
THANKS.
SMILE
HUH?
OH, I GUESS SHE WANTS ME TO DRINK IT.
THANK YOU.
YOU'RE WEL- COME.
MM...
SLURP
IT'S YUMMY!
SMILE
HUH?

Author's Note Part 3

I get things wrong in the refrigerator a lot, but it's always my kid brother who suffers.

This is what happened...

One time I saw a white supermarket bag with a picture of crab legs on it in the refrigerator. I was so happy, so I asked my brother if he wanted some crab soup. He yelled, "Yeah!!" So I immediately put a pot of water on the stove for the crab soup. Well, when the water came to a boil, and I was ready to add the crab legs, I looked in the bag and found--of all things--bread crusts. I was so shocked that I actually got dizzy. I guess I don't have to tell you that my brother was crushed...

And then there was this incident...

One night my brother was sleeping soundly after a hard day. I thought that it would be sad if there was nothing for him to eat in the morning, so I decided to set the rice to cook on a timer. I washed the rice and set the timer on the cooker. Then, wondering if there was anything for him to eat with the rice, I opened the refrigerator and found nothing, not even an egg.

Continued in Part 4...

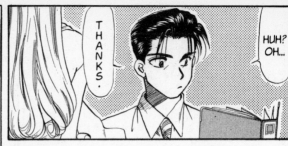

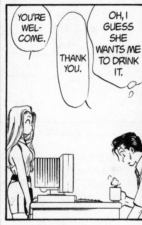

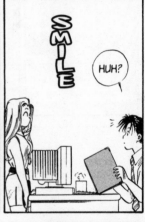

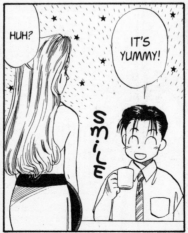

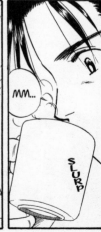

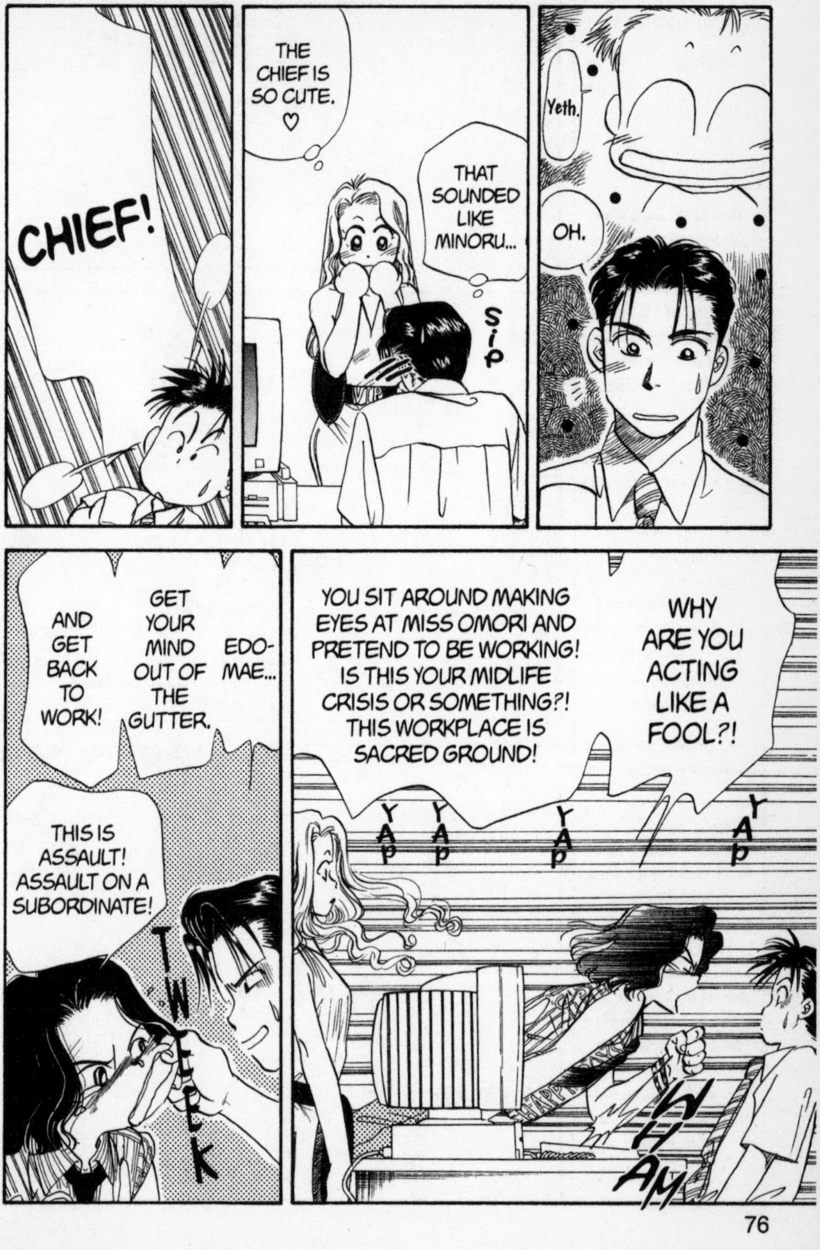
Yeth.
OH.
THE CHIEF IS SO CUTE. ♡
THAT SOUNDED LIKE MINORU...
SIP
CHIEF!
WHY ARE YOU ACTING LIKE A FOOL?!
YOU SIT AROUND MAKING EYES AT MISS OMORI AND PRETEND TO BE WORKING! IS THIS YOUR MIDLIFE CRISIS OR SOMETHING?! THIS WORKPLACE IS SACRED GROUND!
YAP YAP YAP YAP
WHAM
EDO-MAE...
GET YOUR MIND OUT OF THE GUTTER.
AND GET BACK TO WORK!
THIS IS ASSAULT! ASSAULT ON A SUBORDINATE!
TWEEK

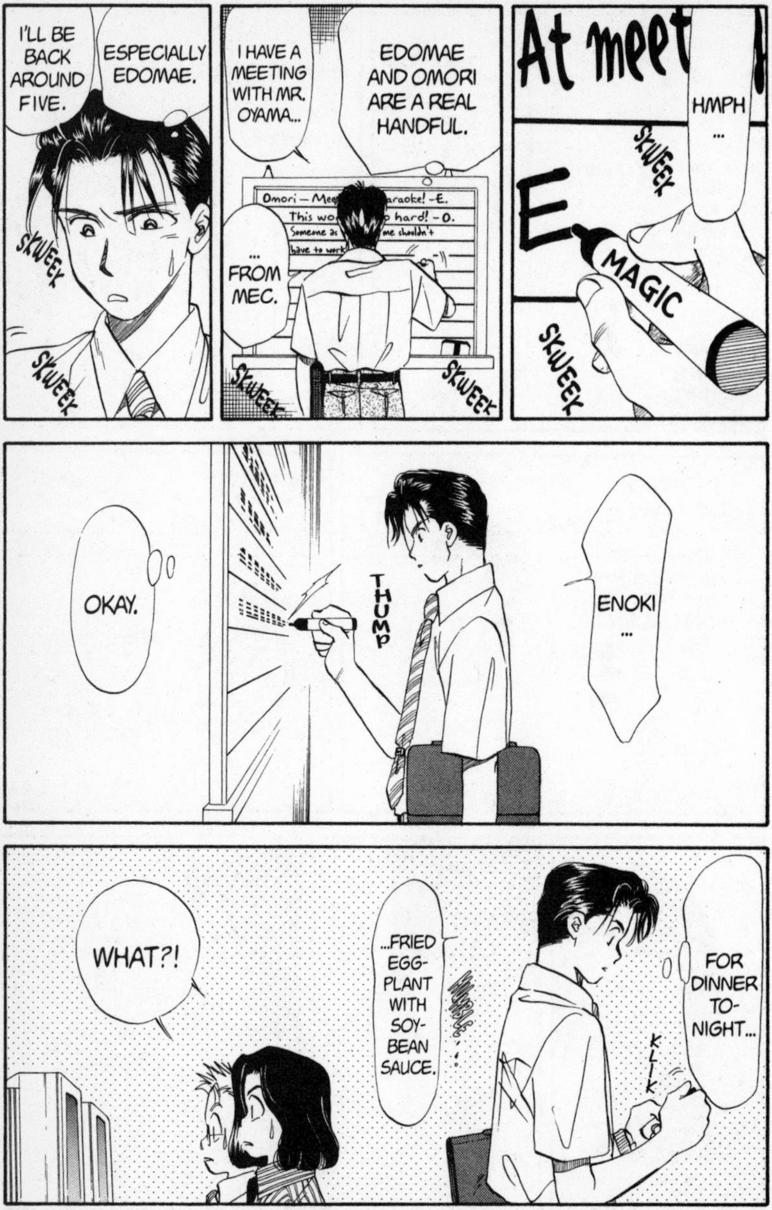
At meet
HMPH ...
SKWEEK
E
MAGIC
SKWEEK
EDOMAE AND OMORI ARE A REAL HANDFUL.
I HAVE A MEETING WITH MR. OYAMA...
... FROM MEC.
SKWEEK
SKWEEK
ESPECIALLY EDOMAE.
I'LL BE BACK AROUND FIVE.
SKWEEK
SKWEEK
ENOKI ...
THUMP
OKAY.
FOR DINNER TO-NIGHT...
KLIK
...FRIED EGG-PLANT WITH SOY-BEAN SAUCE.
WHAT?!

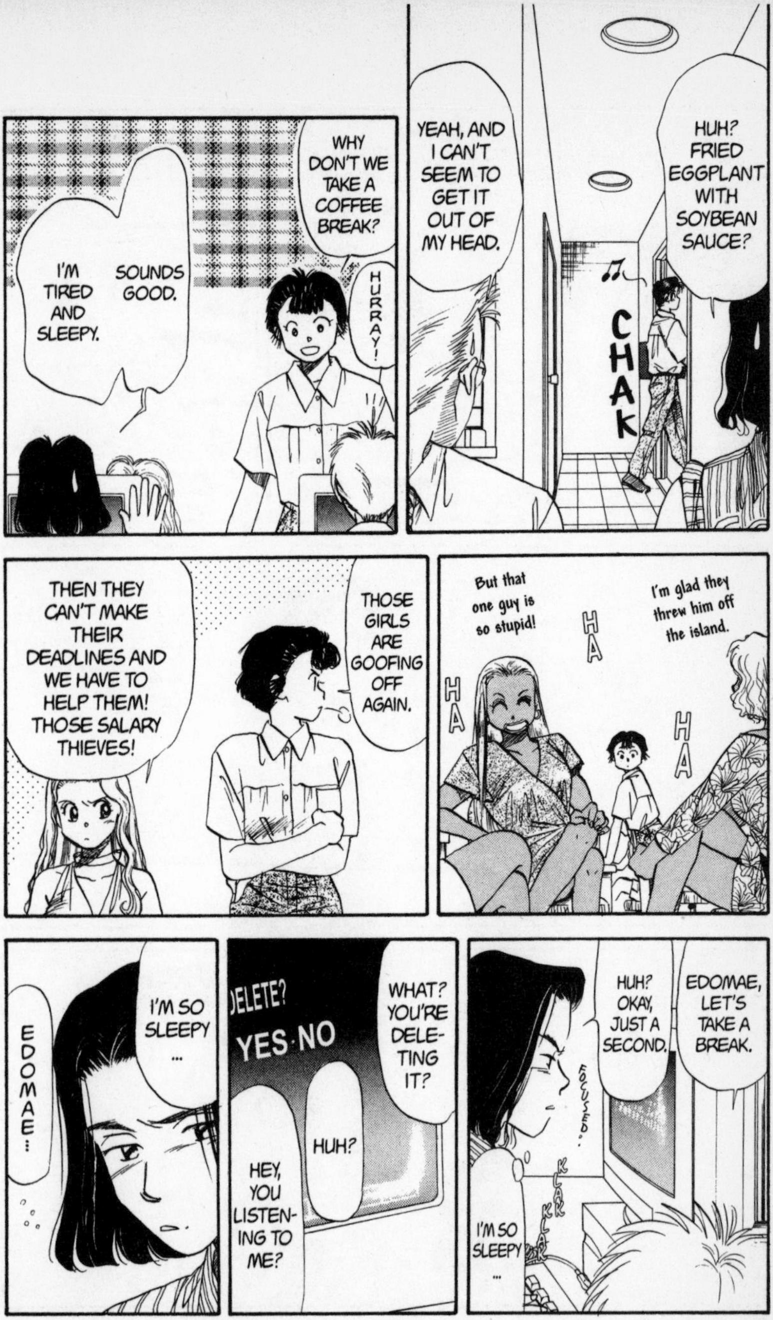
HUH? FRIED EGGPLANT WITH SOYBEAN SAUCE?
YEAH, AND I CAN'T SEEM TO GET IT OUT OF MY HEAD.
CHAK
WHY DON'T WE TAKE A COFFEE BREAK?
HURRAY!
SOUNDS GOOD.
I'M TIRED AND SLEEPY.
I'm glad they threw him off the island.
HA
HA
But that one guy is so stupid!
HA
THOSE GIRLS ARE GOOFING OFF AGAIN.
THEN THEY CAN'T MAKE THEIR DEADLINES AND WE HAVE TO HELP THEM! THOSE SALARY THIEVES!
EDOMAE, LET'S TAKE A BREAK.
HUH? OKAY, JUST A SECOND.
FOCUSED..
KLAK KLAK
I'M SO SLEEPY...
WHAT? YOU'RE DELETING IT?
DELETE?
YES NO
HUH?
HEY, YOU LISTENING TO ME?
I'M SO SLEEPY...
EDOMAE...

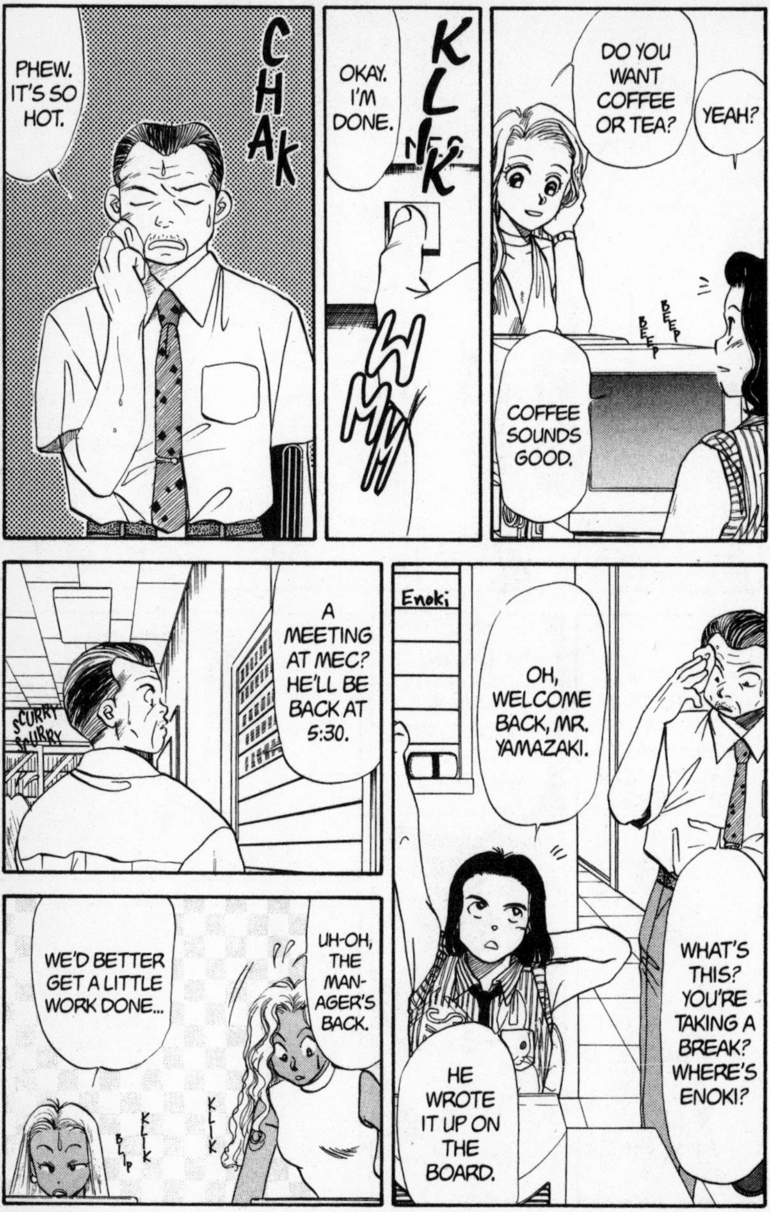
YEAH?
DO YOU WANT COFFEE OR TEA?
BEEP BEEP
COFFEE SOUNDS GOOD.
KLIK
OKAY. I'M DONE.
WMMM
CHAK
PHEW. IT'S SO HOT.
Enoki
OH, WELCOME BACK, MR. YAMAZAKI.
WHAT'S THIS? YOU'RE TAKING A BREAK? WHERE'S ENOKI?
HE WROTE IT UP ON THE BOARD.
A MEETING AT MEC? HE'LL BE BACK AT 5:30.
SCURRY SCURRY
UH-OH, THE MANAGER'S BACK.
WE'D BETTER GET A LITTLE WORK DONE...
KLIK
KLIK BLIP

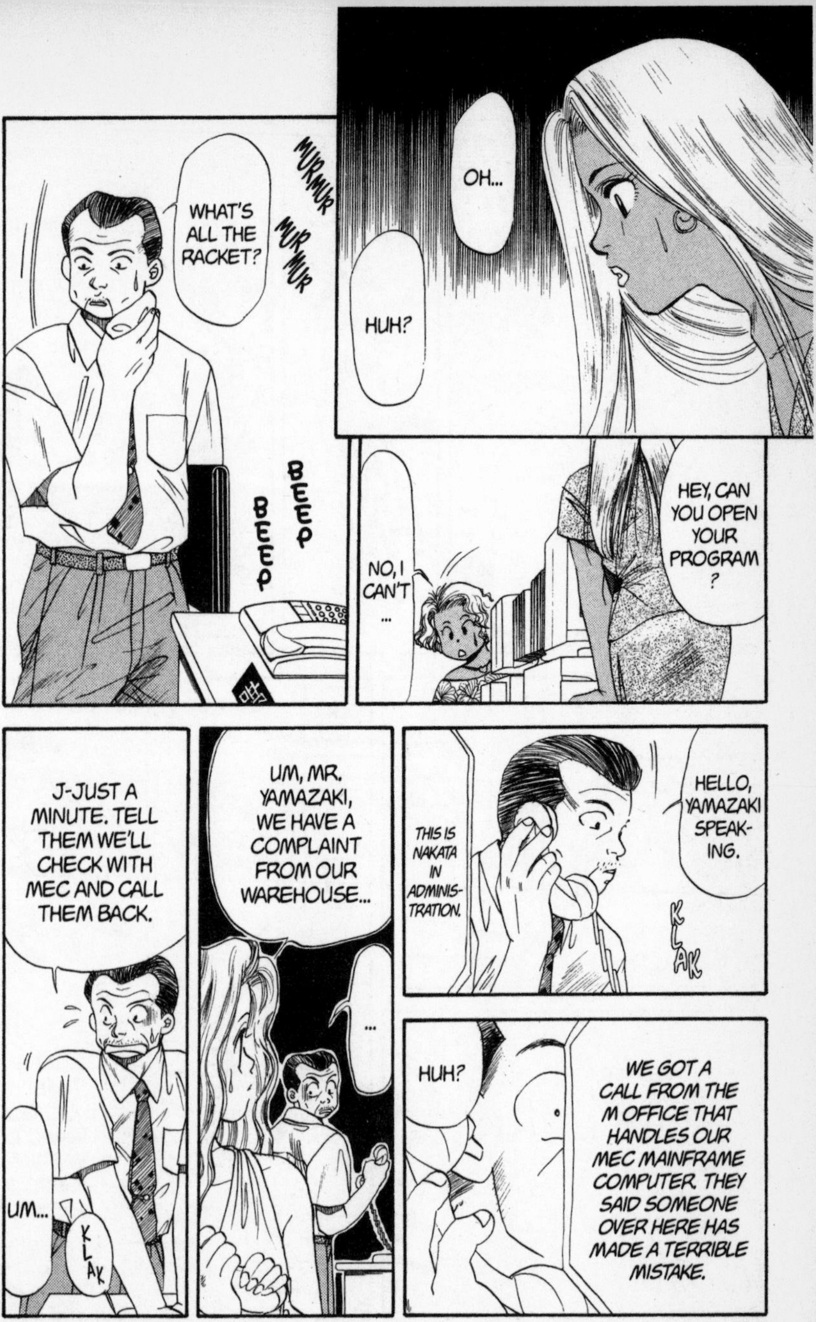

OH...
HUH?
HEY, CAN YOU OPEN YOUR PROGRAM?
NO, I CAN'T...
MURMUR
MURMUR
WHAT'S ALL THE RACKET?
BEEP
BEEP
HELLO, YAMAZAKI SPEAKING.
KLAK
THIS IS NAKATA IN ADMINISTRATION.
WE GOT A CALL FROM THE M OFFICE THAT HANDLES OUR MEC MAINFRAME COMPUTER. THEY SAID SOMEONE OVER HERE HAS MADE A TERRIBLE MISTAKE.
HUH?
UM, MR. YAMAZAKI, WE HAVE A COMPLAINT FROM OUR WAREHOUSE...
...
J-JUST A MINUTE. TELL THEM WE'LL CHECK WITH MEC AND CALL THEM BACK.
UM...
KLAK

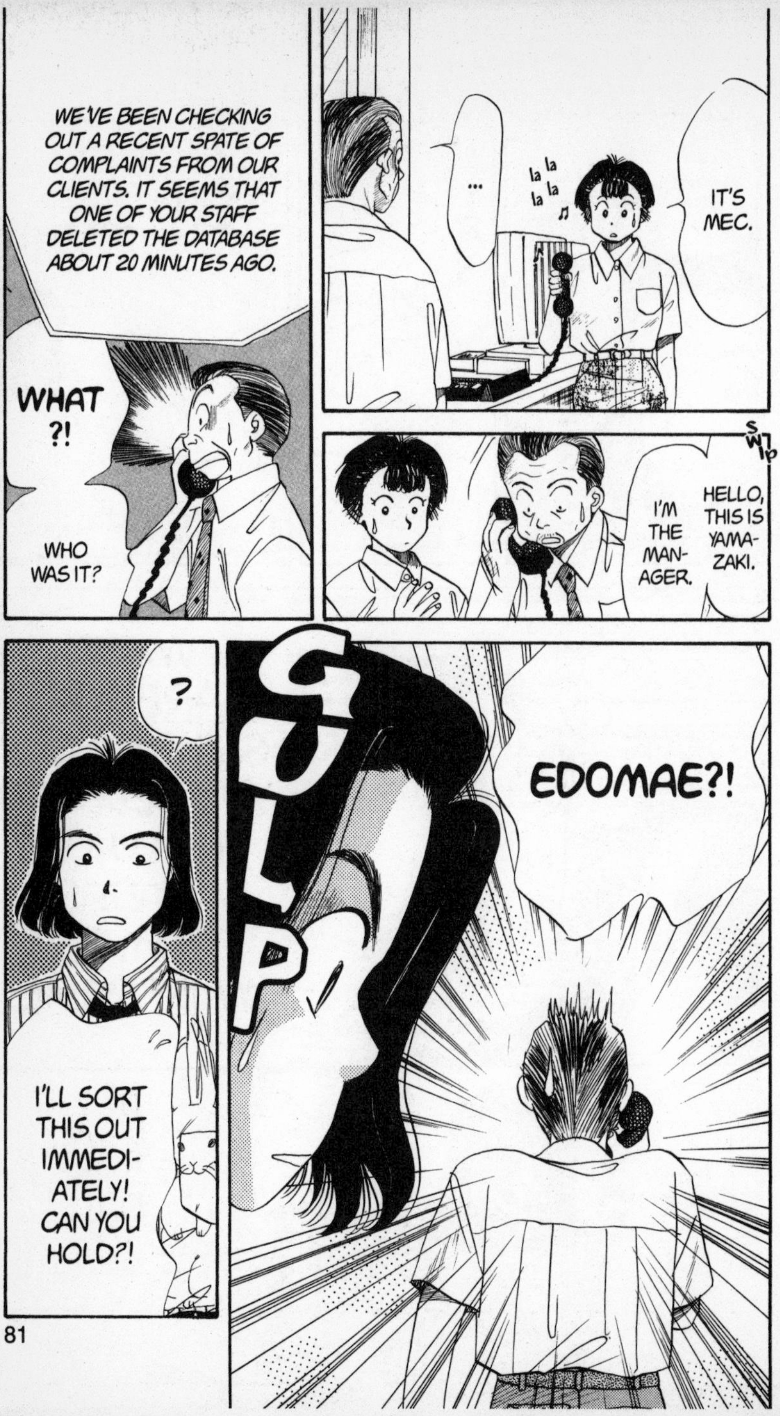
IT'S MEC.
la la la la ♫
...
SWIP
HELLO, THIS IS YAMAZAKI.
I'M THE MANAGER.
WE'VE BEEN CHECKING OUT A RECENT SPATE OF COMPLAINTS FROM OUR CLIENTS. IT SEEMS THAT ONE OF YOUR STAFF DELETED THE DATABASE ABOUT 20 MINUTES AGO.
WHAT?!
WHO WAS IT?
EDOMAE?!
GULP
?
I'LL SORT THIS OUT IMMEDIATELY! CAN YOU HOLD?!

*Database: A place where programs are systematically organized and stored. The stored programs are sometimes also called the library. Programs in the library can be called up when needed, edited and used.

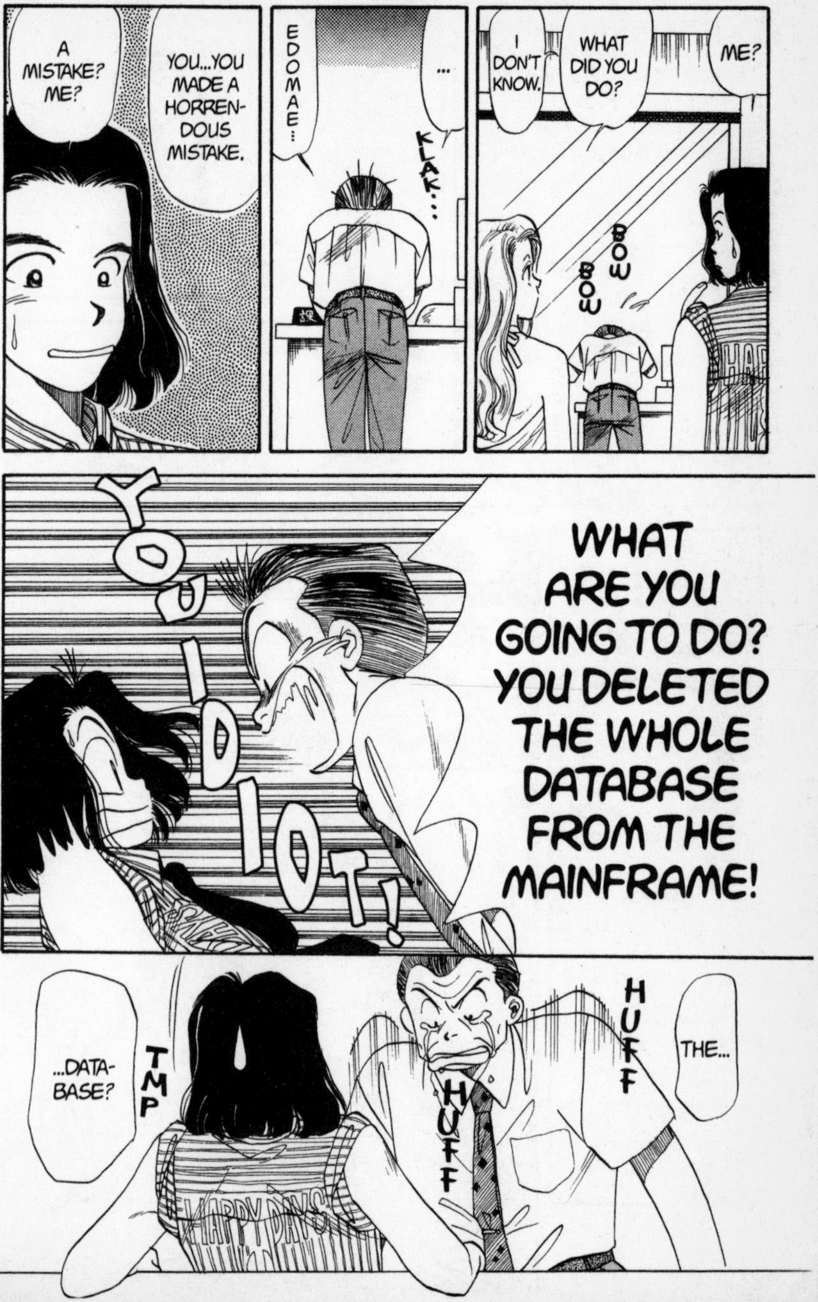
ME?
WHAT DID YOU DO?
I DON'T KNOW.
BOW
BOW
...
EDOMAE...
KLAK...
YOU...YOU MADE A HORRENDOUS MISTAKE.
A MISTAKE? ME?
WHAT ARE YOU GOING TO DO? YOU DELETED THE WHOLE DATABASE FROM THE MAINFRAME!
YOU IDIOT!
THE...
HUFF
HUFF
TMP
...DATABASE?

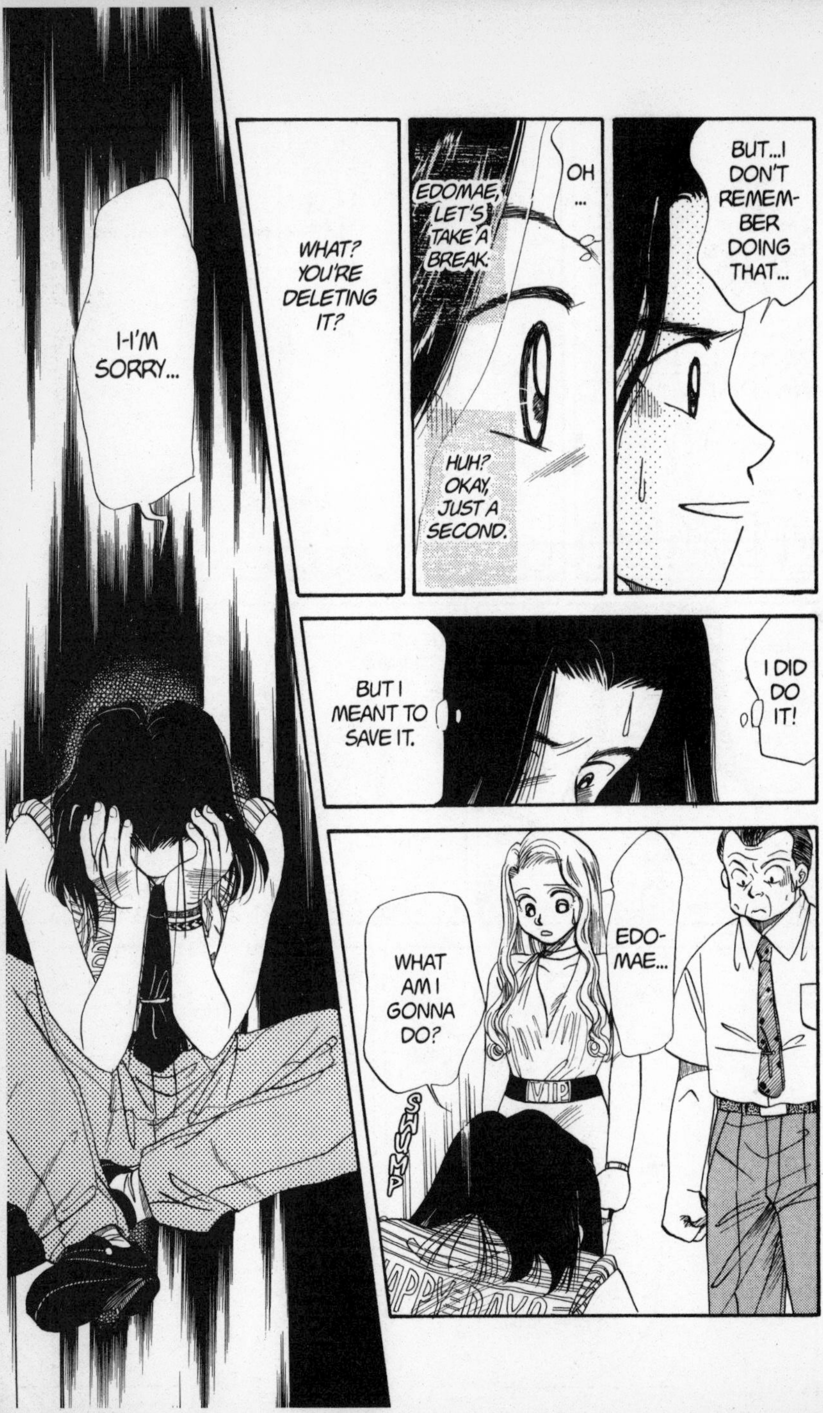
BUT...I DON'T REMEM-BER DOING THAT...
OH ...
EDOMAE, LET'S TAKE A BREAK.
HUH? OKAY, JUST A SECOND.
WHAT? YOU'RE DELETING IT?
I DID DO IT!
BUT I MEANT TO SAVE IT.
EDO-MAE...
WHAT AM I GONNA DO?
SHUMP
I-I'M SORRY...

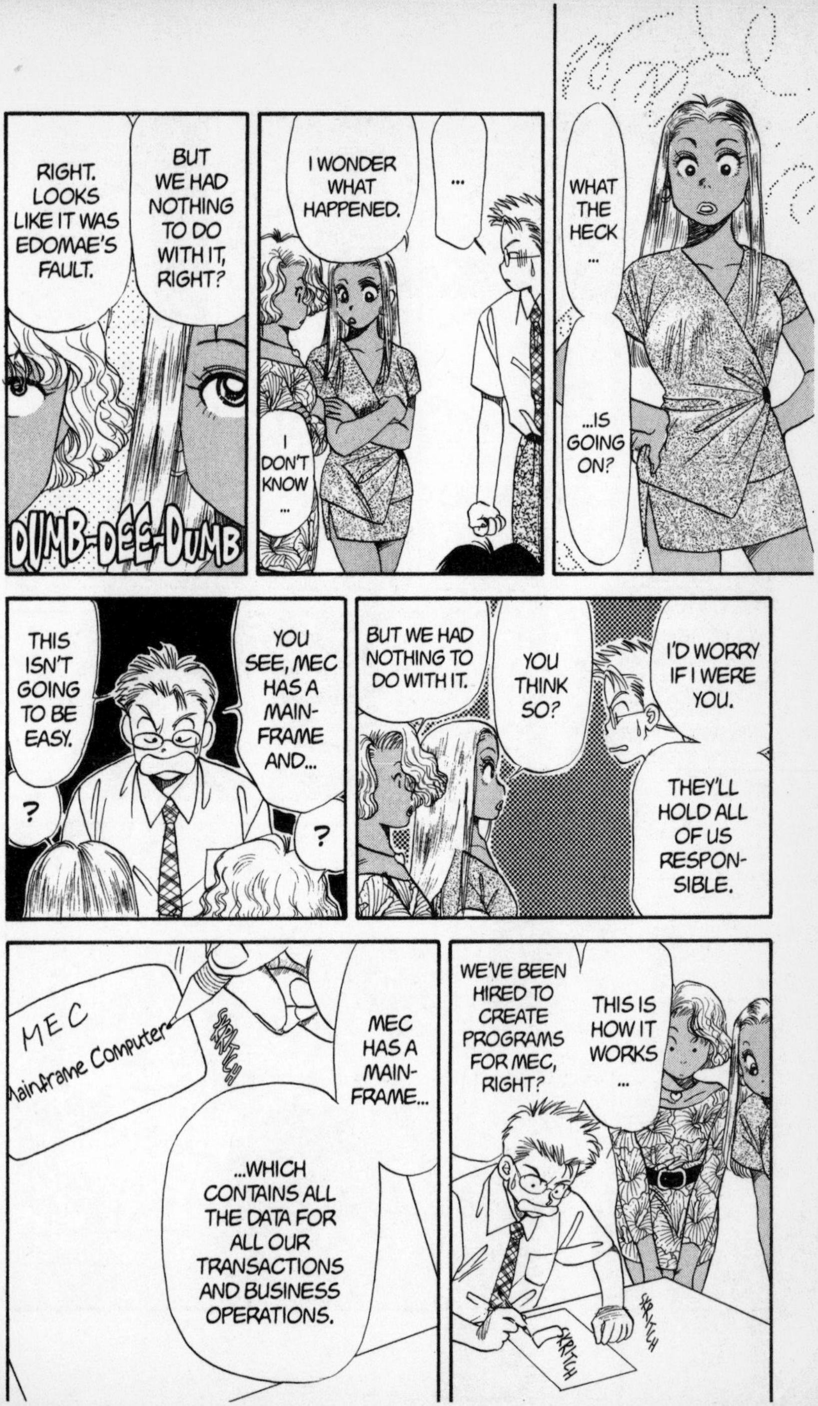
WHAT THE HECK ...
...IS GOING ON?
...
I WONDER WHAT HAPPENED.
I DON'T KNOW ...
BUT WE HAD NOTHING TO DO WITH IT, RIGHT?
RIGHT. LOOKS LIKE IT WAS EDOMAE'S FAULT.
DUMB-DEE-DUMB
I'D WORRY IF I WERE YOU.
YOU THINK SO?
BUT WE HAD NOTHING TO DO WITH IT.
THEY'LL HOLD ALL OF US RESPONSIBLE.
YOU SEE, MEC HAS A MAIN-FRAME AND...
THIS ISN'T GOING TO BE EASY.
?
?
THIS IS HOW IT WORKS ...
WE'VE BEEN HIRED TO CREATE PROGRAMS FOR MEC, RIGHT?
SKRITCH
SKRITCH
MEC HAS A MAIN-FRAME...
SKRITCH
MEC
Mainframe Computer
...WHICH CONTAINS ALL THE DATA FOR ALL OUR TRANSACTIONS AND BUSINESS OPERATIONS.

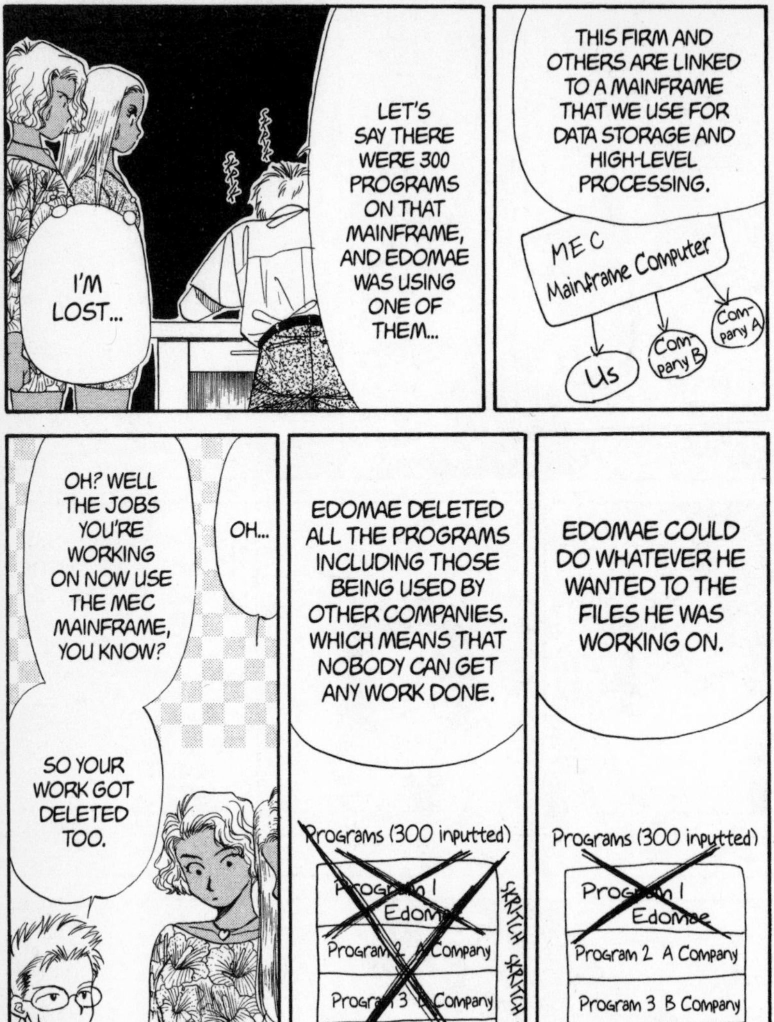
THIS FIRM AND OTHERS ARE LINKED TO A MAINFRAME THAT WE USE FOR DATA STORAGE AND HIGH-LEVEL PROCESSING.
MEC
Mainframe Computer
Company A
Company B
Us
LET'S SAY THERE WERE 300 PROGRAMS ON THAT MAINFRAME, AND EDOMAE WAS USING ONE OF THEM...
I'M LOST...
EDOMAE COULD DO WHATEVER HE WANTED TO THE FILES HE WAS WORKING ON.
Programs (300 inputted)
Program 1 Edomae
Program 2 A Company
Program 3 B Company
297 programs, etc
EDOMAE DELETED ALL THE PROGRAMS INCLUDING THOSE BEING USED BY OTHER COMPANIES. WHICH MEANS THAT NOBODY CAN GET ANY WORK DONE.
Programs (300 inputted)
Program 1 Edomae
Program 2 A Company
Program 3 B Company
297 programs, etc
SKRITCH SKRITCH...
OH...
OH? WELL THE JOBS YOU'RE WORKING ON NOW USE THE MEC MAINFRAME, YOU KNOW?
SO YOUR WORK GOT DELETED TOO.

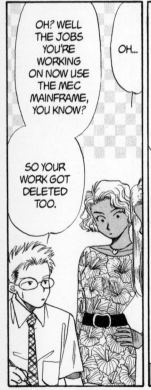

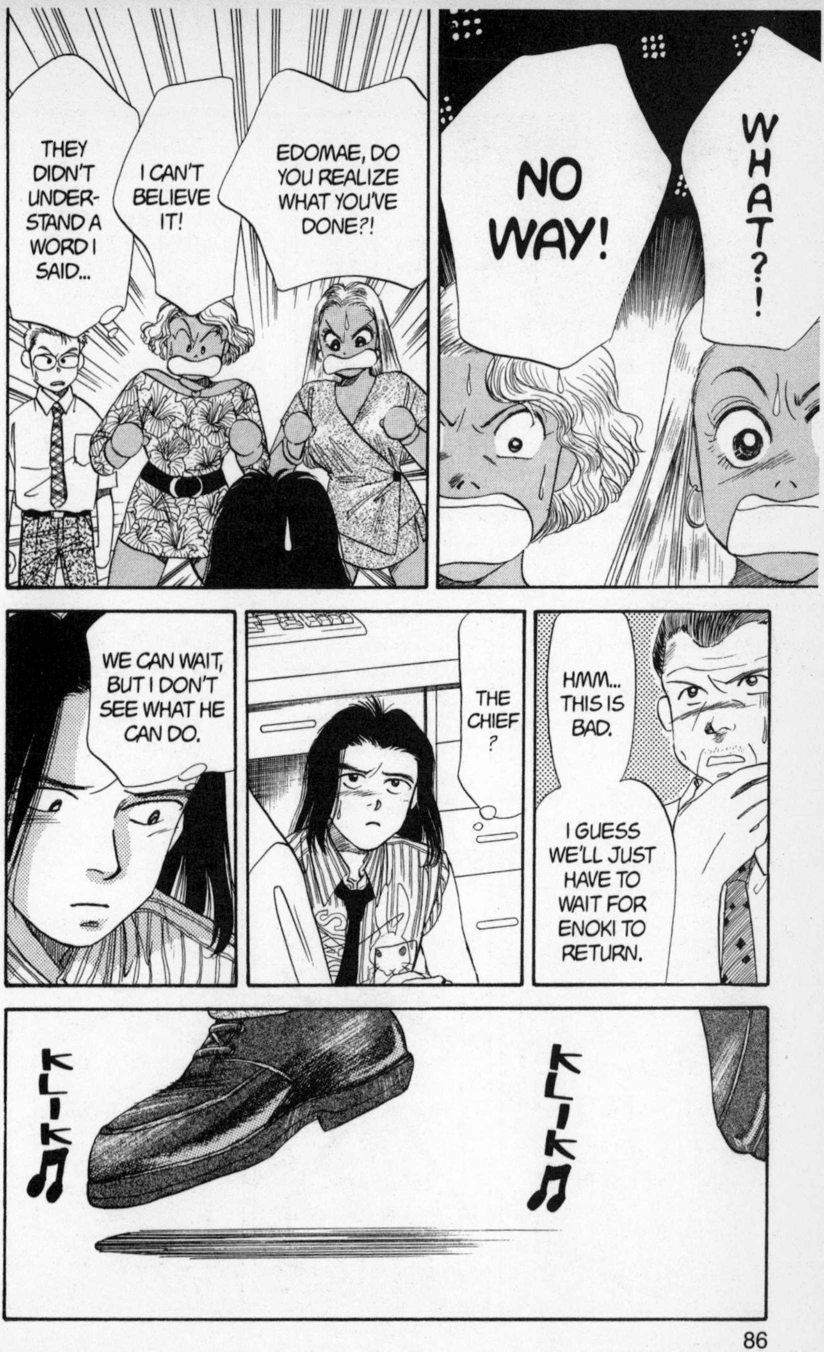
WHAT?!
NO WAY!
EDOMAE, DO YOU REALIZE WHAT YOU'VE DONE?!
I CAN'T BELIEVE IT!
THEY DIDN'T UNDER-STAND A WORD I SAID...
HMM... THIS IS BAD.
I GUESS WE'LL JUST HAVE TO WAIT FOR ENOKI TO RETURN.
THE CHIEF?
WE CAN WAIT, BUT I DON'T SEE WHAT HE CAN DO.
KLIK♫
KLIK♫

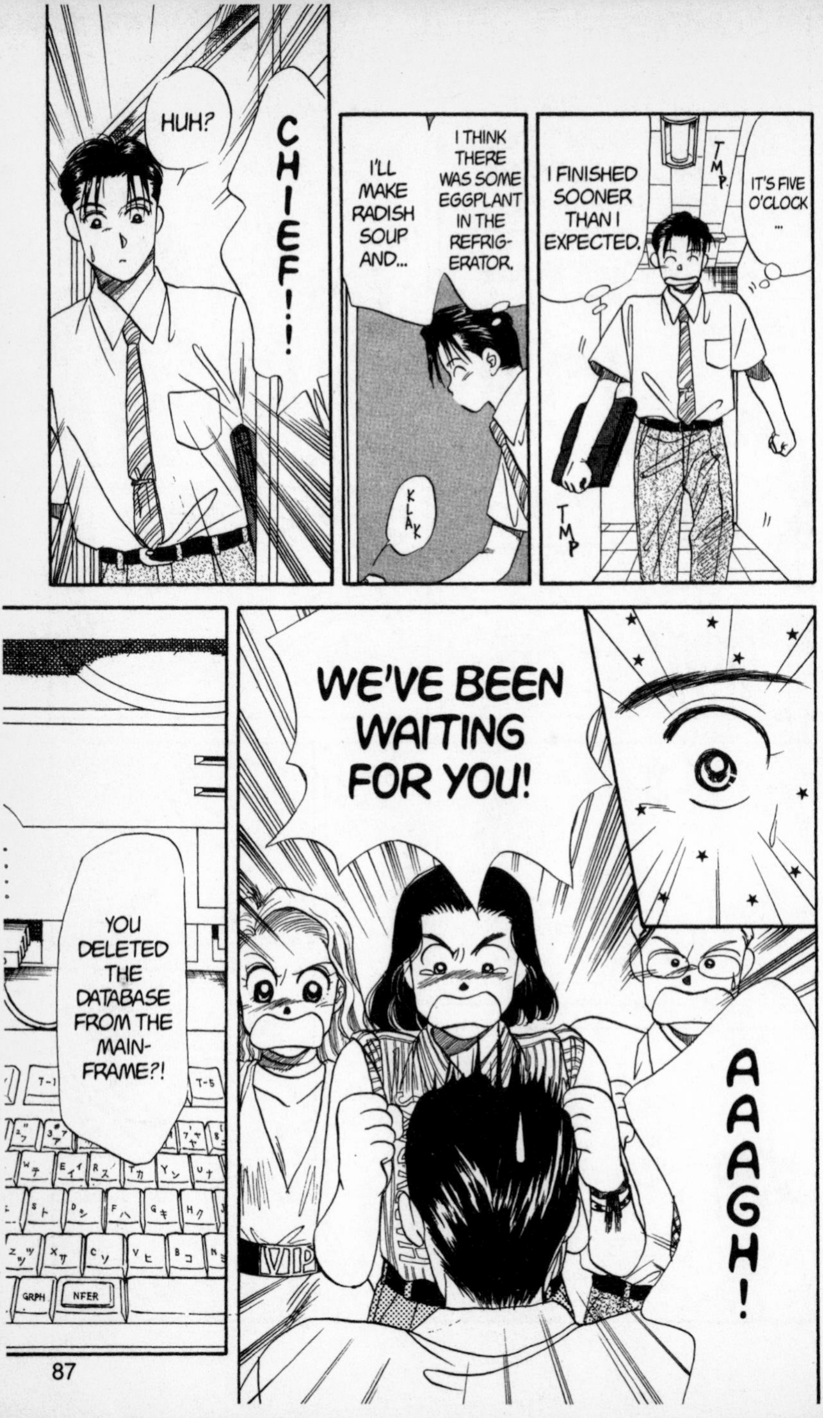

IT'S FIVE O'CLOCK ...
I FINISHED SOONER THAN I EXPECTED.
TMP
TMP
I THINK THERE WAS SOME EGGPLANT IN THE REFRIGERATOR.
I'LL MAKE RADISH SOUP AND...
KLAK
CHIEF!!
HUH?
WE'VE BEEN WAITING FOR YOU!
AAAGH!
YOU DELETED THE DATABASE FROM THE MAINFRAME?!

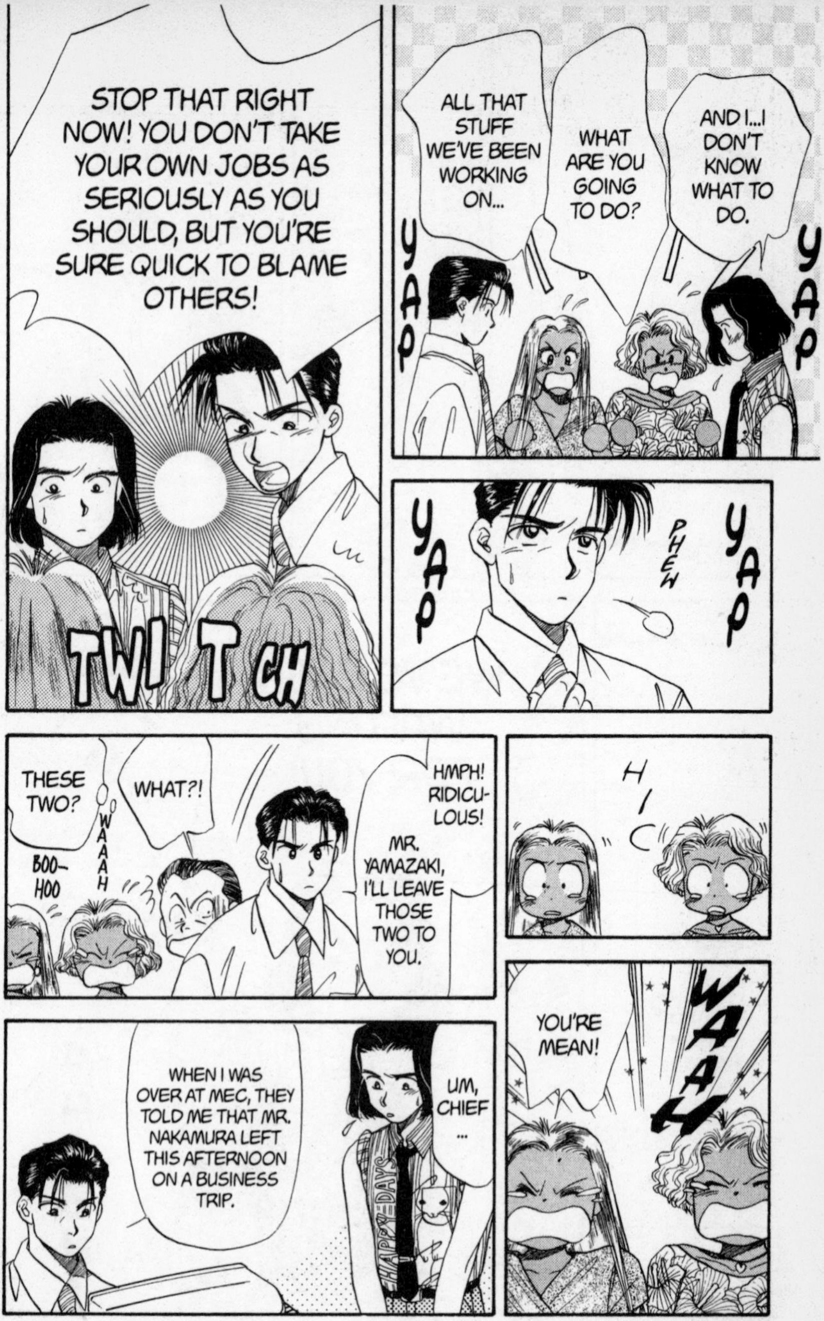
AND I...I DON'T KNOW WHAT TO DO.
WHAT ARE YOU GOING TO DO?
ALL THAT STUFF WE'VE BEEN WORKING ON...
YAP YAP
YAP YAP
PHEW
YAP YAP
STOP THAT RIGHT NOW! YOU DON'T TAKE YOUR OWN JOBS AS SERIOUSLY AS YOU SHOULD, BUT YOU'RE SURE QUICK TO BLAME OTHERS!
TWITCH
HIC
HMPH! RIDICULOUS!
MR. YAMAZAKI, I'LL LEAVE THOSE TWO TO YOU.
WHAT?!
THESE TWO?
WAAAH
BOO-HOO
WAAAH
YOU'RE MEAN!
UM, CHIEF ...
WHEN I WAS OVER AT MEC, THEY TOLD ME THAT MR. NAKAMURA LEFT THIS AFTERNOON ON A BUSINESS TRIP.
HAPPY DAYS

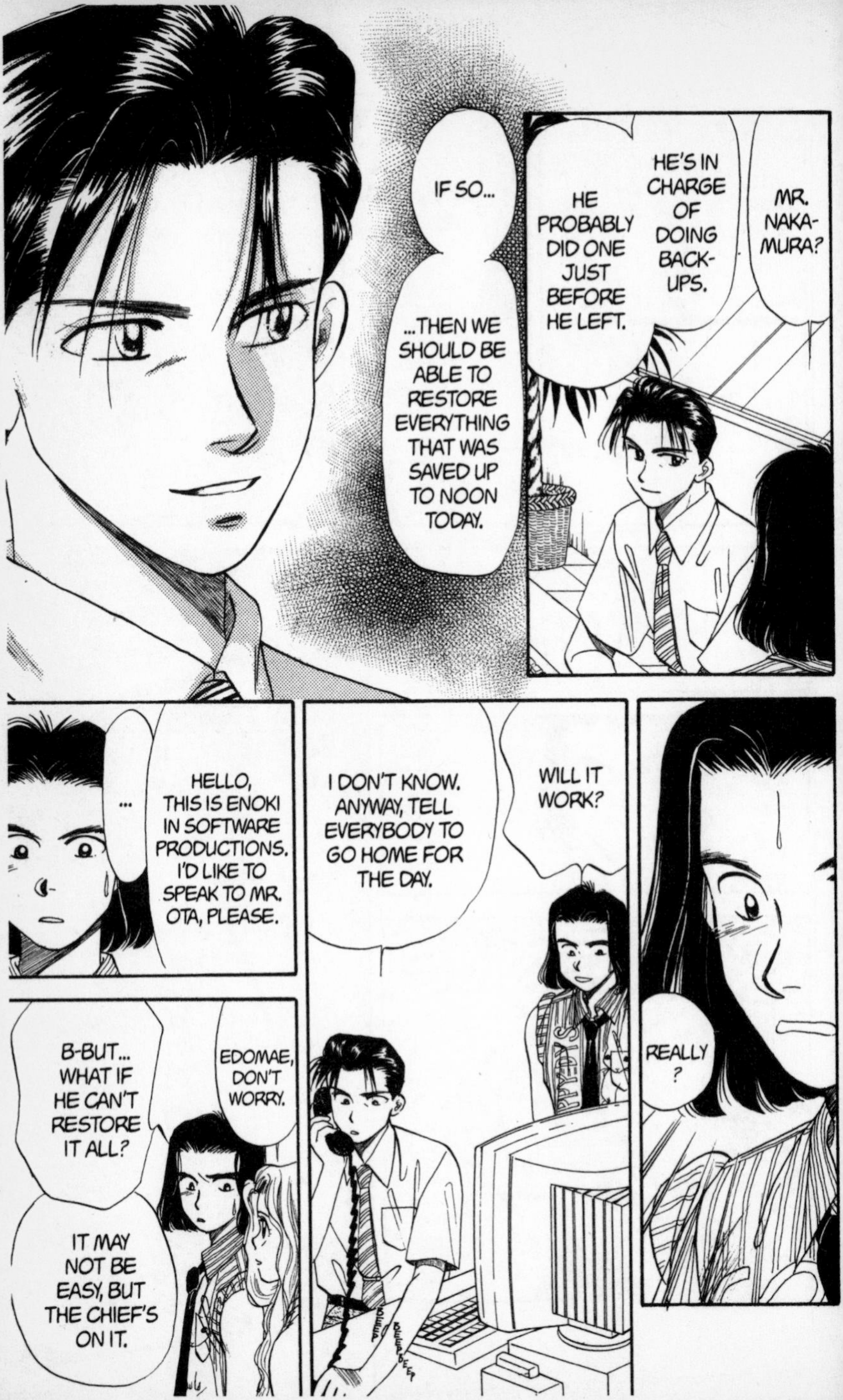
MR. NAKA-MURA?
HE'S IN CHARGE OF DOING BACK-UPS.
HE PROBABLY DID ONE JUST BEFORE HE LEFT.
IF SO...
...THEN WE SHOULD BE ABLE TO RESTORE EVERYTHING THAT WAS SAVED UP TO NOON TODAY.
REALLY ?
WILL IT WORK?
I DON'T KNOW. ANYWAY, TELL EVERYBODY TO GO HOME FOR THE DAY.
HELLO, THIS IS ENOKI IN SOFTWARE PRODUCTIONS. I'D LIKE TO SPEAK TO MR. OTA, PLEASE.
...
EDOMAE, DON'T WORRY.
B-BUT... WHAT IF HE CAN'T RESTORE IT ALL?
IT MAY NOT BE EASY, BUT THE CHIEF'S ON IT.

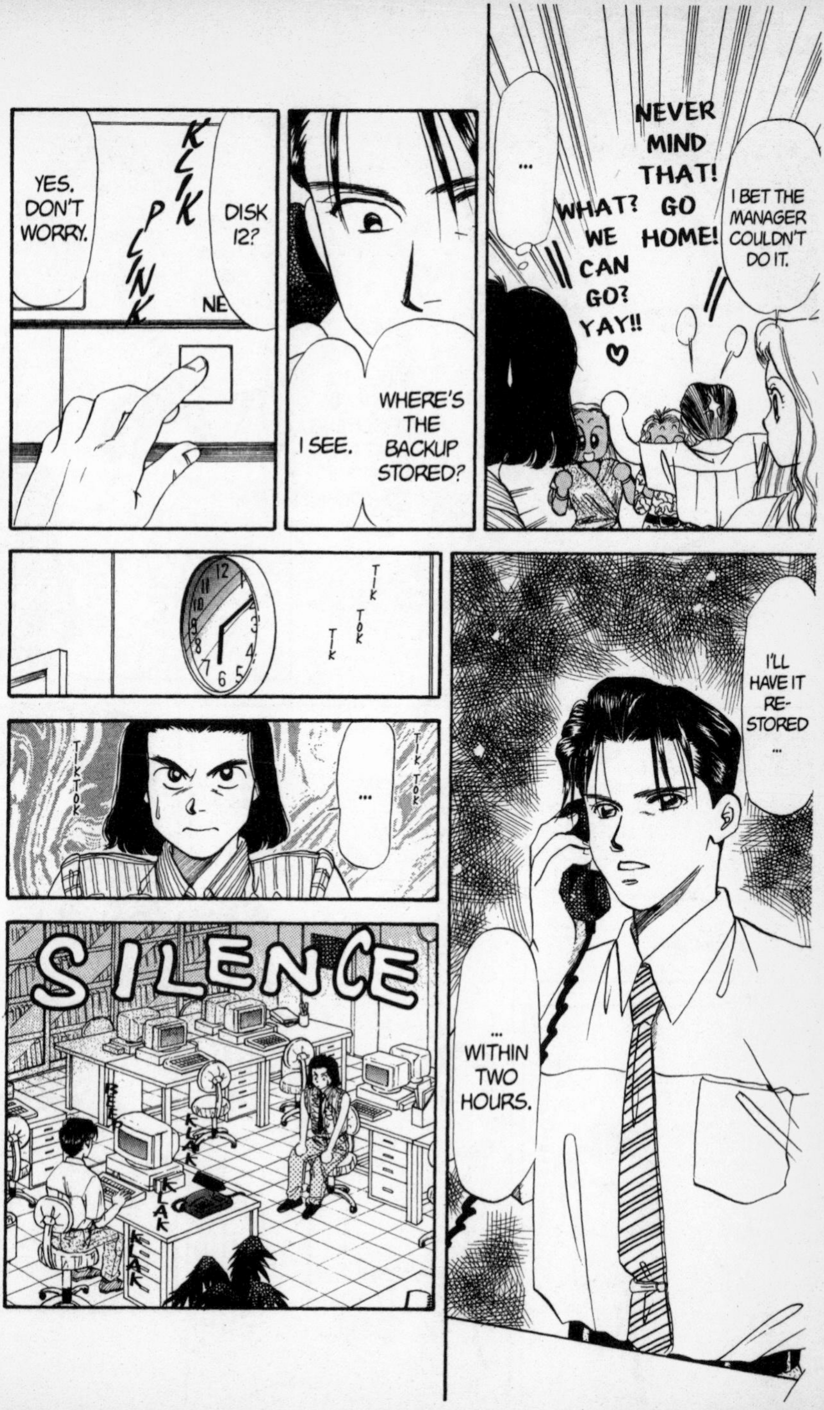
I BET THE MANAGER COULDN'T DO IT.
NEVER MIND THAT! GO HOME!
...
WHAT? WE CAN GO? YAY!! ♡
WHERE'S THE BACKUP STORED?
I SEE.
DISK 12?
NE
KLIK
PLINK
YES. DON'T WORRY.
I'LL HAVE IT RE-STORED ...
... WITHIN TWO HOURS.
TIK
TOK
TIK
TIK TOK
...
TIK TOK
SILENCE
KLAK
KLAK
KLAK

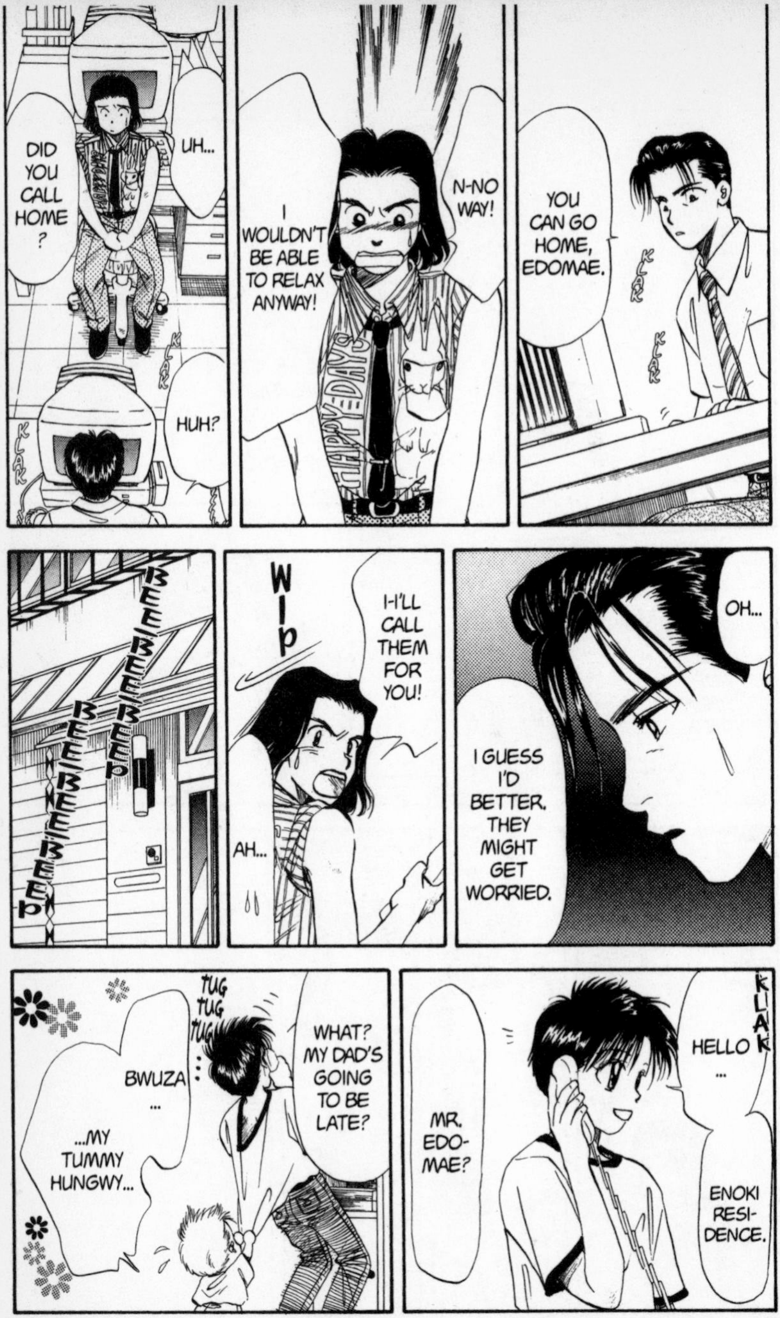
YOU CAN GO HOME, EDOMAE.
KLAK
KLAK
N-NO WAY!
I WOULDN'T BE ABLE TO RELAX ANYWAY!
UH...
DID YOU CALL HOME?
HUH?
KLAK
KLAK
OH...
I GUESS I'D BETTER. THEY MIGHT GET WORRIED.
Wip
I-I'LL CALL THEM FOR YOU!
AH...
BEEEBEEEP
BEEEBEEEP
KLAK
HELLO...
ENOKI RESIDENCE.
MR. EDOMAE?
WHAT? MY DAD'S GOING TO BE LATE?
TUG TUG TUG...
BWUZA...
...MY TUMMY HUNGWY...

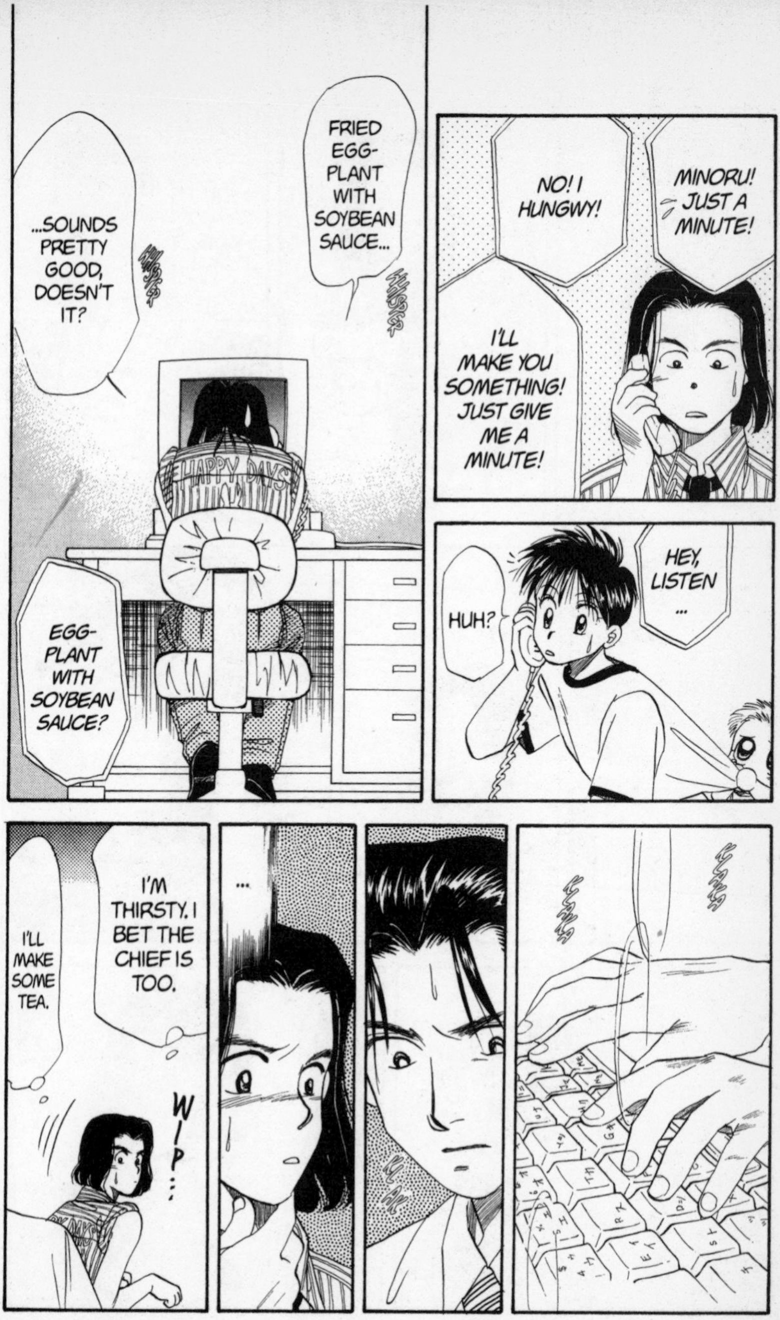
MINORU! JUST A MINUTE!
NO! I HUNGWY!
I'LL MAKE YOU SOMETHING! JUST GIVE ME A MINUTE!
HEY, LISTEN ...
HUH?
FRIED EGG-PLANT WITH SOYBEAN SAUCE...
WHISPER
...SOUNDS PRETTY GOOD, DOESN'T IT?
WHISPER
EGG-PLANT WITH SOYBEAN SAUCE?
...
I'M THIRSTY. I BET THE CHIEF IS TOO.
I'LL MAKE SOME TEA.
WIP...

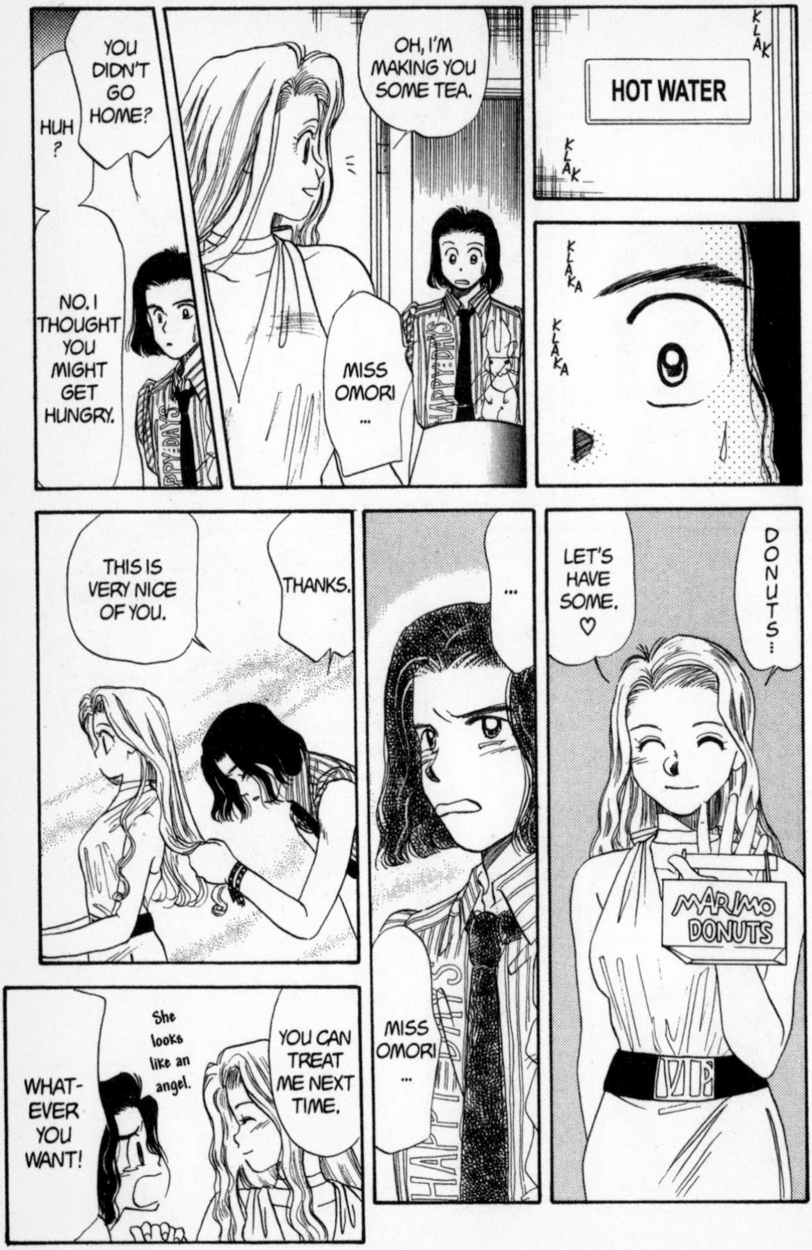
KLAK
HOT WATER
KLAK
KLAKA
KLAKA
OH, I'M MAKING YOU SOME TEA.
MISS OMORI ...
YOU DIDN'T GO HOME?
HUH?
NO. I THOUGHT YOU MIGHT GET HUNGRY.
DONUTS...
LET'S HAVE SOME. ♡
MARIMO DONUTS
...
MISS OMORI ...
THANKS.
THIS IS VERY NICE OF YOU.
YOU CAN TREAT ME NEXT TIME.
She looks like an angel.
WHAT-EVER YOU WANT!

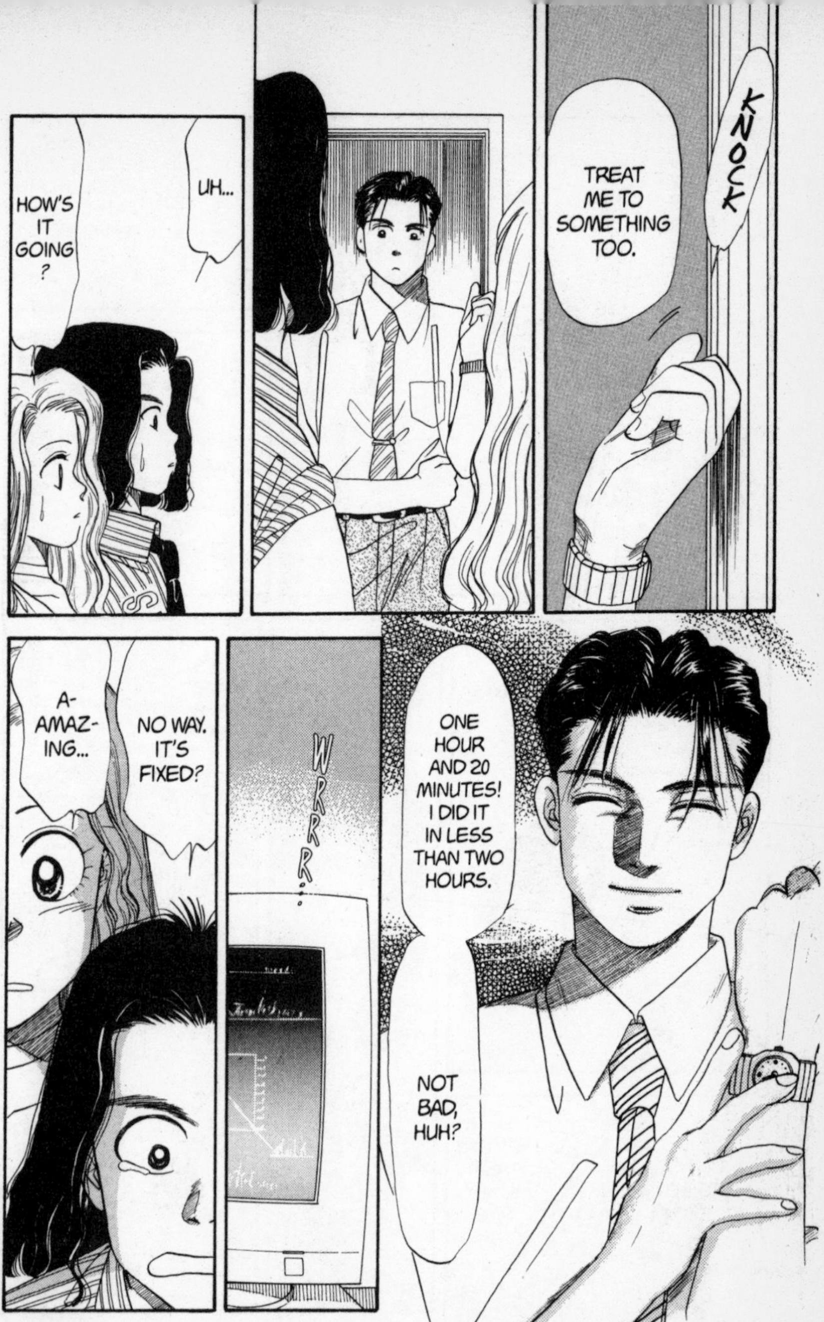
KNOCK
TREAT ME TO SOMETHING TOO.
UH...
HOW'S IT GOING?
ONE HOUR AND 20 MINUTES! I DID IT IN LESS THAN TWO HOURS.
NOT BAD, HUH?
WRRRR...
NO WAY. IT'S FIXED?
A-AMAZING...

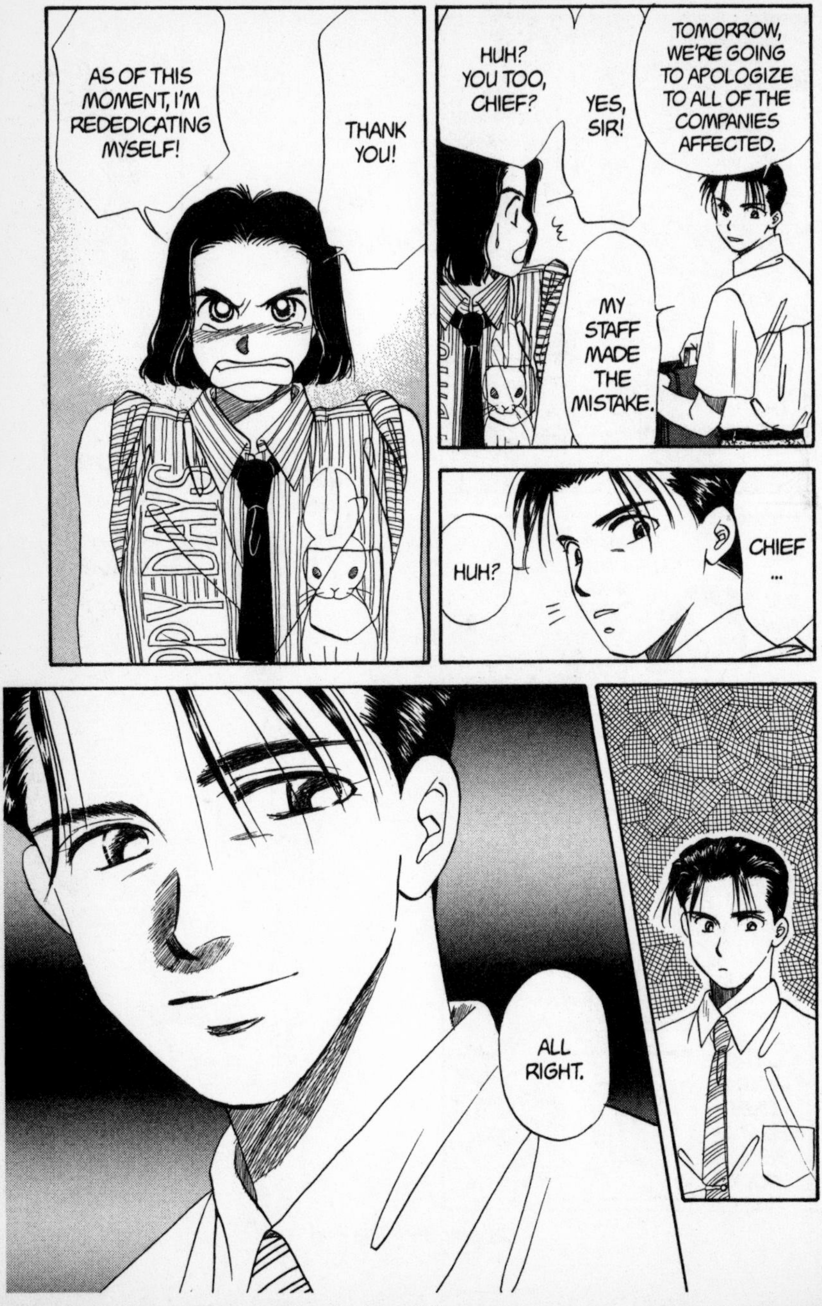
TOMORROW, WE'RE GOING TO APOLOGIZE TO ALL OF THE COMPANIES AFFECTED.
YES, SIR!
HUH? YOU TOO, CHIEF?
MY STAFF MADE THE MISTAKE.
CHIEF ...
HUH?
THANK YOU!
AS OF THIS MOMENT, I'M REDEDICATING MYSELF!
ALL RIGHT.

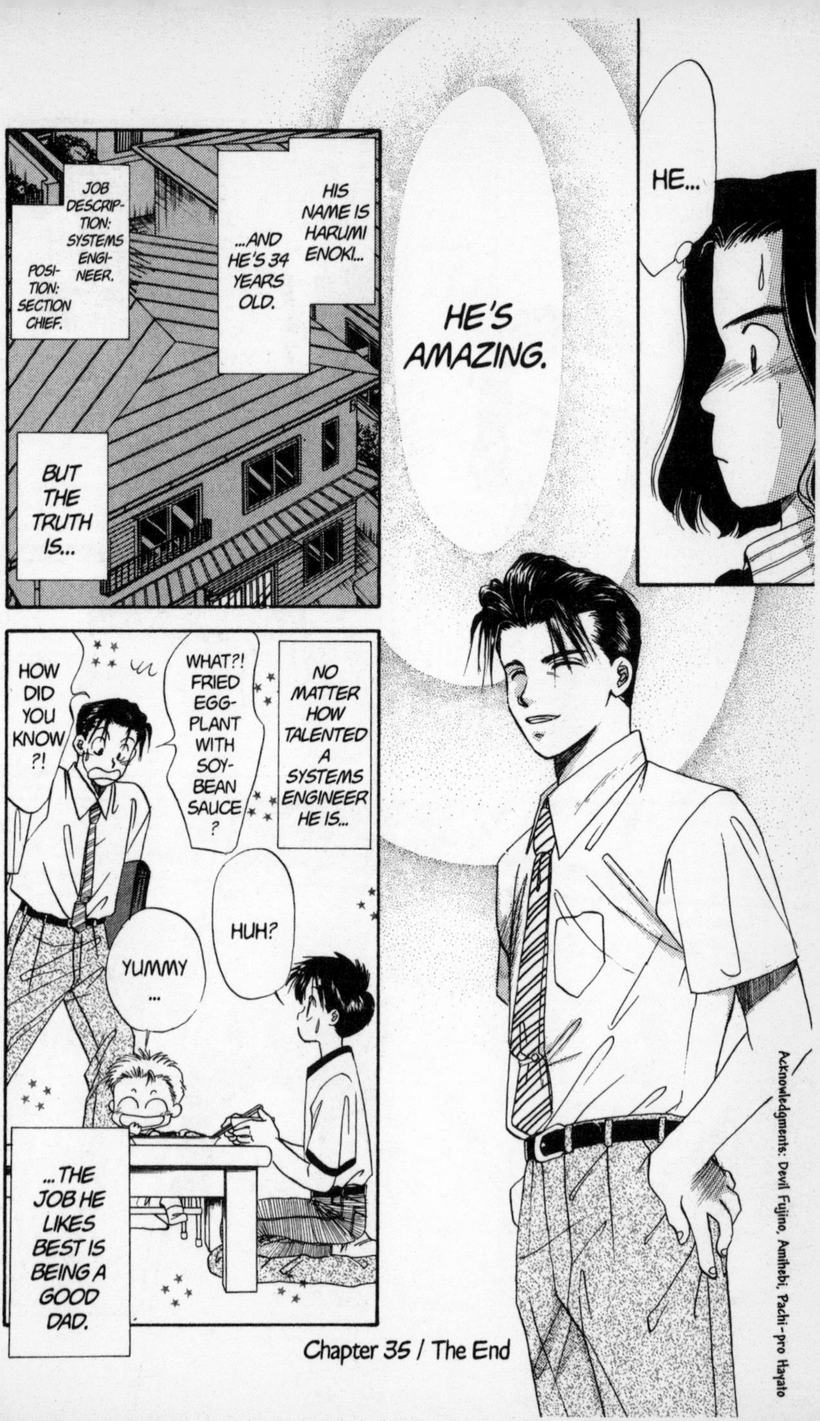
HE...
HE'S AMAZING.
HIS NAME IS HARUMI ENOKI...
...AND HE'S 34 YEARS OLD.
JOB DESCRIPTION: SYSTEMS ENGINEER.
POSITION: SECTION CHIEF.
BUT THE TRUTH IS...
NO MATTER HOW TALENTED A SYSTEMS ENGINEER HE IS...
WHAT?! FRIED EGGPLANT WITH SOYBEAN SAUCE?
HOW DID YOU KNOW?!
HUH?
YUMMY...
...THE JOB HE LIKES BEST IS BEING A GOOD DAD.

Chapter 35 / The End

Acknowledgments: Devil Fujino, Amihebi, Pachi-pro Hayato

BABY & Me

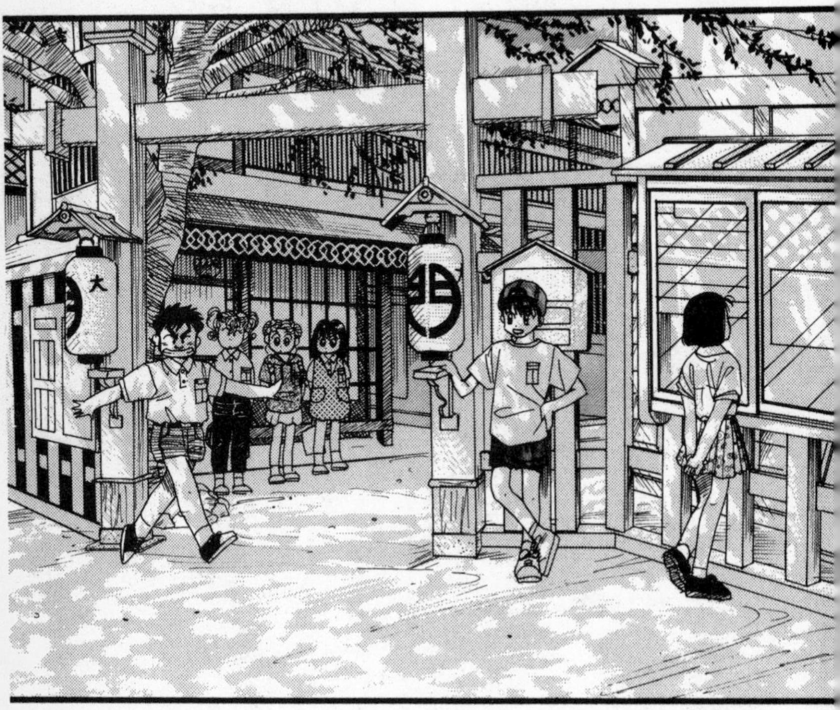
大

At Uzumasa Movie Village

Chapter 36

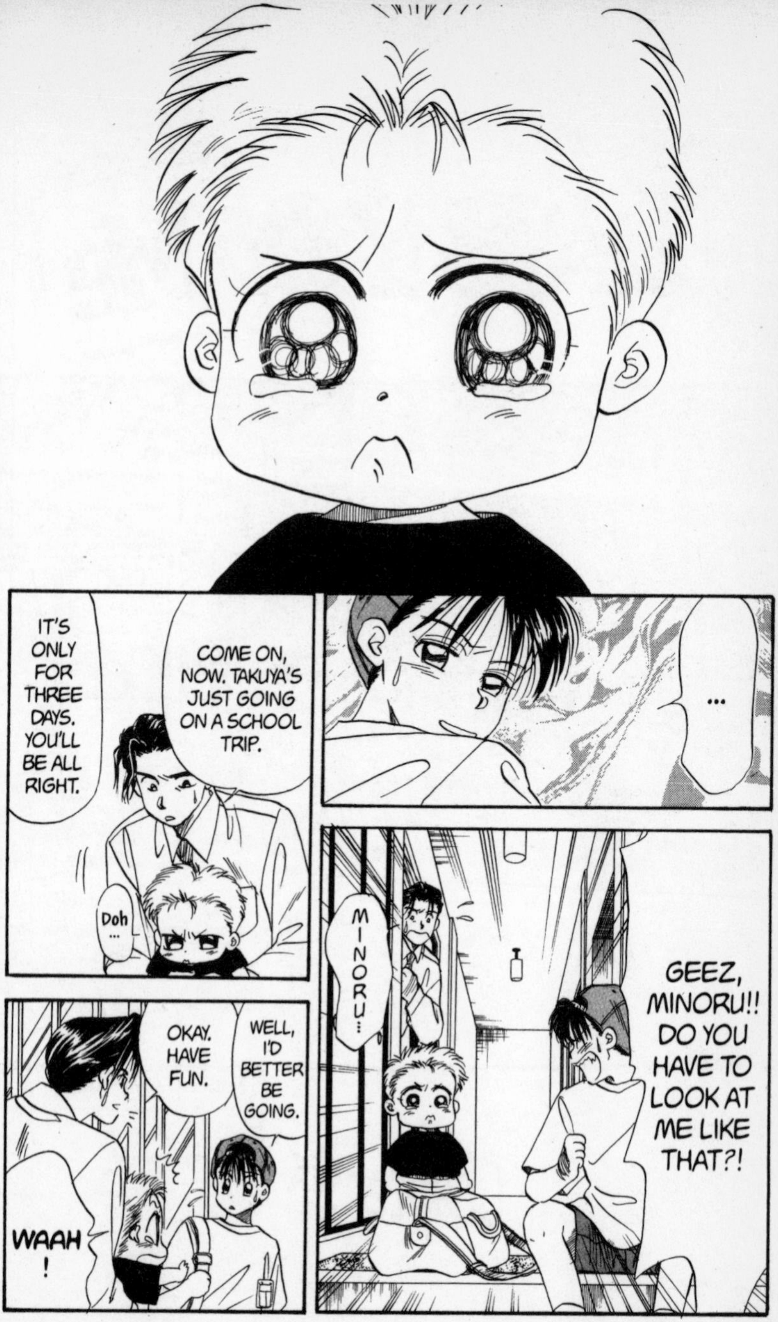
...
COME ON, NOW. TAKUYA'S JUST GOING ON A SCHOOL TRIP.
IT'S ONLY FOR THREE DAYS. YOU'LL BE ALL RIGHT.
Doh ...
GEEZ, MINORU!! DO YOU HAVE TO LOOK AT ME LIKE THAT?!
MINORU...
WELL, I'D BETTER BE GOING.
OKAY. HAVE FUN.
WAAH!

HE'S NOT ALL RIGHT ...

BWAAAH

BWAZA

WILL HE BE ALL RIGHT?

SHHF..

SOB!

SOB!

OUR SCHOOL'S PRETTY COOL.

MOST SCHOOLS ONLY GET TO GO FOR THE DAY.

THREE DAYS AND TWO NIGHTS IN KYOTO! ♡

YEAH! THIS IS GONNA BE GREAT!

HEH HEH HEH

Exit

HOP

HOP

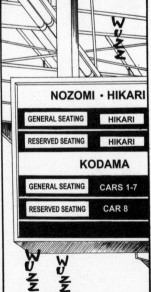

WUZZ

NOZOMI · HIKARI	
GENERAL SEATING	HIKARI
RESERVED SEATING	HIKARI
KODAMA	
GENERAL SEATING	CARS 1-7
RESERVED SEATING	CAR 8

WUZZ

WUZZ

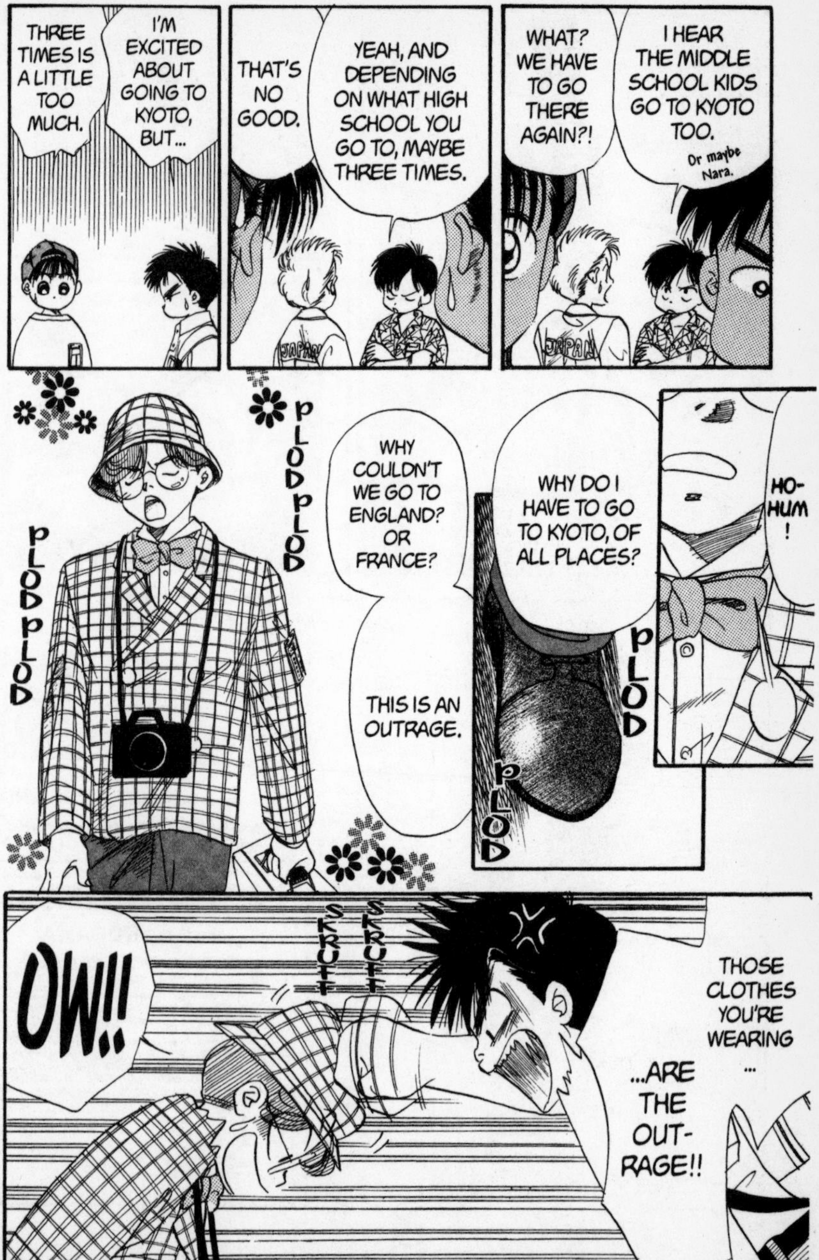
I HEAR THE MIDDLE SCHOOL KIDS GO TO KYOTO TOO.
Or maybe Nara.
WHAT? WE HAVE TO GO THERE AGAIN?!
YEAH, AND DEPENDING ON WHAT HIGH SCHOOL YOU GO TO, MAYBE THREE TIMES.
THAT'S NO GOOD.
I'M EXCITED ABOUT GOING TO KYOTO, BUT...
THREE TIMES IS A LITTLE TOO MUCH.
HO-HUM!
PLOD
WHY DO I HAVE TO GO TO KYOTO, OF ALL PLACES?
PLOD
WHY COULDN'T WE GO TO ENGLAND? OR FRANCE?
THIS IS AN OUTRAGE.
PLOD PLOD
PLOD PLOD
THOSE CLOTHES YOU'RE WEARING...
...ARE THE OUT-RAGE!!
SKRUFF SKRUFF
OW!!

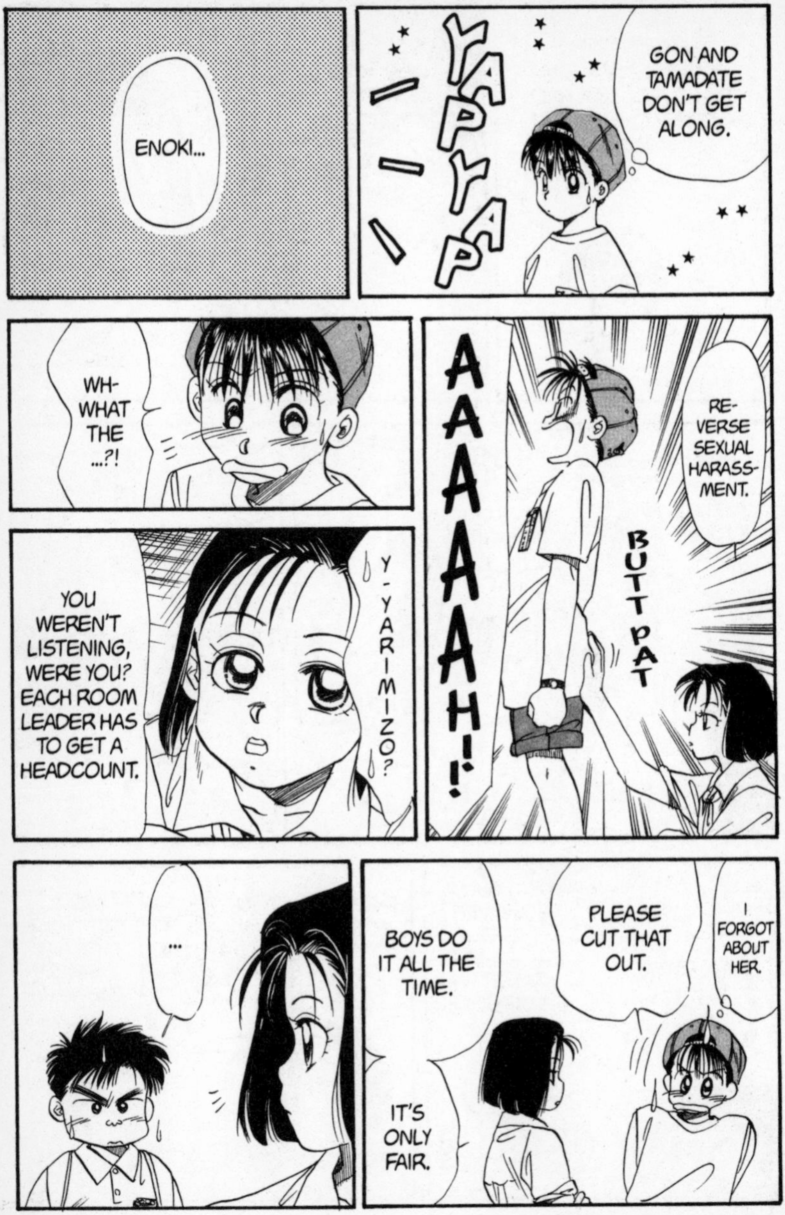
GON AND TAMADATE DON'T GET ALONG.
YAPYAP
I I I
ENOKI...
RE-VERSE SEXUAL HARASS-MENT.
AAAAAH!!
BUTT PAT
WH-WHAT THE ...?!
Y-YARIMIZO?
YOU WEREN'T LISTENING, WERE YOU? EACH ROOM LEADER HAS TO GET A HEADCOUNT.
I FORGOT ABOUT HER.
PLEASE CUT THAT OUT.
BOYS DO IT ALL THE TIME.
IT'S ONLY FAIR.
...

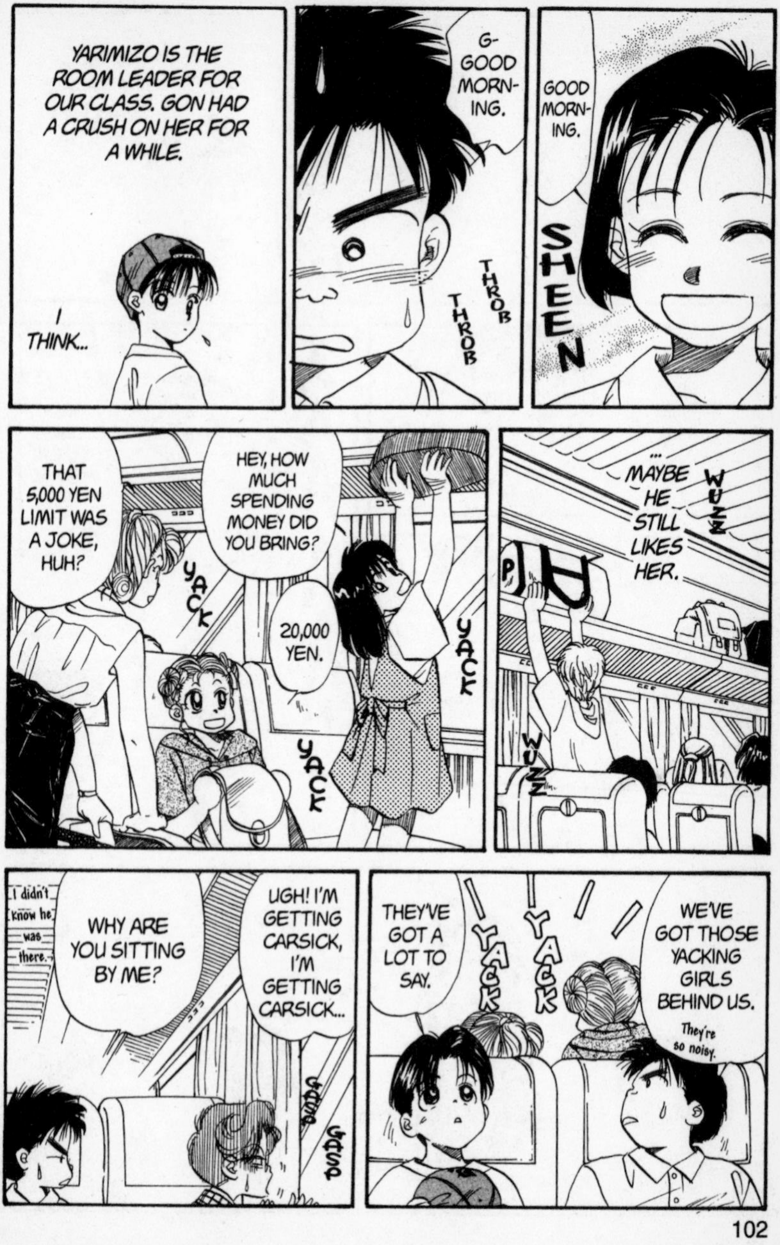
GOOD MORNING.
SHEEN
G-GOOD MORNING.
THROB THROB
YARIMIZO IS THE ROOM LEADER FOR OUR CLASS. GON HAD A CRUSH ON HER FOR A WHILE.
I THINK...
...MAYBE HE STILL LIKES HER.
WUZZ
WUZZ
HEY, HOW MUCH SPENDING MONEY DID YOU BRING?
THAT 5,000 YEN LIMIT WAS A JOKE, HUH?
YACK
YACK
20,000 YEN.
YACK
WE'VE GOT THOSE YACKING GIRLS BEHIND US.
They're so noisy.
YACK
YACK
THEY'VE GOT A LOT TO SAY.
UGH! I'M GETTING CARSICK, I'M GETTING CARSICK...
GASA
GASA
WHY ARE YOU SITTING BY ME?
I didn't know he was there.

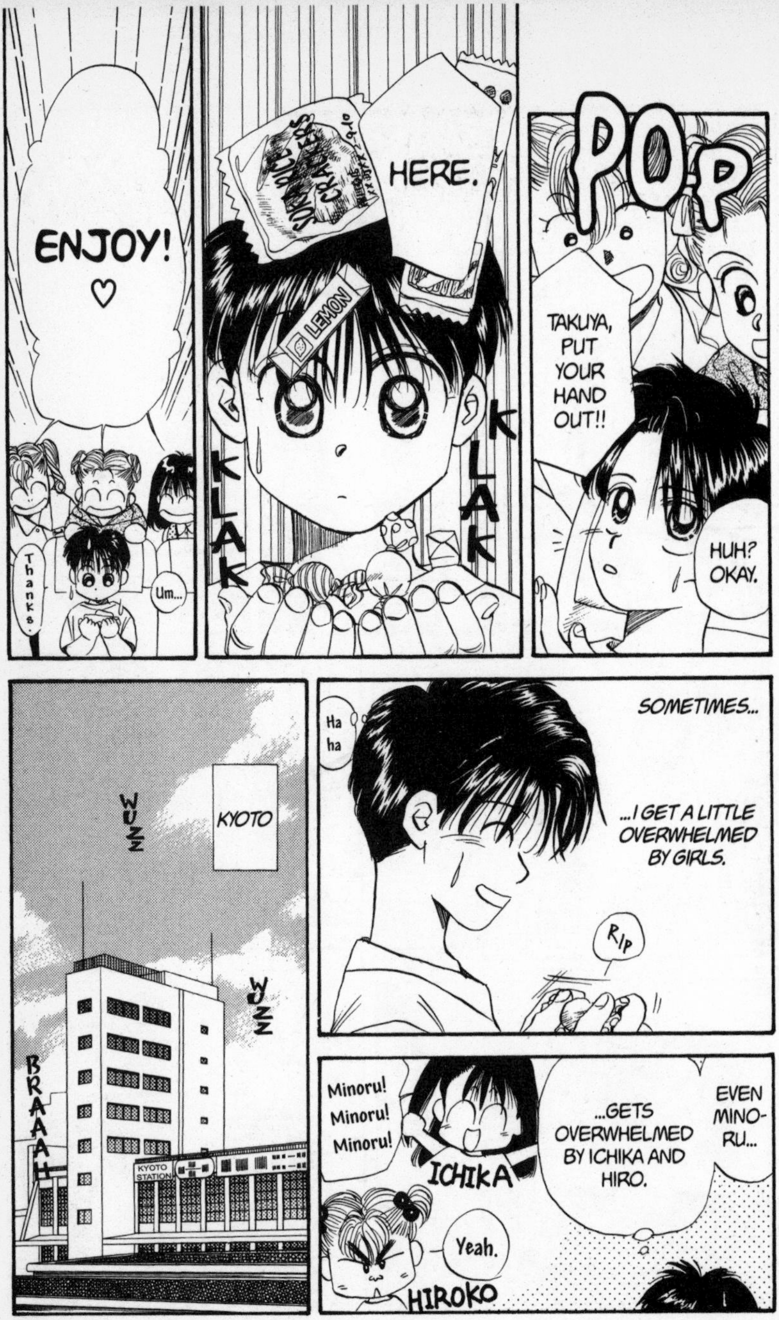
POP
TAKUYA, PUT YOUR HAND OUT!!
HUH? OKAY.
HERE.
SUGAR RICE CRACKERS
LEMON
KLAK
KLAK
ENJOY! ♡
Um...
Thanks.
SOMETIMES...
Ha ha
...I GET A LITTLE OVERWHELMED BY GIRLS.
Rip
EVEN MINORU...
...GETS OVERWHELMED BY ICHIKA AND HIRO.
Minoru! Minoru! Minoru!
ICHIKA
Yeah.
HIROKO
KYOTO
WUZZ
WUZZ
BRAAAAH
KYOTO STATION

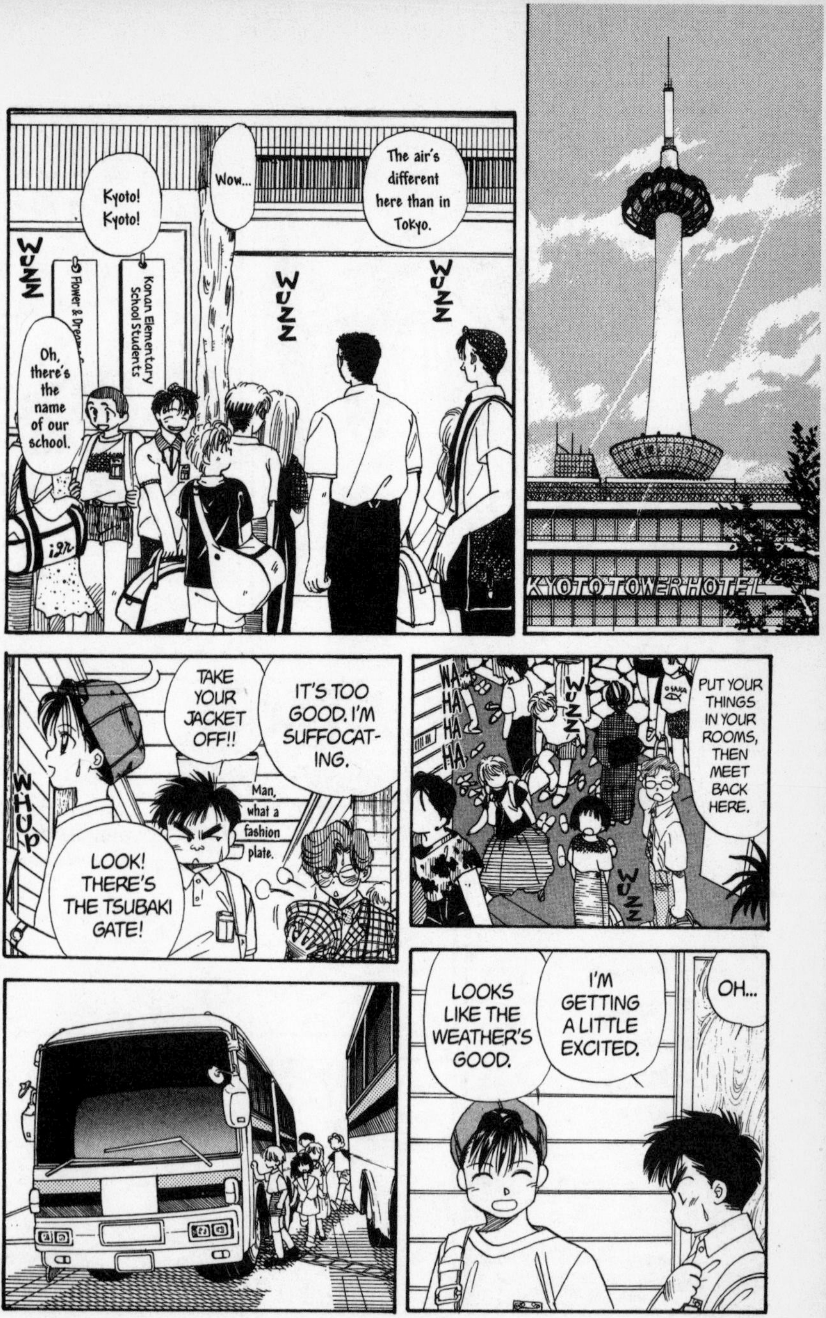

KYOTO TOWER HOTEL
The air's different here than in Tokyo.
WUZZ
WUZZ
Wow...
Kyoto! Kyoto!
Konan Elementary School Students
WUZZ
Oh, there's the name of our school.
PUT YOUR THINGS IN YOUR ROOMS, THEN MEET BACK HERE.
WUZZ
WA HA HA HA HA
WUZZ
IT'S TOO GOOD. I'M SUFFOCATING.
TAKE YOUR JACKET OFF!!
Man, what a fashion plate.
WHUP
LOOK! THERE'S THE TSUBAKI GATE!
OH...
I'M GETTING A LITTLE EXCITED.
LOOKS LIKE THE WEATHER'S GOOD.

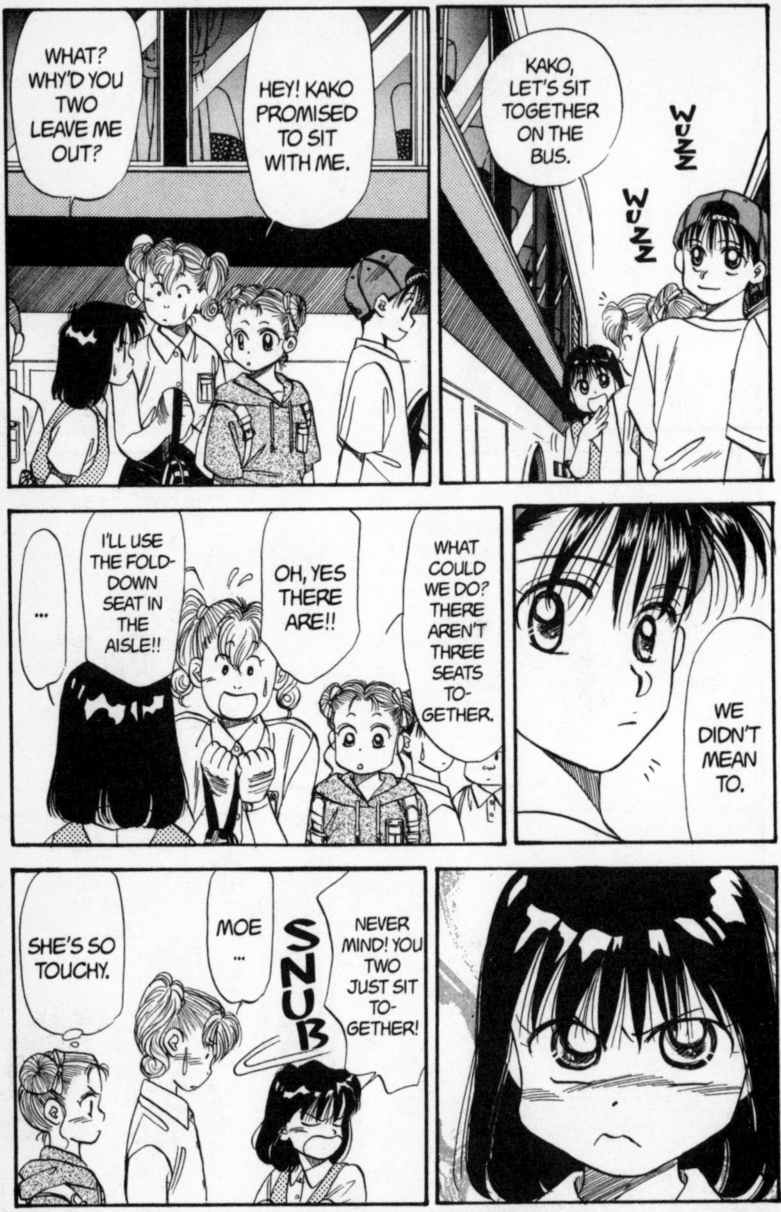
KAKO, LET'S SIT TOGETHER ON THE BUS.
WUZZ
WUZZ
HEY! KAKO PROMISED TO SIT WITH ME.
WHAT? WHY'D YOU TWO LEAVE ME OUT?
WE DIDN'T MEAN TO.
WHAT COULD WE DO? THERE AREN'T THREE SEATS TO-GETHER.
OH, YES THERE ARE!!
I'LL USE THE FOLD-DOWN SEAT IN THE AISLE!!
...
NEVER MIND! YOU TWO JUST SIT TO-GETHER!
SNUB
MOE ...
SHE'S SO TOUCHY.

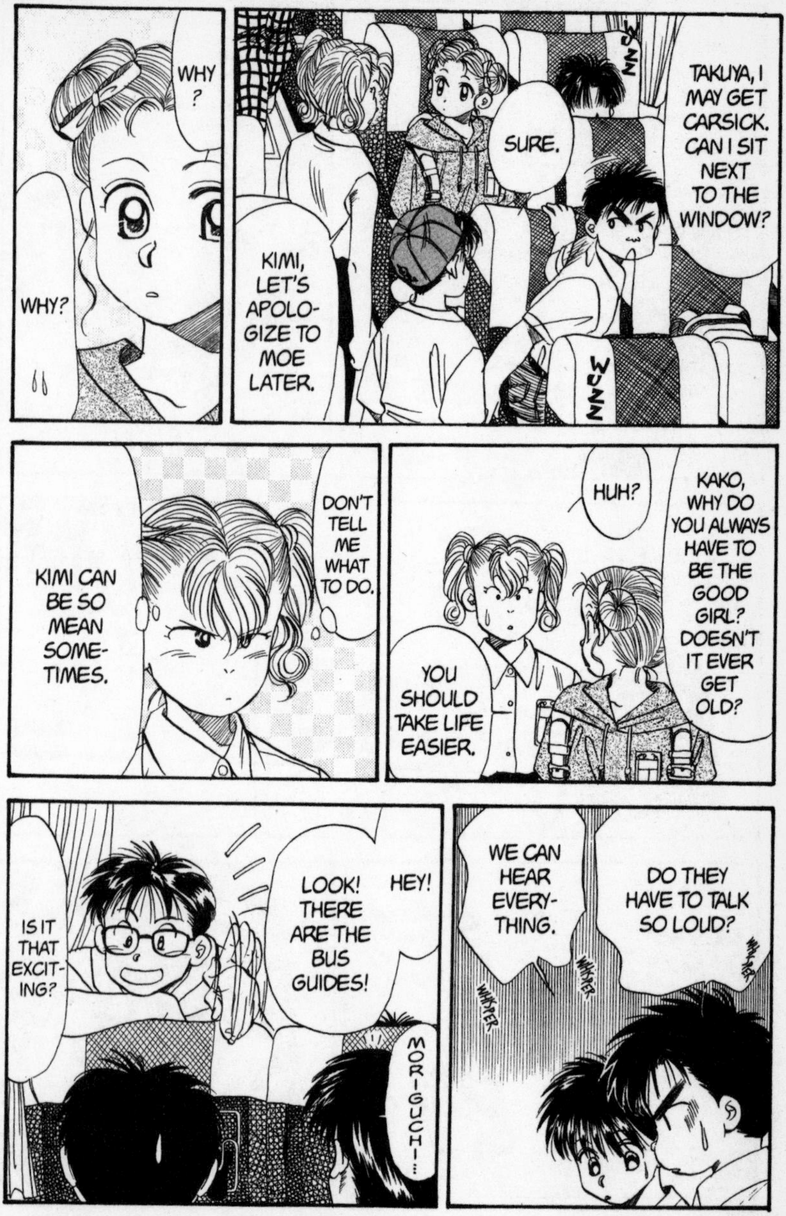
TAKUYA, I MAY GET CARSICK. CAN I SIT NEXT TO THE WINDOW?
WUZZ
SURE.
KIMI, LET'S APOLOGIZE TO MOE LATER.
WUZZ
WHY?
WHY?
KAKO, WHY DO YOU ALWAYS HAVE TO BE THE GOOD GIRL? DOESN'T IT EVER GET OLD?
HUH?
YOU SHOULD TAKE LIFE EASIER.
DON'T TELL ME WHAT TO DO.
KIMI CAN BE SO MEAN SOMETIMES.
DO THEY HAVE TO TALK SO LOUD?
WE CAN HEAR EVERYTHING.
WHISPER
WHISPER
WHISPER
HEY!
LOOK! THERE ARE THE BUS GUIDES!
MORIGUCHI...
IS IT THAT EXCITING?

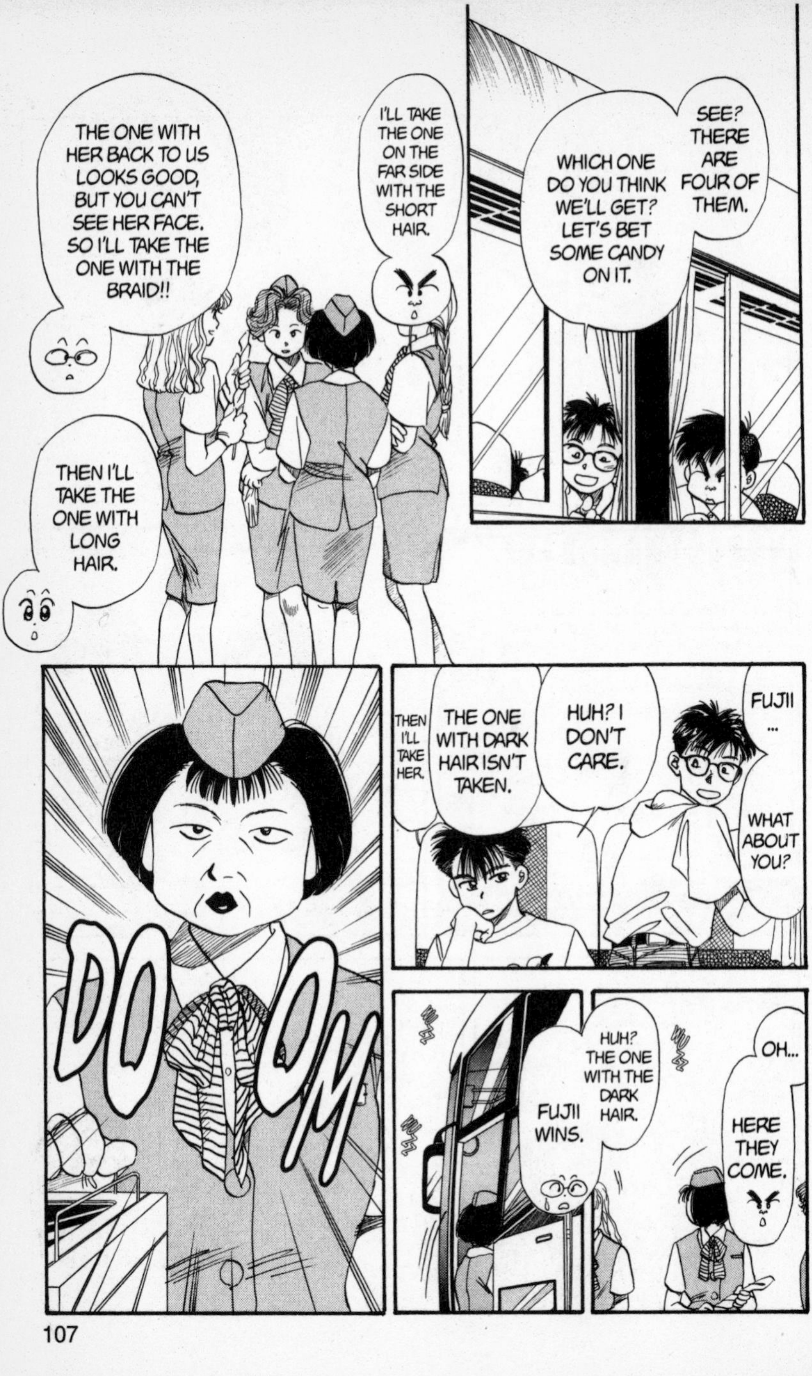
SEE? THERE ARE FOUR OF THEM.
WHICH ONE DO YOU THINK WE'LL GET? LET'S BET SOME CANDY ON IT.
I'LL TAKE THE ONE ON THE FAR SIDE WITH THE SHORT HAIR.
THE ONE WITH HER BACK TO US LOOKS GOOD, BUT YOU CAN'T SEE HER FACE. SO I'LL TAKE THE ONE WITH THE BRAID!!
THEN I'LL TAKE THE ONE WITH LONG HAIR.
FUJII ... WHAT ABOUT YOU?
HUH? I DON'T CARE.
THE ONE WITH DARK HAIR ISN'T TAKEN.
THEN I'LL TAKE HER.
OH... HERE THEY COME.
HUH? THE ONE WITH THE DARK HAIR.
FUJII WINS.
DOOM

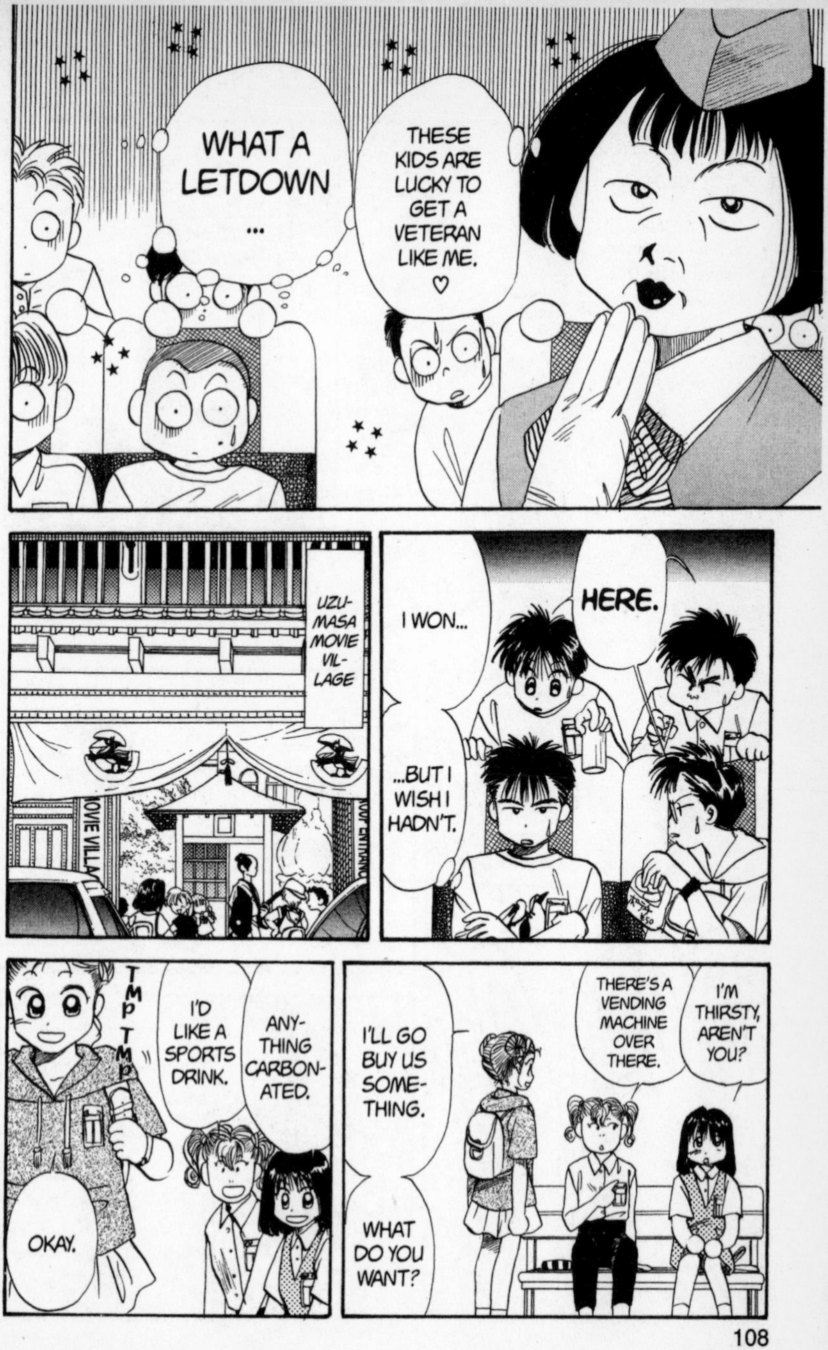
THESE KIDS ARE LUCKY TO GET A VETERAN LIKE ME. ♡
WHAT A LETDOWN ...
HERE.
I WON...
...BUT I WISH I HADN'T.
UZU-MASA MOVIE VIL-LAGE
I'M THIRSTY, AREN'T YOU?
THERE'S A VENDING MACHINE OVER THERE.
I'LL GO BUY US SOME-THING.
WHAT DO YOU WANT?
ANY-THING CARBON-ATED.
I'D LIKE A SPORTS DRINK.
TMP TMP
OKAY.

Author's Note Part 4

In the back of the fridge, I saw a white container. I thought it was *natto* (fermented soybeans). So I woke my brother up from a deep sleep—which wasn't easy—and I told him, "Listen, I washed some rice for you, so eat it in the morning with the *natto* that's in the fridge." My brother said something in a thick groggy voice, then rolled over and went back to sleep. I had done a good deed. Pleased with myself, I crawled into bed around dawn—I'm a night owl. At about 7:30, my brother woke me up. I'd only been asleep for two hours, so I was in a rotten mood. "What is it?" I shouted. He said there was no *natto* in the fridge. That made me so mad. "What are you talking about? I saw it there last night!" So I got up and opened the fridge, and there was the white container in the back. I grabbed it and stuck it out at my brother saying, "Look!" But what I held in my hand was margarine. Needless to say, my brother's head exploded.

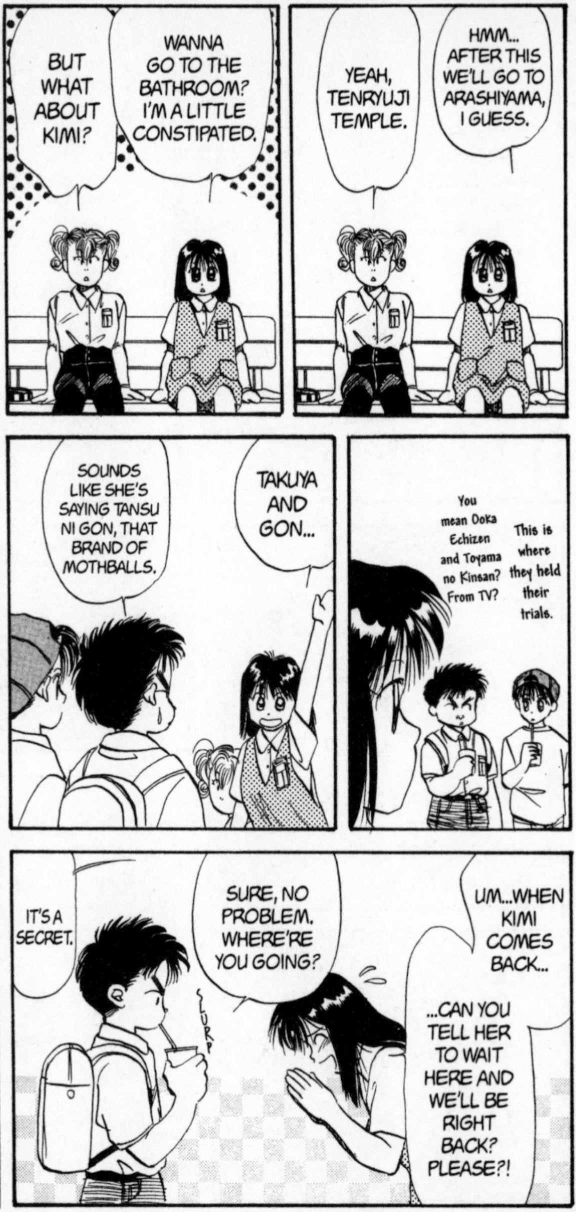
HMM... AFTER THIS WE'LL GO TO ARASHIYAMA, I GUESS.
YEAH, TENRYUJI TEMPLE.
WANNA GO TO THE BATHROOM? I'M A LITTLE CONSTIPATED.
BUT WHAT ABOUT KIMI?
This is where they held their trials.
You mean Ooka Echizen and Toyama no Kinsan? From TV?
TAKUYA AND GON...
SOUNDS LIKE SHE'S SAYING TANSU NI GON, THAT BRAND OF MOTHBALLS.
UM...WHEN KIMI COMES BACK...
...CAN YOU TELL HER TO WAIT HERE AND WE'LL BE RIGHT BACK? PLEASE?!
SURE, NO PROBLEM. WHERE'RE YOU GOING?
SLURP
IT'S A SECRET.

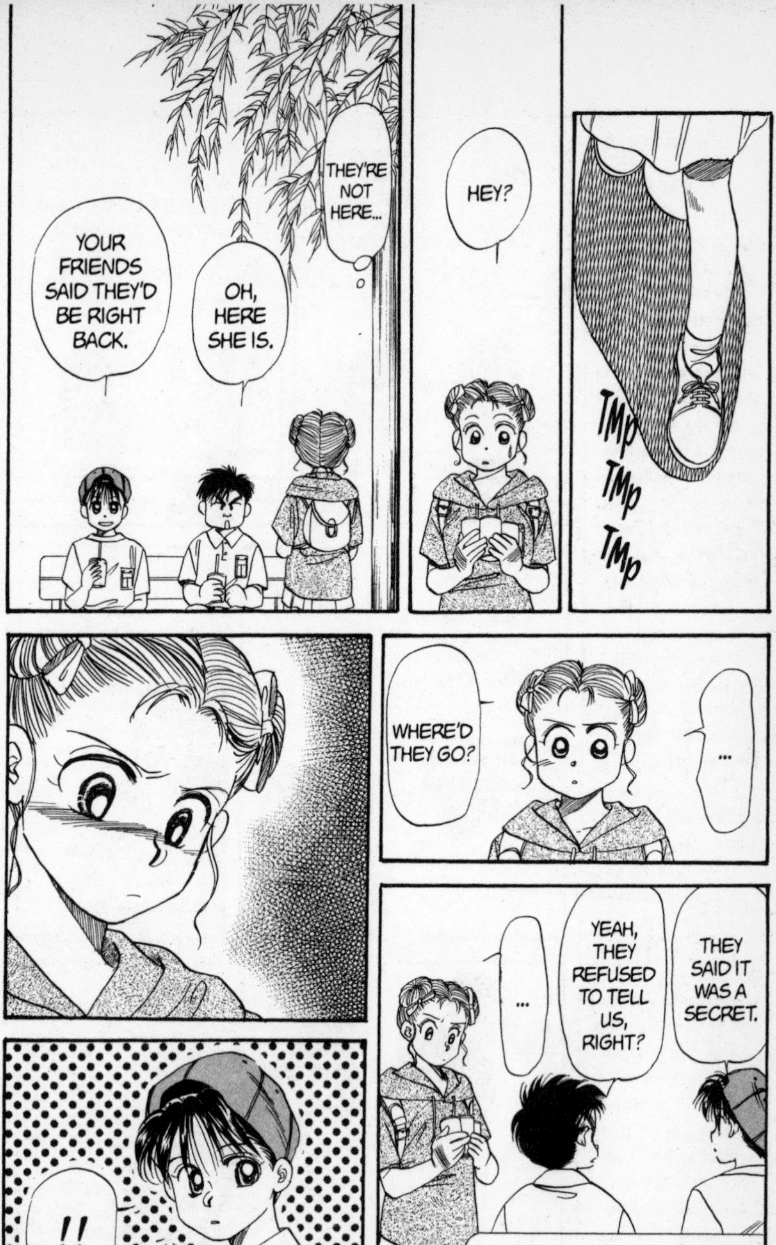
TMp
TMp
TMp
HEY?
THEY'RE NOT HERE...
OH, HERE SHE IS.
YOUR FRIENDS SAID THEY'D BE RIGHT BACK.
...
WHERE'D THEY GO?
THEY SAID IT WAS A SECRET.
YEAH, THEY REFUSED TO TELL US, RIGHT?
...
!!

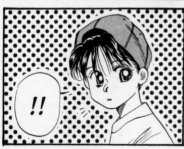

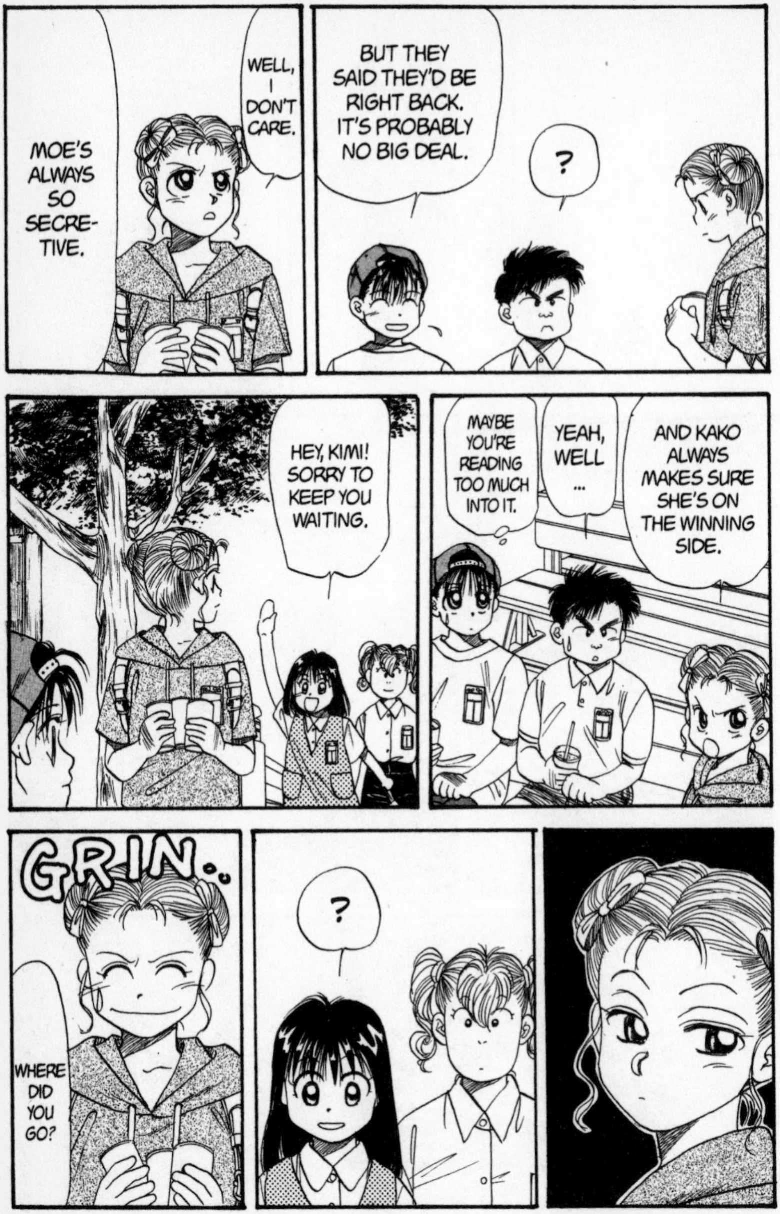

BUT THEY SAID THEY'D BE RIGHT BACK. IT'S PROBABLY NO BIG DEAL.
?
WELL, I DON'T CARE.
MOE'S ALWAYS SO SECRE-TIVE.
AND KAKO ALWAYS MAKES SURE SHE'S ON THE WINNING SIDE.
YEAH, WELL ...
MAYBE YOU'RE READING TOO MUCH INTO IT.
HEY, KIMI! SORRY TO KEEP YOU WAITING.
?
GRIN..
WHERE DID YOU GO?

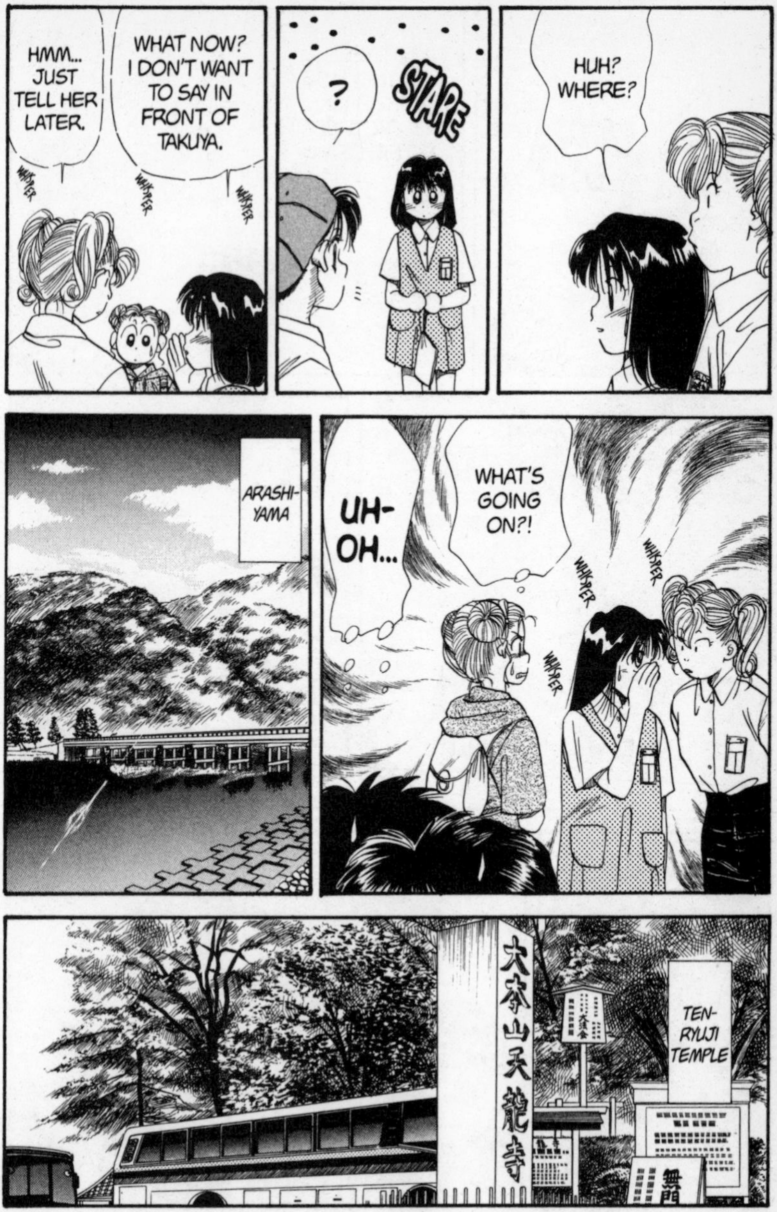
HUH? WHERE?
?
STARE
WHAT NOW? I DON'T WANT TO SAY IN FRONT OF TAKUYA.
HMM... JUST TELL HER LATER.
WHISPER
WHISPER
WHISPER
WHAT'S GOING ON?!
UH-OH...
WHISPER
WHISPER
WHISPER
ARASHI-YAMA
TEN-RYUJI TEMPLE
大本山天龍寺

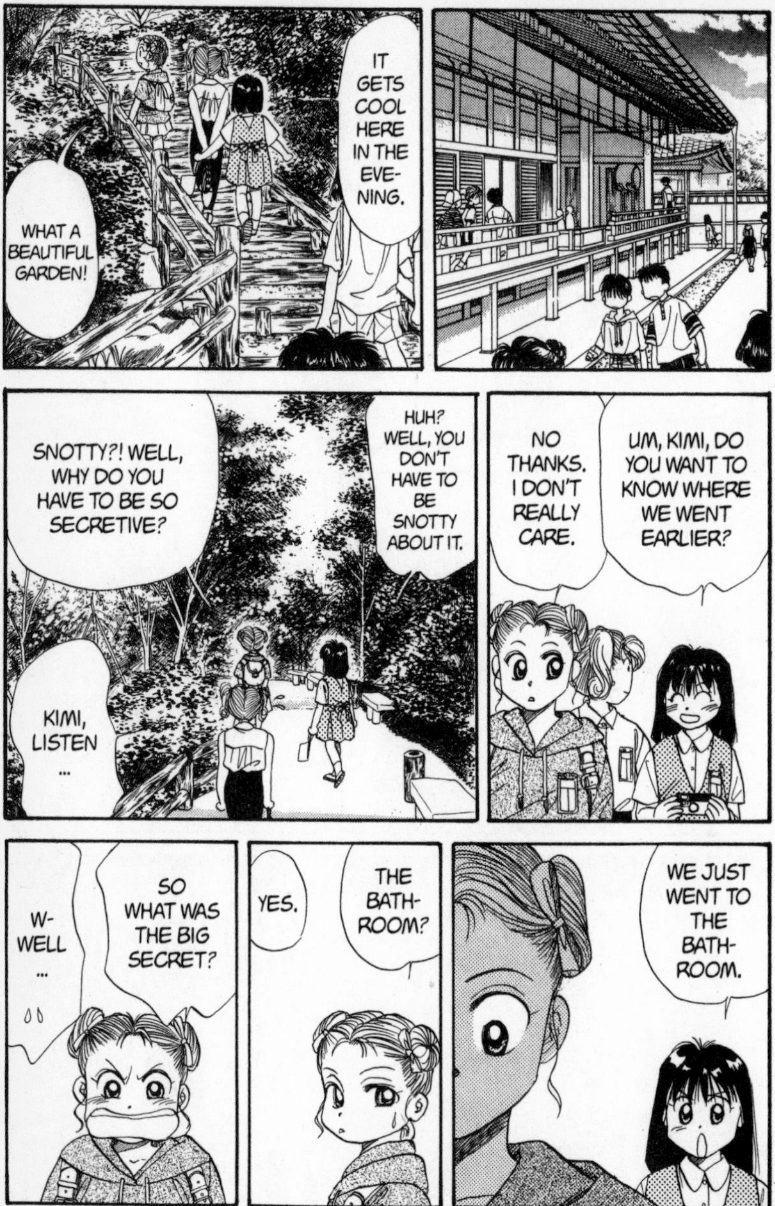
IT GETS COOL HERE IN THE EVENING.
WHAT A BEAUTIFUL GARDEN!
UM, KIMI, DO YOU WANT TO KNOW WHERE WE WENT EARLIER?
NO THANKS. I DON'T REALLY CARE.
HUH? WELL, YOU DON'T HAVE TO BE SNOTTY ABOUT IT.
SNOTTY?! WELL, WHY DO YOU HAVE TO BE SO SECRETIVE?
KIMI, LISTEN ...
WE JUST WENT TO THE BATHROOM.
THE BATHROOM?
YES.
SO WHAT WAS THE BIG SECRET?
W-WELL ...

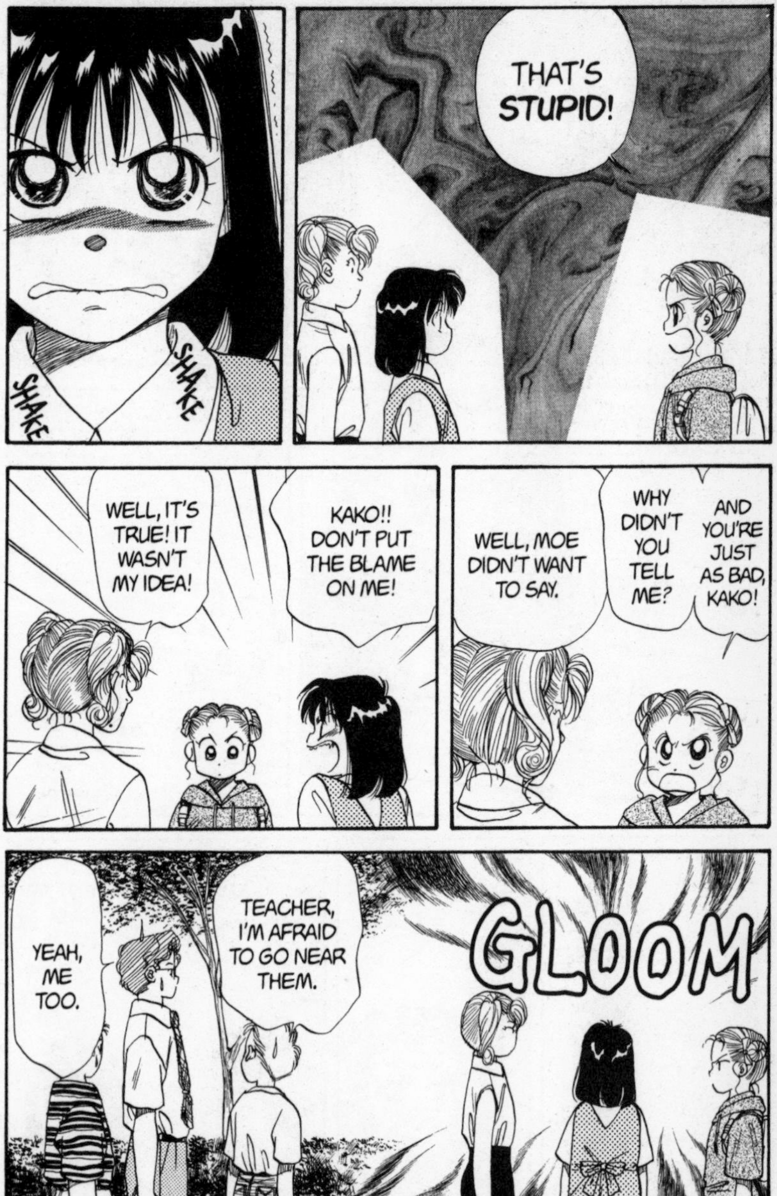
THAT'S STUPID!
SHAKE
SHAKE
AND YOU'RE JUST AS BAD, KAKO!
WHY DIDN'T YOU TELL ME?
WELL, MOE DIDN'T WANT TO SAY.
KAKO!! DON'T PUT THE BLAME ON ME!
WELL, IT'S TRUE! IT WASN'T MY IDEA!
GLOOM
TEACHER, I'M AFRAID TO GO NEAR THEM.
YEAH, ME TOO.

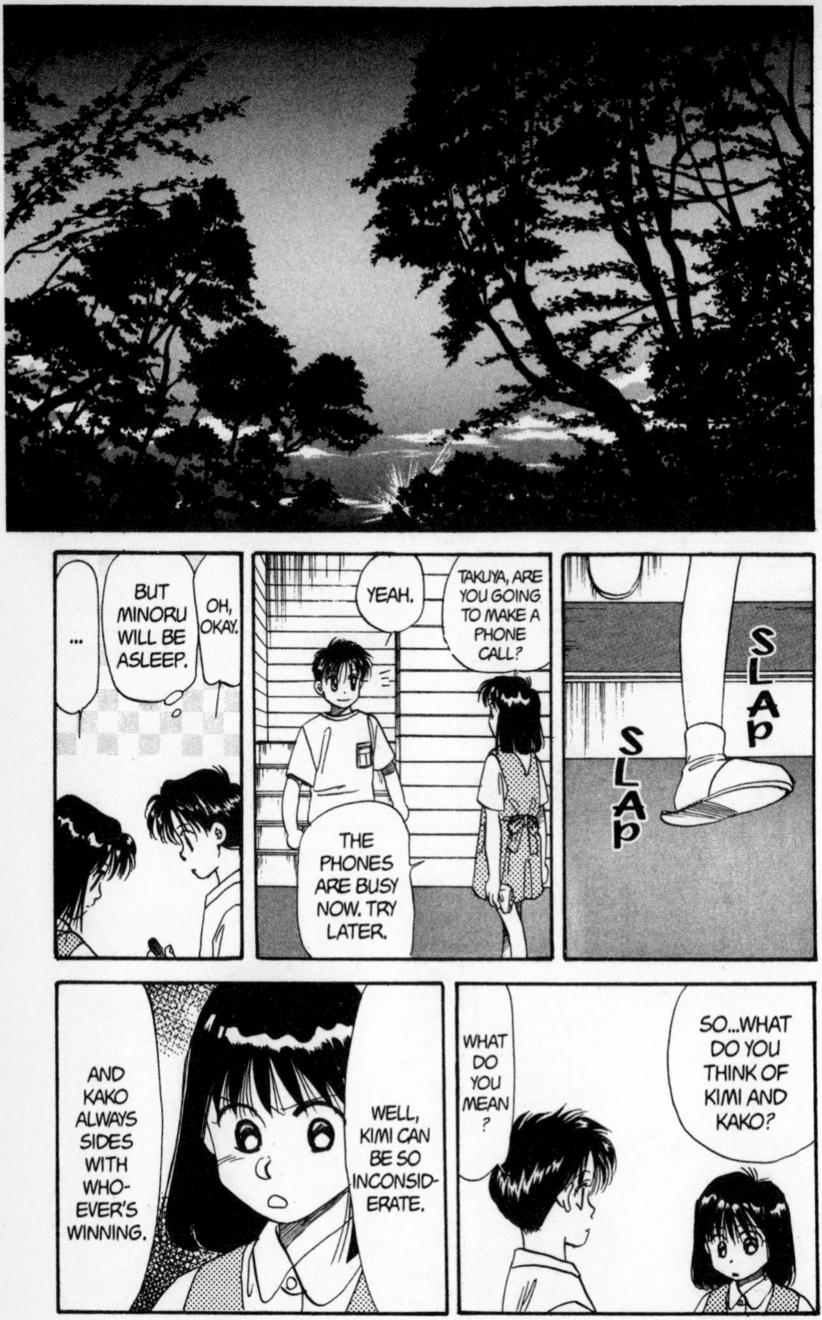
SLAP
SLAP
TAKUYA, ARE YOU GOING TO MAKE A PHONE CALL?
YEAH.
THE PHONES ARE BUSY NOW. TRY LATER.
OH, OKAY.
BUT MINORU WILL BE ASLEEP.
...
SO...WHAT DO YOU THINK OF KIMI AND KAKO?
WHAT DO YOU MEAN?
WELL, KIMI CAN BE SO INCONSIDERATE.
AND KAKO ALWAYS SIDES WITH WHOEVER'S WINNING.

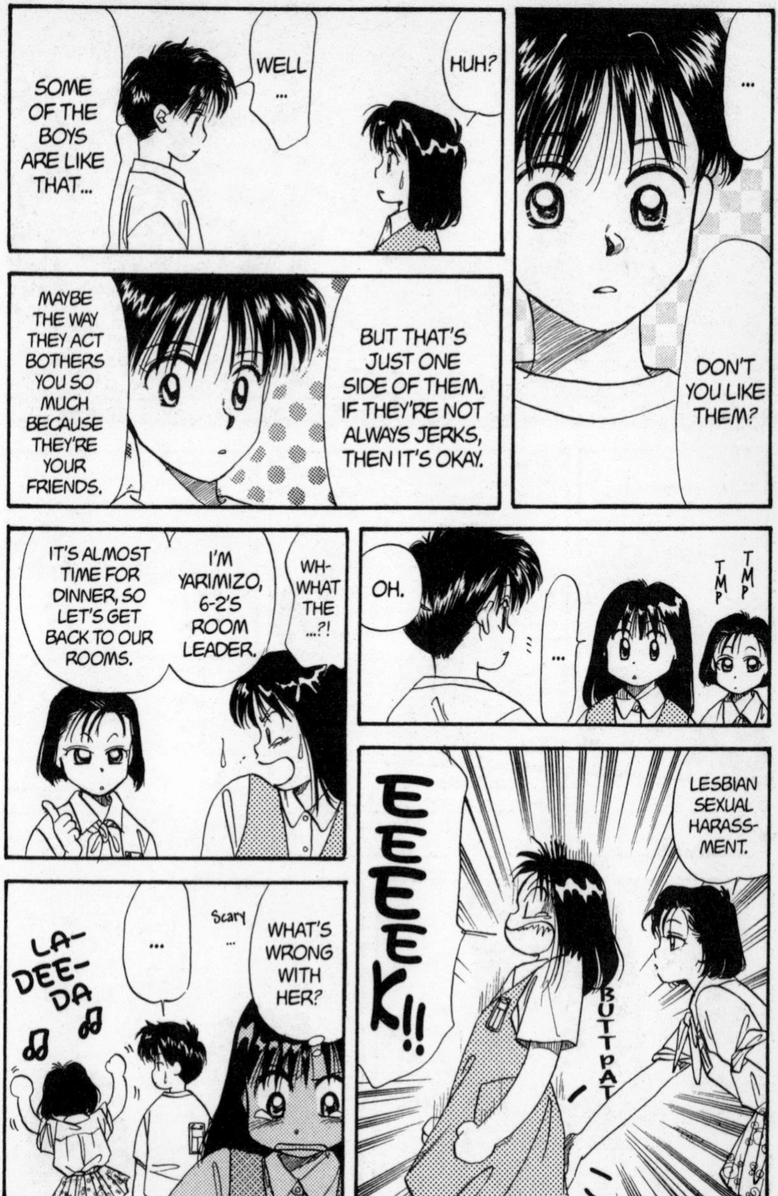
...
DON'T YOU LIKE THEM?
HUH?
WELL ...
SOME OF THE BOYS ARE LIKE THAT...
BUT THAT'S JUST ONE SIDE OF THEM. IF THEY'RE NOT ALWAYS JERKS, THEN IT'S OKAY.
MAYBE THE WAY THEY ACT BOTHERS YOU SO MUCH BECAUSE THEY'RE YOUR FRIENDS.
TMP TMP
...
OH.
WH-WHAT THE ...?!
I'M YARIMIZO, 6-2'S ROOM LEADER.
IT'S ALMOST TIME FOR DINNER, SO LET'S GET BACK TO OUR ROOMS.
LESBIAN SEXUAL HARASS-MENT.
BUTT PAT
EEEEEK!!
WHAT'S WRONG WITH HER?
Scary ...
...
LA-DEE-DA

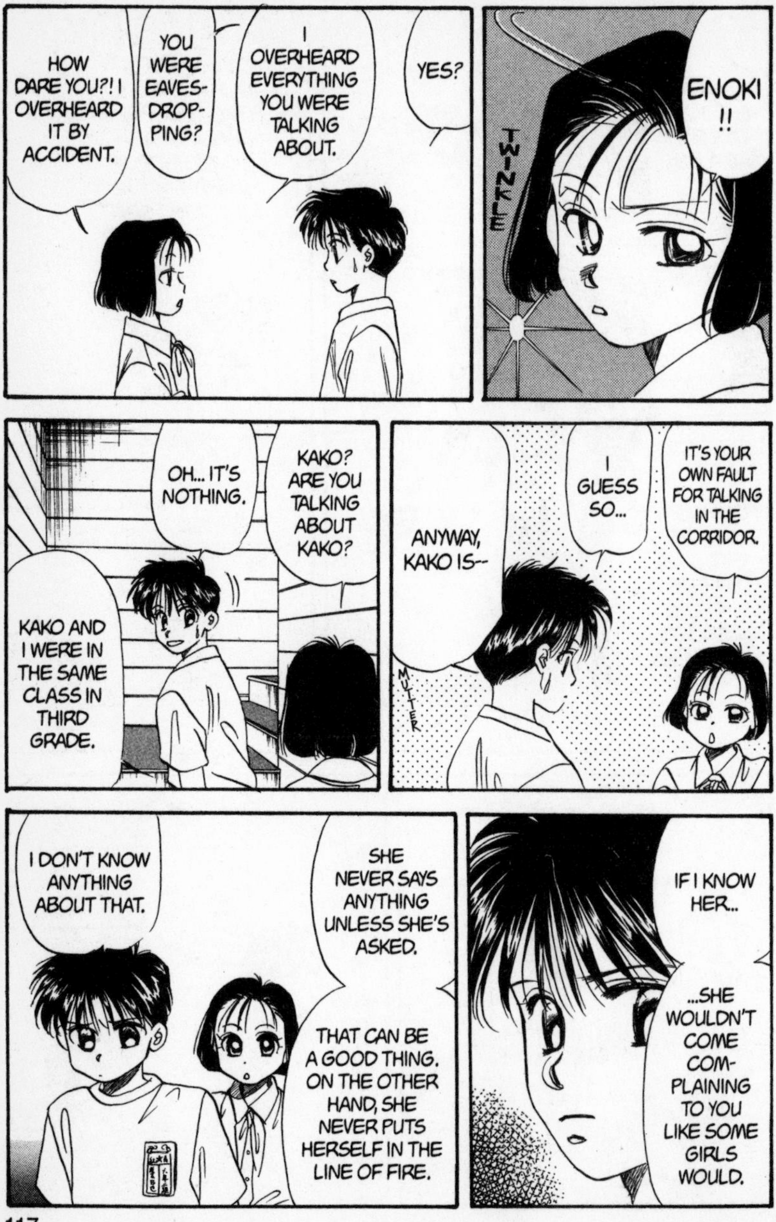
ENOKI !!
TWINKLE
YES?
I OVERHEARD EVERYTHING YOU WERE TALKING ABOUT.
YOU WERE EAVES-DROP-PING?
HOW DARE YOU?! I OVERHEARD IT BY ACCIDENT.
IT'S YOUR OWN FAULT FOR TALKING IN THE CORRIDOR.
I GUESS SO...
ANYWAY, KAKO IS--
MUTTER
KAKO? ARE YOU TALKING ABOUT KAKO?
OH... IT'S NOTHING.
KAKO AND I WERE IN THE SAME CLASS IN THIRD GRADE.
IF I KNOW HER..
...SHE WOULDN'T COME COM-PLAINING TO YOU LIKE SOME GIRLS WOULD.
SHE NEVER SAYS ANYTHING UNLESS SHE'S ASKED.
THAT CAN BE A GOOD THING. ON THE OTHER HAND, SHE NEVER PUTS HERSELF IN THE LINE OF FIRE.
I DON'T KNOW ANYTHING ABOUT THAT.

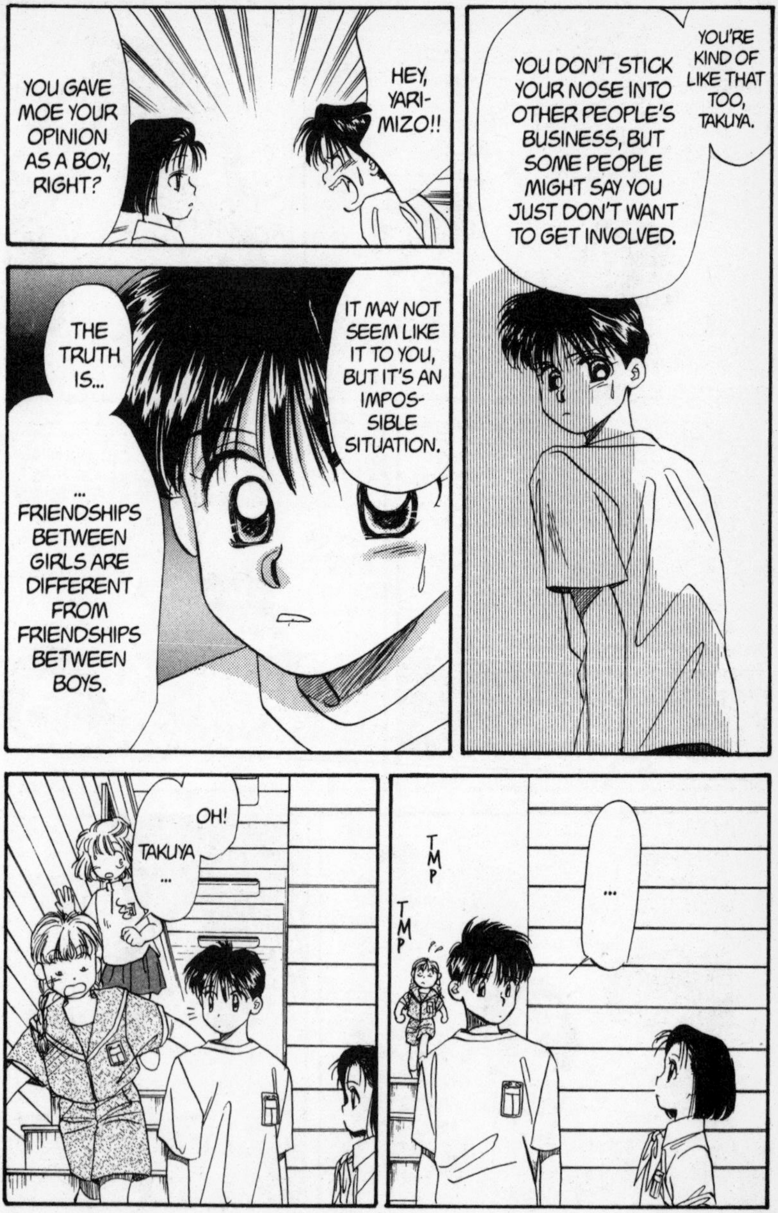
YOU'RE KIND OF LIKE THAT TOO, TAKUYA.
YOU DON'T STICK YOUR NOSE INTO OTHER PEOPLE'S BUSINESS, BUT SOME PEOPLE MIGHT SAY YOU JUST DON'T WANT TO GET INVOLVED.
HEY, YARI-MIZO!!
YOU GAVE MOE YOUR OPINION AS A BOY, RIGHT?
IT MAY NOT SEEM LIKE IT TO YOU, BUT IT'S AN IMPOS-SIBLE SITUATION.
THE TRUTH IS...
...FRIENDSHIPS BETWEEN GIRLS ARE DIFFERENT FROM FRIENDSHIPS BETWEEN BOYS.
TMP
TMP
...
OH!
TAKUYA...

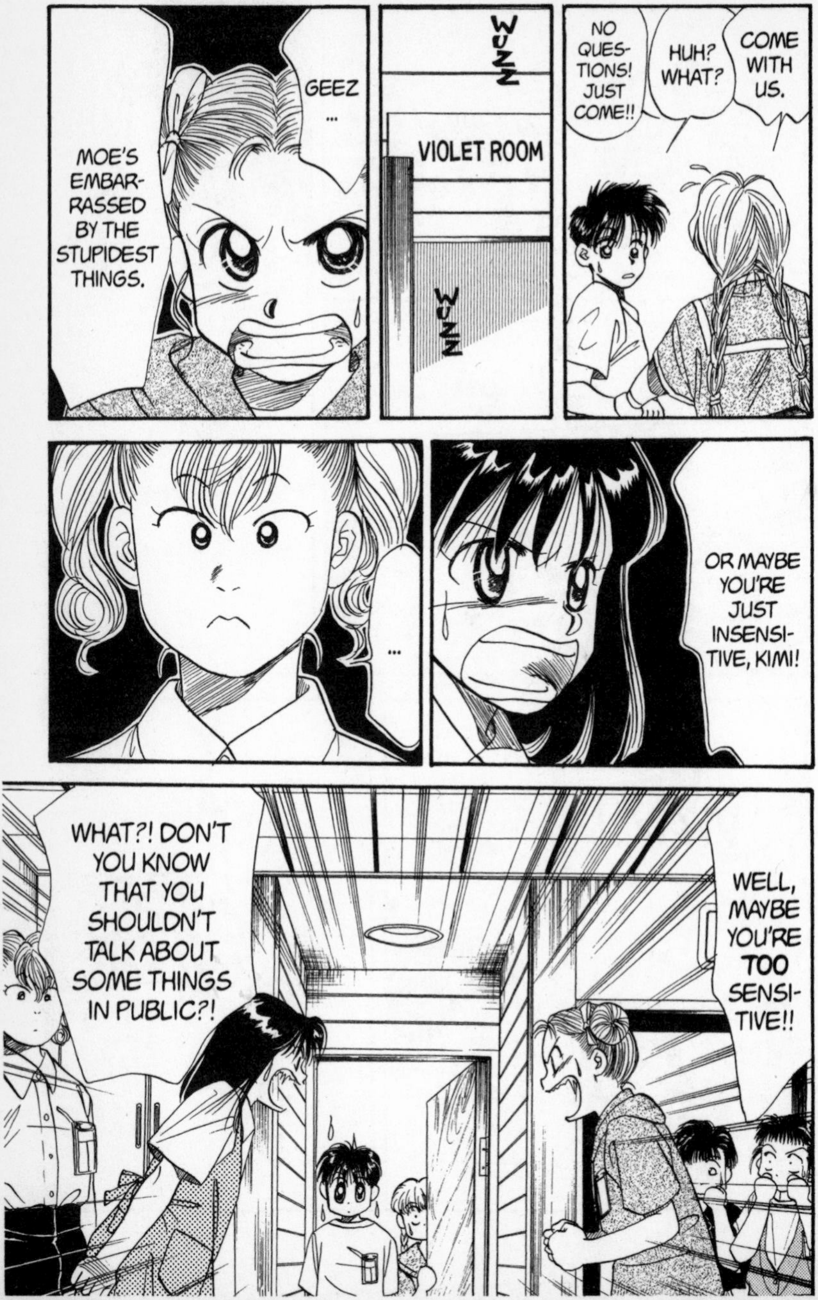
COME WITH US.
HUH? WHAT?
NO QUESTIONS! JUST COME!!
WUZZ
VIOLET ROOM
WUZZ
GEEZ ...
MOE'S EMBARRASSED BY THE STUPIDEST THINGS.
OR MAYBE YOU'RE JUST INSENSITIVE, KIMI!
...
WELL, MAYBE YOU'RE **TOO** SENSITIVE!!
WHAT?! DON'T YOU KNOW THAT YOU SHOULDN'T TALK ABOUT SOME THINGS IN PUBLIC?!

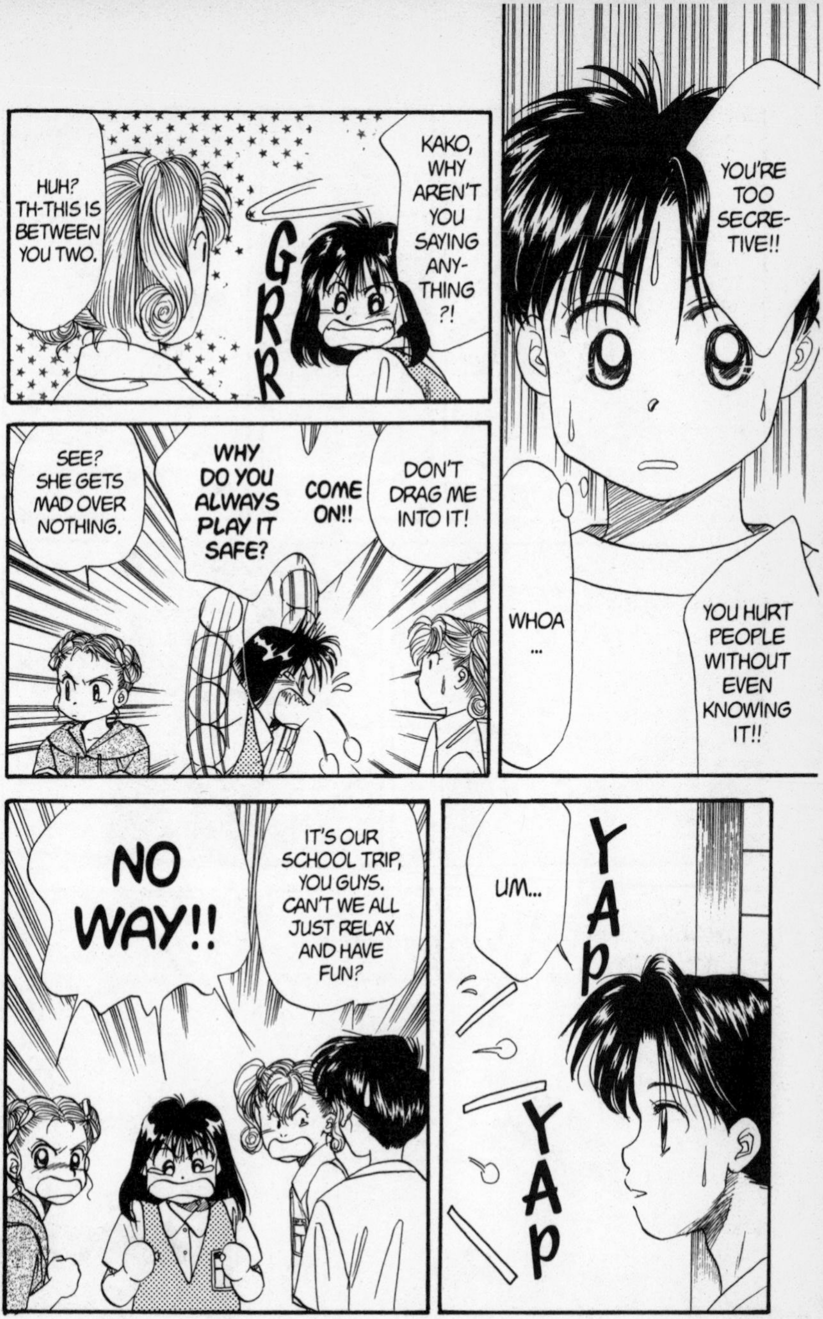
YOU'RE TOO SECRETIVE!!
YOU HURT PEOPLE WITHOUT EVEN KNOWING IT!!
WHOA...
KAKO, WHY AREN'T YOU SAYING ANYTHING?!
GRR
HUH? TH-THIS IS BETWEEN YOU TWO.
DON'T DRAG ME INTO IT!
COME ON!!
WHY DO YOU ALWAYS PLAY IT SAFE?
SEE? SHE GETS MAD OVER NOTHING.
YAP
UM...
YAP
IT'S OUR SCHOOL TRIP, YOU GUYS. CAN'T WE ALL JUST RELAX AND HAVE FUN?
NO WAY!!

THESE TWO ALWAYS COMPLAIN ABOUT EVERYTHING.
WELL, IT'S YOUR FAULT!
YOU TWO LEFT ME OUT!
WHAT IS THIS? WHY ARE YOU TWO SO NEGATIVE ?!
ISN'T EVERYBODY?
M-MEGUMI ?

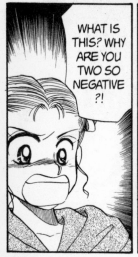

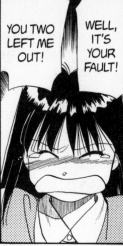

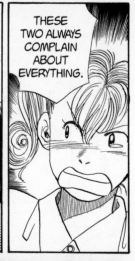

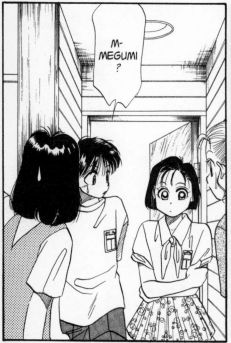

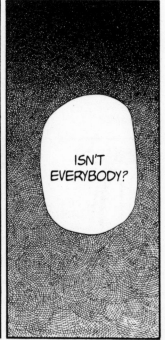

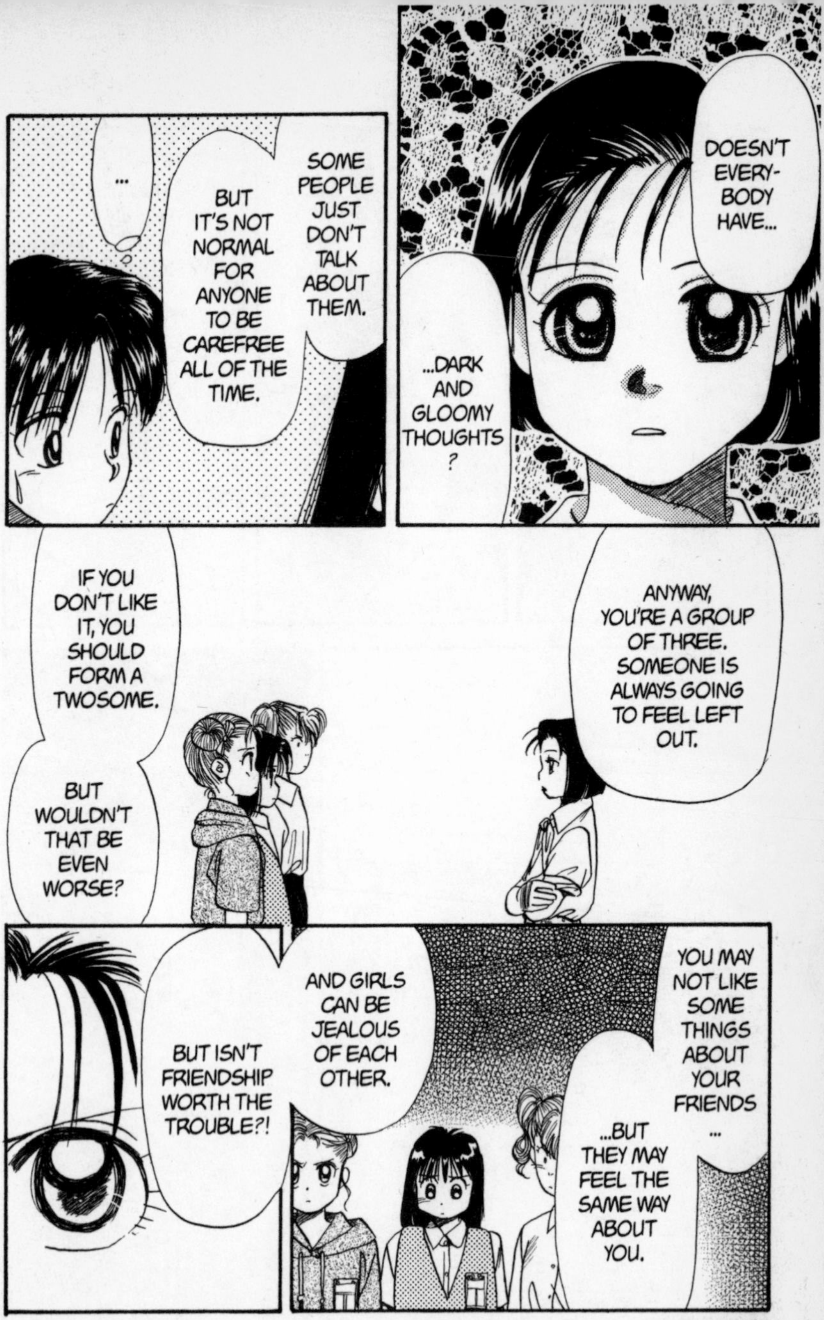
DOESN'T EVERY-BODY HAVE...
...DARK AND GLOOMY THOUGHTS?
SOME PEOPLE JUST DON'T TALK ABOUT THEM.
BUT IT'S NOT NORMAL FOR ANYONE TO BE CAREFREE ALL OF THE TIME.
...
ANYWAY, YOU'RE A GROUP OF THREE. SOMEONE IS ALWAYS GOING TO FEEL LEFT OUT.
IF YOU DON'T LIKE IT, YOU SHOULD FORM A TWOSOME.
BUT WOULDN'T THAT BE EVEN WORSE?
YOU MAY NOT LIKE SOME THINGS ABOUT YOUR FRIENDS...
...BUT THEY MAY FEEL THE SAME WAY ABOUT YOU.
AND GIRLS CAN BE JEALOUS OF EACH OTHER.
BUT ISN'T FRIENDSHIP WORTH THE TROUBLE?!

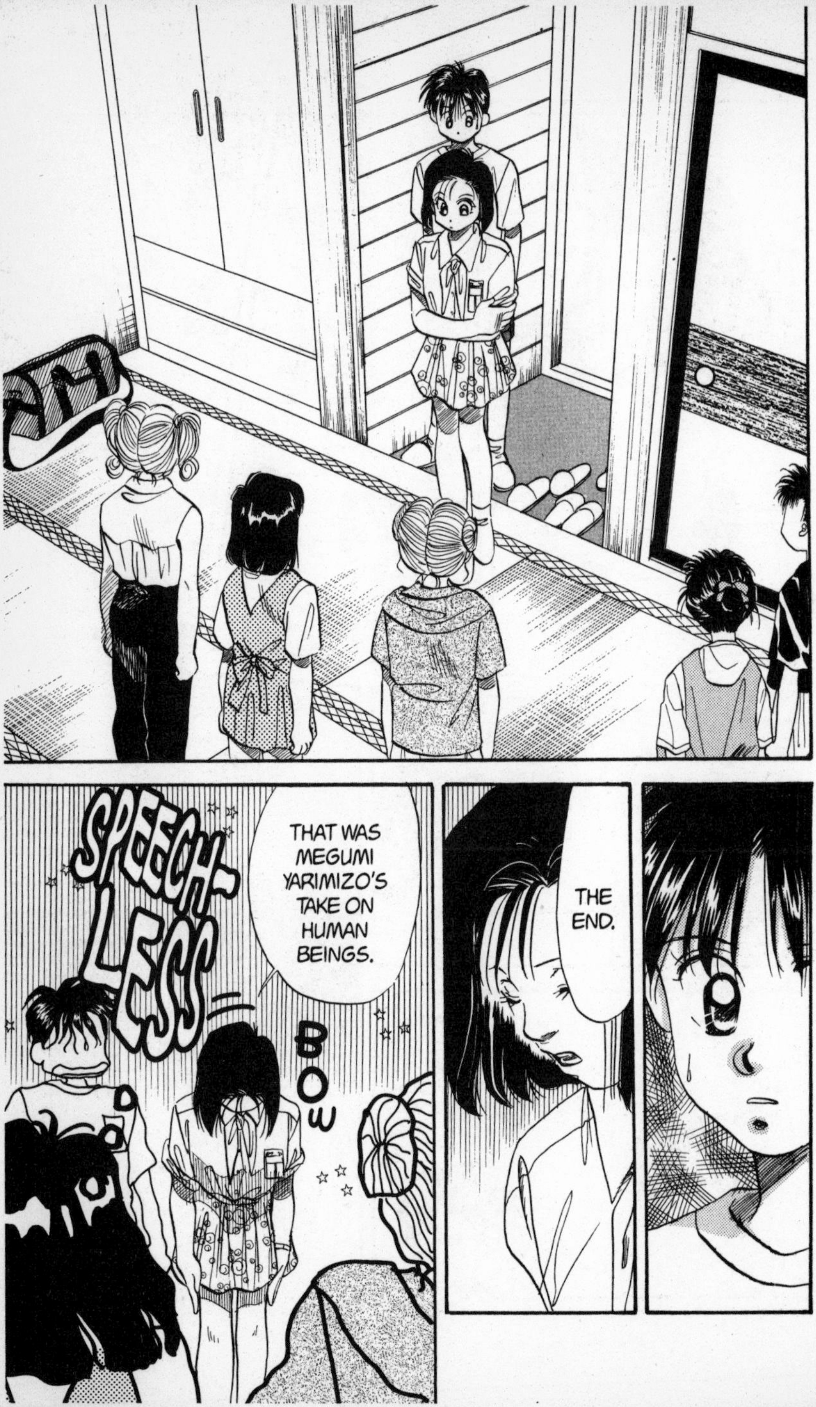
THE END.
THAT WAS MEGUMI YARIMIZO'S TAKE ON HUMAN BEINGS.
SPEECH-LESS
BOW

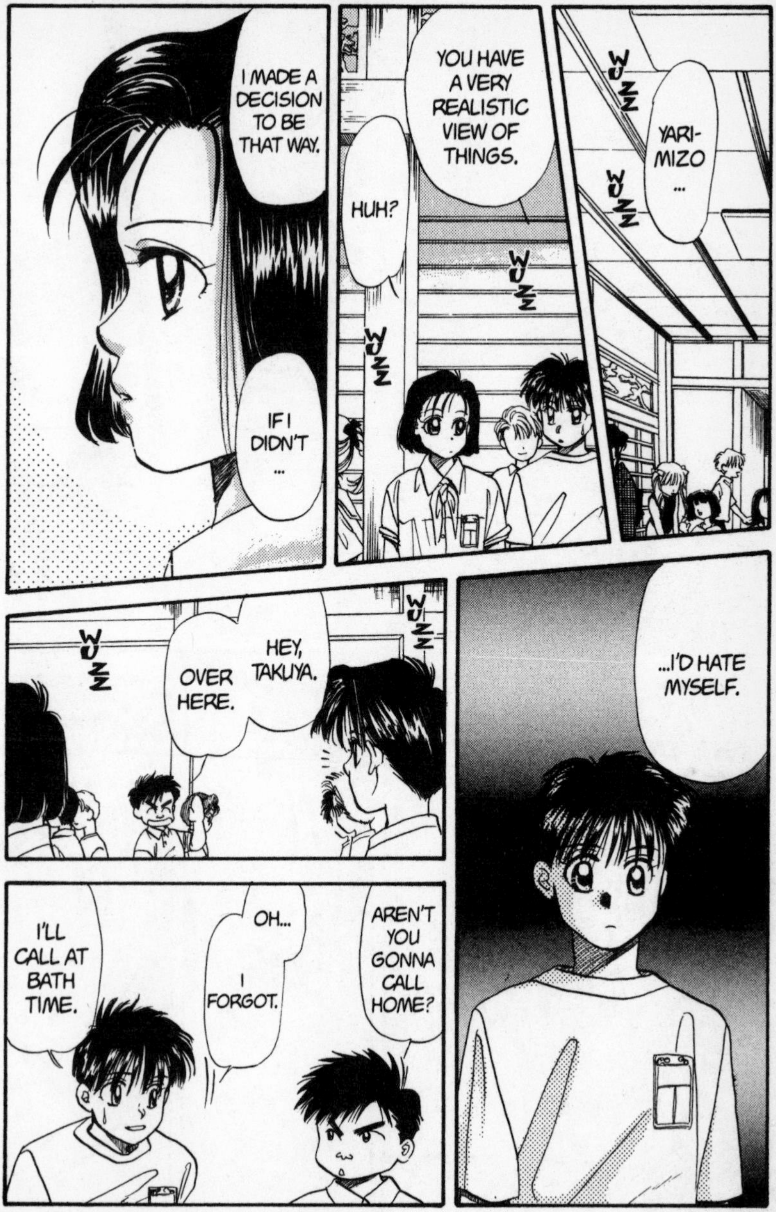
WUZZ
YARI-MIZO ...
WUZZ
YOU HAVE A VERY REALISTIC VIEW OF THINGS.
HUH?
WUZZ
WUZZ
I MADE A DECISION TO BE THAT WAY.
IF I DIDN'T ...
...I'D HATE MYSELF.
WUZZ
HEY, TAKUYA.
OVER HERE.
WUZZ
AREN'T YOU GONNA CALL HOME?
OH...
I FORGOT.
I'LL CALL AT BATH TIME.

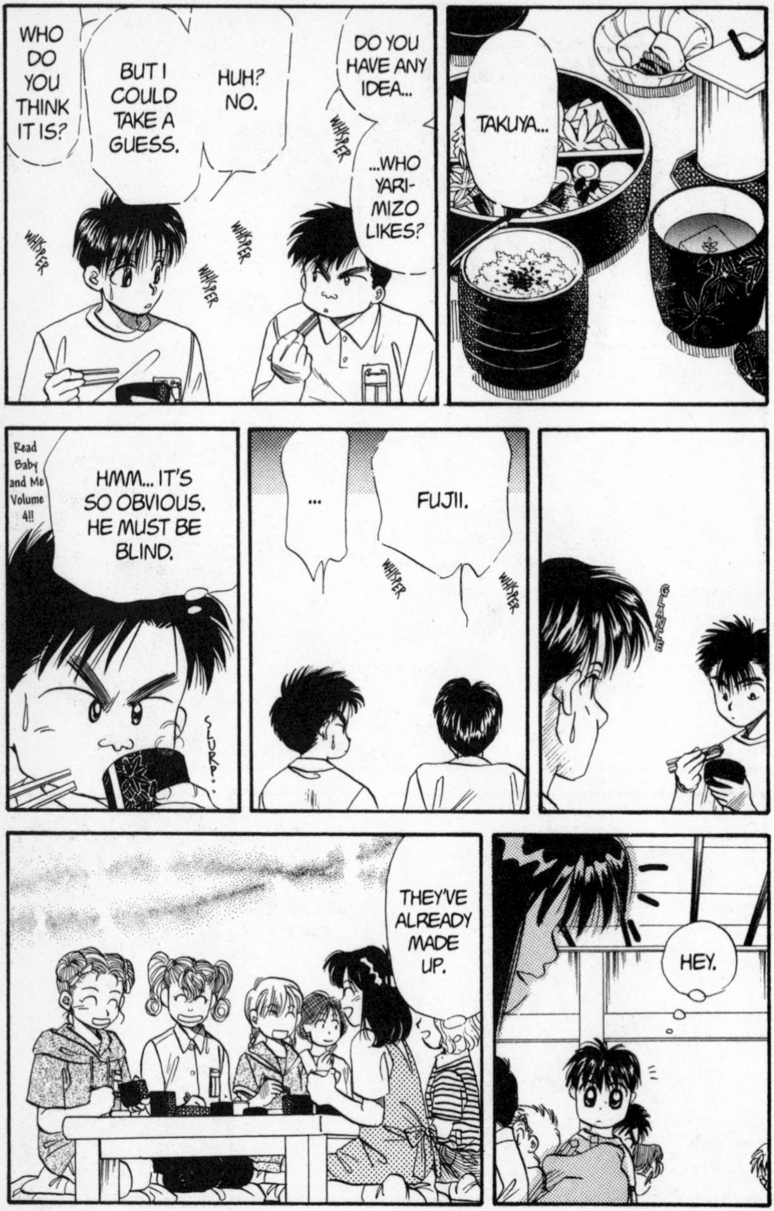
TAKUYA...
DO YOU HAVE ANY IDEA...
WHISPER
...WHO YARI-MIZO LIKES?
HUH? NO.
WHISPER
WHISPER
BUT I COULD TAKE A GUESS.
WHO DO YOU THINK IT IS?
WHISPER
GLANCE
FUJII.
WHISPER
...
WHISPER
HMM... IT'S SO OBVIOUS. HE MUST BE BLIND.
Read Baby and Me Volume 4!!
SLURP..
HEY.
THEY'VE ALREADY MADE UP.

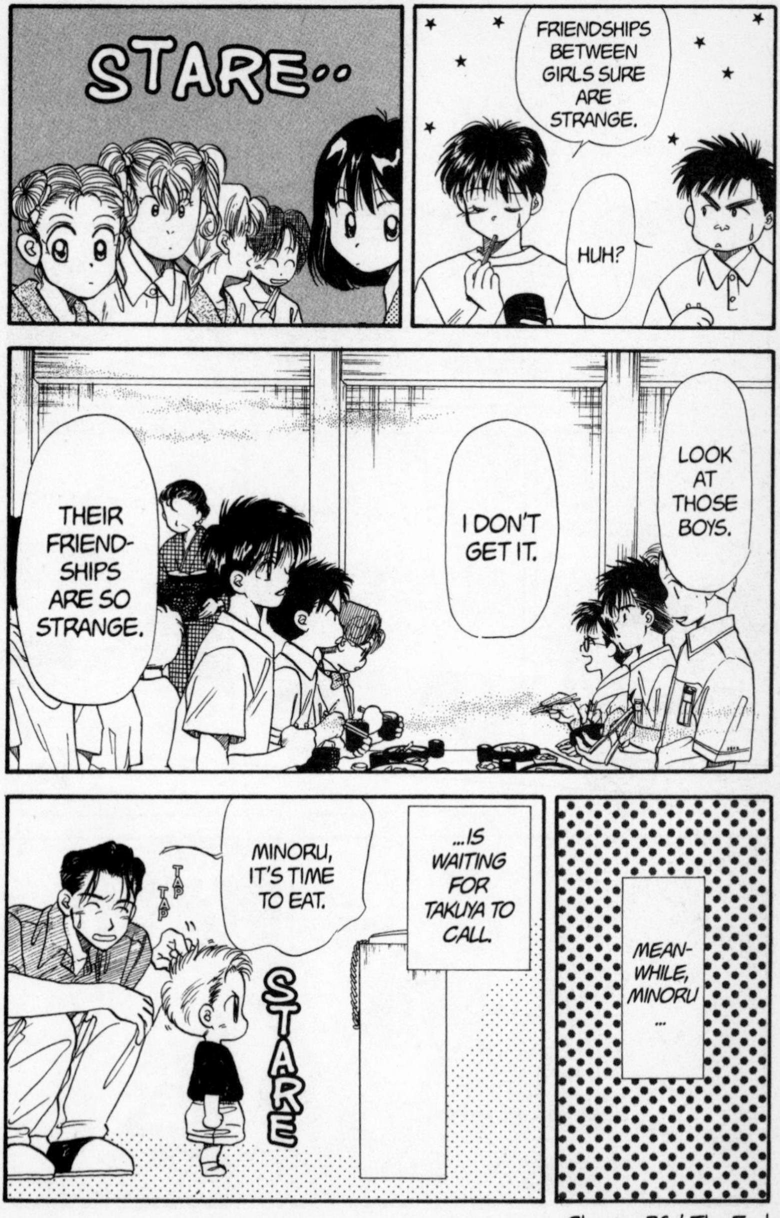
FRIENDSHIPS BETWEEN GIRLS SURE ARE STRANGE.
HUH?
STARE..
LOOK AT THOSE BOYS.
I DON'T GET IT.
THEIR FRIEND-SHIPS ARE SO STRANGE.
MEAN-WHILE, MINORU ...
...IS WAITING FOR TAKUYA TO CALL.
MINORU, IT'S TIME TO EAT.
TAP
TAP
STARE

Chapter 36 / The End

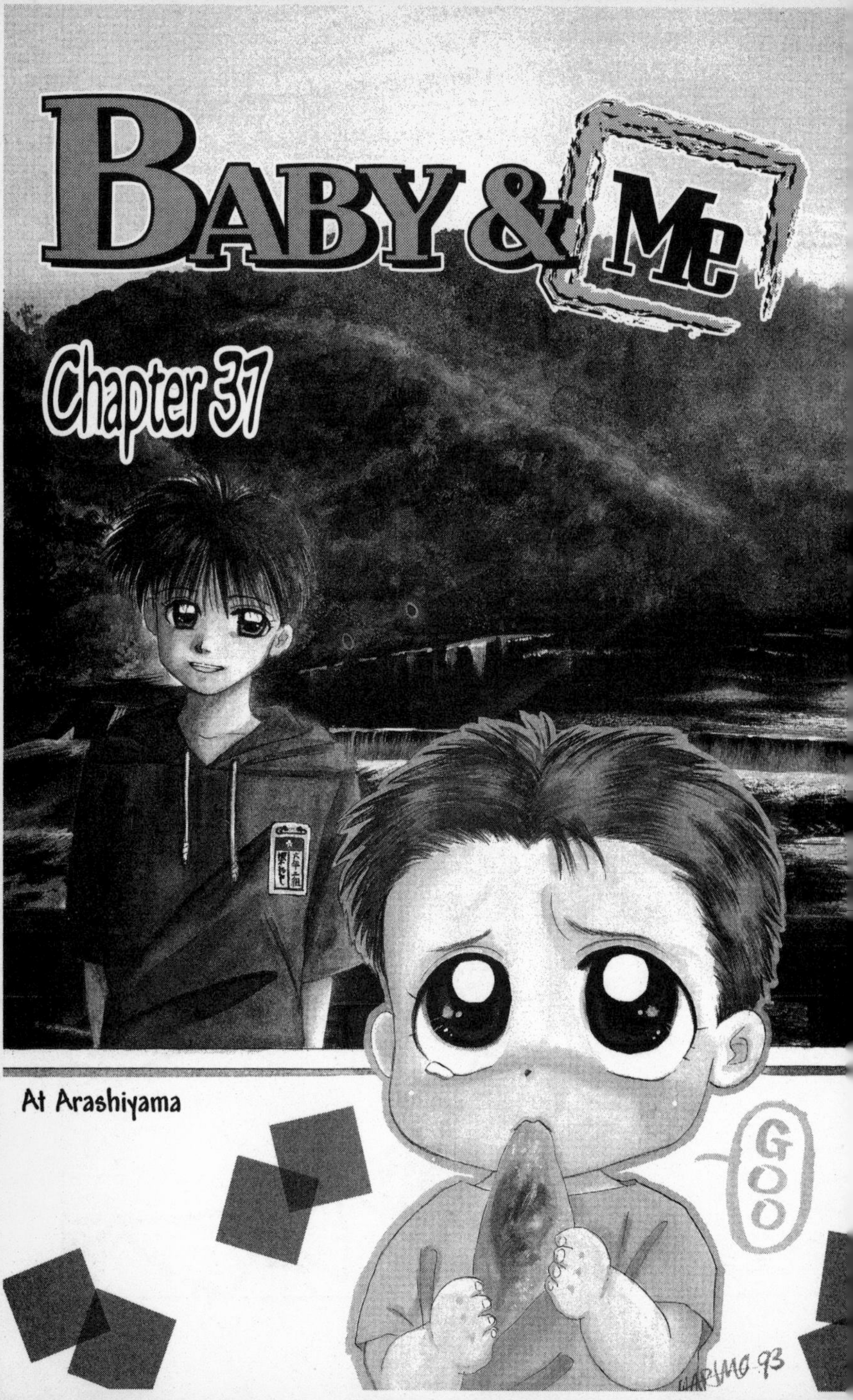

BABY & ME
Chapter 37
At Arashiyama
GOO

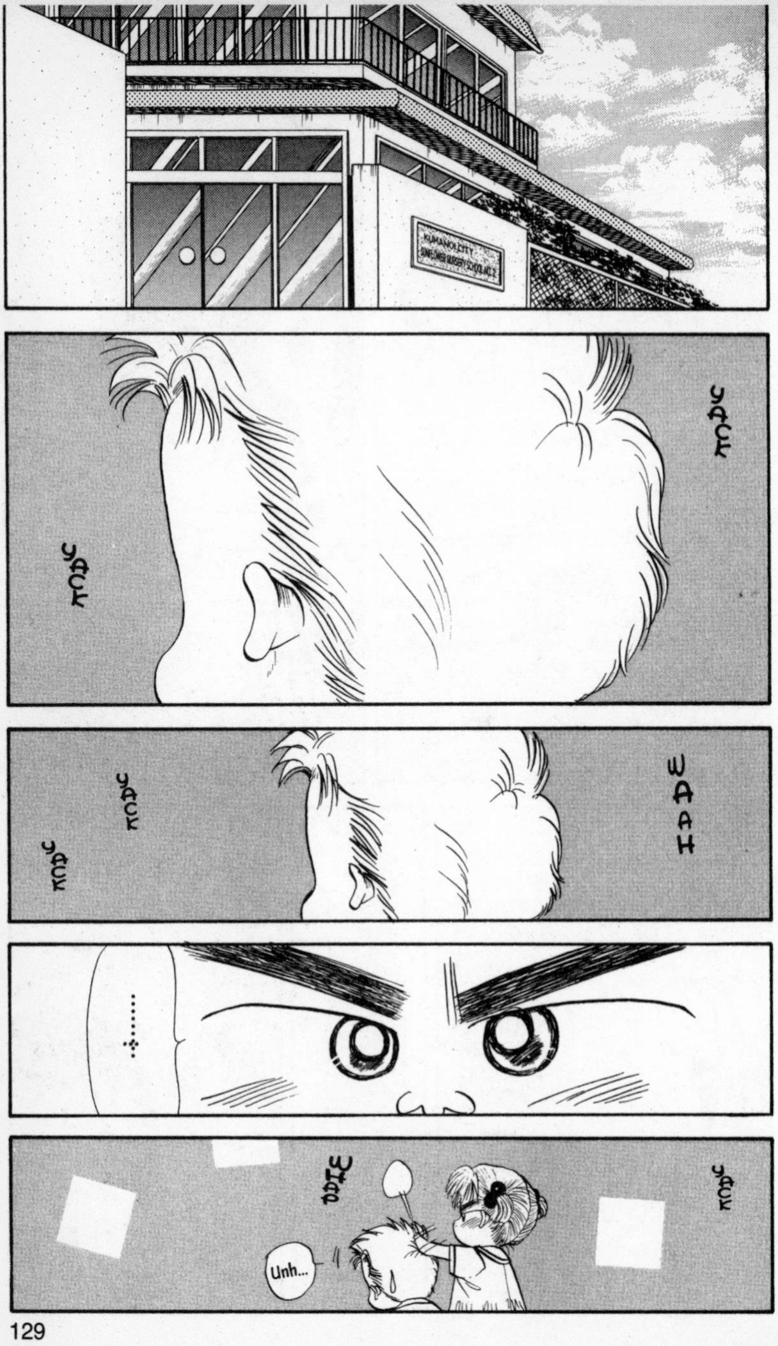
KUMANO CITY
SUNFLOWER NURSERY SCHOOL NO. 2
YACK
YACK
WAAH
YACK
YACK
……!
YACK
WHAP
Unh...

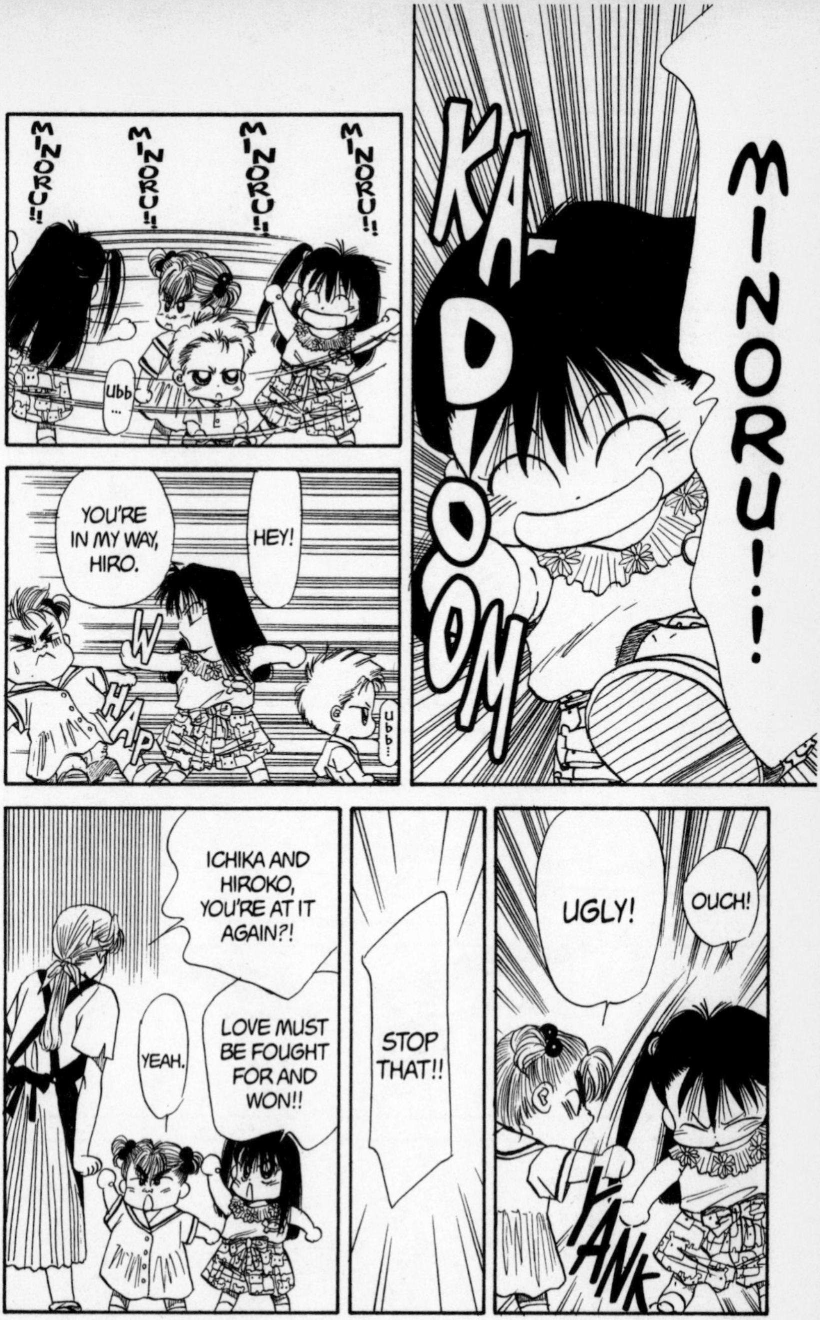
MINORU!!
KA-DOOM
MINORU!!
MINORU!!
MINORU!!
MINORU!!
Ubb...
HEY!
YOU'RE IN MY WAY, HIRO.
WHAP
Ubb...
OUCH!
UGLY!
YANK
STOP THAT!!
ICHIKA AND HIROKO, YOU'RE AT IT AGAIN?!
LOVE MUST BE FOUGHT FOR AND WON!!
YEAH.

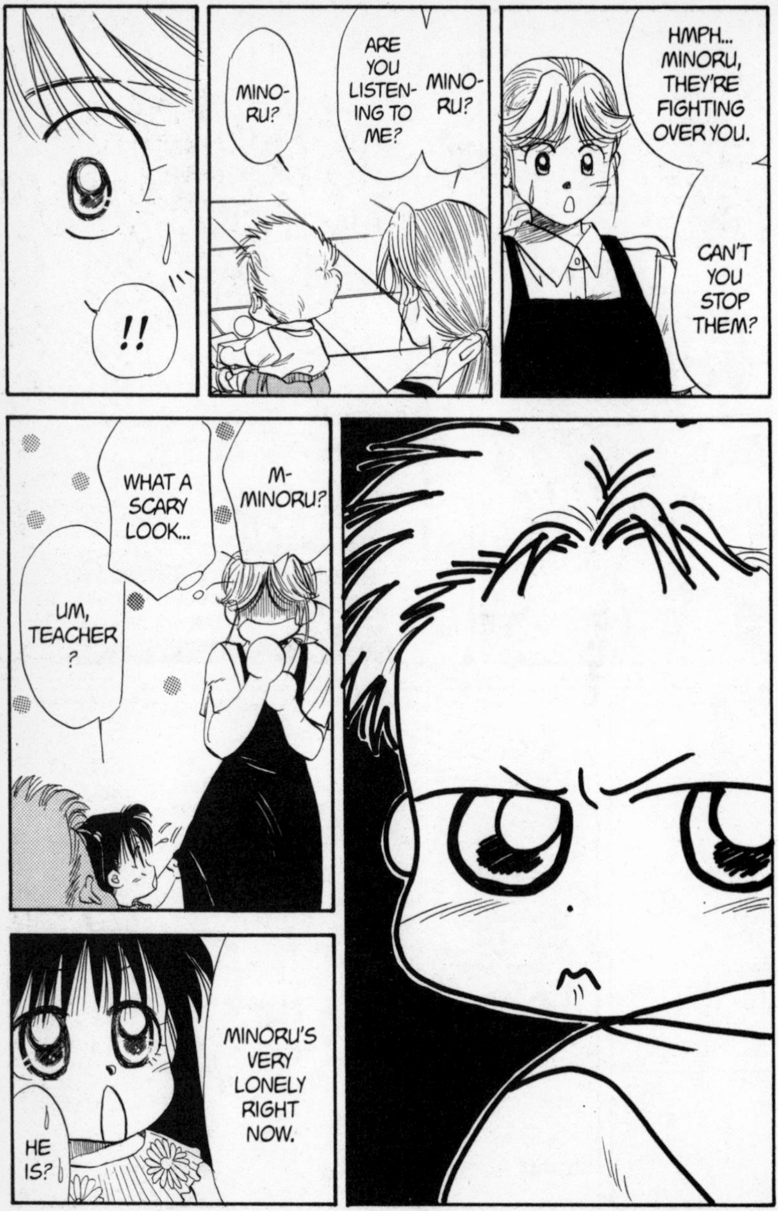
HMPH... MINORU, THEY'RE FIGHTING OVER YOU.
CAN'T YOU STOP THEM?
MINO-RU? ARE YOU LISTENING TO ME?
MINO-RU?
!!
M-MINORU?
WHAT A SCARY LOOK...
UM, TEACHER?
MINORU'S VERY LONELY RIGHT NOW.
HE IS?

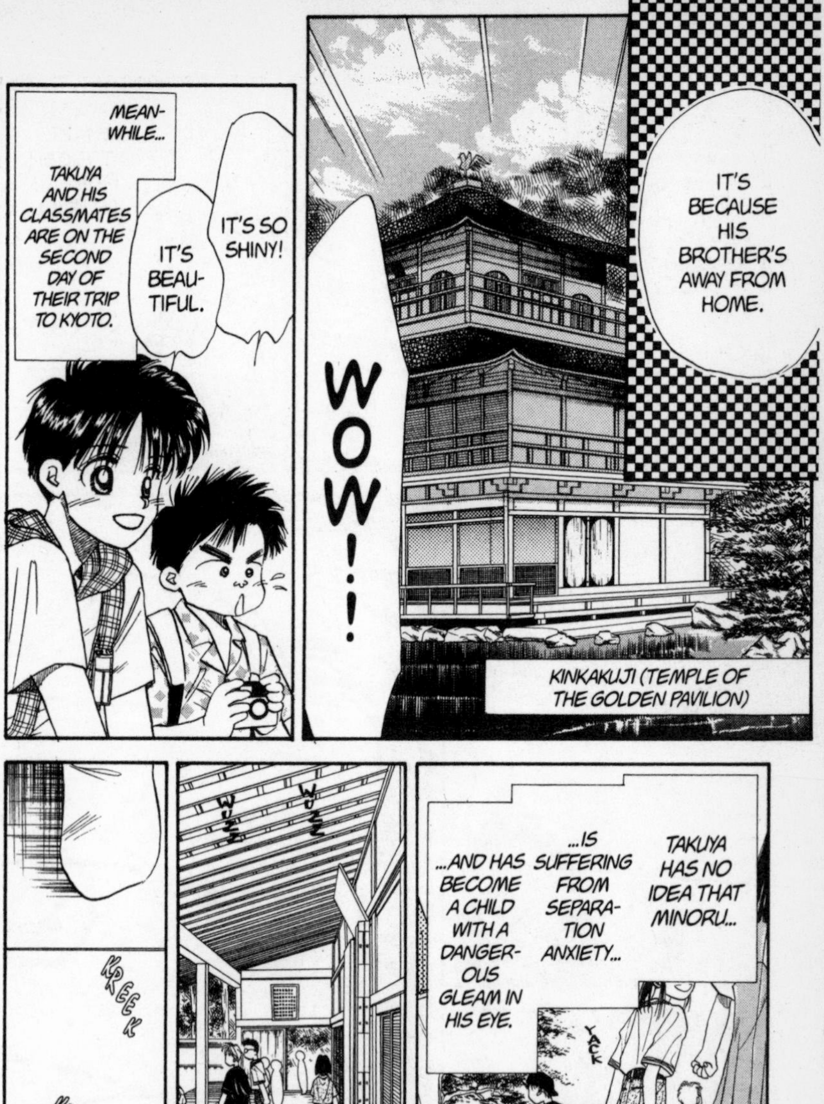
IT'S BECAUSE HIS BROTHER'S AWAY FROM HOME.
WOW!!
KINKAKUJI (TEMPLE OF THE GOLDEN PAVILION)
MEANWHILE...
TAKUYA AND HIS CLASSMATES ARE ON THE SECOND DAY OF THEIR TRIP TO KYOTO.
IT'S SO SHINY!
IT'S BEAUTIFUL.
TAKUYA HAS NO IDEA THAT MINORU...
...IS SUFFERING FROM SEPARATION ANXIETY...
...AND HAS BECOME A CHILD WITH A DANGEROUS GLEAM IN HIS EYE.
YACK
YACK
WUZZ
WUZZ
RYOANJI TEMPLE
KREEK
KREEK

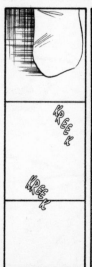

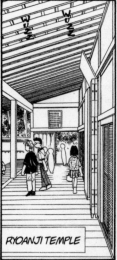

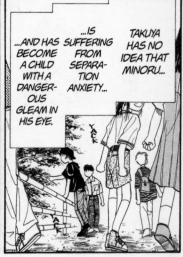

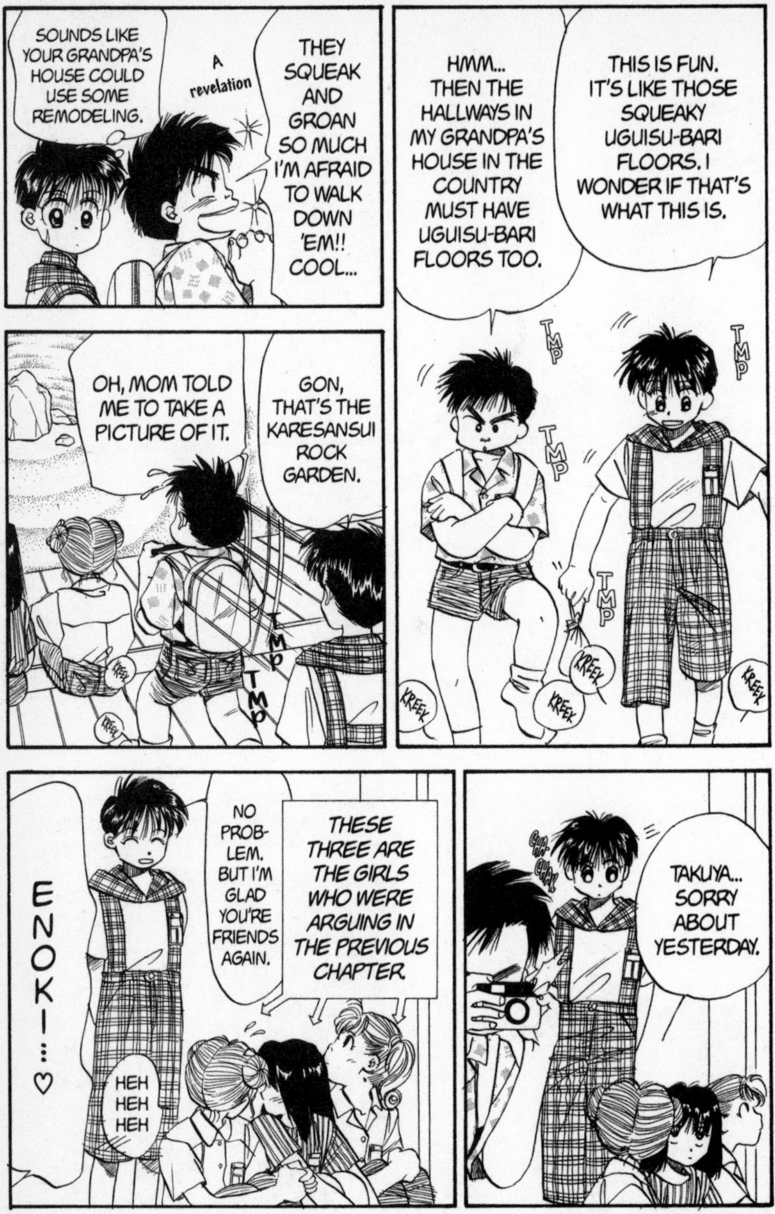
THIS IS FUN. IT'S LIKE THOSE SQUEAKY UGUISU-BARI FLOORS. I WONDER IF THAT'S WHAT THIS IS.
HMM... THEN THE HALLWAYS IN MY GRANDPA'S HOUSE IN THE COUNTRY MUST HAVE UGUISU-BARI FLOORS TOO.
TMP
TMP
TMP
TMP
KREEK
KREEK
KREEK
KREEK
KREEK
THEY SQUEAK AND GROAN SO MUCH I'M AFRAID TO WALK DOWN 'EM!! COOL...
A revelation
SOUNDS LIKE YOUR GRANDPA'S HOUSE COULD USE SOME REMODELING.
GON, THAT'S THE KARESANSUI ROCK GARDEN.
OH, MOM TOLD ME TO TAKE A PICTURE OF IT.
TMP
TMP
KREEK
KREEK
TAKUYA... SORRY ABOUT YESTERDAY.
CHA CHAK
NO PROB-LEM. BUT I'M GLAD YOU'RE FRIENDS AGAIN.
THESE THREE ARE THE GIRLS WHO WERE ARGUING IN THE PREVIOUS CHAPTER.
ENOKI...♡
HEH HEH HEH

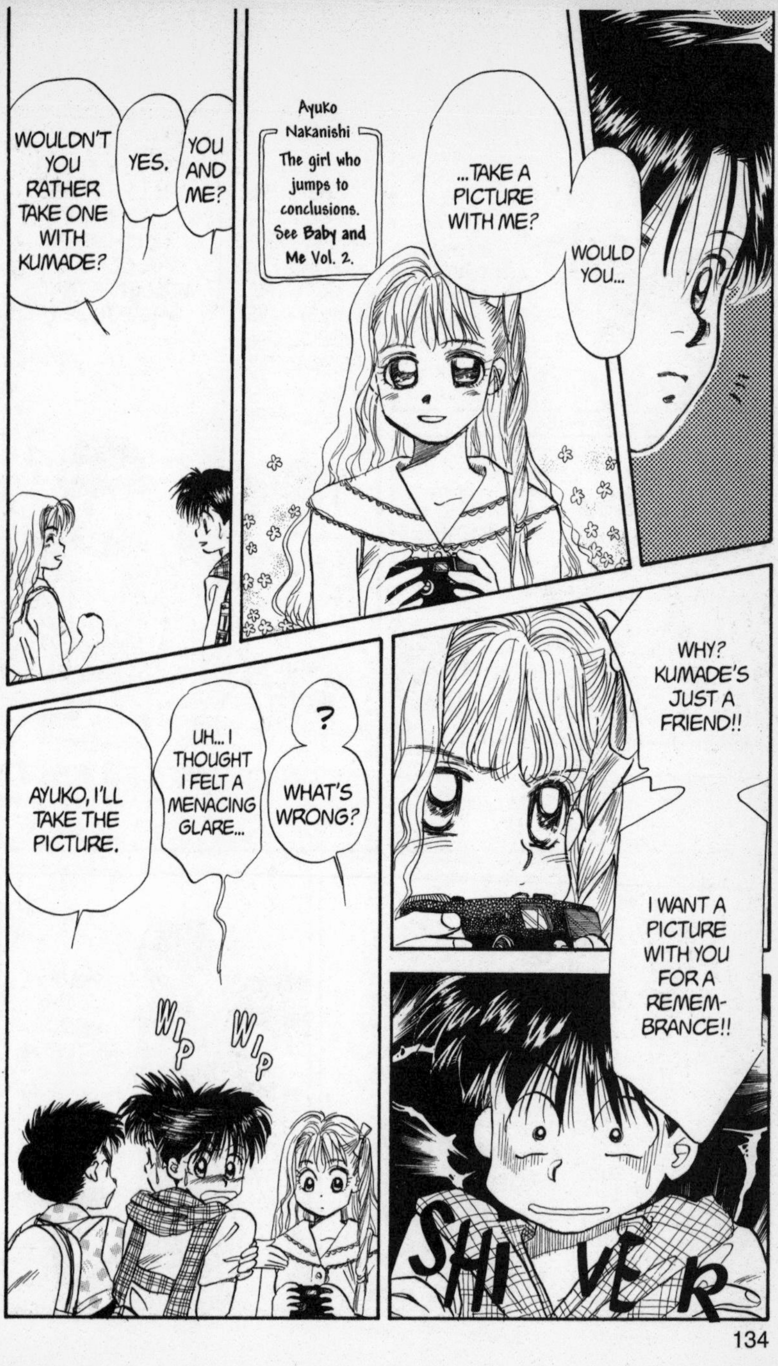
WOULD YOU...
...TAKE A PICTURE WITH ME?
Ayuko Nakanishi
The girl who jumps to conclusions. See Baby and Me Vol. 2.
YOU AND ME?
YES.
WOULDN'T YOU RATHER TAKE ONE WITH KUMADE?
WHY? KUMADE'S JUST A FRIEND!!
I WANT A PICTURE WITH YOU FOR A REMEM-BRANCE!!
SHIVER
?
WHAT'S WRONG?
UH... I THOUGHT I FELT A MENACING GLARE...
AYUKO, I'LL TAKE THE PICTURE.
WIP WIP

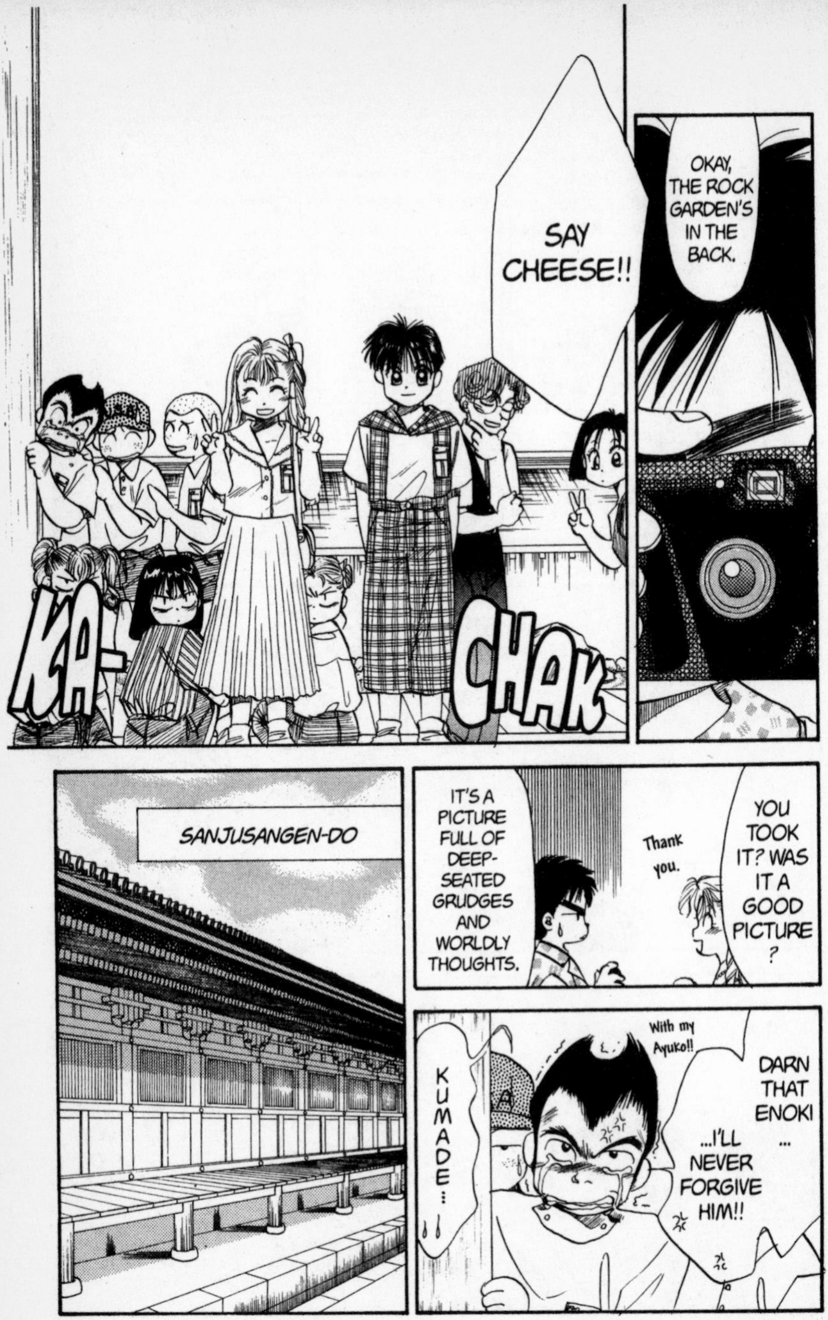

OKAY, THE ROCK GARDEN'S IN THE BACK.
SAY CHEESE!!
KA-CHAK
YOU TOOK IT? WAS IT A GOOD PICTURE?
Thank you.
IT'S A PICTURE FULL OF DEEP-SEATED GRUDGES AND WORLDLY THOUGHTS.
DARN THAT ENOKI...
With my Ayuko!!
...I'LL NEVER FORGIVE HIM!!
KUMADE...
SANJUSANGEN-DO

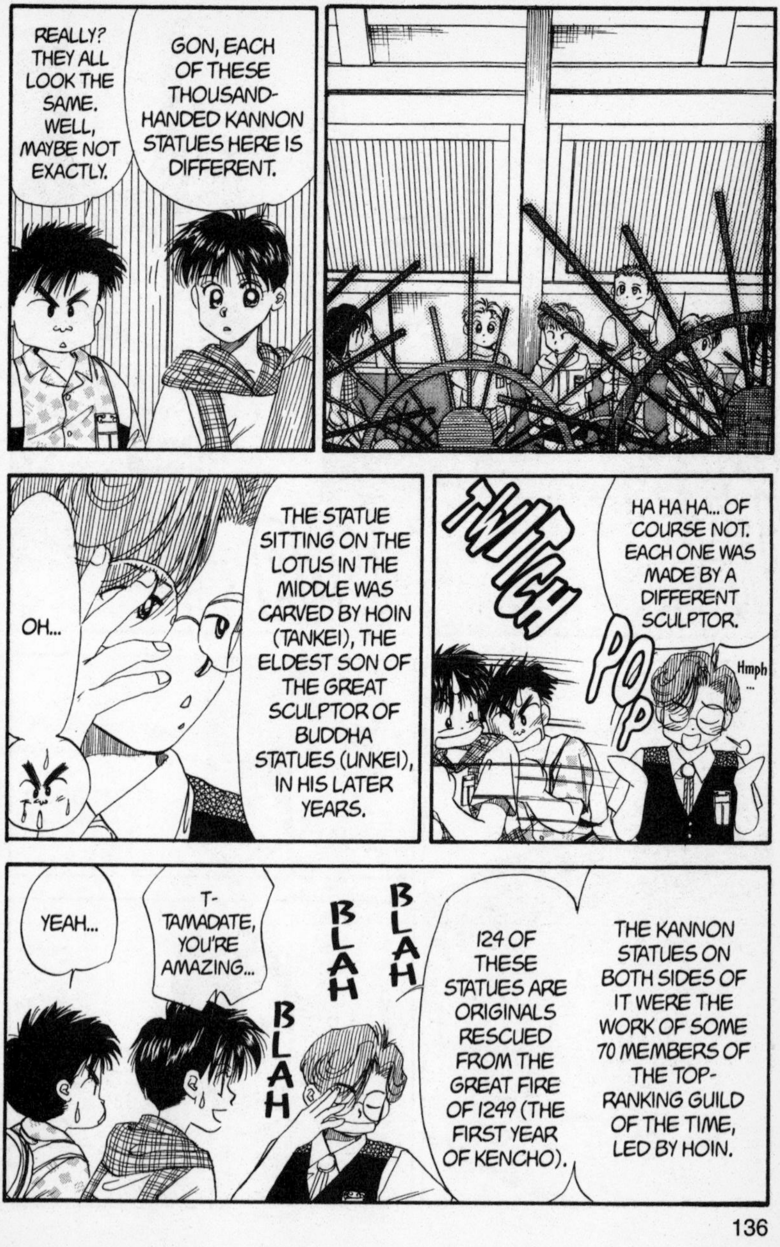
GON, EACH OF THESE THOUSAND-HANDED KANNON STATUES HERE IS DIFFERENT.
REALLY? THEY ALL LOOK THE SAME. WELL, MAYBE NOT EXACTLY.
HA HA HA... OF COURSE NOT. EACH ONE WAS MADE BY A DIFFERENT SCULPTOR.
TWITCH
POP
Hmph...
THE STATUE SITTING ON THE LOTUS IN THE MIDDLE WAS CARVED BY HOIN (TANKEI), THE ELDEST SON OF THE GREAT SCULPTOR OF BUDDHA STATUES (UNKEI), IN HIS LATER YEARS.
OH...
THE KANNON STATUES ON BOTH SIDES OF IT WERE THE WORK OF SOME 70 MEMBERS OF THE TOP-RANKING GUILD OF THE TIME, LED BY HOIN.
124 OF THESE STATUES ARE ORIGINALS RESCUED FROM THE GREAT FIRE OF 1249 (THE FIRST YEAR OF KENCHO).
BLAH
BLAH
BLAH
T-TAMADATE, YOU'RE AMAZING...
YEAH...

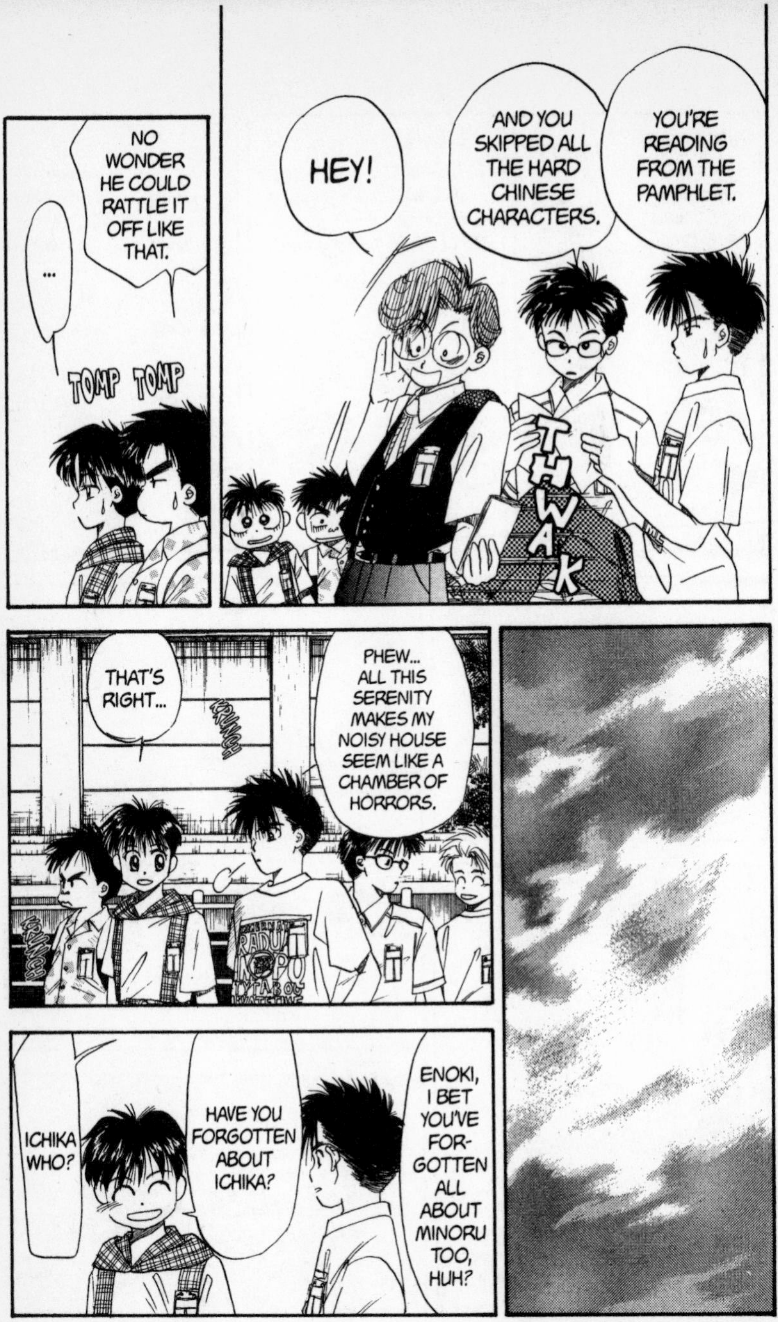
YOU'RE READING FROM THE PAMPHLET.
AND YOU SKIPPED ALL THE HARD CHINESE CHARACTERS.
HEY!
THWAK
NO WONDER HE COULD RATTLE IT OFF LIKE THAT.
...
TOMP TOMP
PHEW... ALL THIS SERENITY MAKES MY NOISY HOUSE SEEM LIKE A CHAMBER OF HORRORS.
THAT'S RIGHT...
KRUNCH
KRUNCH
ENOKI, I BET YOU'VE FOR-GOTTEN ALL ABOUT MINORU TOO, HUH?
HAVE YOU FORGOTTEN ABOUT ICHIKA?
ICHIKA WHO?

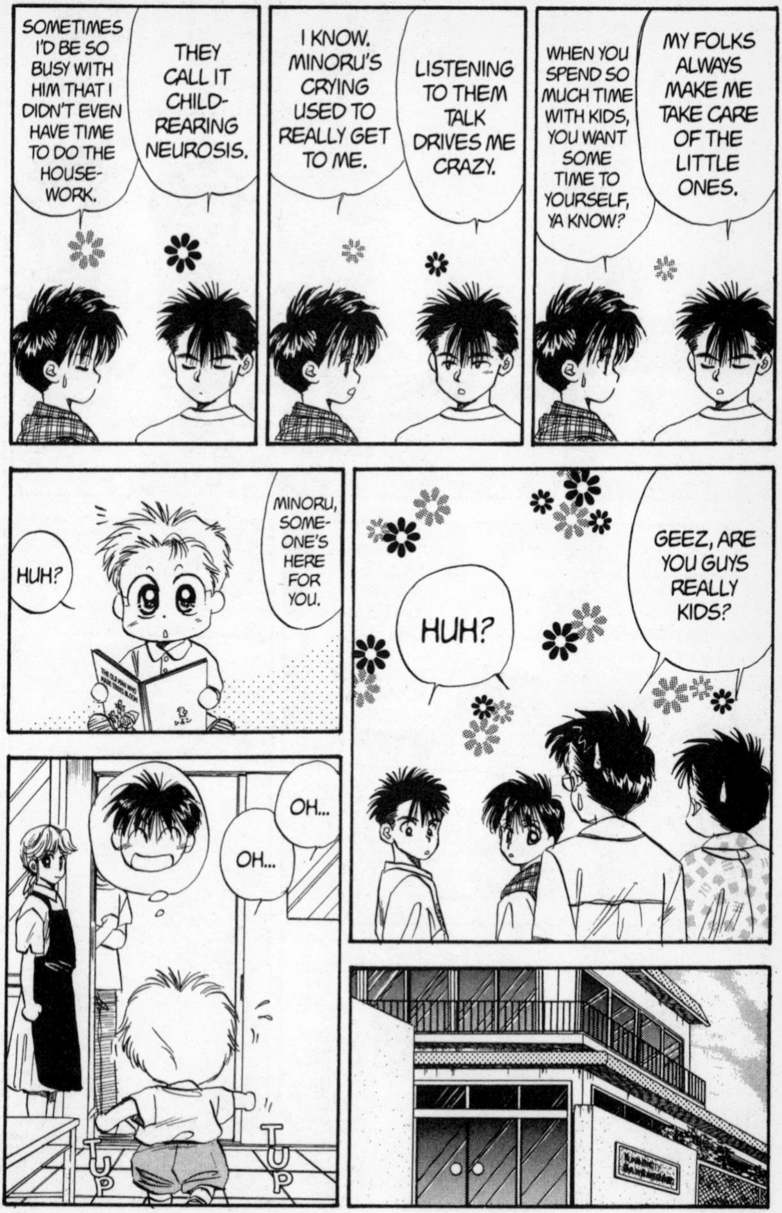
MY FOLKS ALWAYS MAKE ME TAKE CARE OF THE LITTLE ONES.
WHEN YOU SPEND SO MUCH TIME WITH KIDS, YOU WANT SOME TIME TO YOURSELF, YA KNOW?
LISTENING TO THEM TALK DRIVES ME CRAZY.
I KNOW. MINORU'S CRYING USED TO REALLY GET TO ME.
THEY CALL IT CHILD-REARING NEUROSIS.
SOMETIMES I'D BE SO BUSY WITH HIM THAT I DIDN'T EVEN HAVE TIME TO DO THE HOUSE-WORK.
GEEZ, ARE YOU GUYS REALLY KIDS?
HUH?
MINORU, SOME-ONE'S HERE FOR YOU.
HUH?
OH...
OH...
TUP
TUP

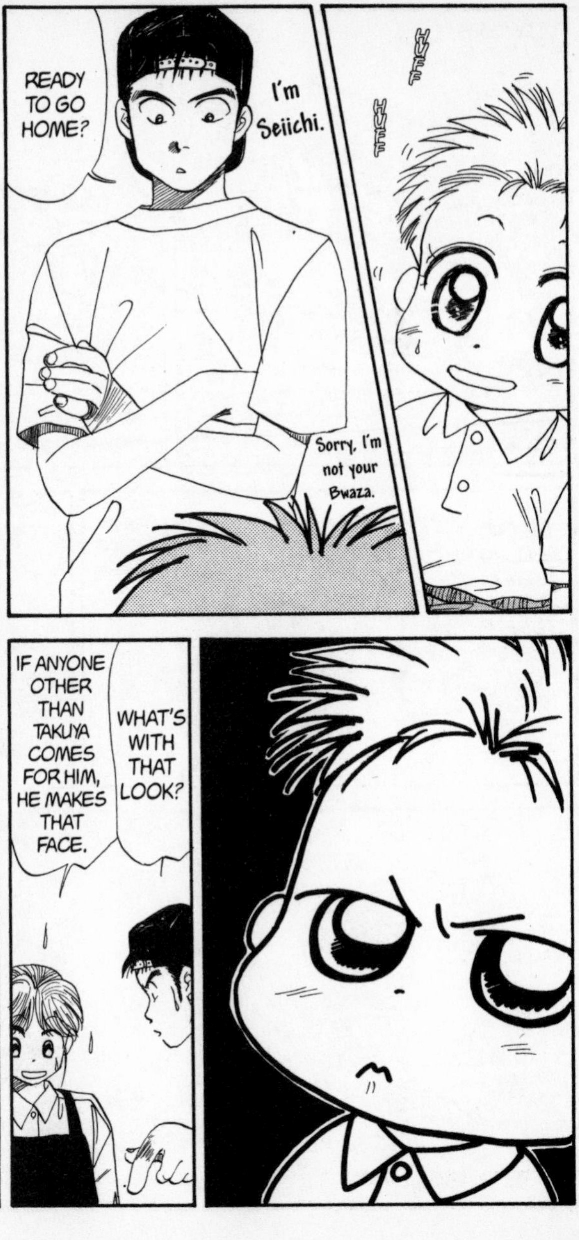
HUFF
HUFF
READY TO GO HOME?
I'm Seiichi.
Sorry, I'm not your Bwaza.
WHAT'S WITH THAT LOOK?
IF ANYONE OTHER THAN TAKUYA COMES FOR HIM, HE MAKES THAT FACE.

Author's Note Part 5

What I Want to Do Now

- I want to do character designs for role-playing games, or other original animation. Isn't there a company out there that would like to use my designs? What? No way? ♪♪
- I want to go on a trip. **Flowers & Dreams**, please give me a vacation.
- I want to sleep. I'm writing this at 6:00 a.m. I've got a busy day ahead of me, so I won't be getting any sleep.
- I'm hungry. I think I'll go to a convenience store and get something to eat when I'm done with this.

I guess that's about it. I especially want to do the first of the above. Won't someone give me a call? Speaking of calls, I want to see my friends. Friends, please call me.

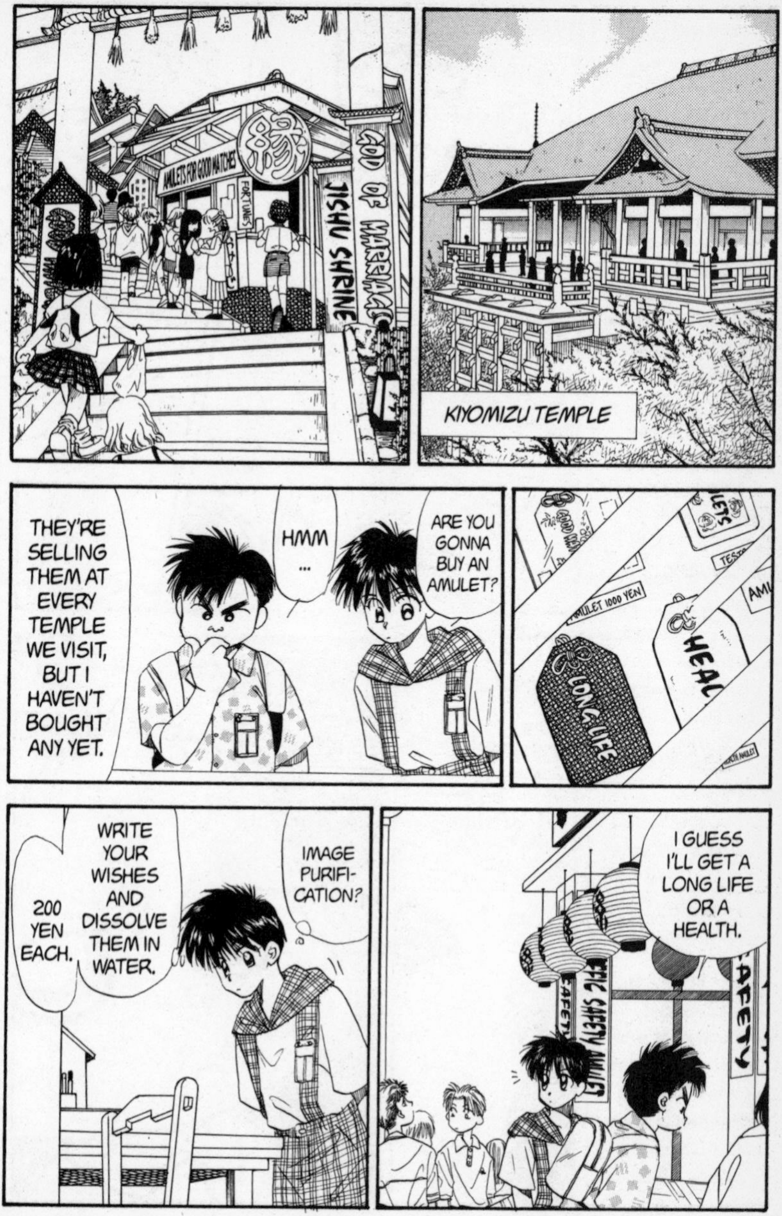
KIYOMIZU TEMPLE
GOD OF MARRIAG
JISHU SHRINE
AMULETS FOR GOOD MATCHES
FORTUNES
AMULET 1000 YEN
LONG LIFE
ARE YOU GONNA BUY AN AMULET?
HMM ...
THEY'RE SELLING THEM AT EVERY TEMPLE WE VISIT, BUT I HAVEN'T BOUGHT ANY YET.
I GUESS I'LL GET A LONG LIFE OR A HEALTH.
SAFETY
IMAGE PURIFICATION?
WRITE YOUR WISHES AND DISSOLVE THEM IN WATER.
200 YEN EACH.

May our family of three in good health and harmony.

Takuya Enoki

Male

Age 12

OFFERINGS

...

I'LL DO IT.

SPARKLE

TAKUYA?

WOW...

IT DIS-SOLVED INSTANTLY.

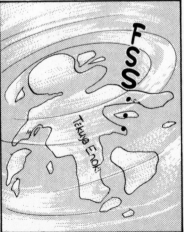

Takuya Enoki

FSS...

Takuya Enoki

KYOTO IS FAMOUS...

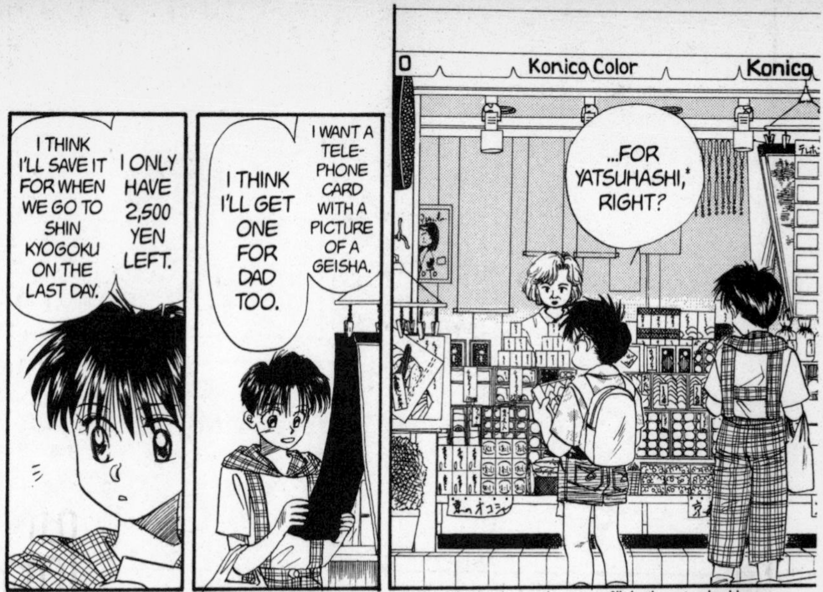
Konica Color
Konica
...FOR YATSUHASHI,* RIGHT?
I WANT A TELEPHONE CARD WITH A PICTURE OF A GEISHA.
I THINK I'LL GET ONE FOR DAD TOO.
I ONLY HAVE 2,500 YEN LEFT.
I THINK I'LL SAVE IT FOR WHEN WE GO TO SHIN KYOGOKU ON THE LAST DAY.

*Yatsuhashi are sweet, rubbery rice cakes topped with powdered soybean, and sometimes filled with sweetened red beans.

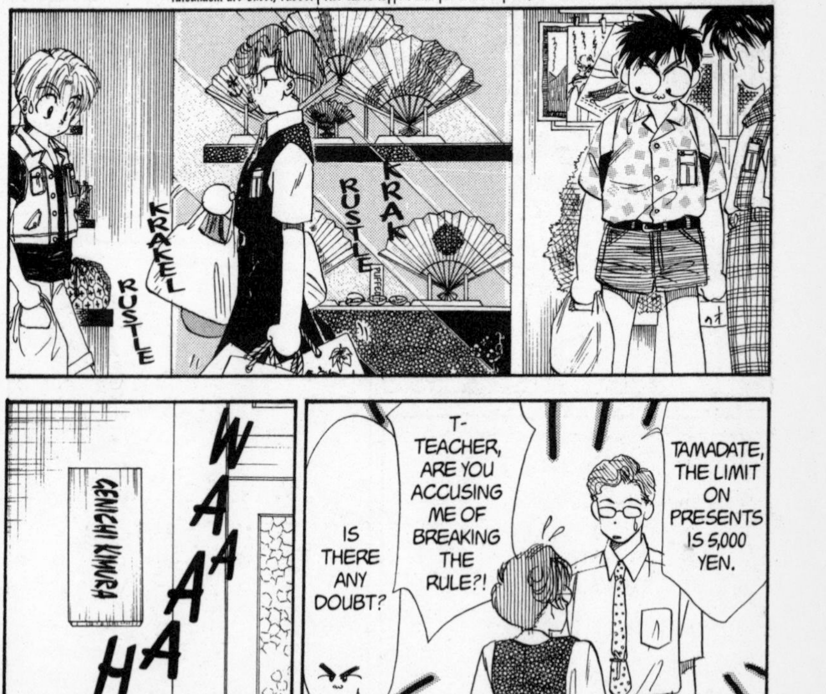
KRAK
RUSTLE
KRAKEL
RUSTLE
TAMADATE, THE LIMIT ON PRESENTS IS 5,000 YEN.
T-TEACHER, ARE YOU ACCUSING ME OF BREAKING THE RULE?!
IS THERE ANY DOUBT?
WAAAAAH
GENICHI KIMURA

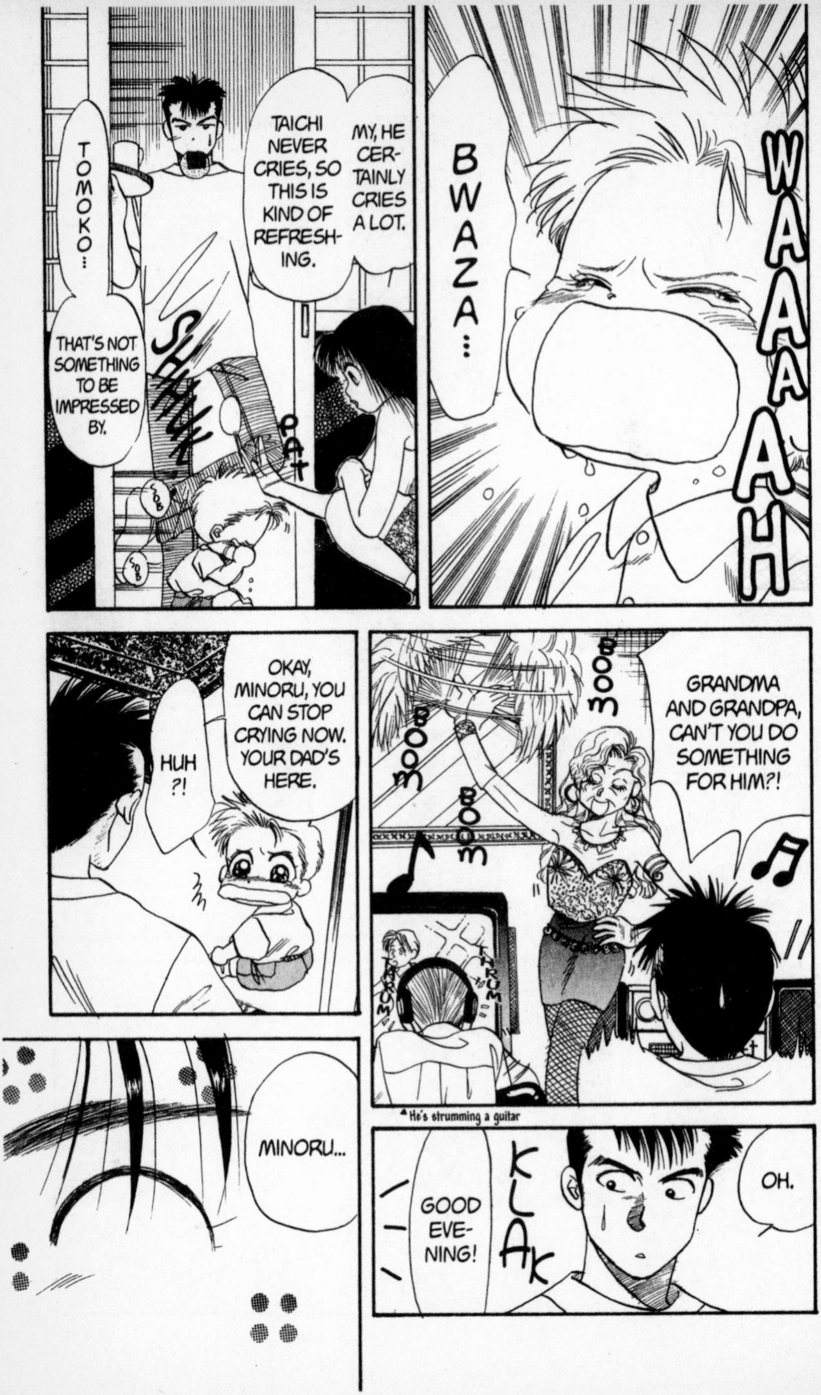
WAAAAAH
BWAZA...
MY, HE CERTAINLY CRIES A LOT.
TAICHI NEVER CRIES, SO THIS IS KIND OF REFRESHING.
TOMOKO...
THAT'S NOT SOMETHING TO BE IMPRESSED BY.
SHHUNK
PAT
SOB
SOB
GRANDMA AND GRANDPA, CAN'T YOU DO SOMETHING FOR HIM?!
BOOM
BOOM
BOOM
THRUM
THRUM
He's strumming a guitar
OKAY, MINORU, YOU CAN STOP CRYING NOW. YOUR DAD'S HERE.
HUH ?!
OH.
KLAK
GOOD EVENING!
MINORU...

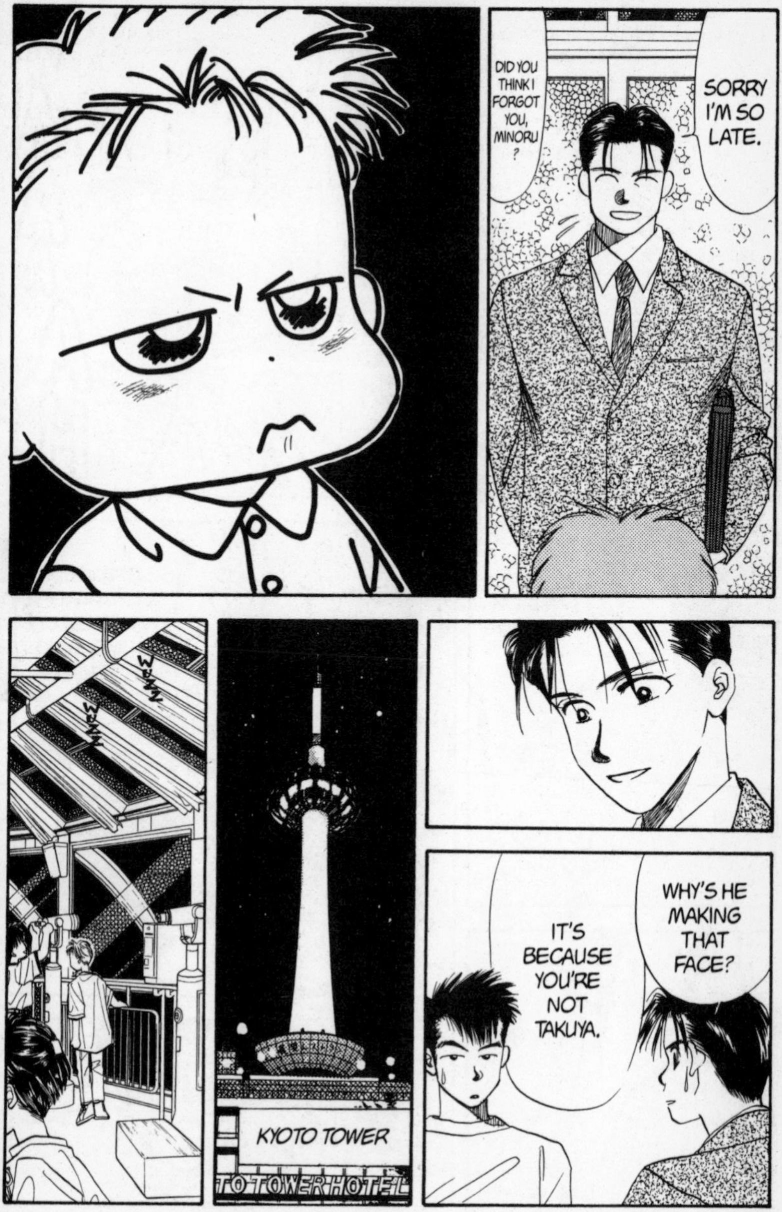
SORRY I'M SO LATE.
DID YOU THINK I FORGOT YOU, MINORU?
WHY'S HE MAKING THAT FACE?
IT'S BECAUSE YOU'RE NOT TAKUYA.
KYOTO TOWER
TOTOWERHOTEL
WUZZ
WUZZ

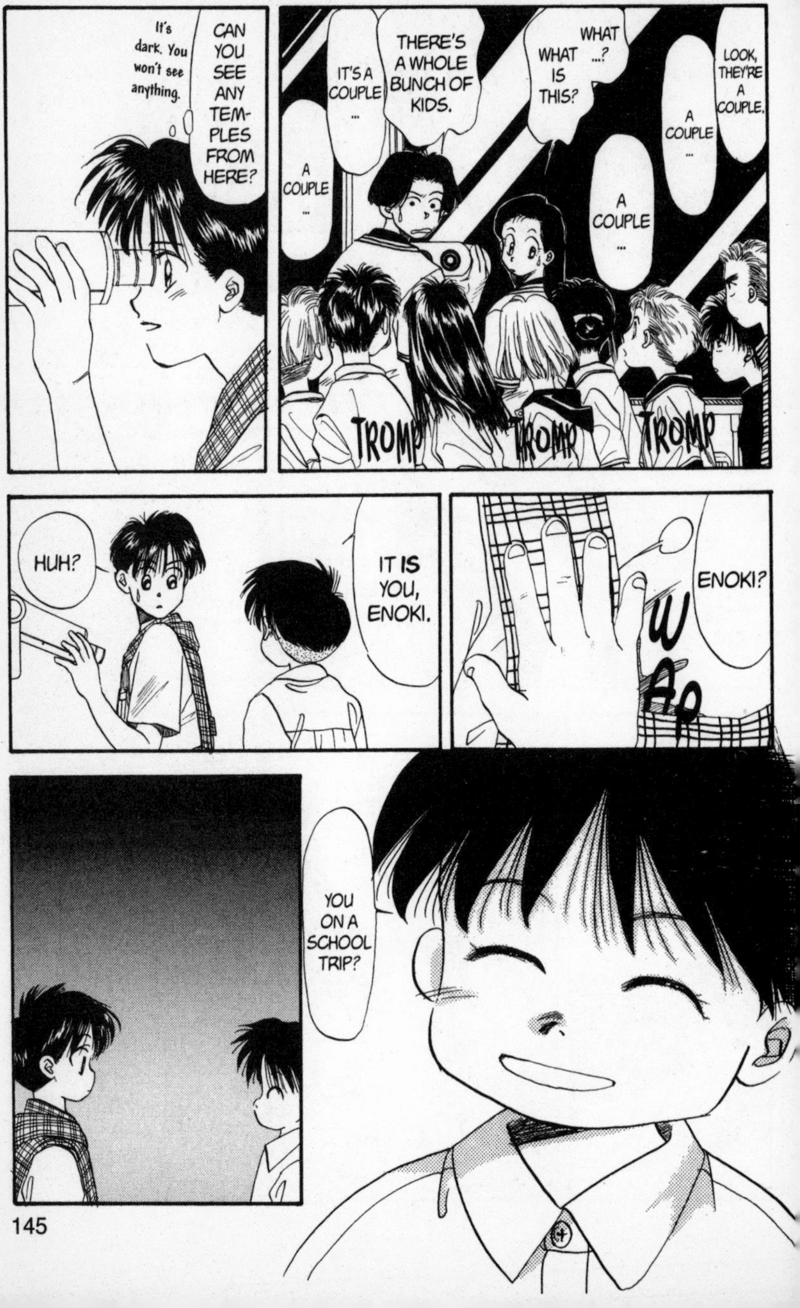
LOOK, THEY'RE A COUPLE.
A COUPLE ...
A COUPLE ...
WHAT ...?
WHAT IS THIS?
THERE'S A WHOLE BUNCH OF KIDS.
IT'S A COUPLE ...
A COUPLE ...
TROMP
TROMP
TROMP
CAN YOU SEE ANY TEMPLES FROM HERE?
It's dark. You won't see anything.
ENOKI?
WAP
IT IS YOU, ENOKI.
HUH?
YOU ON A SCHOOL TRIP?

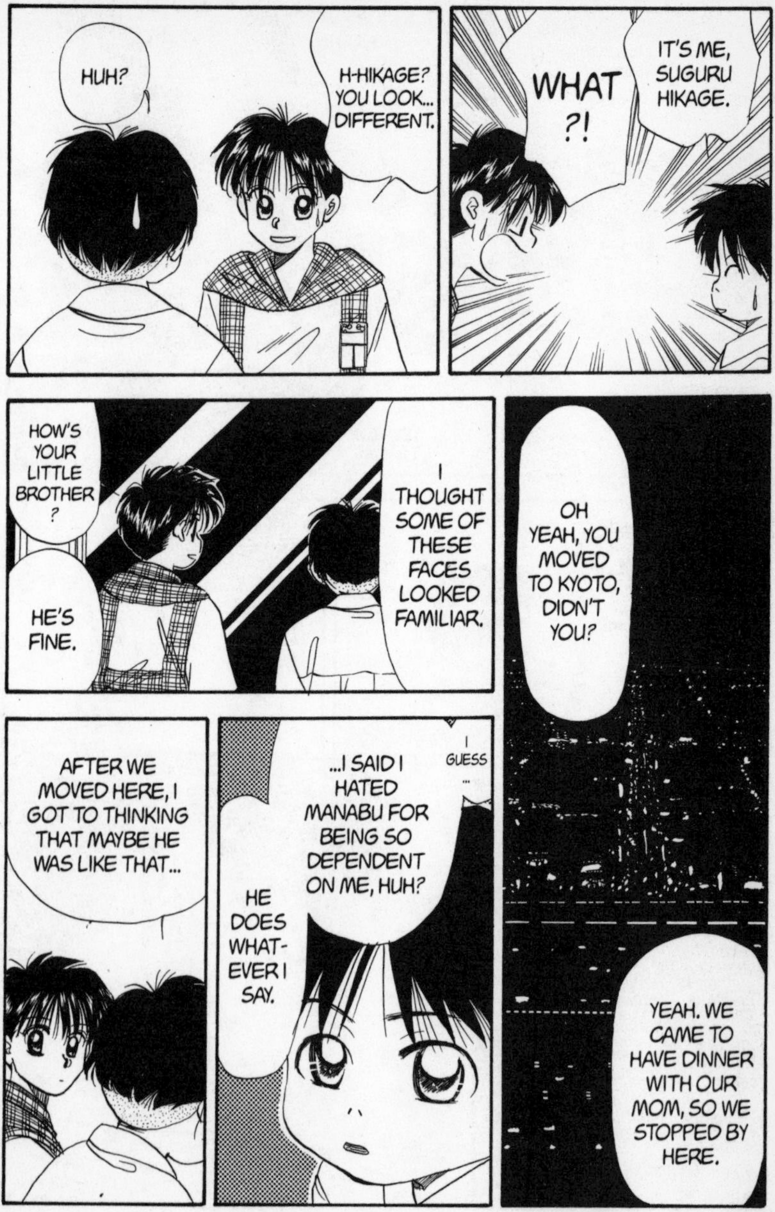
IT'S ME, SUGURU HIKAGE.
WHAT ?!
H-HIKAGE? YOU LOOK... DIFFERENT.
HUH?
OH YEAH, YOU MOVED TO KYOTO, DIDN'T YOU?
YEAH. WE CAME TO HAVE DINNER WITH OUR MOM, SO WE STOPPED BY HERE.
I THOUGHT SOME OF THESE FACES LOOKED FAMILIAR.
HOW'S YOUR LITTLE BROTHER?
HE'S FINE.
I GUESS...
...I SAID I HATED MANABU FOR BEING SO DEPENDENT ON ME, HUH?
HE DOES WHATEVER I SAY.
AFTER WE MOVED HERE, I GOT TO THINKING THAT MAYBE HE WAS LIKE THAT...

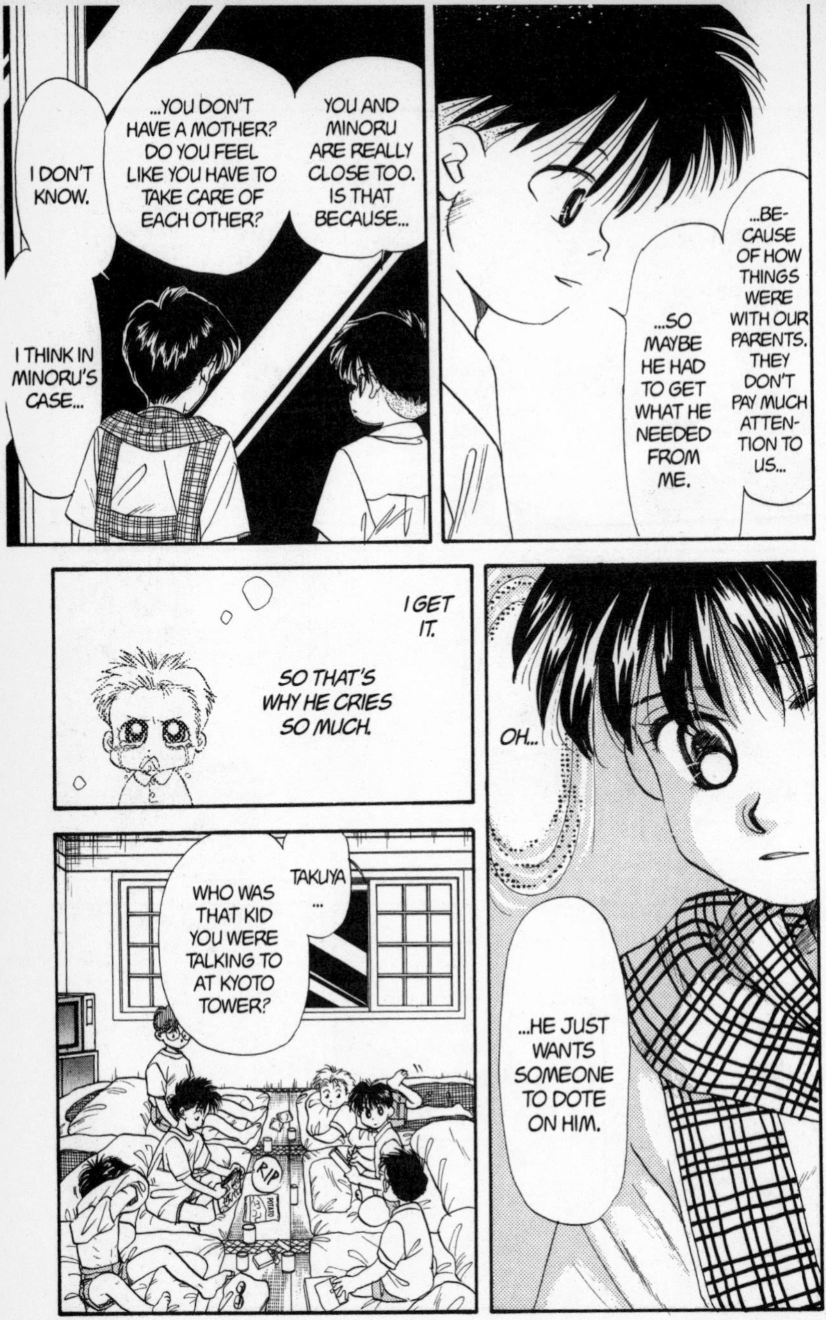
YOU AND MINORU ARE REALLY CLOSE TOO. IS THAT BECAUSE...
...YOU DON'T HAVE A MOTHER? DO YOU FEEL LIKE YOU HAVE TO TAKE CARE OF EACH OTHER?
I DON'T KNOW.
I THINK IN MINORU'S CASE...
...BE-CAUSE OF HOW THINGS WERE WITH OUR PARENTS. THEY DON'T PAY MUCH ATTEN-TION TO US...
...SO MAYBE HE HAD TO GET WHAT HE NEEDED FROM ME.
I GET IT.
SO THAT'S WHY HE CRIES SO MUCH.
OH...
...HE JUST WANTS SOMEONE TO DOTE ON HIM.
TAKUYA...
WHO WAS THAT KID YOU WERE TALKING TO AT KYOTO TOWER?
RIP
POTATO

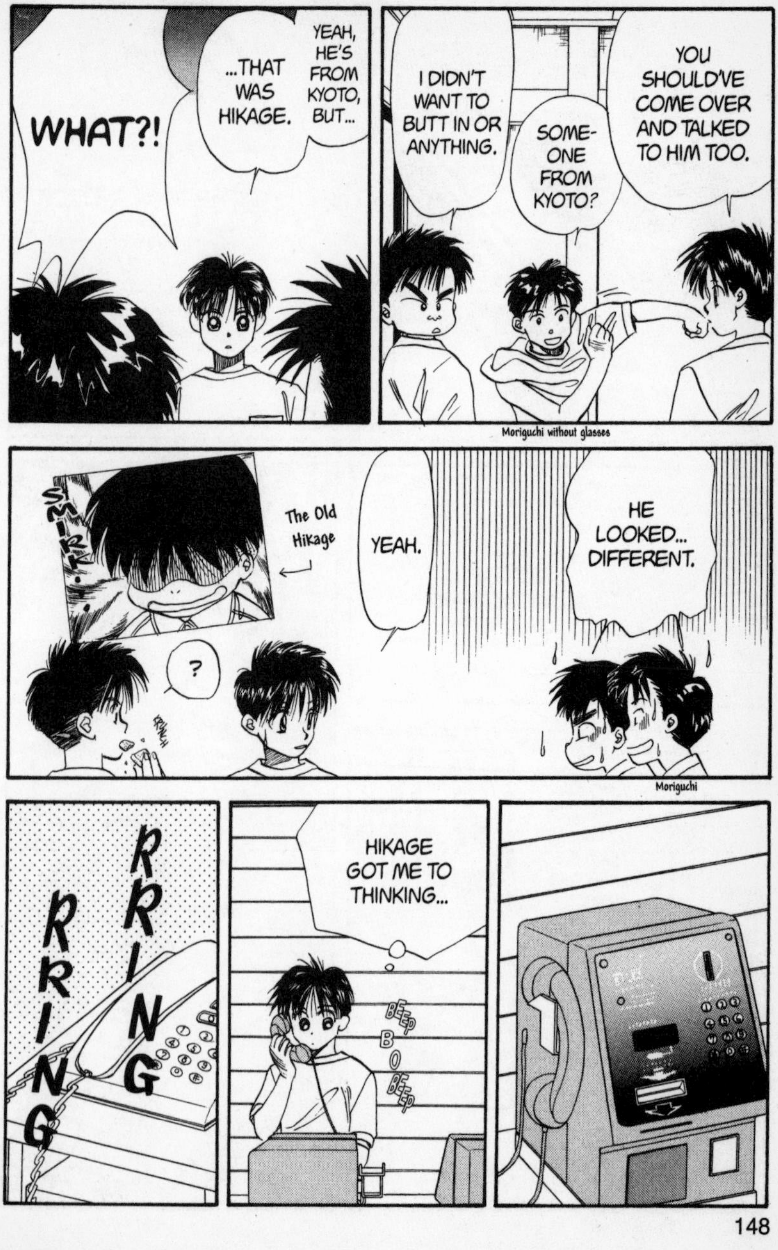
YOU SHOULD'VE COME OVER AND TALKED TO HIM TOO.
SOME-ONE FROM KYOTO?
I DIDN'T WANT TO BUTT IN OR ANYTHING.
Moriguchi without glasses
YEAH, HE'S FROM KYOTO, BUT...
...THAT WAS HIKAGE.
WHAT?!
HE LOOKED... DIFFERENT.
YEAH.
The Old Hikage
SMIRK...
?
KRUNCH
Moriguchi
HIKAGE GOT ME TO THINKING...
BEEP BO BEEP
RRRING
RRRING

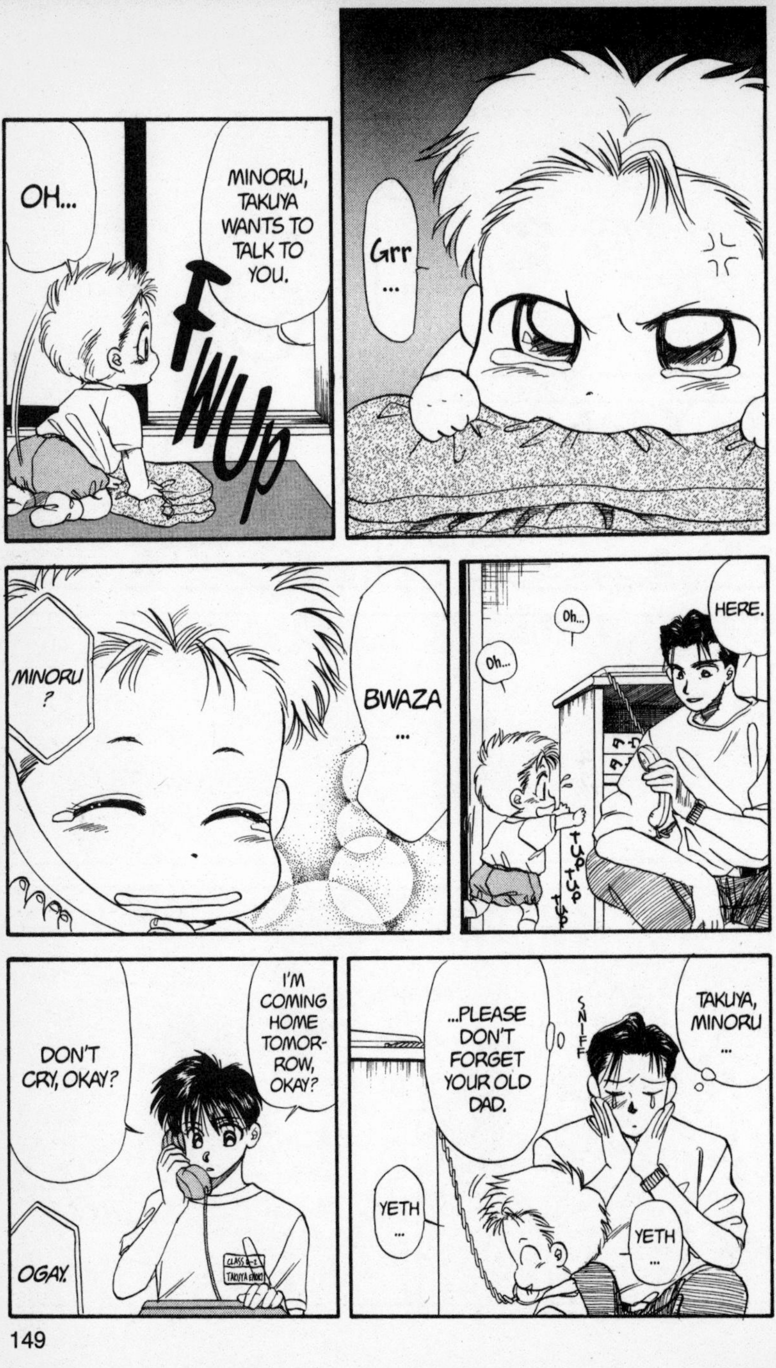
Grr...
MINORU, TAKUYA WANTS TO TALK TO YOU.
OH...
FWUP
HERE.
Oh...
Oh...
TUP TUP TUP
BWAZA...
MINORU?
TAKUYA, MINORU...
SNIFF
...PLEASE DON'T FORGET YOUR OLD DAD.
YETH...
YETH...
I'M COMING HOME TOMORROW, OKAY?
DON'T CRY, OKAY?
OGAY.

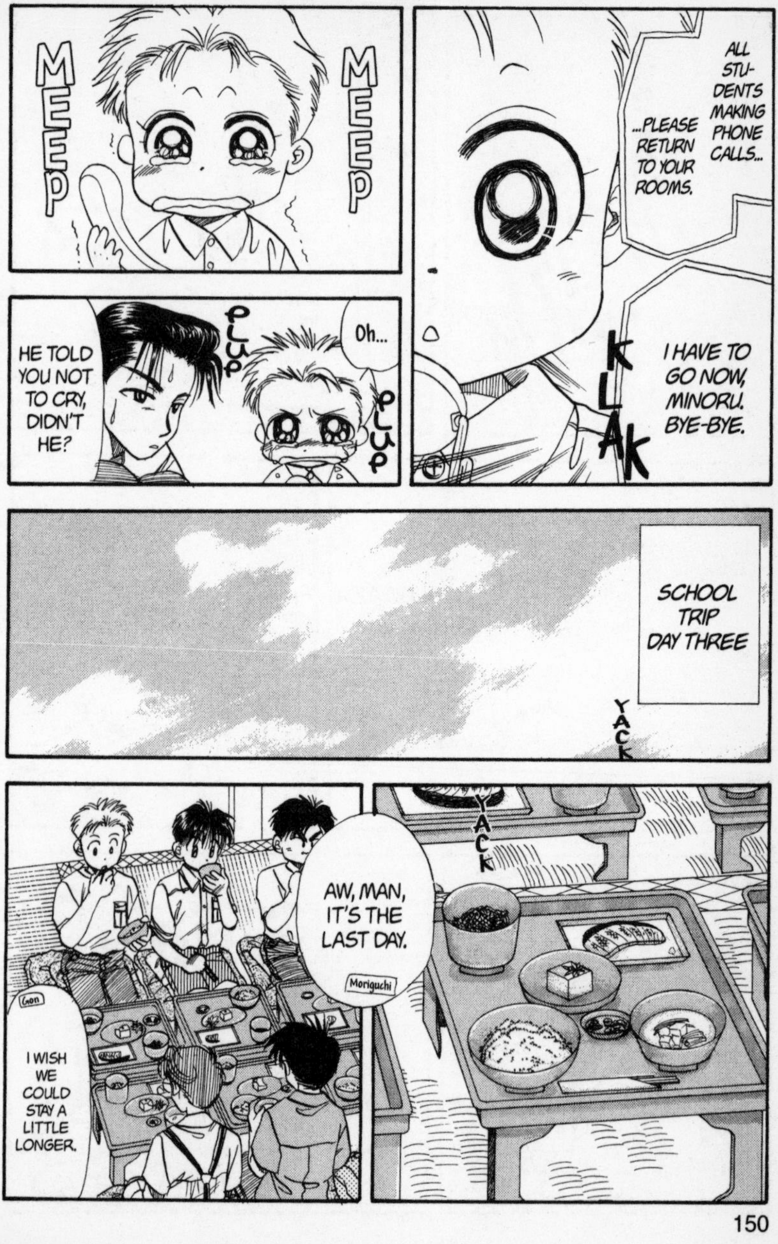
ALL STU-DENTS MAKING PHONE CALLS...
...PLEASE RETURN TO YOUR ROOMS.
KLAK
I HAVE TO GO NOW, MINORU. BYE-BYE.
MEEP
MEEP
Oh...
PLUP
PLUP
HE TOLD YOU NOT TO CRY, DIDN'T HE?
SCHOOL TRIP DAY THREE
YACK
YACK
AW, MAN, IT'S THE LAST DAY.
Moriguchi
Gon
I WISH WE COULD STAY A LITTLE LONGER.

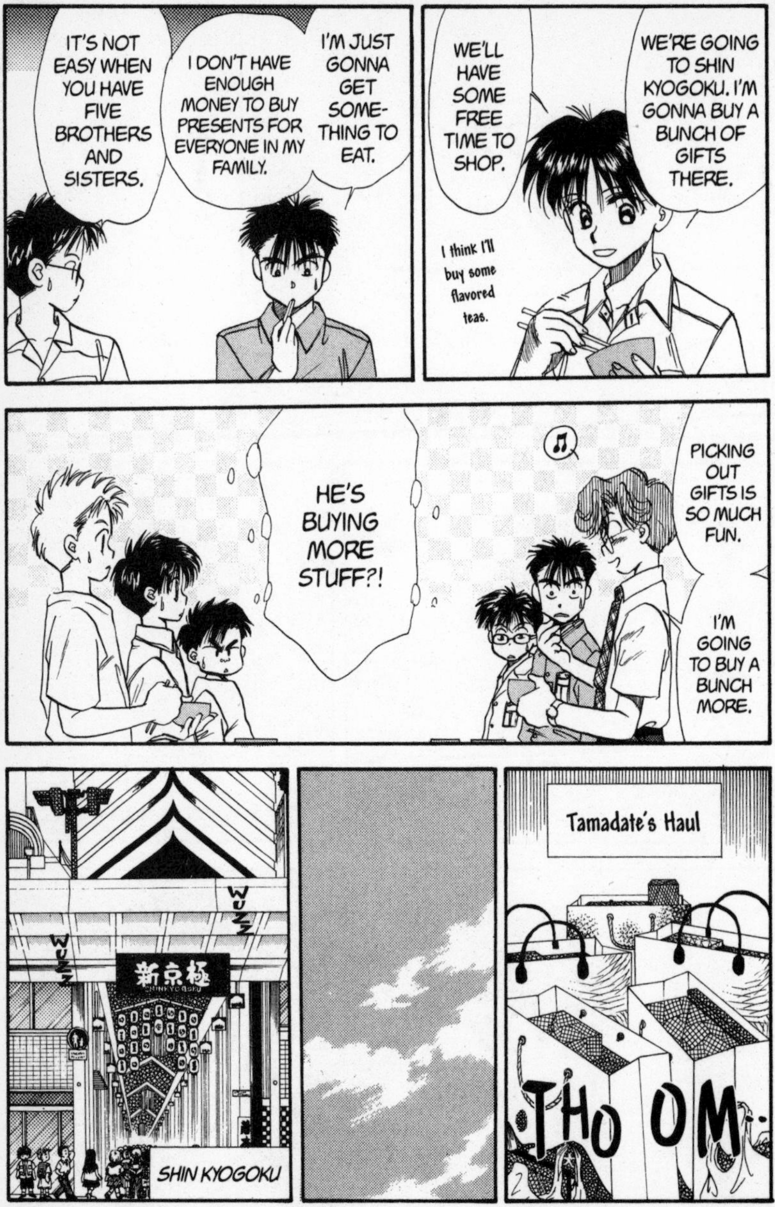
WE'RE GOING TO SHIN KYOGOKU. I'M GONNA BUY A BUNCH OF GIFTS THERE.
WE'LL HAVE SOME FREE TIME TO SHOP.
I think I'll buy some flavored teas.
I'M JUST GONNA GET SOME-THING TO EAT.
I DON'T HAVE ENOUGH MONEY TO BUY PRESENTS FOR EVERYONE IN MY FAMILY.
IT'S NOT EASY WHEN YOU HAVE FIVE BROTHERS AND SISTERS.
PICKING OUT GIFTS IS SO MUCH FUN.
I'M GOING TO BUY A BUNCH MORE.
HE'S BUYING MORE STUFF?!
Tamadate's Haul
THOOM
新京極
WUZZ
WUZZ
SHIN KYOGOKU

WUZZ

WUZZ

BABBLE

BABBLE

GLOOP!

OTO DUMPLINGS
OTO DUMPLINGS
OTO DUMPLINGS

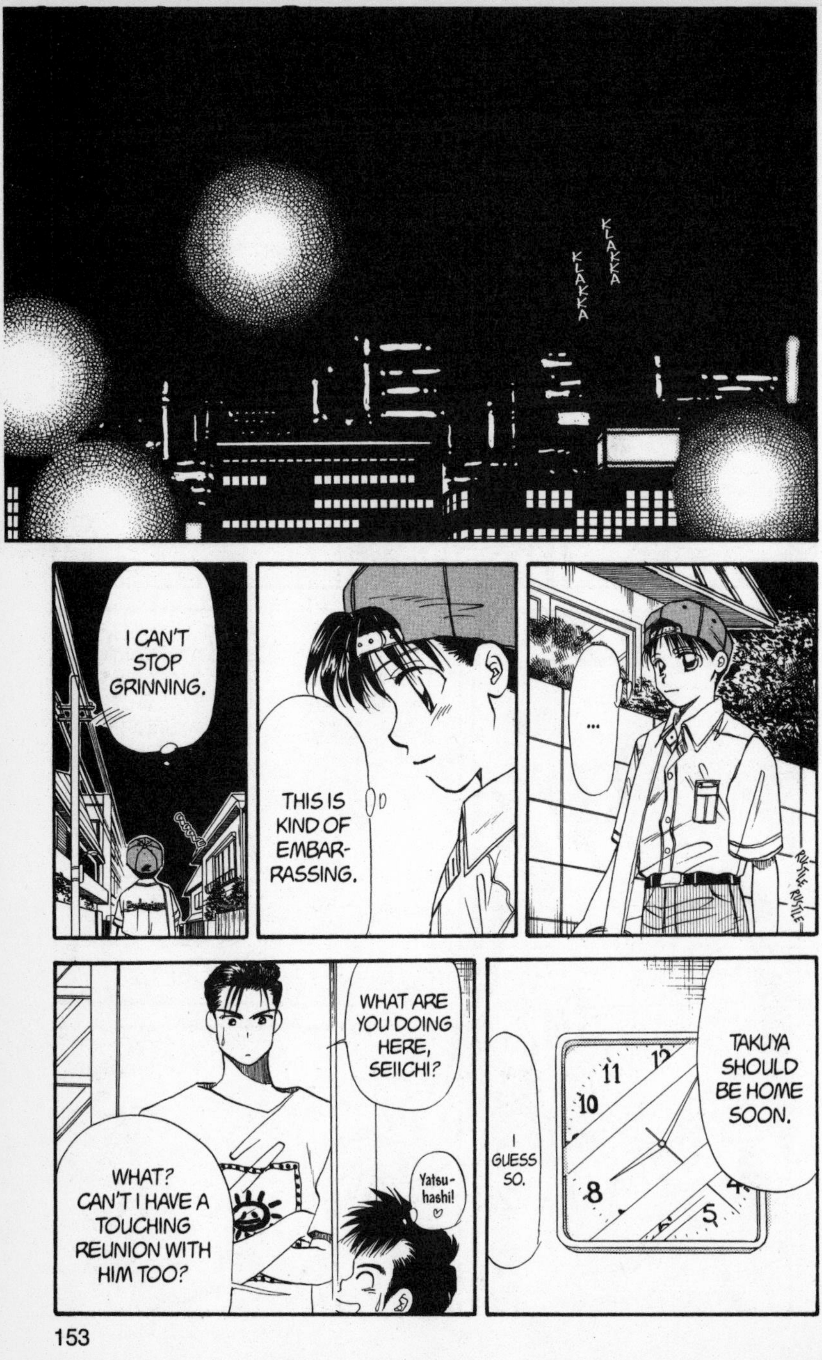
KLAKKA KLAKKA
...
RUSTLE RUSTLE
THIS IS KIND OF EMBAR-RASSING.
I CAN'T STOP GRINNING.
TAKUYA SHOULD BE HOME SOON.
I GUESS SO.
WHAT ARE YOU DOING HERE, SEIICHI?
Yatsu-hashi! ♡
WHAT? CAN'T I HAVE A TOUCHING REUNION WITH HIM TOO?

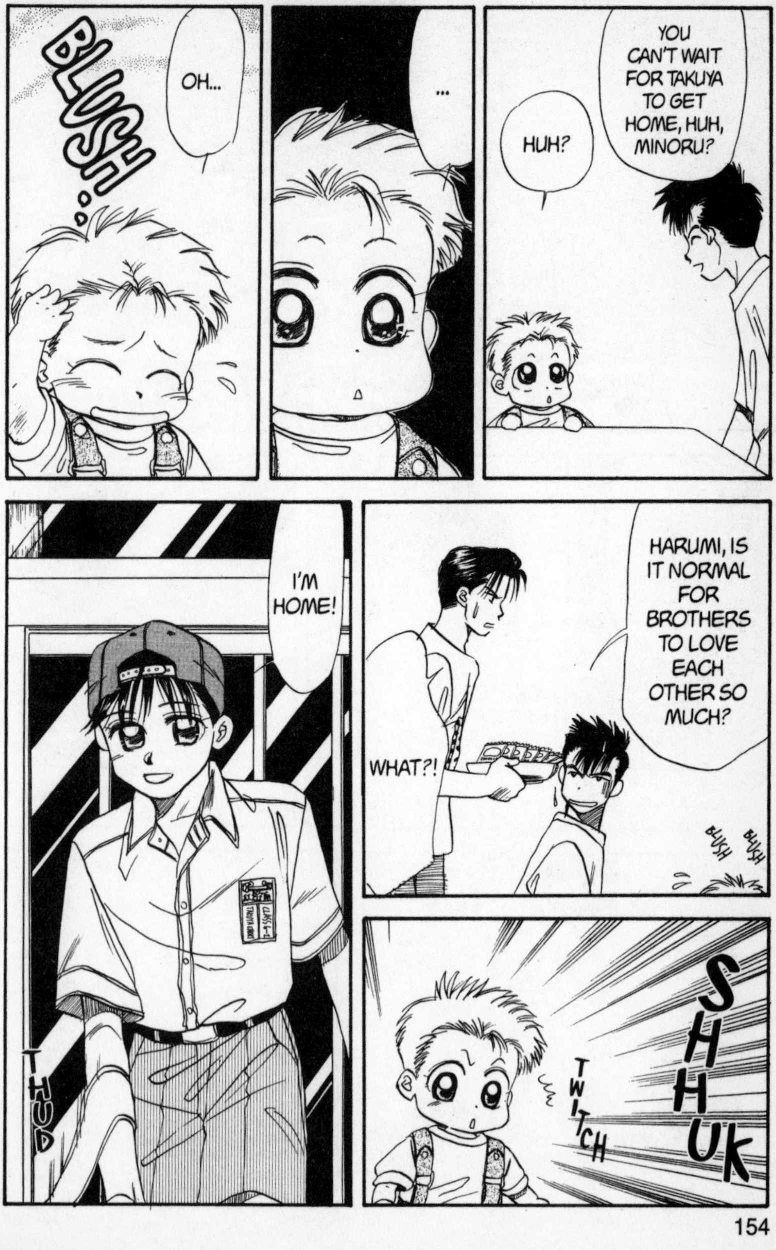
YOU CAN'T WAIT FOR TAKUYA TO GET HOME, HUH, MINORU?
HUH?
...
OH...
BLUSH...
HARUMI, IS IT NORMAL FOR BROTHERS TO LOVE EACH OTHER SO MUCH?
WHAT?!
BLUSH
BLUSH
SHHUK
TWITCH
I'M HOME!
THUD

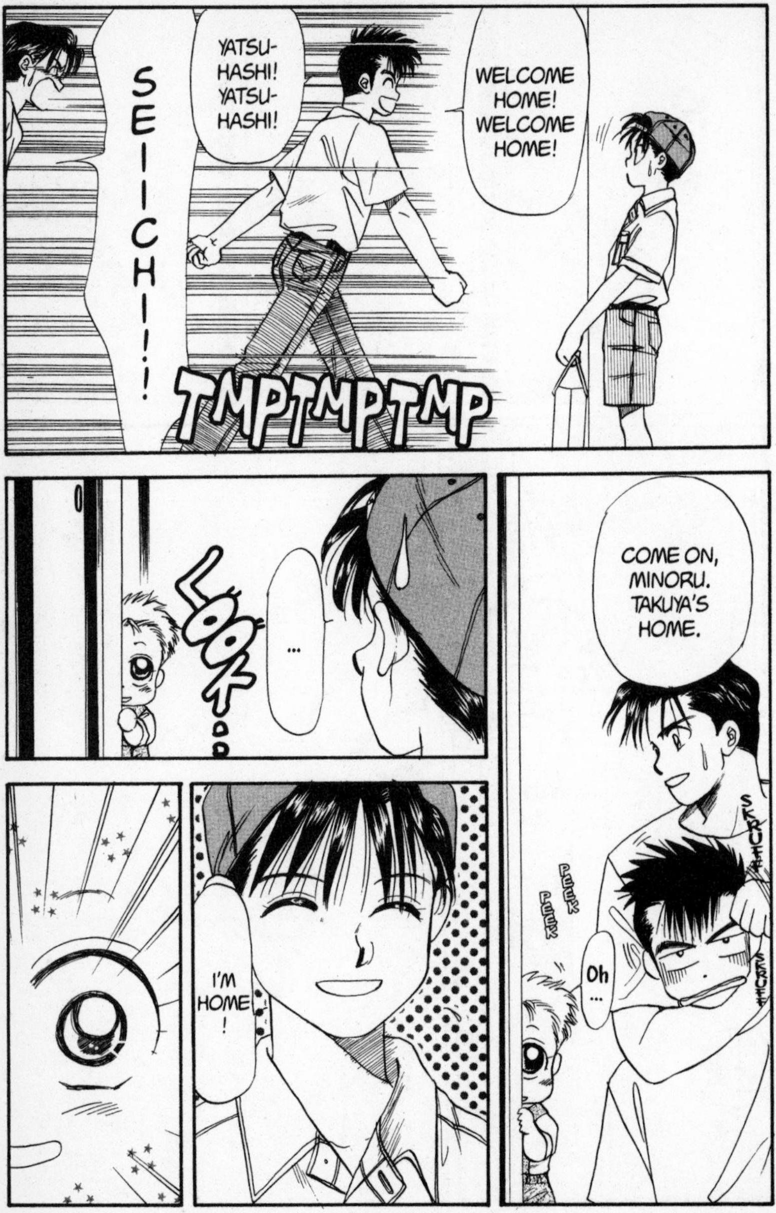
WELCOME HOME! WELCOME HOME!
YATSU-HASHI! YATSU-HASHI!
SEIICHI!!!
TMPTMPTMP
COME ON, MINORU. TAKUYA'S HOME.
SKRUFF
SKRUFF
PEEK PEEK
Oh...
...
LOOK
I'M HOME!

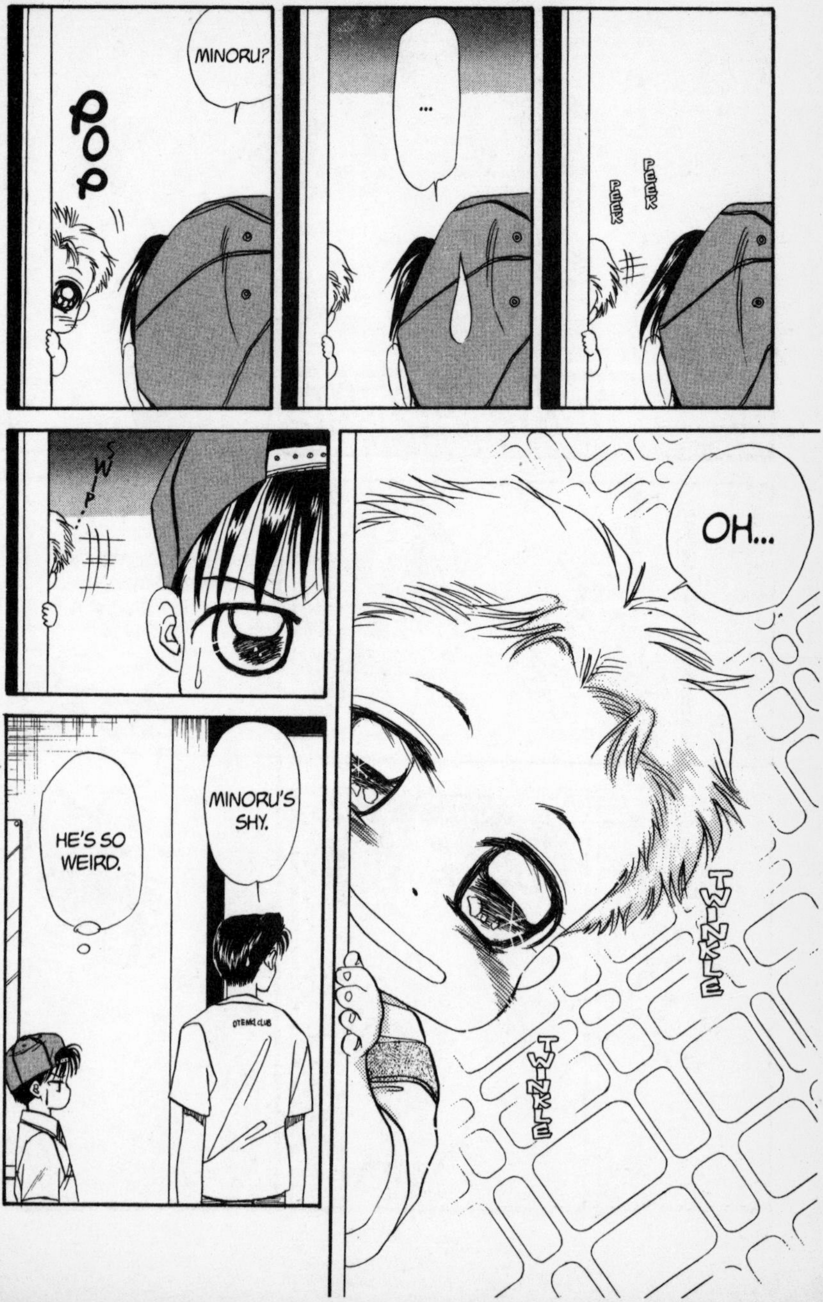
PEEK
PEEK
...
MINORU?
POP
OH...
TWINKLE
TWINKLE
SWIP...
MINORU'S SHY.
HE'S SO WEIRD.
OTENKI CLUB

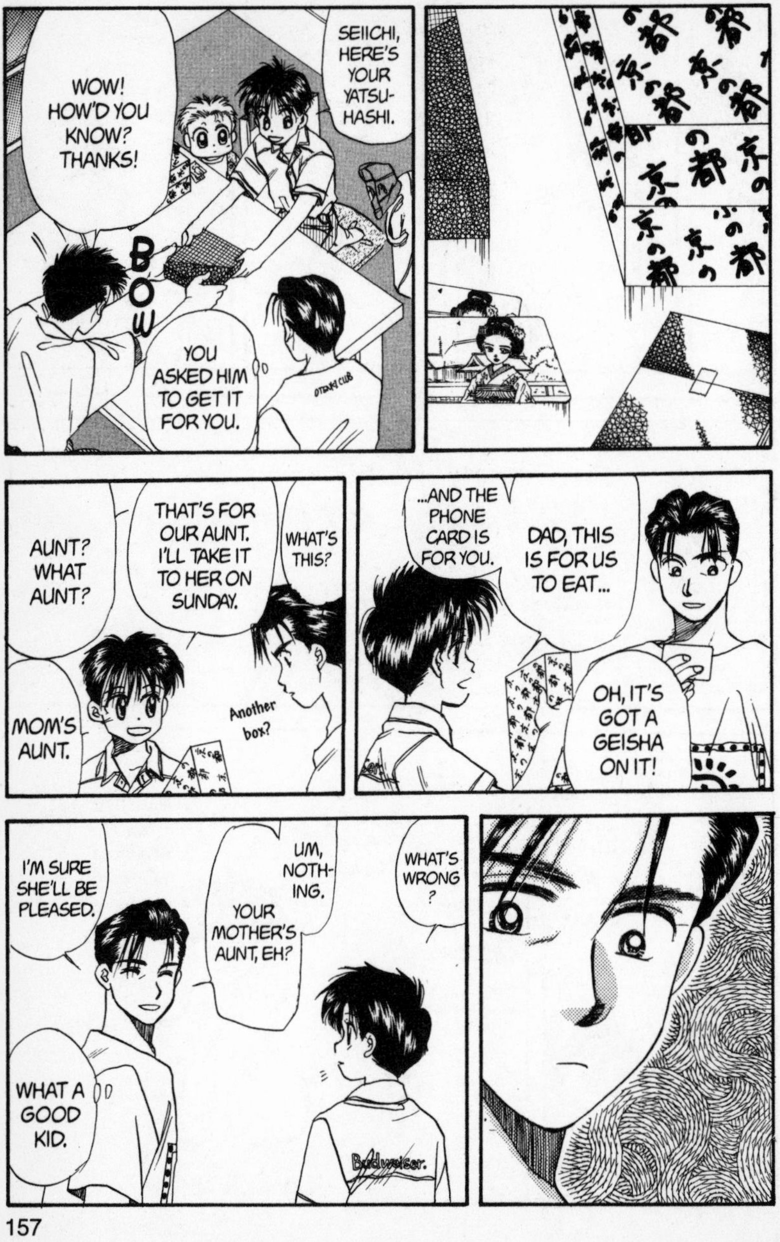
SEIICHI, HERE'S YOUR YATSU-HASHI.
WOW! HOW'D YOU KNOW? THANKS!
BOW
YOU ASKED HIM TO GET IT FOR YOU.
DAD, THIS IS FOR US TO EAT...
...AND THE PHONE CARD IS FOR YOU.
OH, IT'S GOT A GEISHA ON IT!
WHAT'S THIS?
THAT'S FOR OUR AUNT. I'LL TAKE IT TO HER ON SUNDAY.
Another box?
AUNT? WHAT AUNT?
MOM'S AUNT.
WHAT'S WRONG?
UM, NOTHING.
YOUR MOTHER'S AUNT, EH?
I'M SURE SHE'LL BE PLEASED.
WHAT A GOOD KID.

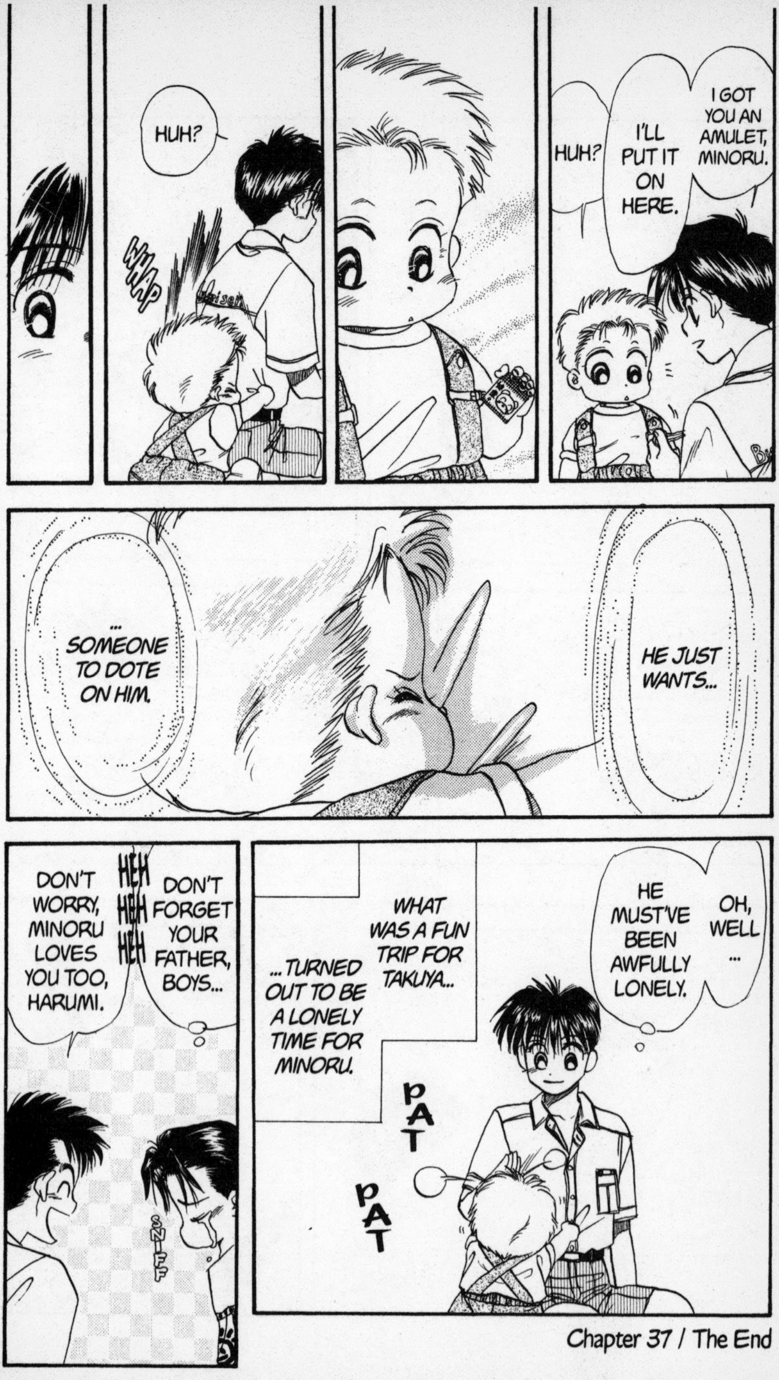
I GOT YOU AN AMULET, MINORU.
I'LL PUT IT ON HERE.
HUH?
HUH?
WHAP
HE JUST WANTS...
... SOMEONE TO DOTE ON HIM.
OH, WELL ...
HE MUST'VE BEEN AWFULLY LONELY.
WHAT WAS A FUN TRIP FOR TAKUYA...
...TURNED OUT TO BE A LONELY TIME FOR MINORU.
PAT
PAT
DON'T FORGET YOUR FATHER, BOYS...
HEH HEH HEH
DON'T WORRY, MINORU LOVES YOU TOO, HARUMI.
SNIFF

Chapter 37 / The End

Baby & Me

Chapter 38

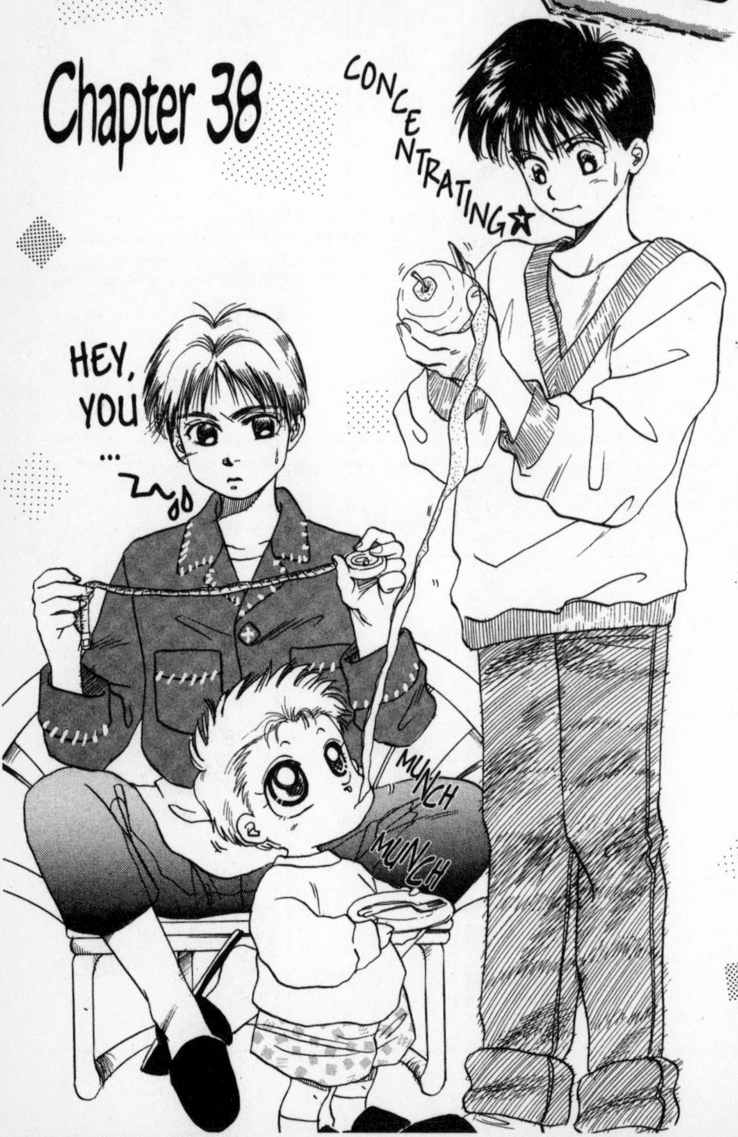
CONCENTRATING☆
HEY, YOU...
MUNCH
MUNCH

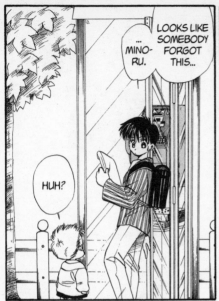

PHONE DIRE
LOOKS LIKE SOMEBODY FORGOT THIS...
... MINO-RU.
HUH?
SHOULD I TAKE IT TO THE POLICE? MAYBE SOMEONE WILL COME BACK FOR IT IF I WAIT HERE.
MAYBE THERE'S A PHONE NUMBER OR SOMETHING INSIDE...
RUSTLE...
OH!
IT IS THE YEAR 2356
IT'S A COMIC!!

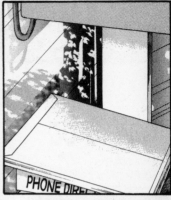

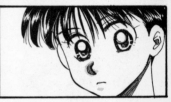

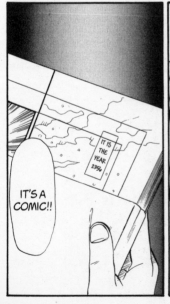

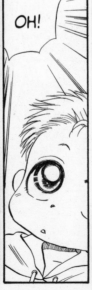

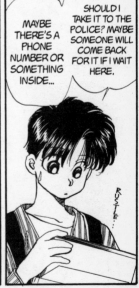

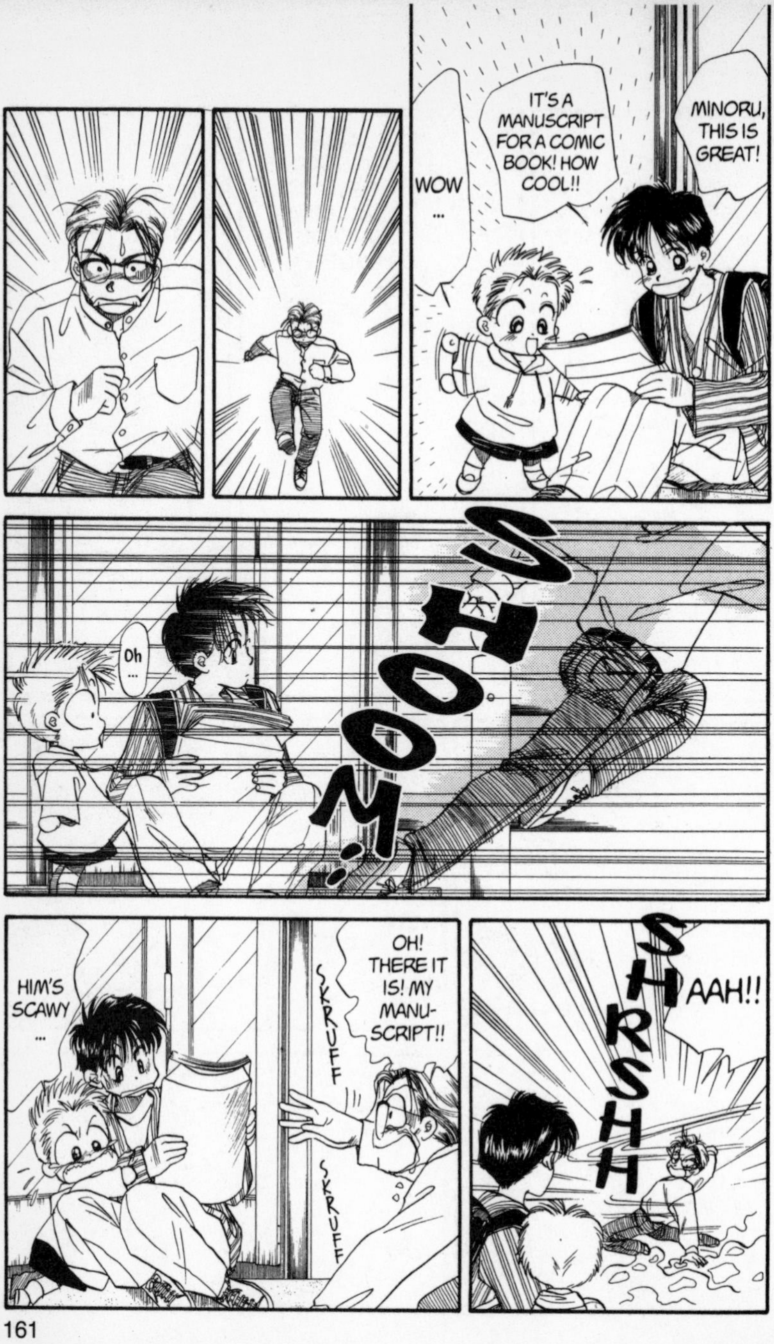
MINORU, THIS IS GREAT!
IT'S A MANUSCRIPT FOR A COMIC BOOK! HOW COOL!!
WOW ...
SHOOOM!
Oh ...
AAH!!
SHRSHH
OH! THERE IT IS! MY MANU-SCRIPT!!
SKRUFF
SKRUFF
HIM'S SCAWY ...

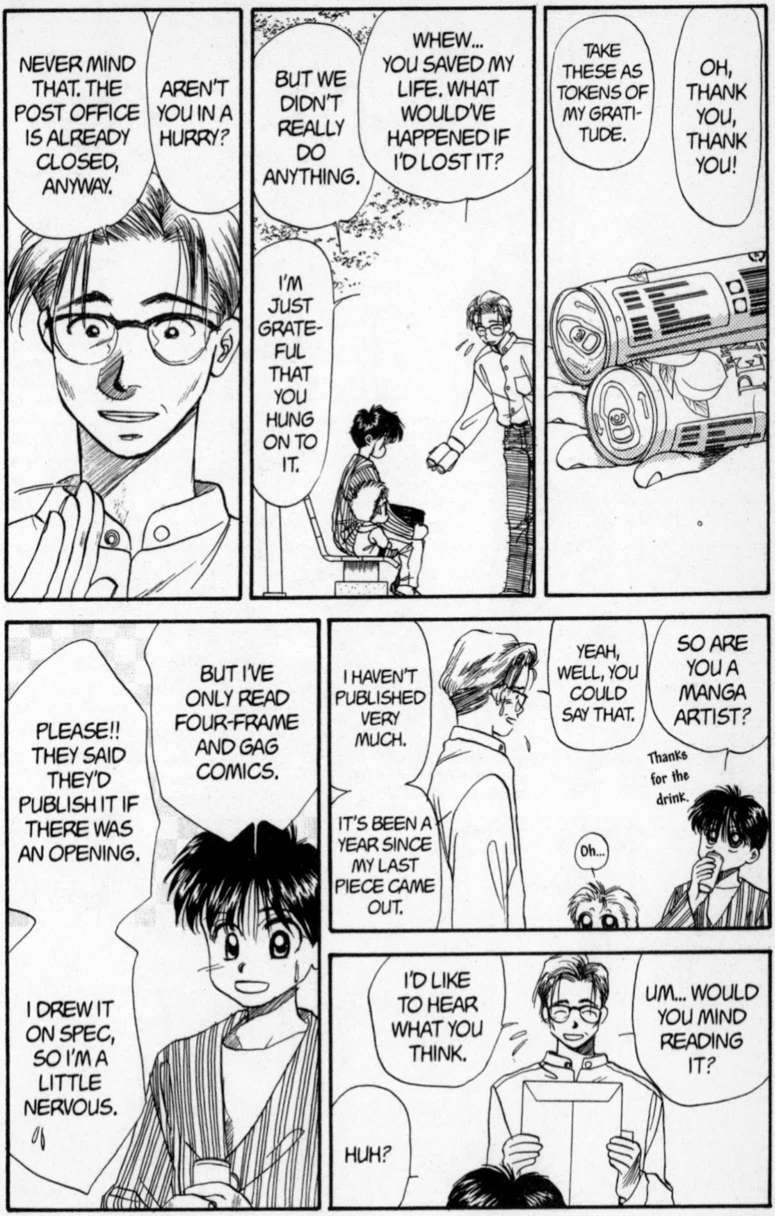
OH, THANK YOU, THANK YOU!
TAKE THESE AS TOKENS OF MY GRATITUDE.
WHEW... YOU SAVED MY LIFE. WHAT WOULD'VE HAPPENED IF I'D LOST IT?
BUT WE DIDN'T REALLY DO ANYTHING.
I'M JUST GRATEFUL THAT YOU HUNG ON TO IT.
AREN'T YOU IN A HURRY?
NEVER MIND THAT. THE POST OFFICE IS ALREADY CLOSED, ANYWAY.
SO ARE YOU A MANGA ARTIST?
Thanks for the drink.
YEAH, WELL, YOU COULD SAY THAT.
Oh...
I HAVEN'T PUBLISHED VERY MUCH.
IT'S BEEN A YEAR SINCE MY LAST PIECE CAME OUT.
UM... WOULD YOU MIND READING IT?
I'D LIKE TO HEAR WHAT YOU THINK.
HUH?
BUT I'VE ONLY READ FOUR-FRAME AND GAG COMICS.
PLEASE!! THEY SAID THEY'D PUBLISH IT IF THERE WAS AN OPENING.
I DREW IT ON SPEC, SO I'M A LITTLE NERVOUS.

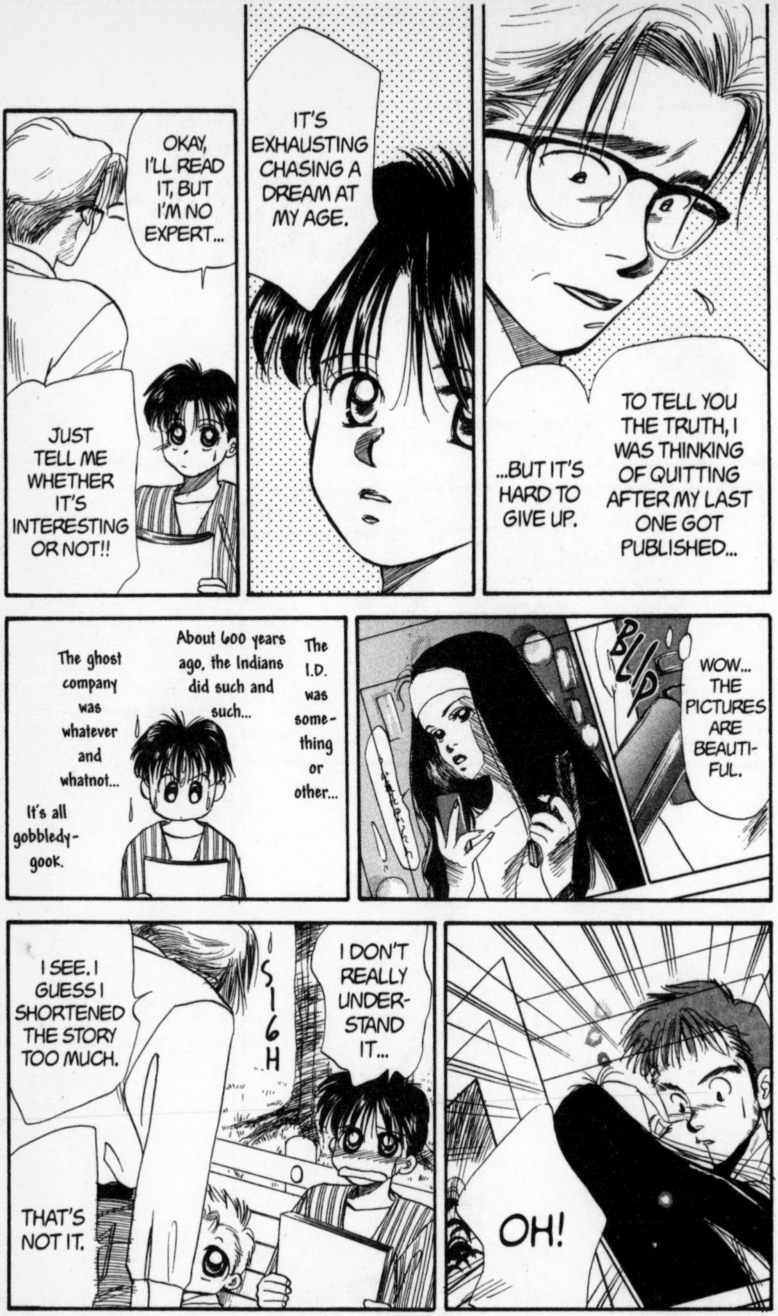
TO TELL YOU THE TRUTH, I WAS THINKING OF QUITTING AFTER MY LAST ONE GOT PUBLISHED...
...BUT IT'S HARD TO GIVE UP.
IT'S EXHAUSTING CHASING A DREAM AT MY AGE.
OKAY, I'LL READ IT, BUT I'M NO EXPERT...
JUST TELL ME WHETHER IT'S INTERESTING OR NOT!!
BLIP
WOW... THE PICTURES ARE BEAUTIFUL.
The I.D. was something or other...
About 600 years ago, the Indians did such and such...
The ghost company was whatever and whatnot...
It's all gobbledygook.
OH!
I DON'T REALLY UNDERSTAND IT...
SIGH
I SEE. I GUESS I SHORTENED THE STORY TOO MUCH.
THAT'S NOT IT.

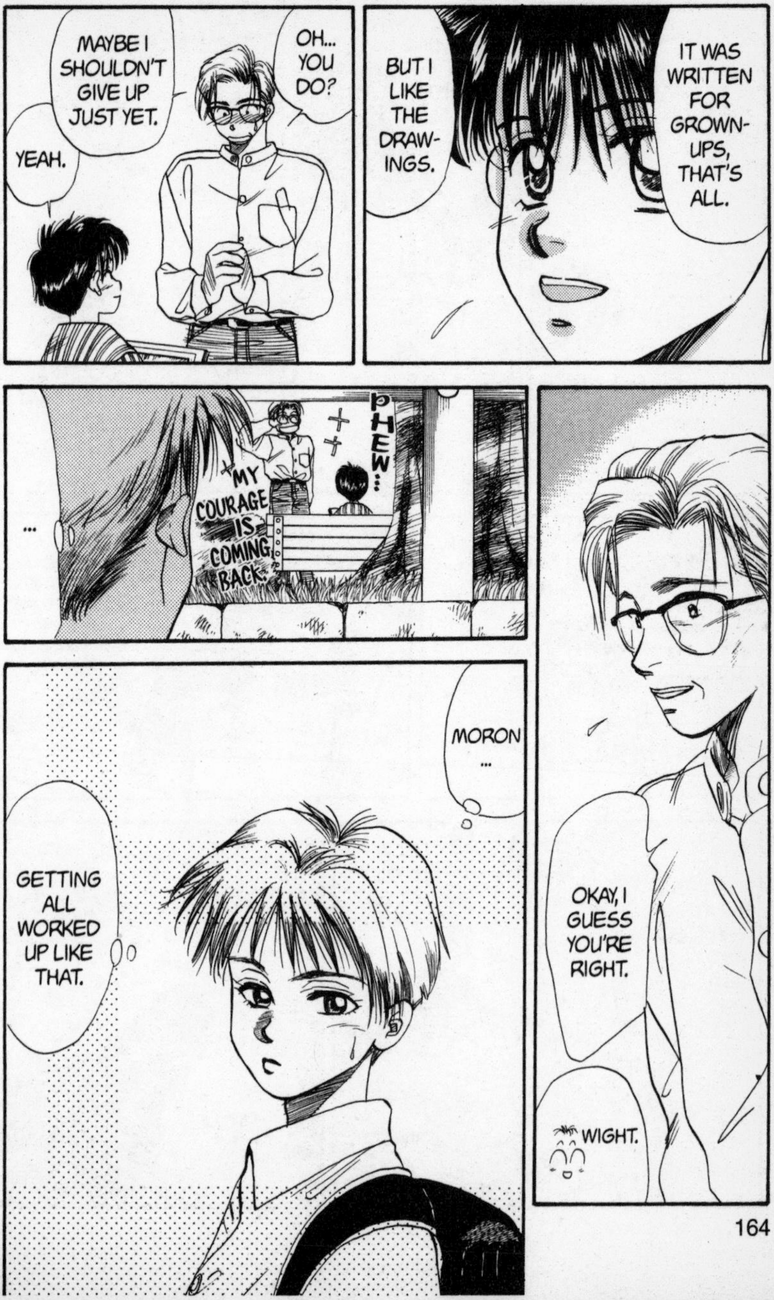
IT WAS WRITTEN FOR GROWN-UPS, THAT'S ALL.
BUT I LIKE THE DRAWINGS.
OH... YOU DO?
MAYBE I SHOULDN'T GIVE UP JUST YET.
YEAH.
OKAY, I GUESS YOU'RE RIGHT.
WIGHT.
PHEW...
MY COURAGE IS COMING BACK.
...
MORON ...
GETTING ALL WORKED UP LIKE THAT.

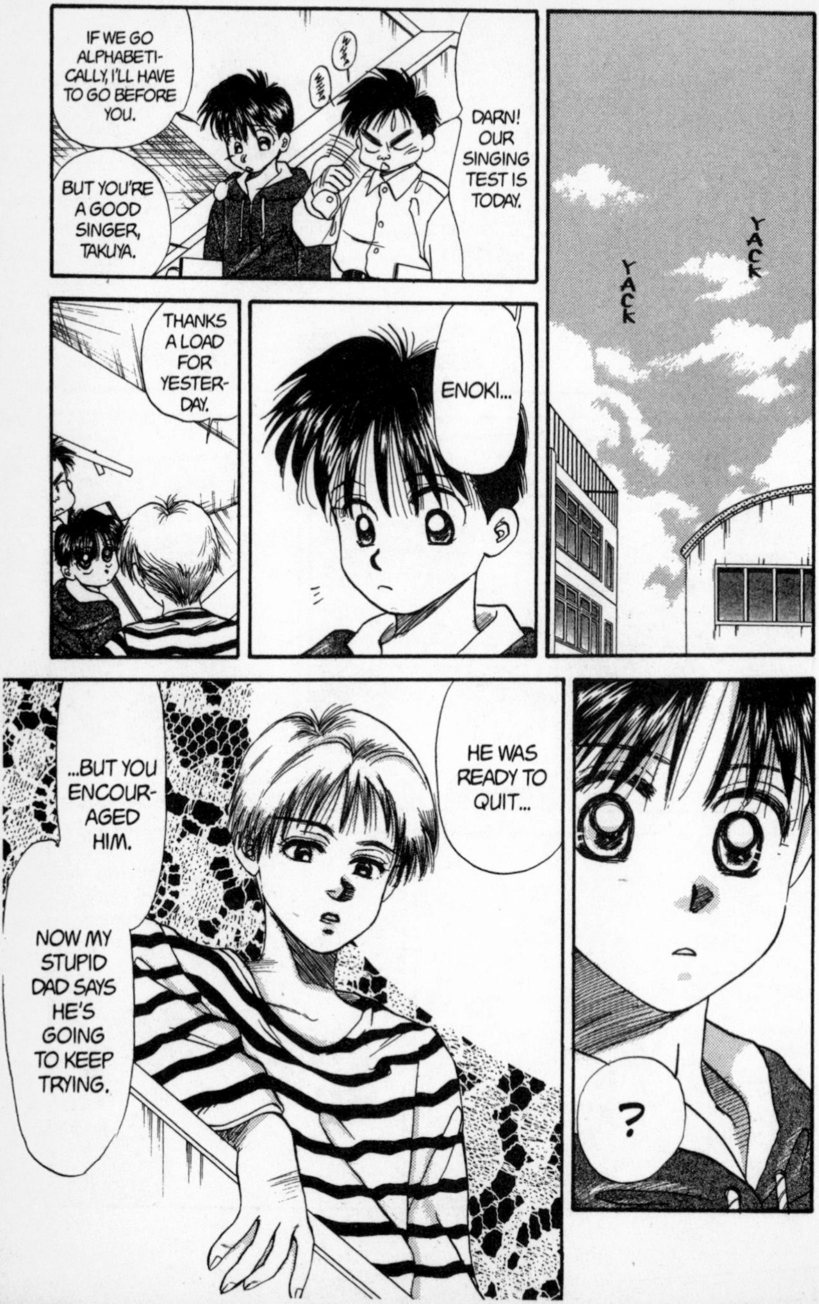
YACK
YACK
DARN! OUR SINGING TEST IS TODAY.
IF WE GO ALPHABETICALLY, I'LL HAVE TO GO BEFORE YOU.
BUT YOU'RE A GOOD SINGER, TAKUYA.
ENOKI...
THANKS A LOAD FOR YESTERDAY.
?
HE WAS READY TO QUIT...
...BUT YOU ENCOURAGED HIM.
NOW MY STUPID DAD SAYS HE'S GOING TO KEEP TRYING.

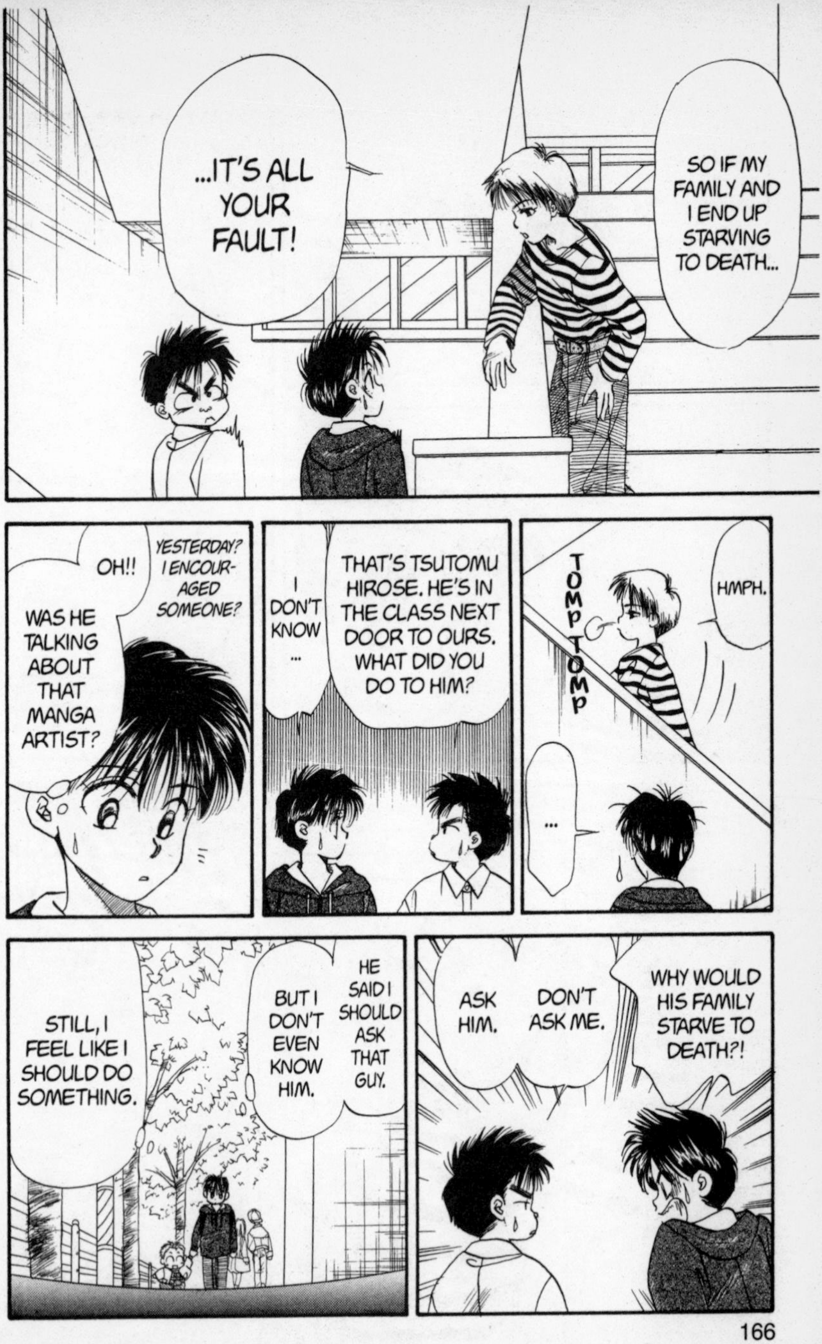
SO IF MY FAMILY AND I END UP STARVING TO DEATH...
...IT'S ALL YOUR FAULT!
HMPH.
TOMP TOMP
...
THAT'S TSUTOMU HIROSE. HE'S IN THE CLASS NEXT DOOR TO OURS. WHAT DID YOU DO TO HIM?
I DON'T KNOW ...
YESTERDAY? I ENCOURAGED SOMEONE?
OH!!
WAS HE TALKING ABOUT THAT MANGA ARTIST?
WHY WOULD HIS FAMILY STARVE TO DEATH?!
DON'T ASK ME.
ASK HIM.
HE SAID I SHOULD ASK THAT GUY.
BUT I DON'T EVEN KNOW HIM.
STILL, I FEEL LIKE I SHOULD DO SOMETHING.

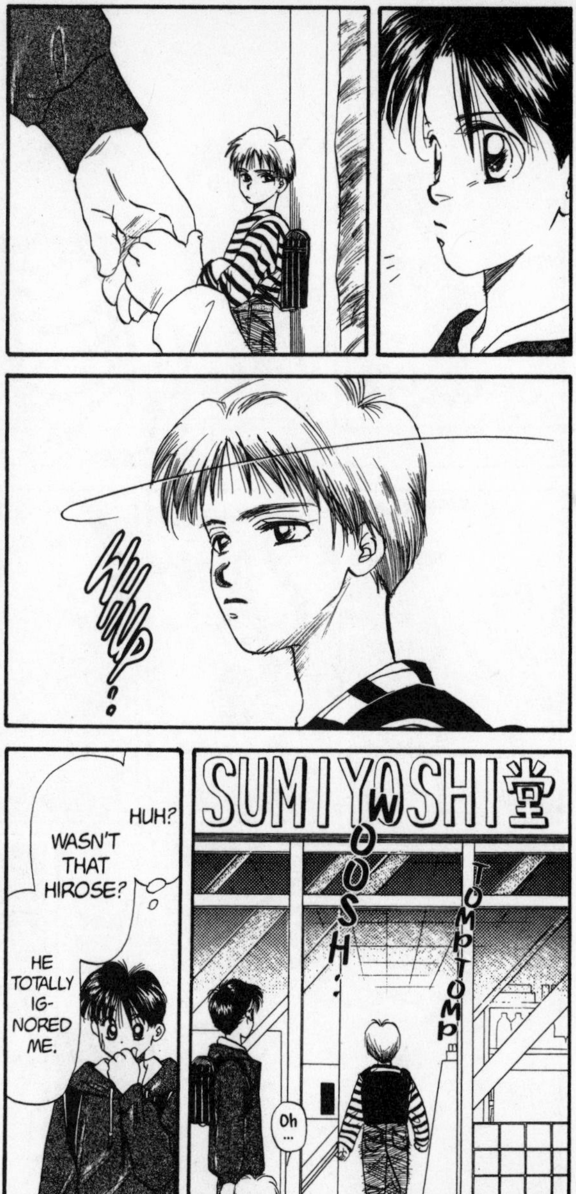
WHUP!!
SUMIYOSHI 堂
WOOSH!
TOMPTOMP
Oh...
HUH?
WASN'T THAT HIROSE?
HE TOTALLY IG-NORED ME.

Author's Note Part 6

Sigh...Uh-oh, I have nothing to write today. The biggest request I get is for profiles of my characters, but since Takuya is still growing, his height and weight are always changing. Minoru's even more difficult.

Minoru from behind

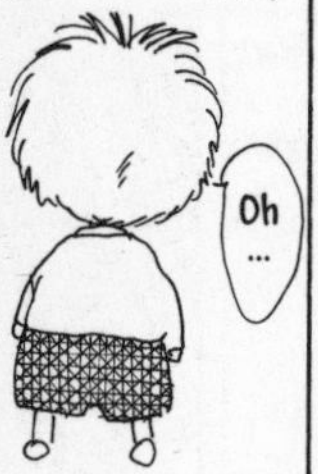
Oh...

Thank you very much for reading Volume 7. See you again in Volume 8!♡

Goodbye.
Marimo

P.S. It seems the Shin Kyogoku Arcade is only decorated the way it was in the school trip story during the Gion Festival. I didn't know that!!

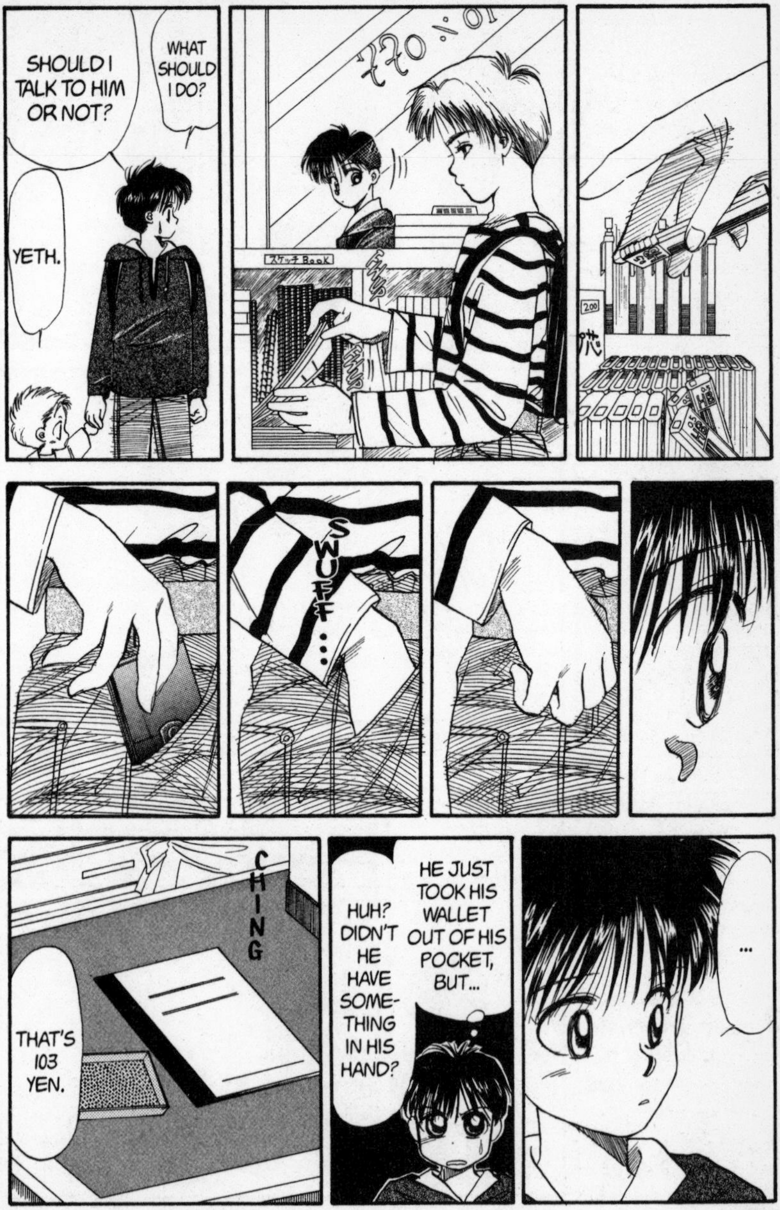
200
スケッチ Book
WHAT SHOULD I DO?
SHOULD I TALK TO HIM OR NOT?
YETH.
SWUFF...
...
HE JUST TOOK HIS WALLET OUT OF HIS POCKET, BUT...
HUH? DIDN'T HE HAVE SOME-THING IN HIS HAND?
CHING
THAT'S 103 YEN.

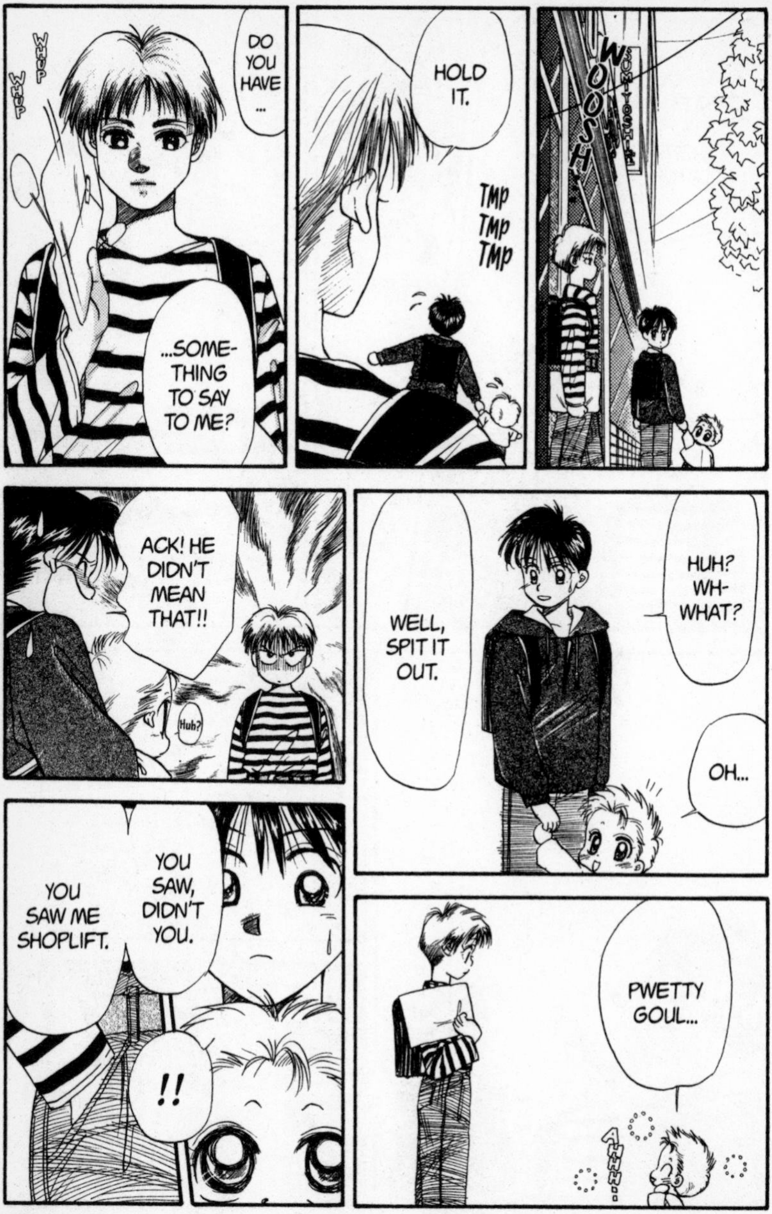
WOOSH
SUMIYOSHI
HOLD IT.
TMP TMP TMP
WHUP WHUP
DO YOU HAVE ...
...SOME-THING TO SAY TO ME?
HUH? WH-WHAT?
WELL, SPIT IT OUT.
OH...
ACK! HE DIDN'T MEAN THAT!!
Huh?
PWETTY GOUL...
AHHH!!
YOU SAW, DIDN'T YOU.
YOU SAW ME SHOPLIFT.
!!

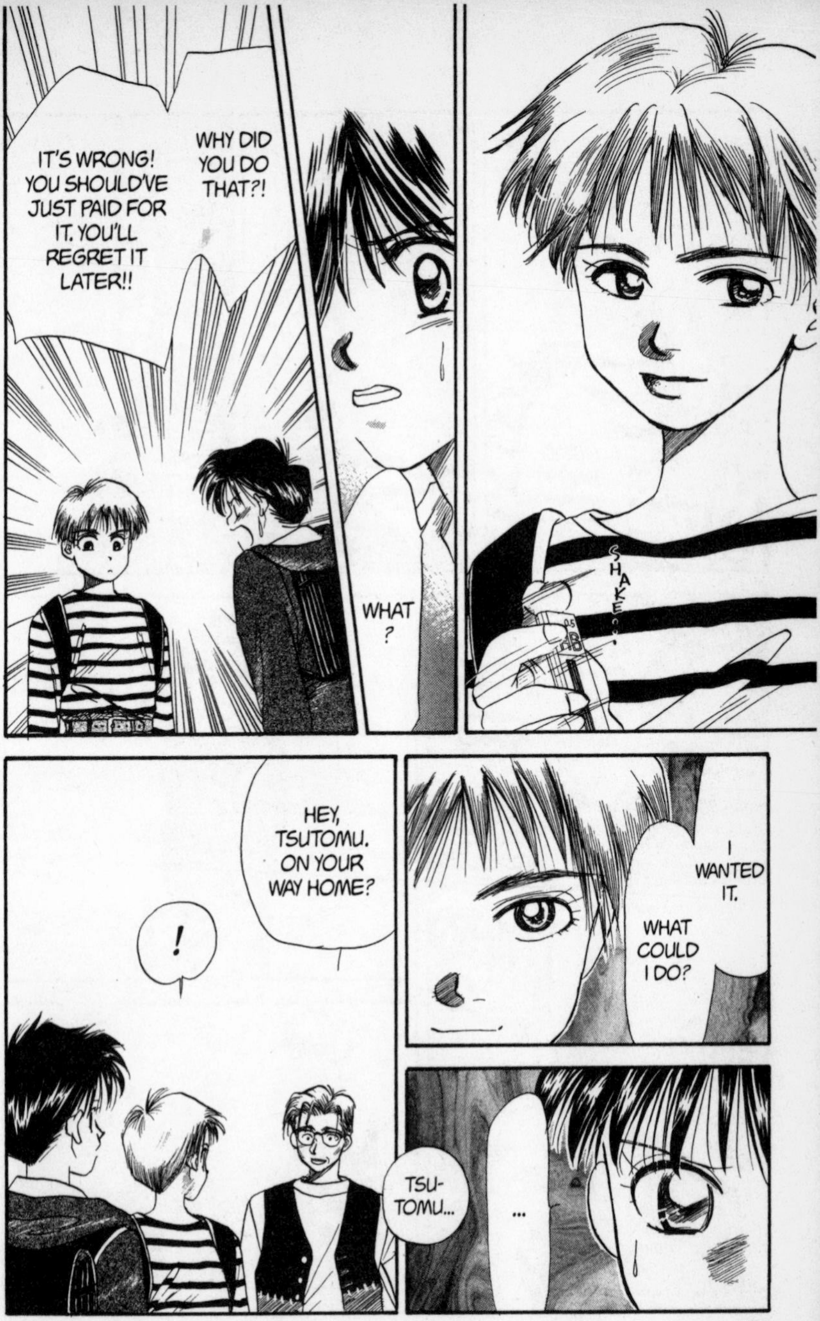
SHAKE...
WHAT ?
WHY DID YOU DO THAT?!
IT'S WRONG! YOU SHOULD'VE JUST PAID FOR IT. YOU'LL REGRET IT LATER!!
I WANTED IT.
WHAT COULD I DO?
...
TSU-TOMU...
HEY, TSUTOMU. ON YOUR WAY HOME?
!

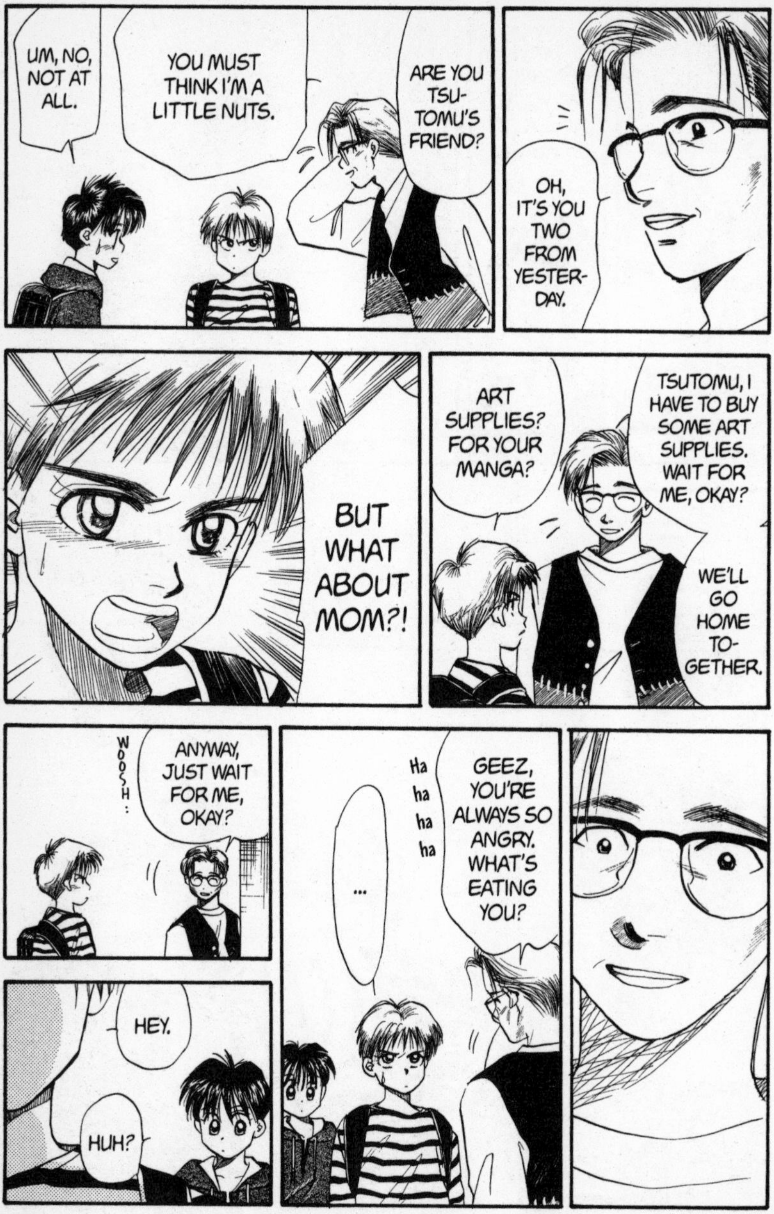
OH, IT'S YOU TWO FROM YESTER-DAY.
ARE YOU TSU-TOMU'S FRIEND?
YOU MUST THINK I'M A LITTLE NUTS.
UM, NO, NOT AT ALL.
TSUTOMU, I HAVE TO BUY SOME ART SUPPLIES. WAIT FOR ME, OKAY?
WE'LL GO HOME TO-GETHER.
ART SUPPLIES? FOR YOUR MANGA?
BUT WHAT ABOUT MOM?!
Ha ha ha ha
GEEZ, YOU'RE ALWAYS SO ANGRY. WHAT'S EATING YOU?
...
ANYWAY, JUST WAIT FOR ME, OKAY?
WOOSH...
HEY.
HUH?

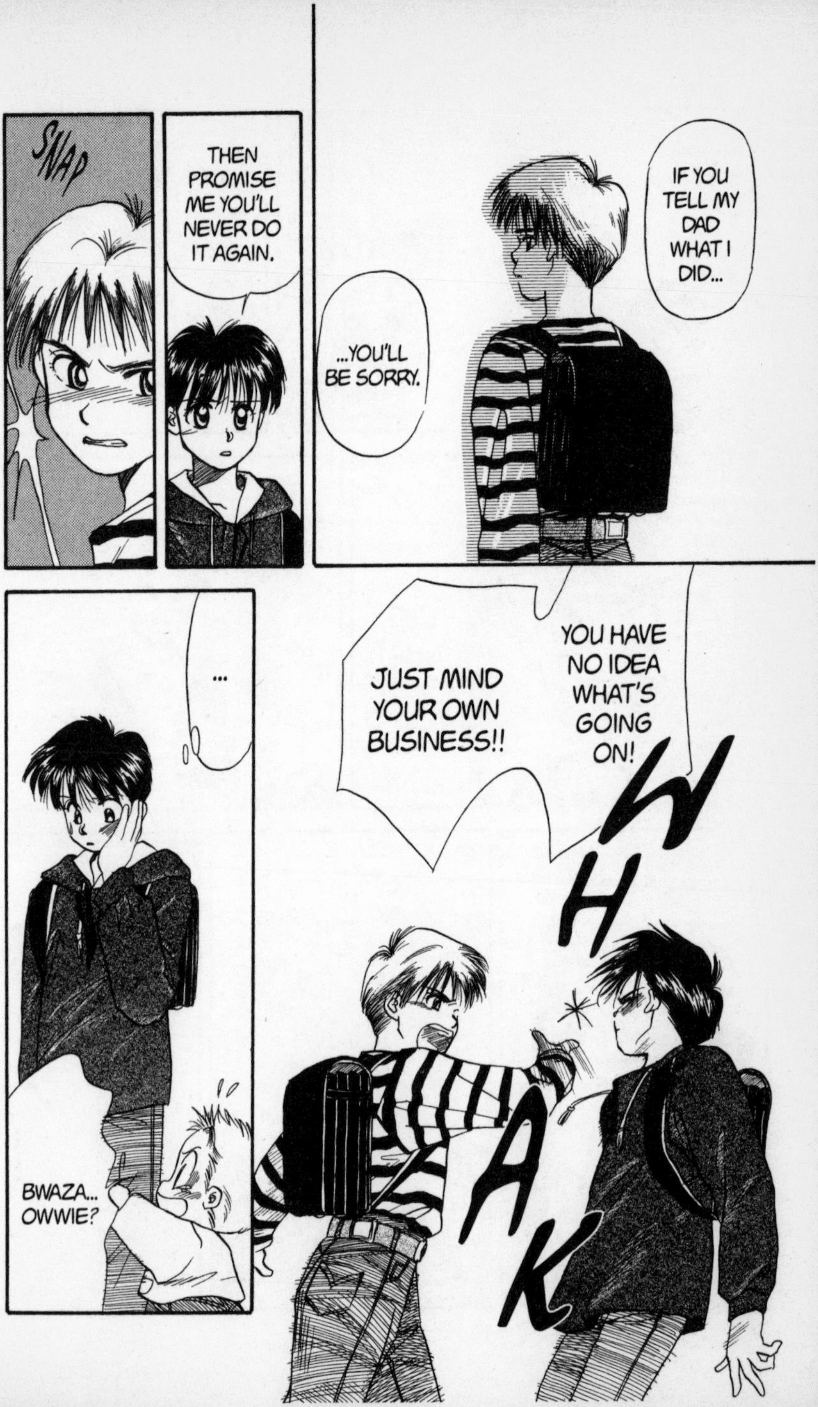
IF YOU TELL MY DAD WHAT I DID...
...YOU'LL BE SORRY.
THEN PROMISE ME YOU'LL NEVER DO IT AGAIN.
SNAP
YOU HAVE NO IDEA WHAT'S GOING ON!
JUST MIND YOUR OWN BUSINESS!!
WHAK
...
BWAZA... OWWIE?

UGH!

THNAK

OH!

OWWIE, OWWIE, GO 'WAY...

...

HUH? WHERE'S TSUTOMU? DID HE GO HOME?

...GEEZ...

OH...

TOMP

OH!

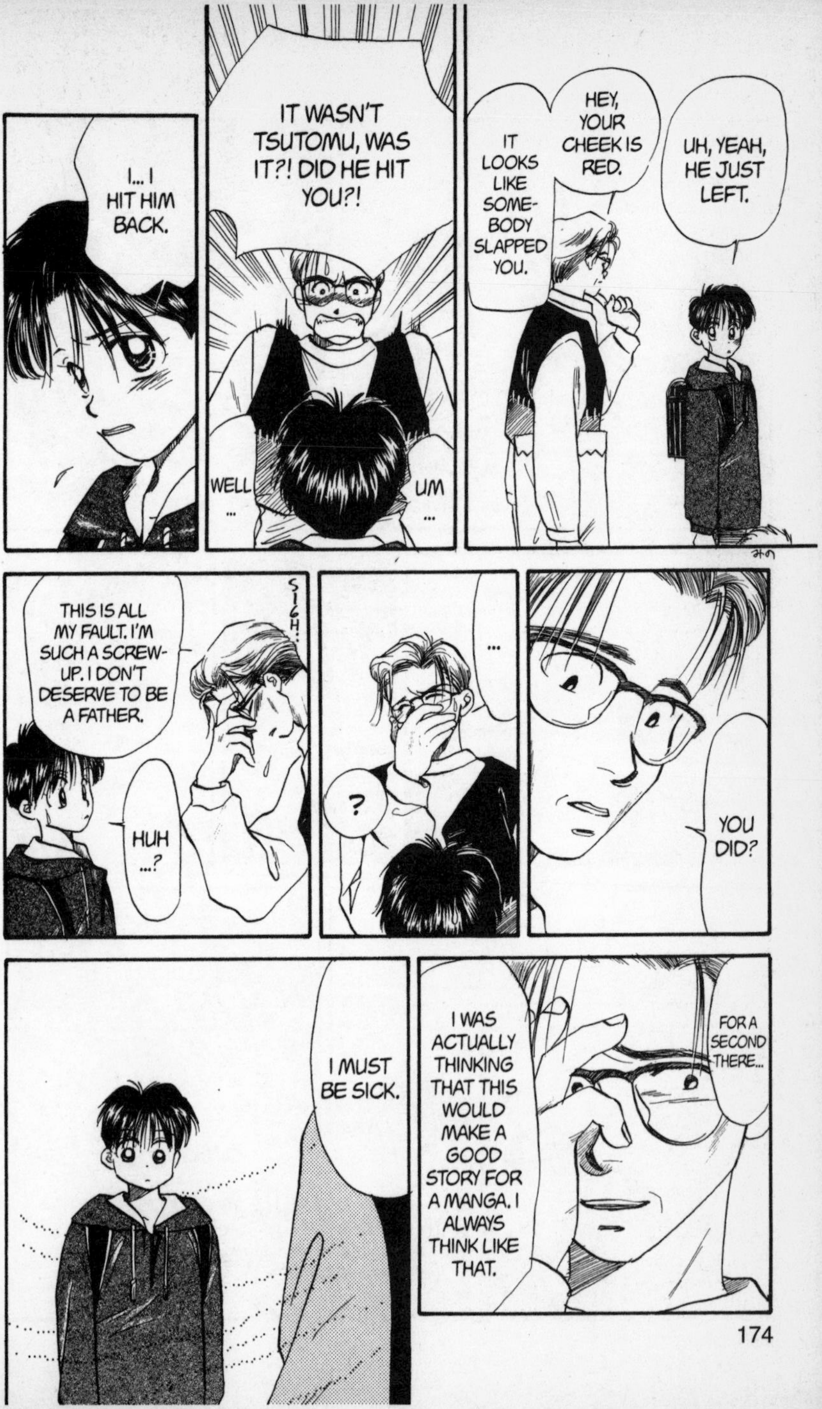
UH, YEAH, HE JUST LEFT.
HEY, YOUR CHEEK IS RED.
IT LOOKS LIKE SOME-BODY SLAPPED YOU.
IT WASN'T TSUTOMU, WAS IT?! DID HE HIT YOU?!
UM ...
WELL ...
I... I HIT HIM BACK.
YOU DID?
...
?
SIGH!
THIS IS ALL MY FAULT. I'M SUCH A SCREW-UP. I DON'T DESERVE TO BE A FATHER.
HUH ...?
FOR A SECOND THERE...
I WAS ACTUALLY THINKING THAT THIS WOULD MAKE A GOOD STORY FOR A MANGA. I ALWAYS THINK LIKE THAT.
I MUST BE SICK.

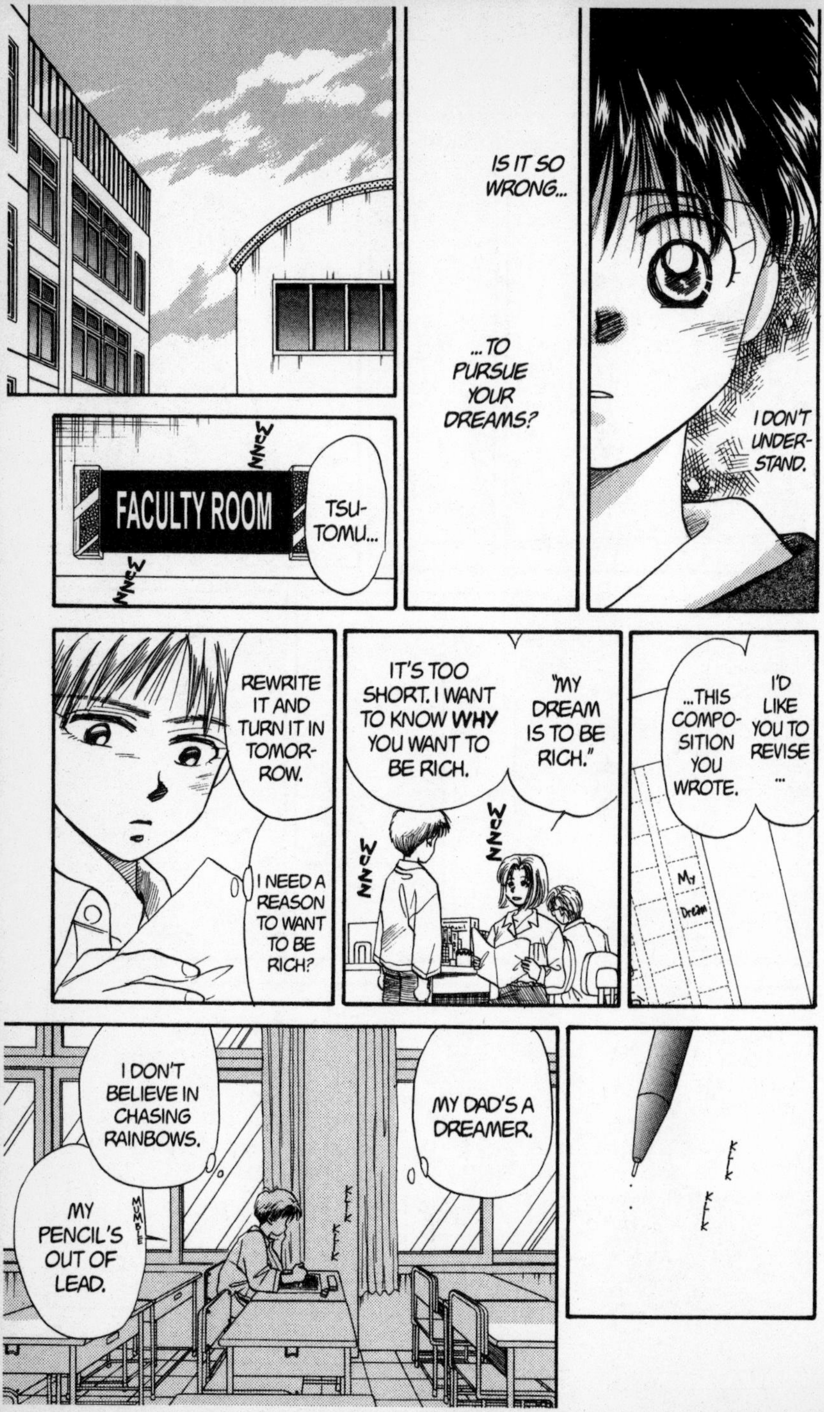
I DON'T UNDER-STAND.
IS IT SO WRONG...
...TO PURSUE YOUR DREAMS?
WUZZ
FACULTY ROOM
TSU-TOMU...
WUZZ
I'D LIKE YOU TO REVISE...
...THIS COMPO-SITION YOU WROTE.
My Dream
"MY DREAM IS TO BE RICH."
IT'S TOO SHORT. I WANT TO KNOW **WHY** YOU WANT TO BE RICH.
WUZZ
WUZZ
REWRITE IT AND TURN IT IN TOMOR-ROW.
I NEED A REASON TO WANT TO BE RICH?
KLK
KLK
MY DAD'S A DREAMER.
I DON'T BELIEVE IN CHASING RAINBOWS.
KLK
KLK
MUMBLE
MY PENCIL'S OUT OF LEAD.

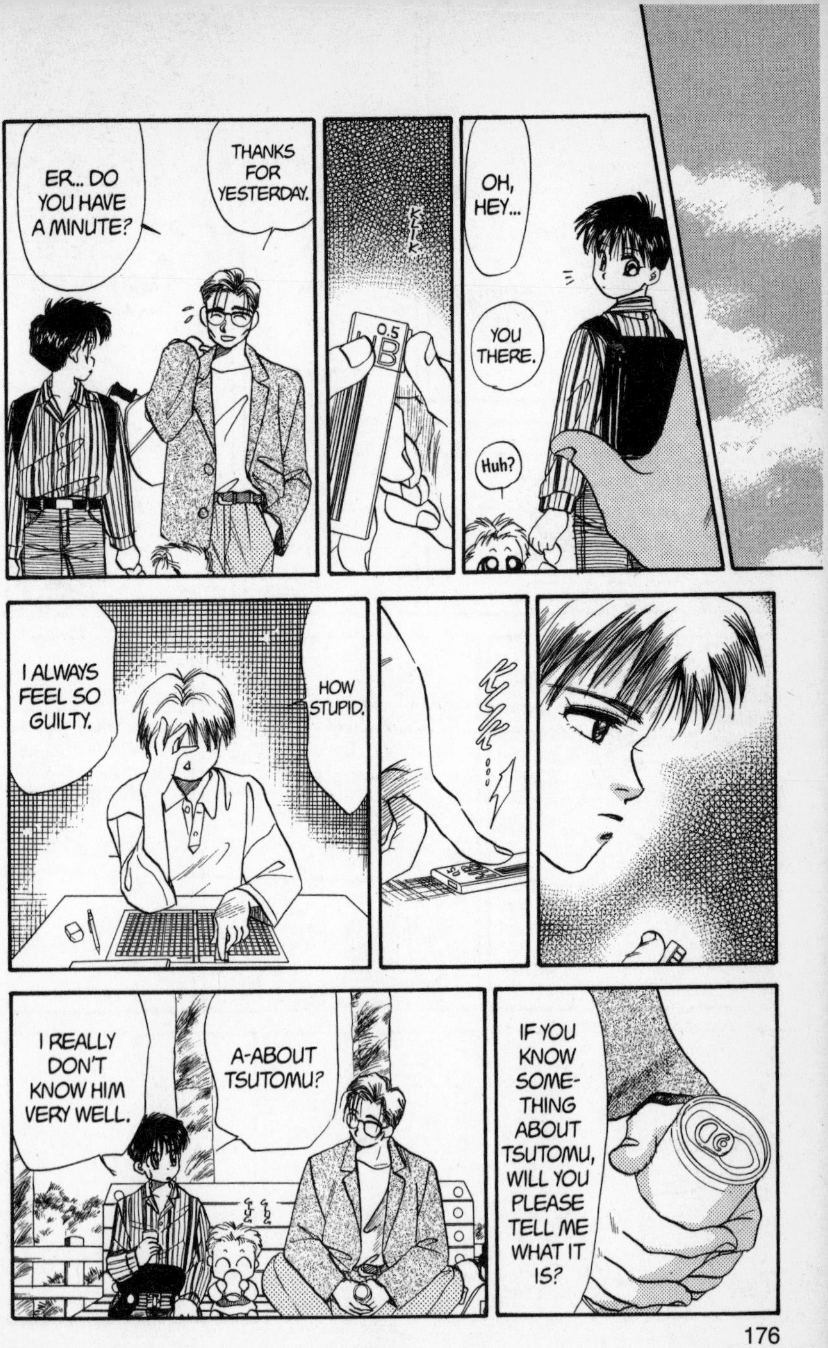
OH, HEY...
YOU THERE.
Huh?
KLIK
THANKS FOR YESTERDAY.
ER... DO YOU HAVE A MINUTE?
KLIK...
HOW STUPID.
I ALWAYS FEEL SO GUILTY.
IF YOU KNOW SOME-THING ABOUT TSUTOMU, WILL YOU PLEASE TELL ME WHAT IT IS?
A-ABOUT TSUTOMU?
I REALLY DON'T KNOW HIM VERY WELL.

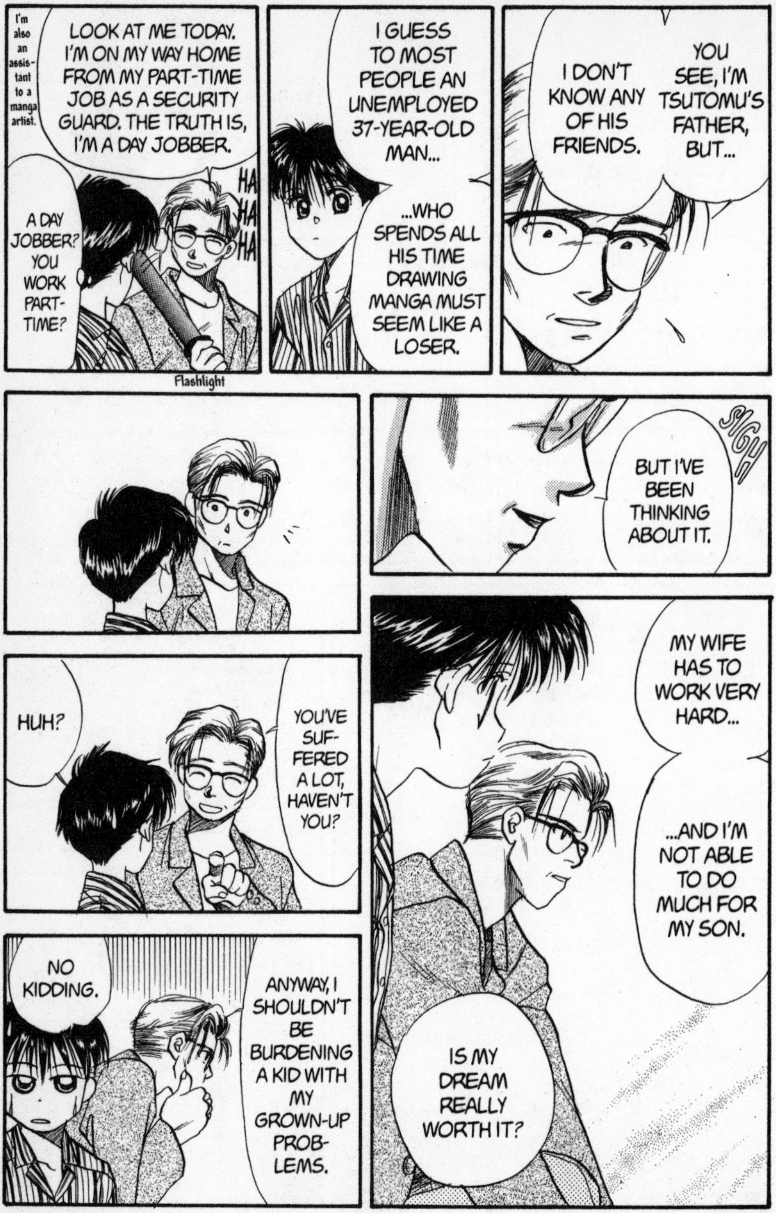

YOU SEE, I'M TSUTOMU'S FATHER, BUT...
I DON'T KNOW ANY OF HIS FRIENDS.
I GUESS TO MOST PEOPLE AN UNEMPLOYED 37-YEAR-OLD MAN...
...WHO SPENDS ALL HIS TIME DRAWING MANGA MUST SEEM LIKE A LOSER.
LOOK AT ME TODAY. I'M ON MY WAY HOME FROM MY PART-TIME JOB AS A SECURITY GUARD. THE TRUTH IS, I'M A DAY JOBBER.
I'm also an assis-tant to a manga artist.
HA HA HA
A DAY JOBBER? YOU WORK PART-TIME?
Flashlight
SIGH
BUT I'VE BEEN THINKING ABOUT IT.
MY WIFE HAS TO WORK VERY HARD...
...AND I'M NOT ABLE TO DO MUCH FOR MY SON.
IS MY DREAM REALLY WORTH IT?
YOU'VE SUF-FERED A LOT, HAVEN'T YOU?
HUH?
ANYWAY, I SHOULDN'T BE BURDENING A KID WITH MY GROWN-UP PROB-LEMS.
NO KIDDING.

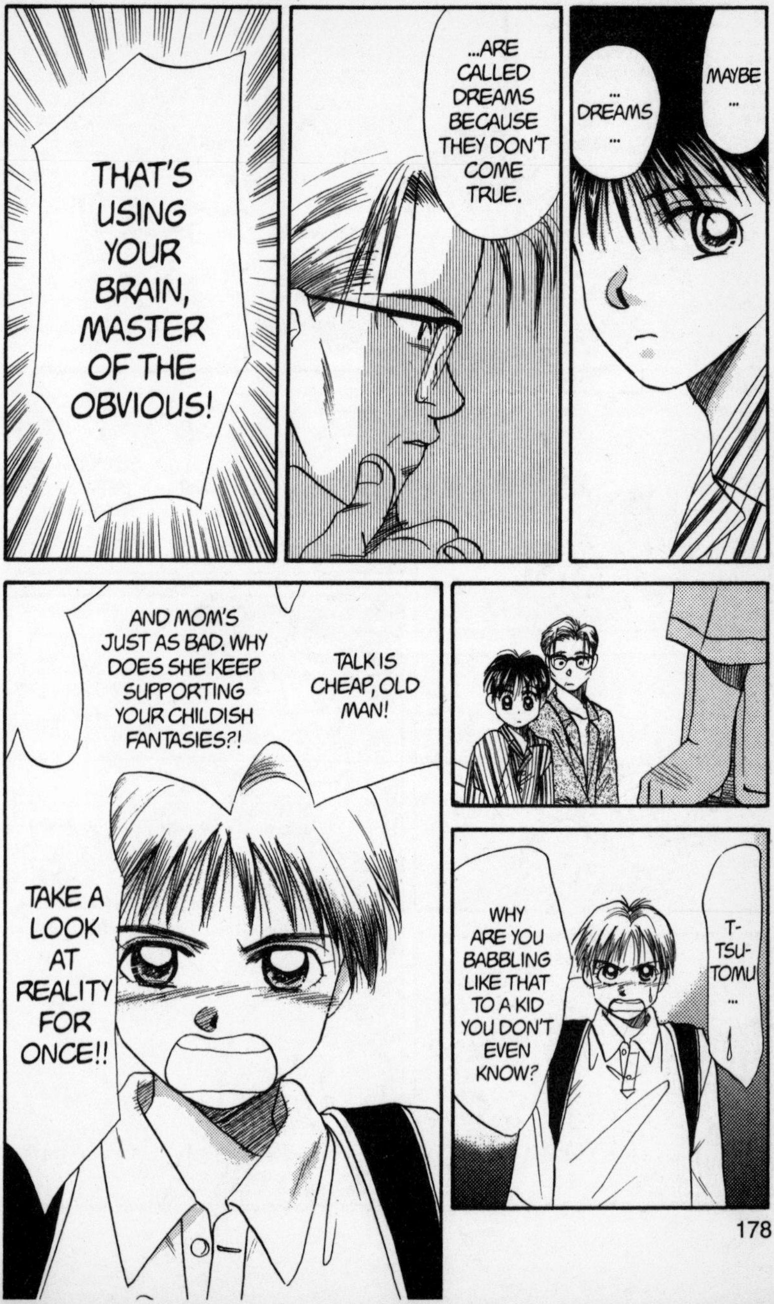
MAYBE ...
... DREAMS ...
...ARE CALLED DREAMS BECAUSE THEY DON'T COME TRUE.
THAT'S USING YOUR BRAIN, MASTER OF THE OBVIOUS!
T-TSU-TOMU ...
WHY ARE YOU BABBLING LIKE THAT TO A KID YOU DON'T EVEN KNOW?
TALK IS CHEAP, OLD MAN!
AND MOM'S JUST AS BAD. WHY DOES SHE KEEP SUPPORTING YOUR CHILDISH FANTASIES?!
TAKE A LOOK AT REALITY FOR ONCE!!

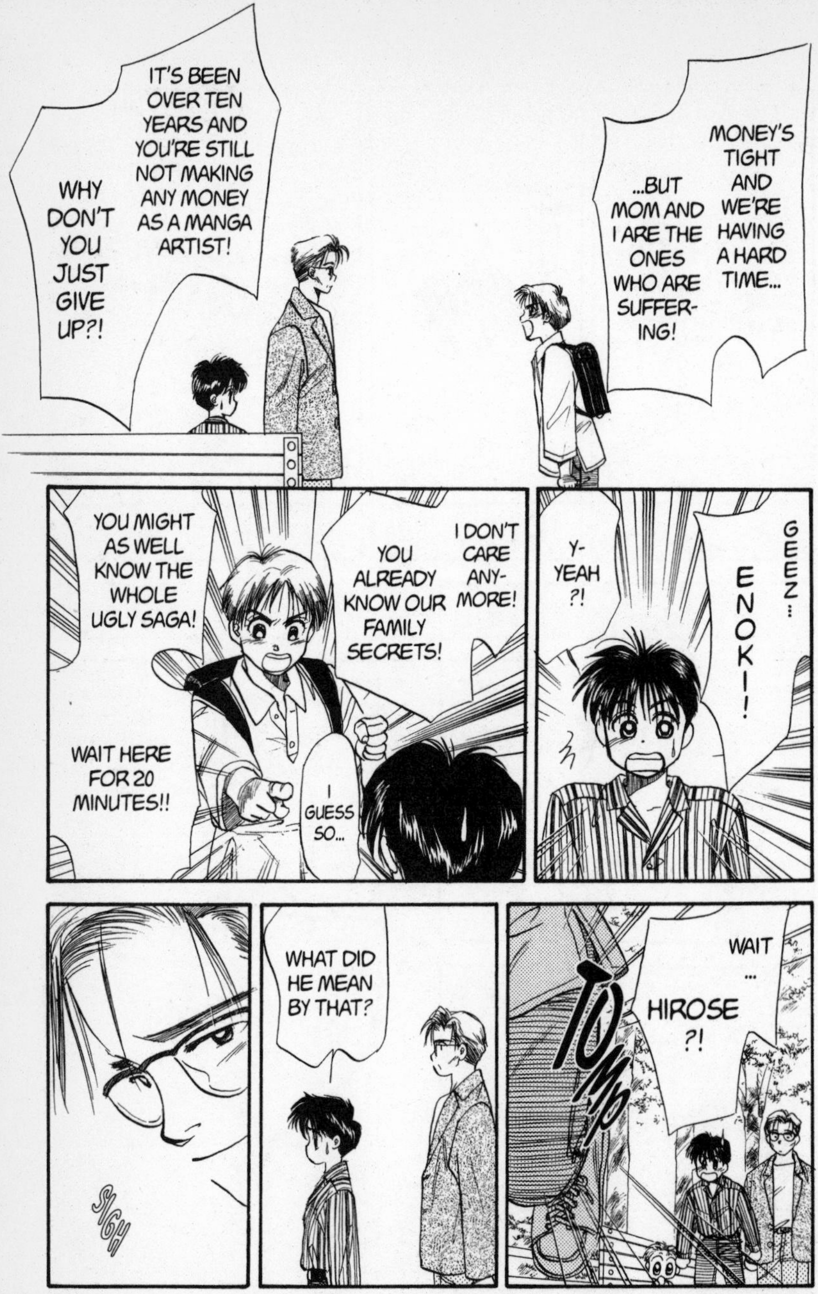
MONEY'S TIGHT AND WE'RE HAVING A HARD TIME...
...BUT MOM AND I ARE THE ONES WHO ARE SUFFERING!
IT'S BEEN OVER TEN YEARS AND YOU'RE STILL NOT MAKING ANY MONEY AS A MANGA ARTIST!
WHY DON'T YOU JUST GIVE UP?!
GEEZ...
ENOKI!!
Y-YEAH?!
I DON'T CARE ANYMORE!
YOU ALREADY KNOW OUR FAMILY SECRETS!
YOU MIGHT AS WELL KNOW THE WHOLE UGLY SAGA!
I GUESS SO...
WAIT HERE FOR 20 MINUTES!!
TOMP
WAIT... HIROSE?!
WHAT DID HE MEAN BY THAT?
SIGH

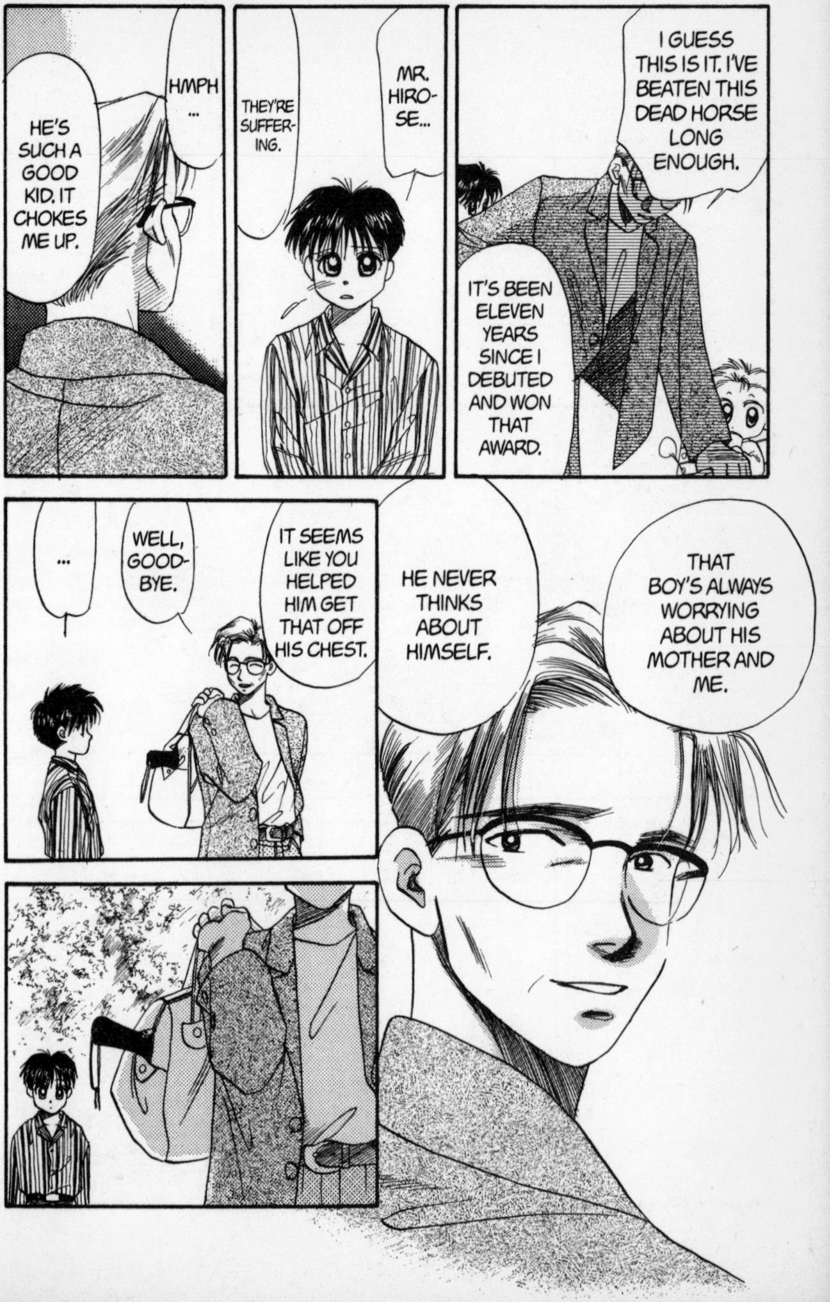
I GUESS THIS IS IT. I'VE BEATEN THIS DEAD HORSE LONG ENOUGH.
IT'S BEEN ELEVEN YEARS SINCE I DEBUTED AND WON THAT AWARD.
MR. HIROSE...
THEY'RE SUFFERING.
HMPH ...
HE'S SUCH A GOOD KID. IT CHOKES ME UP.
THAT BOY'S ALWAYS WORRYING ABOUT HIS MOTHER AND ME.
HE NEVER THINKS ABOUT HIMSELF.
IT SEEMS LIKE YOU HELPED HIM GET THAT OFF HIS CHEST.
WELL, GOODBYE.
...

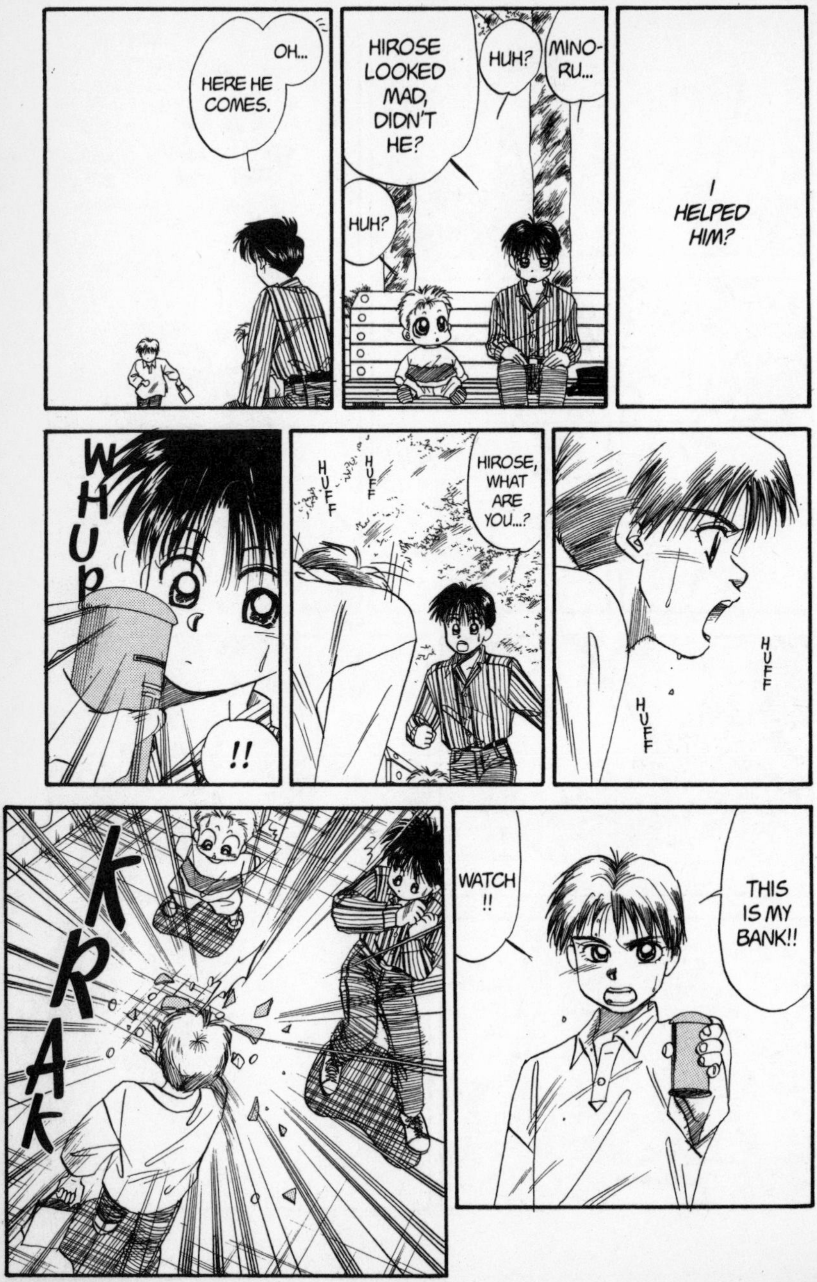
I HELPED HIM?
MINO-RU...
HUH?
HIROSE LOOKED MAD, DIDN'T HE?
HUH?
OH...
HERE HE COMES.
HUFF
HUFF
HIROSE, WHAT ARE YOU...?
HUFF
HUFF
WHUP
!!
THIS IS MY BANK!!
WATCH !!
KRAK

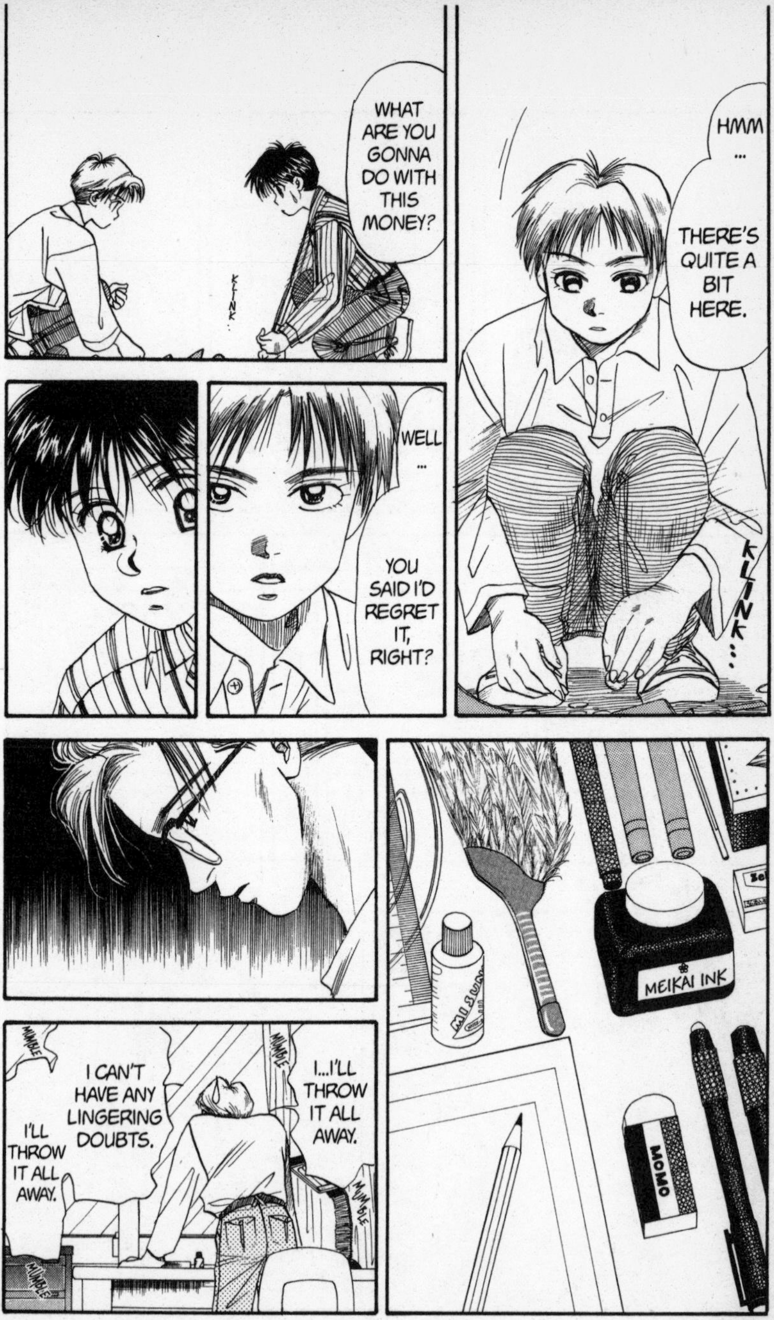
HMM ...
THERE'S QUITE A BIT HERE.
KLINK...
WHAT ARE YOU GONNA DO WITH THIS MONEY?
KLINK...
WELL ...
YOU SAID I'D REGRET IT, RIGHT?
MEIKAI INK
MOMO
MUMBLE
I...I'LL THROW IT ALL AWAY.
I CAN'T HAVE ANY LINGERING DOUBTS.
I'LL THROW IT ALL AWAY.
MUMBLE
MUMBLE
MUMBLE

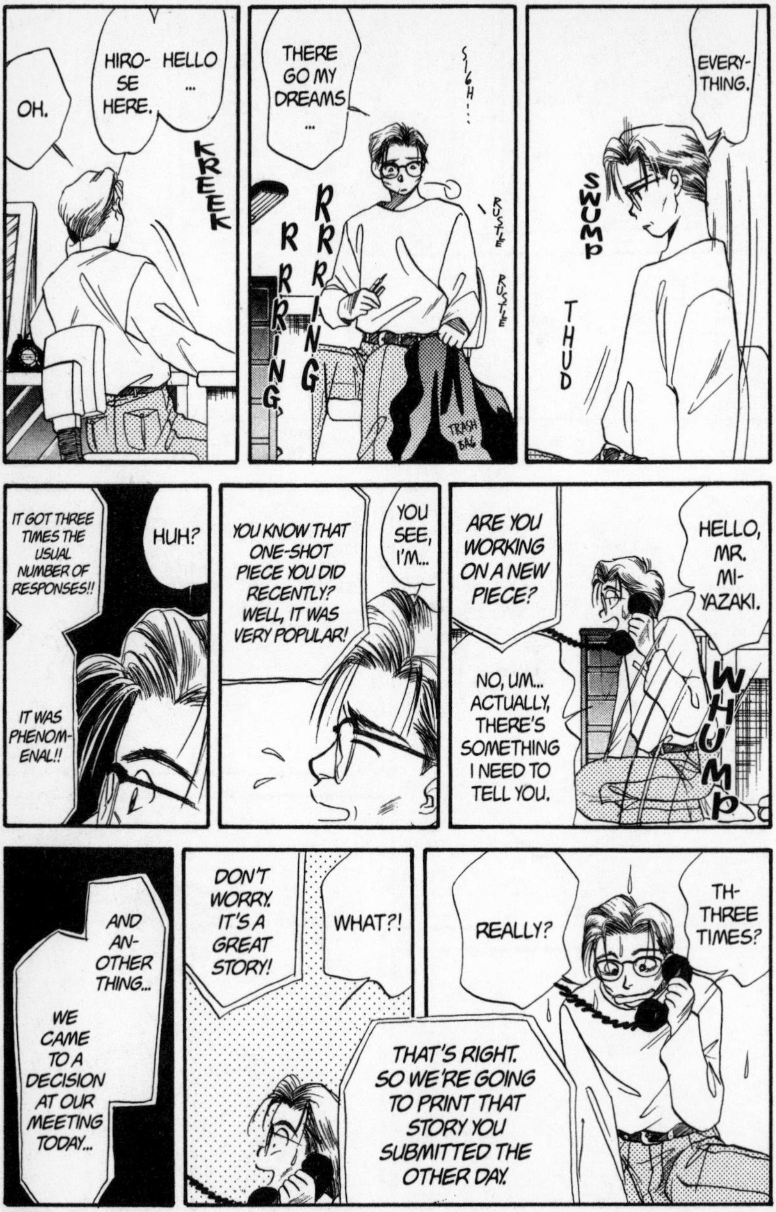
EVERY-THING.
SWUMP
THUD
THERE GO MY DREAMS...
SIGH...
RUSTLE
RUSTLE
TRASH BAG
RRRING
RRRING
HELLO...
HIRO-SE HERE.
OH.
KREEK
HELLO, MR. MI-YAZAKI.
WHUMP
ARE YOU WORKING ON A NEW PIECE?
NO, UM... ACTUALLY, THERE'S SOMETHING I NEED TO TELL YOU.
YOU SEE, I'M...
YOU KNOW THAT ONE-SHOT PIECE YOU DID RECENTLY? WELL, IT WAS VERY POPULAR!
HUH?
IT GOT THREE TIMES THE USUAL NUMBER OF RESPONSES!!
IT WAS PHENOM-ENAL!!
TH-THREE TIMES?
REALLY?
THAT'S RIGHT. SO WE'RE GOING TO PRINT THAT STORY YOU SUBMITTED THE OTHER DAY.
WHAT?!
DON'T WORRY. IT'S A GREAT STORY!
AND AN-OTHER THING...
WE CAME TO A DECISION AT OUR MEETING TODAY...

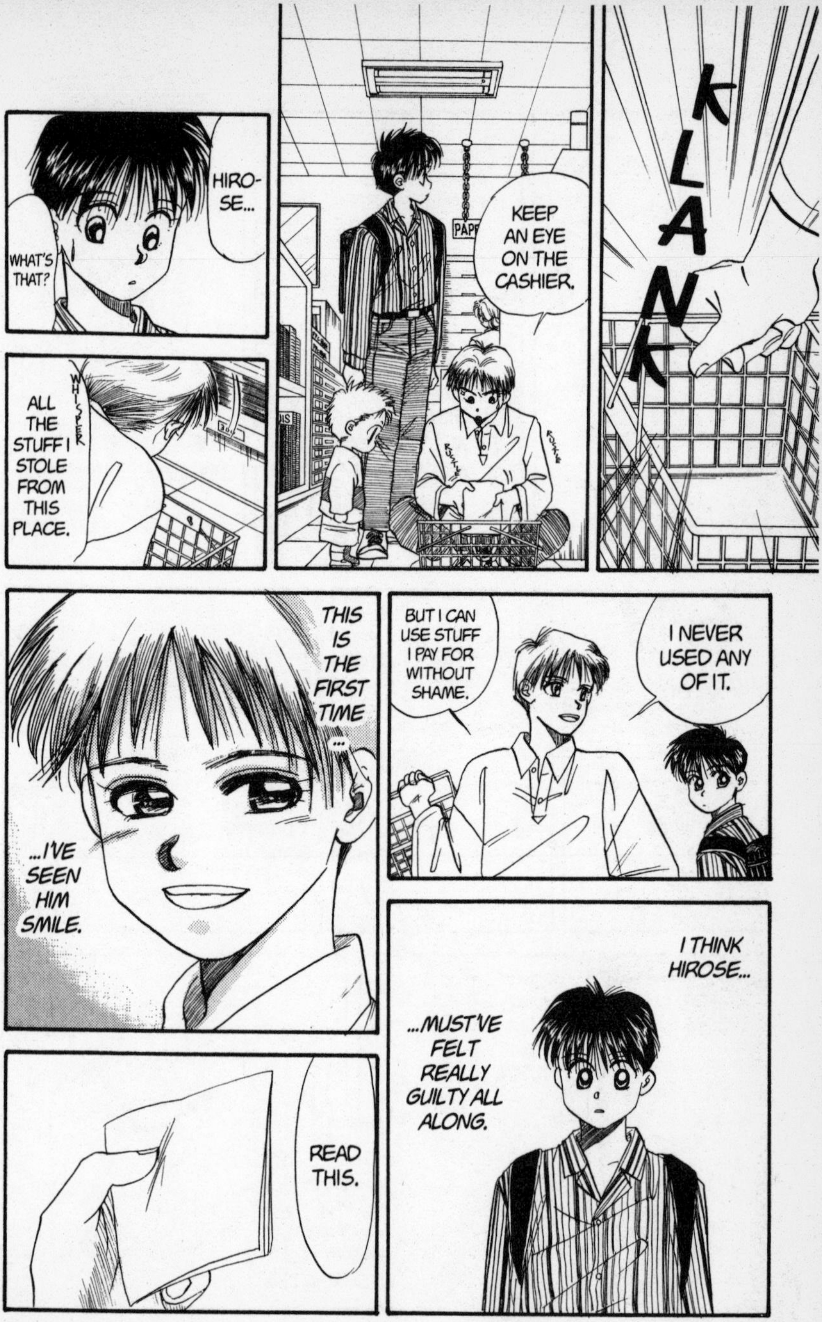
KLANK
KEEP AN EYE ON THE CASHIER.
RUSTLE
RUSTLE
HIRO-SE...
WHAT'S THAT?
WHISPER
ALL THE STUFF I STOLE FROM THIS PLACE.
I NEVER USED ANY OF IT.
BUT I CAN USE STUFF I PAY FOR WITHOUT SHAME.
THIS IS THE FIRST TIME...
...I'VE SEEN HIM SMILE.
I THINK HIROSE...
...MUST'VE FELT REALLY GUILTY ALL ALONG.
READ THIS.

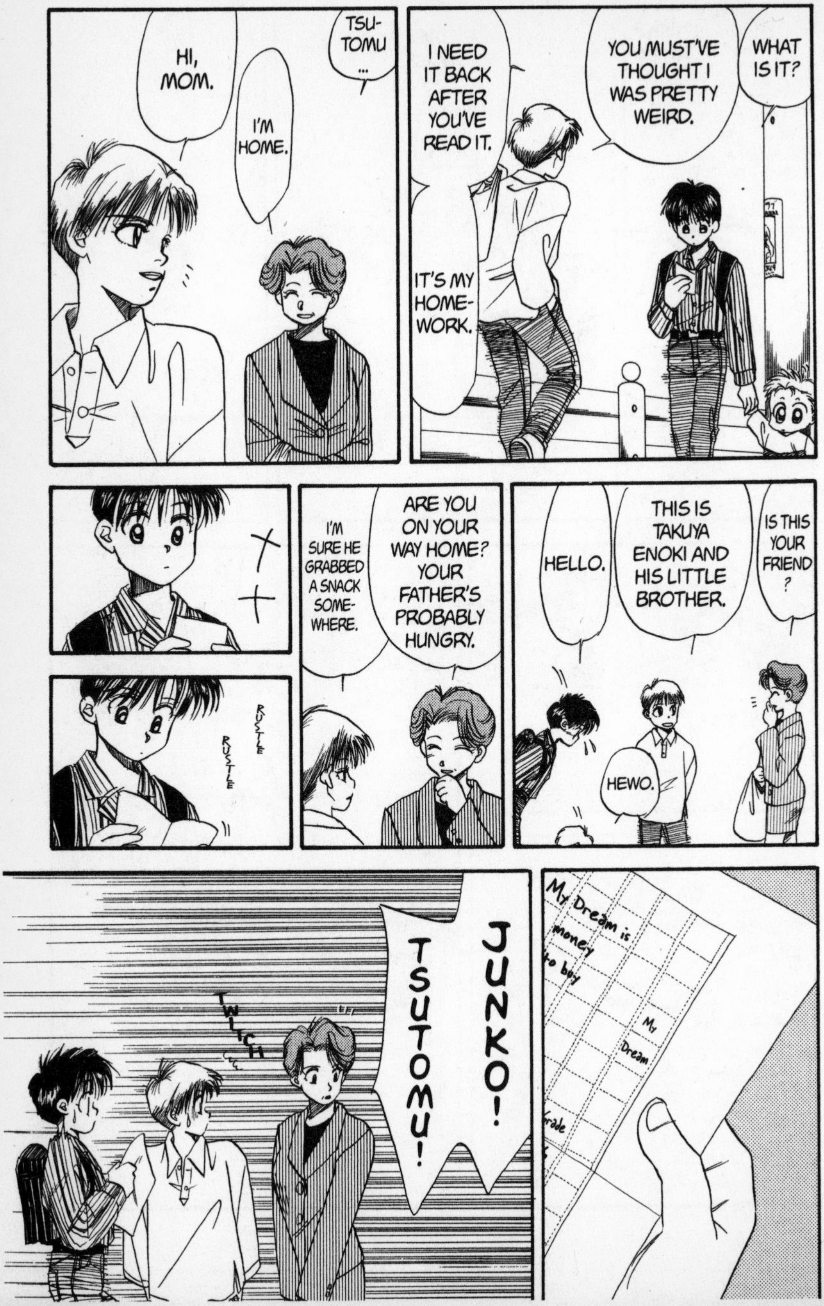
WHAT IS IT?
YOU MUST'VE THOUGHT I WAS PRETTY WEIRD.
I NEED IT BACK AFTER YOU'VE READ IT.
IT'S MY HOMEWORK.
TSU-TOMU ...
HI, MOM.
I'M HOME.
IS THIS YOUR FRIEND?
THIS IS TAKUYA ENOKI AND HIS LITTLE BROTHER.
HELLO.
HEWO.
ARE YOU ON YOUR WAY HOME? YOUR FATHER'S PROBABLY HUNGRY.
I'M SURE HE GRABBED A SNACK SOMEWHERE.
RUSTLE
RUSTLE
My Dream is
money
to buy
My
Dream
JUNKO!
TSUTOMU!
TWITCH

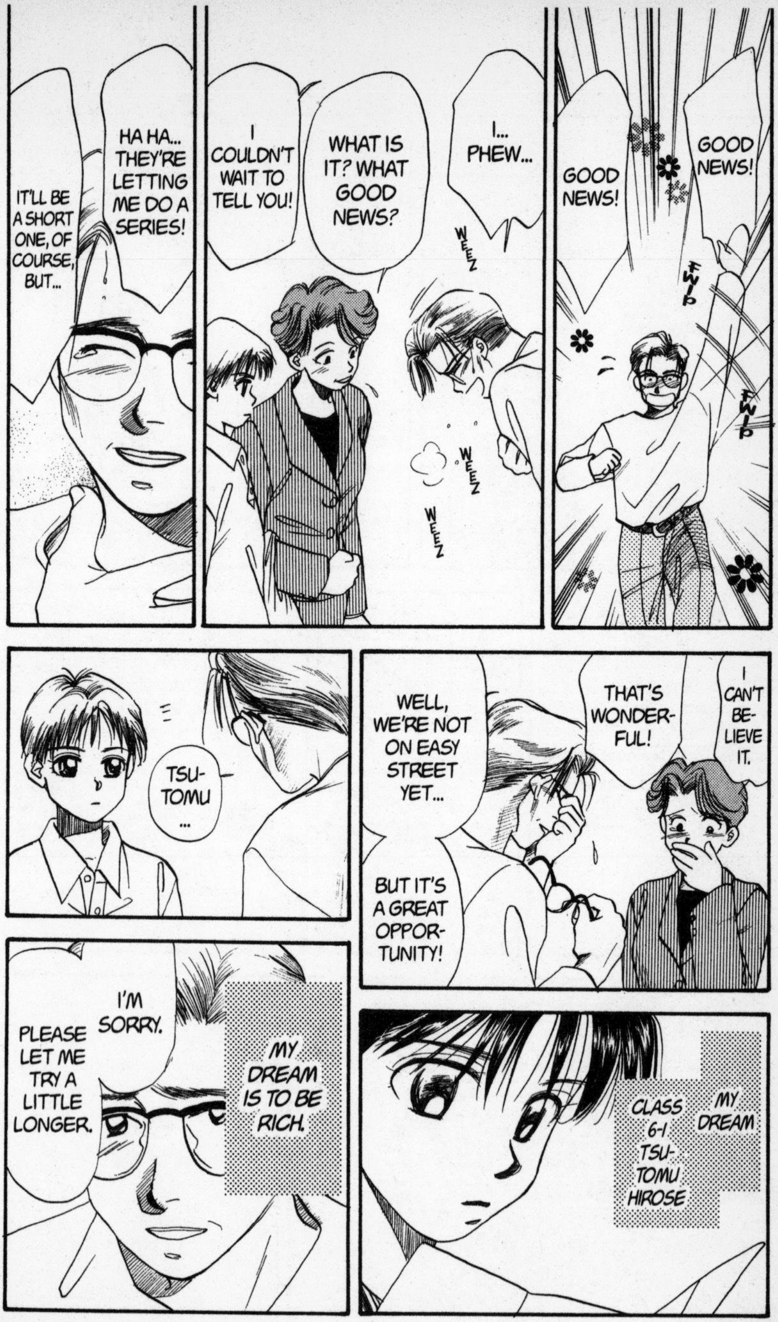
GOOD NEWS!
GOOD NEWS!
FWIP
FWIP
I... PHEW...
WEEZ
WEEZ
WEEZ
WHAT IS IT? WHAT GOOD NEWS?
I COULDN'T WAIT TO TELL YOU!
HA HA... THEY'RE LETTING ME DO A SERIES!
IT'LL BE A SHORT ONE, OF COURSE, BUT...
I CAN'T BELIEVE IT.
THAT'S WONDERFUL!
WELL, WE'RE NOT ON EASY STREET YET...
BUT IT'S A GREAT OPPORTUNITY!
TSUTOMU...
MY DREAM
CLASS 6-1 TSUTOMU HIROSE
MY DREAM IS TO BE RICH.
I'M SORRY.
PLEASE LET ME TRY A LITTLE LONGER.

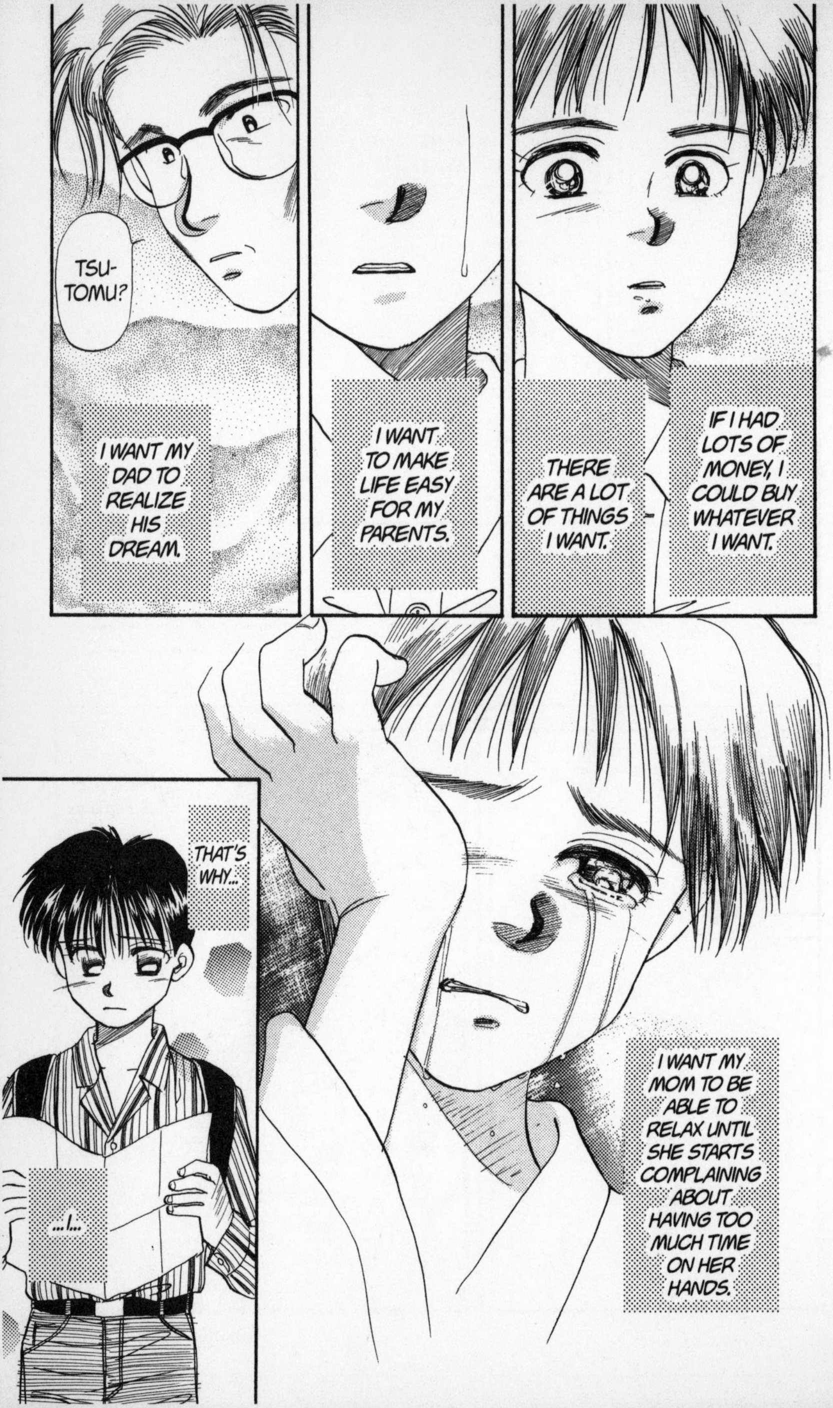
IF I HAD LOTS OF MONEY, I COULD BUY WHATEVER I WANT.
THERE ARE A LOT OF THINGS I WANT.
I WANT TO MAKE LIFE EASY FOR MY PARENTS.
TSU-TOMU?
I WANT MY DAD TO REALIZE HIS DREAM.
I WANT MY MOM TO BE ABLE TO RELAX UNTIL SHE STARTS COMPLAINING ABOUT HAVING TOO MUCH TIME ON HER HANDS.
THAT'S WHY...
...I...

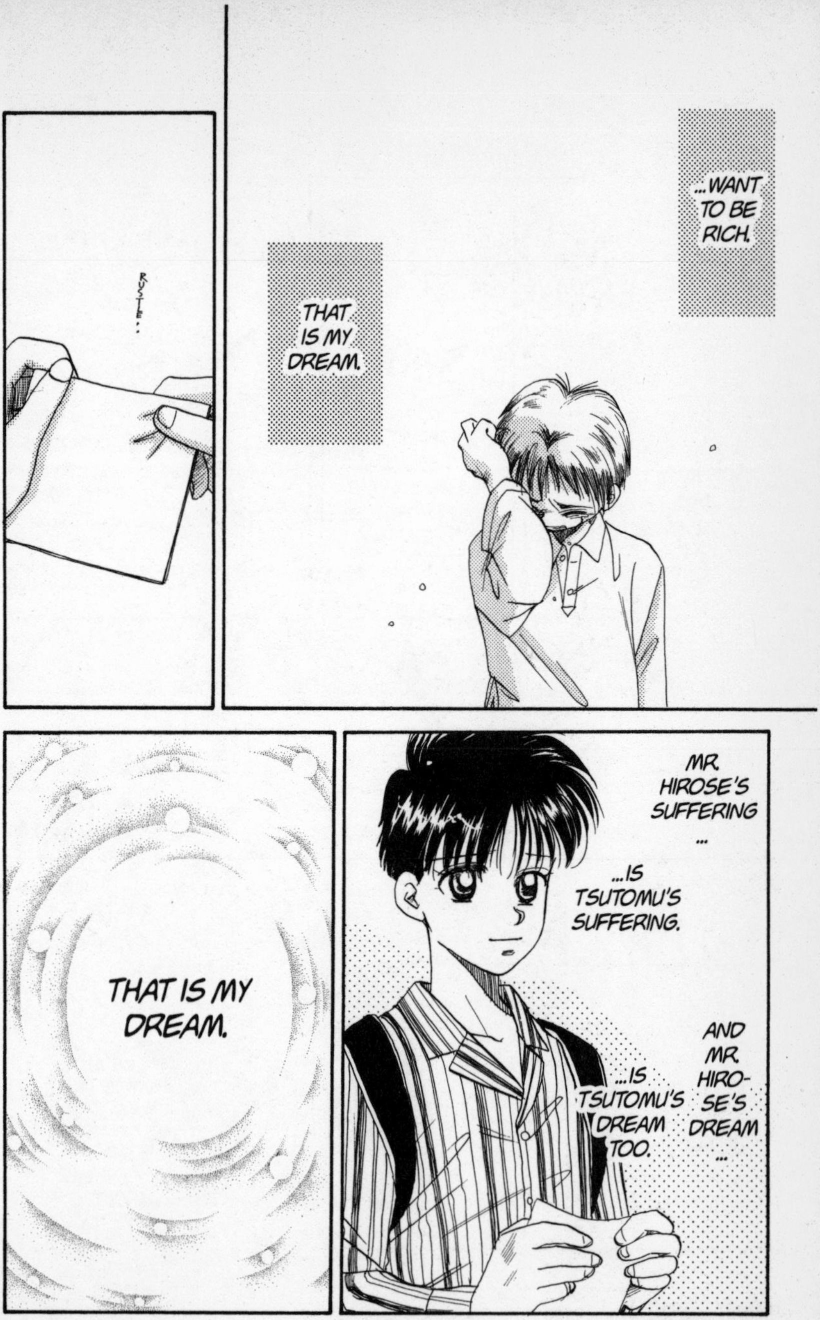
...WANT TO BE RICH.
THAT IS MY DREAM.
RUSTLE...
MR. HIROSE'S SUFFERING ...
...IS TSUTOMU'S SUFFERING.
AND MR. HIROSE'S DREAM ...
...IS TSUTOMU'S DREAM TOO.
THAT IS MY DREAM.

Chapter 38 / The End

BABY & ME

Creator: Marimo Ragawa

SBM Title: *Baby & Me*

Date of Birth: September 21

Blood Type: B

Major Works: *Time Limit*,
Baby & Me, *N.Y. N.Y.*, and
Shanimuni-Go (Desperately—Go)

Marimo Ragawa first started submitting manga to a comic magazine when she was 12 years old. She kept up her submissions for four years, but to no avail. She decided to submit her work to the magazine *Hana to Yume*, where she received Top Prize in the Monthly Manga Contest as well as an honorable mention (Kasaku) in the magazine's Big Challenge contest. Her first manga was titled *Time Limit*. *Baby & Me* was honored with a Shogakukan Manga Award in 1995 and was spun off into an anime.

Ragawa's work showcases some very cute and expressive line work along with an incredible ability to depict complex emotions and relationships. Some of her other works include *N.Y. N.Y.* and the tennis manga *Shanimuni-Go*.

Ragawa has two brothers and two sisters.

BABY & ME, Vol. 7

The Shojo Beat Manga Edition

STORY & ART BY

MARIMO RAGAWA

English Adaptation/Lance Caselman
Translation/JN Productions
Touch-up Art & Lettering/Mark Griffin
Design/Yuki Ameda
Editors/Pancha Diaz and Shaenon K. Garrity

Editor in Chief, Books/Alvin Lu
Editor in Chief, Magazines/Marc Weidenbaum
VP of Publishing Licensing/Rika Inouye
VP of Sales/Gonzalo Ferreyra
Sr. VP of Marketing/Liza Coppola
Publisher/Hyoe Narita

Printed in Canada

Published by VIZ Media, LLC
P.O. Box 77010
San Francisco, CA 94107

Shojo Beat Manga Edition
10 9 8 7 6 5 4 3 2 1
First printing, April 2008

PARENTAL ADVISORY
BABY & ME is rated T for Teen and is recommended for ages 13 and up. This volume contains adult situations.
RATED T FOR TEEN
ratings.viz.com

store.viz.com

TMV

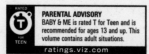